# Comparing Asian Politics

# Comparing
# Asian Politics

## India, China, and Japan

## Sue Ellen M. Charlton
Colorado State University

WestviewPress
*A Division of* HarperCollins*Publishers*

Published in 1997 in the United States of America by Westview Press, 5500 Central Avenue, Boulder, Colorado 80301-2877, and in the United Kingdom by Westview Press, 12 Hid's Copse Road, Cumnor Hill, Oxford OX2 9JJ


Library of Congress Cataloging-in-Publication Data
Charlton, Sue Ellen M.
    Comparing Asian politics : India, China, and Japan / Sue Ellen M.
Charlton.
      p.   cm.
    Includes bibliographical references and index.
    ISBN 0-8133-8584-9 (hc). — ISBN 0-8133-8585-7 (pbk).
    1. Asia—Politics and government—Case studies.   2. India—
Politics and government.   3. China—Politics and government.
4. Japan—Politics and government.   I. Title.
JQ24.C48   1997
320.3'095—dc21
                                                                97-21721
                                                                CIP


The paper used in this publication meets the requirements of the American National Standard for Permanence of Paper for Printed Library Materials Z39.48-1984.

10     9     8     7     6     5     4     3     2     1

*To Vera and Fred Markey,*
*in gratitude for their years of*
*hospitality, support, and good cheer*

# Contents

# Tables and Illustrations

*Photos*

# Preface

All books begin with an author's conviction that there is something new to say or that something old can be said better. So it is with *Comparing Asian Politics*. Some twenty-five years of teaching Asian politics to undergraduates and arguing with friends and family members about the intrinsic interest and value of understanding political processes in Asia finally prompted what has been an ambitious and lengthy project—far too lengthy, judging by the comments of those around me.

The length of this project can be explained by common problems that beset most writers, including competing work and family obligations. One of the delightful, if insidious, reasons for the delay in completion has been the temptation to spend time exploring Asia in person rather than staying home to read, think, and write. For the opportunity to work in Japan in 1991 and 1993, I am especially grateful to the Center for Women's Studies, Tokyo Woman's Christian University; and for making possible my stay in India in 1992, I thank the American Institute for Indian Studies. Travel support to both Japan and India, as well as to China in 1995, was also provided by the College of Liberal Arts, Colorado State University.

One of the most important goals of this book is to provide nonspecialized readers with a balanced discussion of contemporary Asian politics that is sensitive to historical and cultural contexts. Insofar as this sensitivity has been realized, it is due in large part to the generations of scholars whose research has helped to inform this book. Any successes are also due to numerous colleagues, friends, hosts, and passing acquaintances in Asia. They have caused me to learn, to rethink what I was *sure* I understood, and to help me see their world through their lenses, not mine. They may have difficulty understanding how their patience and, occasionally, impatience touched me, but they should know that without them, this book would have been the poorer. I am deeply grateful to the following people: Marcia M. Allen, Karuna Ambarasen, Sonja Arntzen, Tsuyoshi Awaya, Surinder and Gunit Ghuman, Janet Gilligan and John Waples, the Ishibashi Family, Yasuko Muramatsu, Anup and Raji Nair, Yukiko Oda, and Irene Tong.

Scholar-writers need support networks, and I am no exception. The network includes colleagues, especially those in the Asian Studies Program at Colorado State University, who have sustained my interests over the years, who answer my questions and correct my mistakes, particularly Loren Crabtree, Bill Griswold, and Kai-Ho Mah. I owe a debt of appreciation also to two special friends: Jana Everett, University of Colorado at Denver, for her knowledge, friendship, and encouragement in trying times; and the late Betsy Moen of the University of Colorado at Boulder, whose premature death cast a lingering shadow over this book.

My students in several sections of Asian politics have served as test-subjects for the book's ideas and organizational scheme. Over a period of several years, some of them took on the project of reading and critiquing the chapters in various drafts. Their help was invaluable in my efforts to avoid jargon and make sure that the writing was clear and interesting. The network also includes two particularly knowledgeable and patient editors at Westview Press: Susan McEachern, who supported the project early on; and Laura Parsons, who saw it through.

Best of all has been my immediate family network: my parents, who lent their "cabin on the Hill" so that I could think and write with minimal interruption and to whom this book is dedicated; and Jim Boyd, who never lost faith, who read and commented on endless drafts—colleague, friend, and *compagnon de route*.

*Sue Ellen M. Charlton*

*one*

# Introduction: Themes in Asian Politics

## Why Asia?

The colors of Asia are legendary: Indian saris, Beijing opera, and Tokyo's neon lights all captivate the visitor. The Asian continent, from west to east, is the birthplace of many of the most influential cultures we see in the world today. For the student of politics, Asian countries offer an unparalleled variety of government structures and political styles, all different from those found in North America. There are constitutional and absolute monarchies, military and civilian dictatorships. There are bold experiments with multiparty democracy that have been in existence for only a few decades. In addition, Asia is home to the largest remaining self-proclaimed socialist state, the People's Republic of China (PRC).

This book seeks to capture here some of the richness and diversity of politics in South Asia and East Asia by focusing on what I believe are the three most important Asian countries for the North American reader: India, China, and Japan. One measure of importance is size: China and India are the two most populous nations in the world, and this fact alone suggests that their systems of governing, their political choices, and their crises will interest outside observers. China and Japan, in particular, weigh heavily on our calculations about actual and potential power in the

Pacific Rim region. We thus continue to be preoccupied with the domestic politics of both countries, for example, with their degree of democracy, corruption, or stability, with the role of government in economic planning, and with the size of the military establishment.

In view of the acknowledged economic and strategic significance of East Asia to North Americans, why not limit the study here to Japan and China? The answer is clear: India is too frequently overlooked in comparative political studies, even though it has much to teach us about the most important political dilemmas of our age. Issues that dominate Indian politics are increasingly becoming central to Western nations: For example, what is the appropriate balance between communities and individuals for fostering human freedom *and* social order? How do we reconcile the tensions between ethnic demands for regional autonomy and the perceived need for national cohesion and stability? Are federal systems less efficient than more centralized unitary political systems? Thus, a Russian thinking about the ethnic demands unleashed by the demise of the Soviet Union or a Canadian looking for parallels to Quebec's demands for autonomy and to federal-provincial tensions would do well to study Indian politics. Similarly, an American interested in the problems and promises of special programs for disadvantaged citizens and minority groups might want to examine India's policies concerning its so-called **Backward Classes**.[1] Finally, it is in India, not China or Japan, where the potentially most important political debate of the early twenty-first century is occurring—the debate over what it means to have a "secular" political system.

Studied individually, India, China, and Japan are politically as rich and as fascinating as any countries in the world. Taken together, they raise provocative questions that can best be studied in a comparative framework. Studying China, for example, may help us understand what happens when a government pursues apparently contradictory political and economic goals, such as encouraging competition in one arena (the economic) and not in another (the political). We may also view **Confucianism** as a system of moral, political, and social order influential throughout East Asia. Similarly, the study of Japan has long raised provocative questions about the adaptation of an East Asian civilization to Western technology, political institutions, and popular culture. In recent years, the comparative study of Japanese politics has invited inquiry into the connection between economic and military power and the linkage of both of these to international political influence.

Ultimately, what draws many students and scholars to Asia is the conviction that the traditions of the region have much to offer us as we try to define and answer the great questions of human experience, including those of our political life.

# Themes in Asian Politics: Culture and Tradition

For purposes of comparison, six themes run through the chapters in this book. These themes reflect my assumptions about what is most important and most interesting in the study of Asian politics, and they also reflect the motivating question behind the book: What can we learn about politics by studying other countries, particularly those in Asia? The discussion that follows in this section introduces the first three themes, which are historically interwoven. The next section then takes up a second group of themes that build on the first group and focus specifically on contemporary issues of development, the role of the state, and national identity.

The first theme is that of the *endurance of traditional cultures* that are unique for their ancient roots as well for their richness in literature, the arts, and philosophy. Especially in India and China, history is measured not only by decades and centuries but also by millennia. Of particular significance for our study is the fact that both countries have ancient political texts, historical figures, and representational symbols that modern politicians lay claim to. Thus, Chinese Communist leaders in the 1960s and 1970s staked out their ideological territory by referring to ancient political figures and debates. In India, a modern political party uses the lotus as a party symbol, thus consciously drawing on an artistic and religious tradition that dates back at least 2,500 years (see Figure 1.1). Even Japan, a relatively young country by contrast, claims the oldest continuous monarchy in the world.

The point to be emphasized is not just the age or durability of these traditions but their contemporary legitimacy in the eyes of today's citizens. This legitimacy is reinforced by the existence of ancient texts, architectural monuments, and artistic works that are daily reminders of traditional values and accomplishments. Despite traumatic historical events in the modern era, including colonial conquest (India), war and revolution (China), war and military occupation (Japan), much of the traditional culture endures and influences politics. The question to be asked, then, is this: How significant for politics and government is this cultural continuity?

The second theme is an extension of the first and may seem at first glance to contradict it. This theme is the *intermingling and grafting of the Asian traditions*, meaning the way in which the Asian traditions have moved across the continent and influenced one another. The most striking cultural and human migrations have moved from west to east: the expansion of ancient Persian influence from West to South Asia; the spread of **Islam** to South and East Asia; the migration of Buddhism from India to South, Southeast, and East Asia; and the influence of Confucianism, Chinese language, and other aspects of culture in Korea, Japan, and much of Southeast Asia. The cultural movement has continued through the twenti-

*Figure 1.1    Lotus symbol*

eth century, often with today's traders converging by airplane in Bombay, Singapore, and Shanghai rather than by the ships of past centuries. Hindi movies are broadcast in Hong Kong; Chinese restaurants proliferate in India; Iranian workers congregate in Tokyo parks on Sunday afternoons.

The political significance of this movement and intermingling varies and may be both direct and indirect. It is direct when a politician such as Lee Kuan Yew, the former prime minister of Singapore, calls for an official national ideology of Confucianism and asserts the superiority of Confucian over Western political and social values.[2] It is direct also when ethnic minorities, such as Chinese populations in Southeast Asia or Indian Tamils in Sri Lanka, become a political force to be recognized or a "problem" to be "dealt with." It is more indirect when a Japanese journalist carries information about sex tourism in the Philippines back to her country in a manner that contributes to the growing political awareness of Japanese women.[3]

The third theme is the specific *influence of Western values and institutions* in Asia. We may date the origins of Western influence from the first great period of European exploration and conquest, from the fifteenth to the seventeenth centuries. The remnants linger in place-names such as Macao and Goa (Portuguese) and Pondicherry (French). Other footprints of the early Europeans mark the historical passage through the Asian experience. There are hidden memories of Christian converts in early Japan; our English word **"caste"** comes from the Portuguese term "casta," used to describe the Indian social organization encountered by early Portuguese traders. We have all heard of the early spice trade that prompted the explorations. Fewer have heard about the privileged status of a European missionary who served as a scientific adviser at the Chinese imperial court in the mid-seventeenth century.[4]

The second sweep of Western expansion, from the late eighteenth to the early twentieth centuries, caused many of the political tremors that linger even at the end of the twentieth century. To this period belong the direct British conquest of most of South Asia; the creation of a French empire in "Indo-china" (today's Vietnam, Laos, and Cambodia); American merchant and naval ships in Japanese harbors, cracking the isolation of the Tokugawa order; the "carving up" of coastal Chinese territory by the Russians, French, British, Americans, and, ultimately, the Japanese; and the replacement of Spanish colonialism with American colonialism in the Philippines. It is to this period that we must look for the origins of modern Asian nationalism, which helps us understand in turn the preoccupation of today's Asian governments with strong state institutions and national integrity.

For the purposes of this book, the most important aspects of the Western impact occur in the area of political institutions and ideas. Arguably, this influence on contemporary politics is more apparent than that of traditional norms and practices. The lineage is direct, if different, for all three of the countries under study. The Indian Constitution draws directly on documents from the colonial period, and India's national parliamentary institutions largely replicate the British. Western impact on Japanese politics dates to the early Meiji period (1860s–1870s) and was consolidated during the post–World War II U.S. occupation (1945–1952). China, seemingly the nonconforming case, actually borrowed from a different European tradition, combining Marxist-Leninist ideology with Leninist Communist Party and state organizations.

Taken together, these three themes suggest that we need to be alert to evidence of both the distinct influence and the intersection of culture and institutions based in the indigenous (I) traditions of India, China, and Japan; the role of other Asian (A) thought systems, conventions, and institutions; and, of course, the Western (W) impact. Conceptualized schematically, we should look for the flow among these three elements (see Figure 1.2). These relationships can be illustrated in concrete terms, a good example being the political relationships found in contemporary Japan. What is the mixture of traditional norms (such as factional loyalty in the political parties), bureaucratic prerogative (inherited from the Confucian tradition), and (Western) parliamentary convention in public policy decisionmaking? Similar questions will be asked about Chinese and Indian politics as well.

As important as the *flow* and overlap among these three sets of influences is the *fissure*, or conflict, that may occur among them. A striking example of such conflict emerged in Indian politics in the 1980s with the

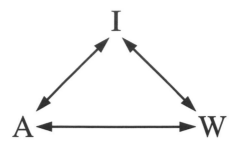

*Figure 1.2    Flow patterns of I, A, and W. Indigenous (I) traditions of India, China, and Japan have mixed with other Asian (A) and Western (W) influences.*

public debate over the appropriateness of (Western) secular institutions and ideology in what some political leaders argued is and should be a traditional *Hindu* nation.

The point of questions of this sort is not to measure the exact input of a factor called I, A, or W in a specific political moment. Rather, it is to remind us that, even where indigenous traditions are strong, politics also mirrors foreign history and culture. Political institutions are permeable to external influences. The very fact of this permeability, in turn, may inspire national political resistance and controversy, as happens periodically throughout Asia.

## Themes in Asian Politics: Development, State, and Nation

The fourth theme that runs through this book is that of *socioeconomic development and political change*. The very notion of development, as the word is used here, is Western, the concept having been brought to Asia in the nineteenth and twentieth centuries. Development carries with it the assumption of linear, progressive change. It is linear in its future-oriented perspective and in its assumption that history means progress. Progress in turn means material advancement in the broad sense: higher material standards of living, accompanied by longer life expectancies and the spread of wealth to increased numbers of people.

One of the most distinctive features of development at the end of the twentieth century is that it constitutes a political mandate for Asian governments. A handful of exceptions notwithstanding, Asian politicians (like their European and American counterparts) are almost universally preoccupied with development. For example, what policies will stimulate economic growth, who will benefit, and, occasionally, how growth can be reconciled with environmental damage are development issues found on every government agenda. Differences over the development policies to be followed may split ruling elites into competing factions or be the main source of ideological distinction between political parties. Thus, politics both responds to socioeconomic change and seeks to direct it.

It is important here to note that development cannot be fully understood without recognizing its relationship to the political concepts of *state* and *nation*. Often these two words are linked, as in *nation-state*, to refer to the territorially based political units that have come to cover the globe in the nineteenth and twentieth centuries. It is useful to remember, however, that the two words reflect distinct, though complementary, concepts. Historically, the word *state* refers to the authoritative legal order that controls and governs the territory. *Nation*, in contrast, refers to the cultural, ideological, and emotional bonds that link the population of the territory to each other, to the territory itself, and to the state. Because these words have different meanings and implications, they are linked to issues of development in different ways. To explain these linkages, we need to turn to the fifth and sixth themes of the book.

The fifth theme is that of the *relationship between individuals and institutions of the state*. For a variety of reasons, state authorities in Asia (like those elsewhere) have sought to expand the influence and control of their policies and institutions. This expansion has been a response to both internal and external pressures. For example, Western imperialism propelled Chinese, Indian, and Japanese leaders to modernize the civilian and military bureaucracies of their states in order to counter and eliminate external threats. The preoccupation with internal and external threats has also defined the primary goals of the new political elites who came into power in the twentieth century: unity and state sovereignty, domestic civil order, economic self-sufficiency, and development. The implementation of these goals has called for building up state authority and capability.

What have been the consequences of this process for ordinary citizens? Obviously, the consequences vary by time and place and also depend on the citizens in question. Some pay more taxes than others or receive better services. Expanded police authority affects the poor, illiterate, and female more than others. Those advantaged by traditional sources of power are better placed to convert their power into "modern" influence through new institutions such as political parties. One of the tasks of this book is to look at politics as the interplay between individuals and the state, with different kinds of groups, parties, bureaucracies, and other institutions acting as key intermediaries.

The last major theme is that of *national identity and nationalism*. Before the nineteenth century, national identity was seldom a concern—if it existed at all—except for intellectuals or those in the highest levels of state leadership. By the early twentieth century, nationalist elites throughout

Asia began to see national identity and cohesion as a tool to be used in eliminating Western colonialism and imperialism. Nationalism begat nationalism: Some Asian politicians were deeply influenced by the schooling in nationalist theories and ideologies they received in Europe and America. As successful nationalist movements in Asia arose, they inspired other Asian movements.

In several ways, the focus on national identity links the earlier themes. Asian nationalism cannot be understood without reference to the flow and mixing of indigenous, Asian, and Western cultures. Many have argued that socioeconomic development facilitates the growth and spread of nationalist sentiment and loyalty, as when public schools are established, roads built, and radios distributed. A strong sense of national identity and cohesion also facilitates the implementation of development policies insofar as individuals feel loyalty toward the state institutions charged with formulating and executing those policies. For this reason, elites charged with enhancing state independence and wealth typically seek to nurture nationalism at the same time.

## Lenses

It is important to reflect on our role as outsiders trying to understand the inside of Asian politics. I am one such outsider, as will be most of the readers of this book. We must therefore look for and even create bridges between our external, non-Asian positions and the internal realities of Indian, Chinese, and Japanese politics. We are not the first to seek to build such bridges. We cannot hope to understand Asian politics without building on the work of those who have preceded us as students and scholars—but at the same time, and in many ways, our understanding is biased by our predecessors.

Lenses clarify and magnify; they also distort and color. At the very least, when we look through them, we see some things and not others. So it is with intellectual lenses: They make it possible for us to see things we would otherwise miss, but when this happens, our focus becomes selective and often distorted.

Among the many ways in which our knowledge and hence our understanding of Asian politics has been filtered, three are especially significant for the text that follows. The first has come to be known as **Orientalism**, a historical "Orientalist," or Eurocentric, bias in Western scholarship. The second is a clearly identifiable political or ideological bias in researching, interpreting, or reporting facts. The third is the distortion that often results from the process of translating one language (and its inevitable cultural context) into another.

## Orientalism and Eurocentrism: Culture, Knowledge, and Politics

In the late 1970s, Edward Said argued in his book *Orientalism* that the idea of the Orient was in effect a European invention. The Orient, he claimed, has existed as part of a dualistic mindset that juxtaposes Us and Other (or We and They), West and East. Further, the historical relationship between West and East has been one of power and, as suggested above in the sketch of Western colonialism and imperialism, frequently of Western domination of Eastern territory, people, and culture. Examples of the attitudes and interpretations that have accompanied Western hegemony would range from those that explicitly postulate Western superiority to those that stereotype "Easterners" as brutal (Mongol hordes), sneaky (East Asians in general), terrorist (West Asians), or exotic (Asian women).

One of Said's central arguments is that it is not only views or attitudes that are formed from the relationships of power between East and West but also the structure of knowledge itself and the ways these East-West relationships have been institutionalized in our universities. Consequently, our thought and language are conditioned by our political-cultural relationship.[5]

In its simplest form, the attack on Orientalism is a reminder that our (Western) understanding of Asia's history and cultures has been filtered through the lenses of our own history and culture. These lenses have magnified some phenomena and excluded others, giving a focus to the Western scholarship that enables comparative study of Asian politics, while simultaneously inculcating biases that are so pervasive we barely notice them.[6] To illustrate: A glance at a map of Asia would suggest that we refer to West, South, or East Asia. But it is commonplace to write and talk about the "Middle East" and "Far East," which are clearly Eurocentric terms because they reflect Asian geographic regions as seen from Europe.

## Scholarship, Politics, and "Truth"

Sometimes the political bias in the development of knowledge is immediate and explicit and manifests itself through political control that clearly serves the interests of a ruling ideology or party or the government in general. Examples of such control are almost universal. It was illegal for Americans, including scholars, to travel to China in the 1960s. The Chinese Communist Party (CCP) and government, in turn, have long directed the scope and focus of research and publication, particularly on political and social questions. The Indian government banned some books during the period of the **Emergency** (1975 1977), and the Japanese government has periodically edited school textbooks to minimize Japan's imperialism in East Asia during the first half of the twentieth century.

It may be difficult to identify political or ideological bias, particularly when there is no overt government control. Scholars themselves may not recognize their own assumptions and prejudices or may not admit the way these influence their research—the questions they ask, the weaknesses of their data, and so forth. If research is sponsored by a government agency or another organization with a vested interest in the research findings (such as a private corporation), the scholarly lenses may be suspect.

A good illustration of these issues is found in American scholarship on China, beginning with charges in the 1940s and 1950s that American officials and journalists working in China had failed to understand the "true" nature and intentions of the Communist Chinese movement. These gullible Americans, their detractors charged, were too sympathetic to the Communists, who were locked in civil war with the Nationalist Chinese forces under **Chiang Kai-shek**; and they consequently contributed to the "loss" of China to the Communists. In retrospect, we can see that China watching, whether conducted by U.S. State Department analysts, journalists, or academics, was heavily influenced by Cold War politics.

The debate over the nature of the pre-1949 Communist movement is echoed in the shifts of opinion since 1949, and these debates continue to affect both popular and scholarly views of China. The controversy over Steven Mosher is an illustration of the ongoing disagreements as to the "real" nature of Chinese politics. In 1983, Mosher, a doctoral student in anthropology at Stanford University, published a book called *Broken Earth: The Rural Chinese*,[7] in which he criticized Chinese politics, particularly those on birth control. In the same year, the anthropology department dismissed Mosher from its program, charging that his fieldwork in China had involved illegal and unethical conduct. Mosher responded that the university action was politically motivated because his writings were critical of Chinese policies and that the Chinese government had threatened to curtail social science research in China if Stanford did not censure Mosher.[8]

Mosher was again part of a controversy over interpreting Chinese politics when his book *China Misperceived* was published in 1990.[9] In this book, he resurrected the old criticisms that American scholars and journalists had been "soft" on Chinese communism in the 1930s and 1940s and argued that American academics and journalists in the 1960s and 1970s repeated much of the earlier infatuation with China. Coming on the heels of the 1989 Tiananmen Square demonstrations and their repression by the Beijing government, Mosher's negative interpretations of China seemed warranted. As others have pointed out, however, the real problem with our lenses is that they are either black or white, leaving little room for the gray truths of Chinese politics and policies. Even the best-trained scholars have been influenced by the cycles of romanticism and cynicism, idealization or condemnation that color the broader climate of opinion. These cycles are rooted in the nineteenth century and have characterized American approaches to China throughout the twentieth century, with the result that scholars should be particularly sensitive about the way the political climate continues to influence our China watching.[10]

Although it will be important in this book to recognize cases of scholarly bias or overt political control of knowledge, it is equally important to recognize how the discussion itself of these issues reflects our respective positions on vital questions of intellectual and cultural integrity, national independence, and religious autonomy. When culture, nation, and religion not only intersect but reinforce each other, there may be no room for compromise and very little scope for understanding the Other's point of view. The clearest case in recent history is that of the bounty levied on the life of Salman Rushdie, the Indian-born (Muslim) author of *The Satanic Verses*.[11] To a Western reader, the book is an imaginary and amusing novel, but it was decreed blasphemous—literally viewed as profane writing concerning God and what is held most sacred—by the highest Iranian authority. To empathize with the death decree, we would need to understand the Iranian national perspective in the light of its rejection of things Western, partly because of Iran's historical association of Western things with Western domination of the "Orient." But we would clearly need to go further and understand the intersection of nation-state, culture, and faith in an Iranian worldview that also rejects the secularism of the West, a secularism that lies behind the humor and fancy of Rushdie's novel.[12] In our secular, liberal-democratic world, where the highest values are freedom of thought and individual expression (*not* God), death decrees for novels belong to a faraway era of inquisitions and witch-hunts.

On a question such as that of Salman Rushdie and his novel, not only are political positions poles apart but the construction of reality may be so different that it becomes practically impossible to talk about knowledge or truth in the same way. Embedded in the contemporary Western, academic definition of knowledge and truth is a secular, scientific worldview that rejects the original meaning of blasphemy. To recapture our earlier metaphor, here it is not solely an issue of different lenses but also concerns blindness to the Other's way of seeing.

Happily, our intellectual and emotional tasks in studying Asian politics will not all be so daunting. But we would be well advised to revisit the Rushdie case occasionally to remind ourselves of the differences in worldviews that exist and that have become politicized with the growth of anticolonialism and what in the West is labeled "religious fundamentalism."

## Language

In addition to various kinds of political and cultural biases, language itself constitutes a lens that illuminates or distorts our understanding of Asian politics. As noted earlier, the Asian countries highlighted here draw on ancient traditions of literacy. They offer an abundance of philosophical, literary, and political or legal texts for scholars to *translate* and study. The process of translation of an Asian language itself constitutes a study, as it does with any language. In the case of China, India, and Japan, however, translation encompasses the additional steps of **transliteration** and **romanization**. Words that are written in the characters of one alphabet are written in the characters of another alphabet (transliterated) in order to approximate the same sounds or words. To "romanize" means to write the characters from the different alphabets (and scripts) in the Roman alphabet, which is used for English and other Western languages. Since romanization is often only an approximation of the original sound, different spellings of the same word are common—such as Moghul/Mughal, Moslem/Muslim, or Sanscrit/Sanskrit.[13]

Chinese and Japanese (or Arabic, for West Asian scholars) alphabets present comparable technical and interpretive problems. The case of Japanese is further complicated by the use of three traditional systems of characters: Along with the Chinese characters (*kanji*) are found Hiragana and Katakana alphabets, each with a different script. The problems confronted by the casual visitor to Asia are multiplied for the scholar, who must both understand the various translations possible for characters and then be able to translate with the greatest accuracy the meaning that is consistent with the context of the word. The challenge is even greater when words change meaning through time.[14]

# Organization and Approach

This book is divided into four parts. Chapters 2–4 in Part One, "People and Politics," introduce the populations of India, China, and Japan, with particular attention paid to those qualitative features, such as gender and ethnic diversity, that are especially significant for contemporary politics. Part Two, "The Foundation of Politics," includes Chapters 5–7, which examine the growth of nationalism and the contemporary state structures of the three countries under study. Each of these chapters, like those in Part One, focuses on a single country.

Part Three, entitled "Government Structures: Form and Substance," includes comparisons of the constitutions of the three countries (Chapter 8), the national governments of India and Japan (Chapter 9), and China's party and state structures (Chapter 10). Chapter 11 compares the subnational levels of government in the three countries, paying particular attention to issues of decentralization.

Part Four looks more closely at the relations between individuals and the state. Chapter 12, "The Decay of One-Party Rule," compares the internal structures of the Congress, Liberal Democratic, and Chinese Communist parties and examines the political changes that have eroded the lengthy dominance of these parties. Chapter 13 examines the most important features of the bureaucratic and coercive structures of the three countries. Chapter 14 discusses the role of socioeconomic development in the changing relationships between government and governed.

Readers will note that Chapters 2–7 are essentially country studies that lay the basis for other approaches to comparative politics undertaken in the succeeding chapters. The shifting nature of comparison between (and sometimes within) the later chapters reflects a deliberate choice. The treatment of India and Japan in Chapter 9, for example, is synchronic, focusing on similarities and differences across national boundaries in roughly the same time period. Chapter 10 on China, in contrast, contains diachronic comparison of one political system over time.

No one book can contain all that is important or interesting about the politics of three countries as complex as Japan, China, and India. The purpose of the approach used here is to encourage readers to explore more fully the individual countries in Asia. The organization of the book is also designed to raise comparative questions that are relevant not just to Asian politics but to other regions as well. I hope that readers will move quickly beyond the questions raised here to others that they find equally or more relevant to their thinking about politics.

The discussions in this book place a relatively heavy emphasis on history and culture in the belief that these are areas of substantial ignorance for most of us raised outside the Asian traditions. Although studying culture and history often leads to the assumption that countries are unique and therefore their political systems are not subject to valid comparison, such an assumption ignores the extensive cross-fertilization among Asian countries and among Asia, Europe, and the rest of the world. Hence, both that which is unique and that which is shared are found in this book.

As the comparative journey begins, a note about romanization of words from the Indian, Chinese, and Japanese languages is in order. There are numerous scholarly conventions about alternative forms of transliteration and romanization, as explained earlier. Those that have become the most widely accepted in recent decades and that readers are the most likely to encounter in the library or on the Internet are the ones used here. The most confusion generally arises over transliteration of Chinese words because for the past two decades, the People's Republic of China has used the *pinyin* system in preference to other spellings. When the PRC shifted to *pinyin*, transliteration became a matter of politics, and the Chinese government of Taiwan retained one of the earlier systems, called Wade-Giles (after two nineteenth-century Englishmen) in translations to English. Thus, readers will find, for example, that the revolutionary Chinese leader, Mao Zedong (*pinyin*), is called Mao Tse-tung in older publications and anywhere the Wade-Giles system is used. Where necessary, endnotes are added to clarify confusing situations.

Finally, there is the subject of personal names. East Asians generally place their surname, or family name, first; for example, Mao Zedong's family name is Mao. This convention has been observed in translations to English for writings on China and is followed here. The Japanese also place their family name first, but this has not been carried over consistently to English. Many widely read English-language materials published in Japan (such as newspapers) have adopted the European name order, as have some scholarly publications on Japan. Thus, in the chapters that follow, Chinese surnames come first in the text, but Japanese names for the contemporary period are given in the Western order. Indian names are also given in this order, which is the convention in India. Macrons (short lines over vowels) and other marks that are used as aids for pronouncing words transliterated from the Indian and Japanese languages have been omitted in order to facilitate reading.

## Notes

1. Words in boldface type may be found in the glossary at the end of the text.

2. James Walsh, "Asia's Different Drum," *Time* (international edition), June 14, 1993, pp. 16–19; Fareed Zakaria, "Culture Is Destiny: A Conversation with Lee Kuan Yew," *Foreign Affairs* 73, no. 2 (March/April 1994), pp. 109–126.

3. Yayori Matsui, *Women's Asia* (London and Atlantic Highlands, N.J.: Zed Books, 1987), chap. 9.

4. Jonathan D. Spence, *The Search for Modern China* (New York: W. W. Norton and Company, 1990), p. 43.

5. Edward W. Said, *Orientalism* (New York: Vintage Books, 1979), p. 11.

6. For a criticism of Said and an analysis of the political and scholarly biases of the (anti-) Orientalist argument, see Bernard Lewis, *Islam and the West* (New York and Oxford: Oxford University Press, 1993), chap. 6.

7. Steven W. Mosher, *Broken Earth: The Rural Chinese* (New York: Free Press, 1983). See also his later book, *A Mother's Ordeal: One Woman's Fight Against China's One-Child Policy* (New York: Harcourt Brace, 1993).

8. Peter Van Ness, "The Mosher Affair," *Wilson Quarterly* 8, no. 1 (1984), pp. 160–172. Mosher sued Stanford; ultimately, his charges were dismissed and in early 1990, he dropped his lawsuit. *Chronicle of Higher Education*, January 10, 1990.

9. Steven W. Mosher, *China Misperceived: American Illusions and Chinese Reality* (New York: Basic Books, 1990). Mosher's book is part of a larger debate about American interpretations of China that flared up in the early 1990s. See Stephen R.

MacKinnon and Oris Friesen, eds., *China Reporting: An Oral History of American Journalism in the 1930s and 1940s* (Berkeley: University of California Press, 1987); and Mosher's references to *China Reporting* in his 1990 book *China Misperceived*. Jonathan Mirsky has placed Mosher's book and his experience at Stanford in the broader context of American scholarship on China in "The Myth of Mao's China," *New York Review of Books* 38, no. 10 (May 30, 1991), pp. 19–27.

10. For the background on the shifts of opinion toward China, see Harold Isaacs, *Scratches on Our Minds: American Images of China and India* (New York: John Day, 1958). Chalmers Johnson, "What's Wrong with Chinese Political Studies?" and Harry Harding, "From China, with Disdain: New Trends in the Study of China," provide thoughtful analyses of the scholarly shifts in China studies. Both articles are in *Asian Survey* 22, no. 10 (October 1992), pp. 919–933 and pp. 934–958, respectively.

11. Salman Rushdie, *The Satanic Verses* (New York: Viking Penguin, 1989).

12. Bernard Lewis, "The Roots of Muslim Rage," *Atlantic* 266, no. 3 (September 1990), pp. 47–60.

13. In these examples transliterated from the North Indian Devanagari script, the second version of each word has replaced the first as the preferred romanized form for scholars.

14. Bernard Lewis has illustrated the problems of translating Arabic as they are magnified across time. The word *siyasa*, for example, in a thirteenth-century text meant "severe discretionary punishment"—hardly synonymous with its contemporary translation as "politics" or "policy." *Islam and the West*, pp. 66–67.

# Part One

# *People and Politics*

By the 1990s, the population of the world was approximately 5.5 billion, and almost 60 percent of these people lived in Asia. India and China alone are home to over 2 billion people. Put differently, more than one-third of all human beings are either Chinese or Indian, and by the beginning of the twenty-first century, two of every five people will be Chinese or Indian.

Politics is about people, and the size and composition of a country's population has both direct and indirect implications for politics. For example, countries that are relatively overpopulated find that their resources are stretched thin and the demands for government services typically far exceed the ability of the government to provide even minimal services for citizens. In response to population pressures, governments often initiate policies in areas such as birth control and abortion. In Asia, China and India provide obvious case studies on the dynamics of extremely large numbers of people and on high population density, and in both cases, the governments have had long-standing population policies.

Both the size (the "quantity") and the composition (the qualitative features) of a country's population have direct and indirect consequences for politics and government. An example of the direct significance for politics of a country's demographic makeup is its degree of ethnic homogeneity or heterogeneity. No one who lived through the 1990s could deny the connection between ethnic heterogeneity and the civil conflicts in the Balkan Peninsula (the former Yugoslavia), for example. Similarly, those who follow Indian politics have noted the direct relationship between the diversity of populations and political conflicts in regions such as Punjab or between Hindus and Muslims throughout much of the country. In contrast, the high degree of ethnic homogeneity in Japan is often pointed to as a contributing factor in that nation's political stability.

Like many countries in the world—and in marked contrast to North America and Western Europe—the majority of Asian countries are predominantly rural. The exceptions, such as Taiwan and Japan, are almost all in East Asia, but countries as diverse as Pakistan, Nepal, and Vietnam have at least two-thirds of their people living in rural areas. At the same time, some of the highest concentrations of people in the world are found in Asia: Ten of the world's largest cities are in South and East Asia, including six that are in predominantly rural India and China (Calcutta, Bombay, Delhi, Beijing, Shanghai, and Tianjin).

Differences between urban and rural areas are economically, socially, and politically important in all three countries that are the focus of this book. Even in Japan, where the rural population had declined to 23 percent by the mid-1990s, farming and fishing communities, which account for most of the rural families, continue to wield significant political power and pose political dilemmas to the leadership. The gradual increase in urban populations throughout Asia tends to increase pressures on governments by concentrating the demands for public facilities or infrastructure, such as roads, sewers, and water lines. Urban agglomerations may also become "flash points" for conflicts among politically mobilized groups.

The geographic distribution of people is made more important by the qualitative features of a country's population. Are ethnic groups concentrated in one region or are they spread throughout the country? Has rural-to-urban migration skewed the age and gender composition of some regions, for example, by leaving disproportionate numbers of women, children, and old people in the countryside? Are poverty and its companions such as unemployment, illiteracy, and hunger concentrated in urban or rural areas? Do diseases (malaria, AIDS, and so on) affect some population groups more than others?

The following discussion makes no attempt to provide an in-depth demographic analysis of the three countries. Rather, it offers a general overview and then emphasizes those factors that, at the end of the twentieth century, seem to be of both immediate and long-term political significance. Three criteria were used to select illustrative cases: the usefulness of the cases as examples of the themes introduced in Chapter 1; the clarity of the political implications as gleaned from both academic scholarship and media coverage; and the issues gauged to be of particular interest to general readers. We begin with India, in many ways the most complex case.

# *two*

# India

## Population Size and Distribution

India's 1991 census showed that the country's population had increased in ten years from 683 million to 844 million. Although there seems to be a slight drop in the annual growth rate (from 2.2 to 2.1 percent), the country is rapidly moving toward 1 billion people.[1] An enormous electronic billboard at a major intersection in New Delhi symbolizes the population boom: Like a basketball scoreboard, the minute-by-minute increase in the "score" of India's population is illuminated by computer-driven lights.

The nation is gradually becoming more urbanized, both because of the natural reproduction of city dwellers and as a result of migration from the rural areas. Whereas the 1981 census found that there were twelve cities with a population of more than 1 million, by the 1991 census, there were twenty-three such—almost twice as many. The number of cities with a population between 100,000 and 1 million had similarly increased. Although many of the people who are newcomers to the cities end up living in slums or on the streets and sidewalks (hence the description "pavement dwellers"), they will almost all stay in the cities, where opportunities are better than in the villages they left.

Another feature of the distribution of India's population is its density throughout the regions and states of the country. India has twenty-six states, in addition to a number of smaller Union Territories that are administered directly by the central government (see Figure 2.1). As in many federal systems, including those of the United States and Canada, the Indian states range in area from the small ones in the Northeast (Sikkim, Tripura, and so on) to the largest states of Madhya Pradesh and Rajasthan.

19

The states that have traditionally had the lowest population density are either mountainous (Jammu and Kashmir, Himachal Pradesh), have a large desert (Rajasthan), or are tropical rain forests (the states in the northeastern region). Some of these states, however, have experienced a fast increase in population density in recent years that, in turn, has caused political controversy. For example, many of the new residents of Assam and Nagaland came from Bangladesh, having left their homes both to escape the 1970–1971 Pakistani civil war (Bangladesh was formerly East Pakistan) and to escape the pressures of land scarcity, poverty, and natural calamity that characterize life in much of Bangladesh. Their presence in the northeast Indian states has contributed to tension with long-established residents, many of whom are from tribal groups, and to conflicts over electoral rolls (lists of eligible voters).

The rhythm of life varies dramatically between urban and rural areas. Urban culture and modern technology are transforming every corner of India, but the pace and the nature of the changes are uneven. In rural areas, it is still common to see scenes like the one in Photo 2.1, in which the women and young children of a family are riding to and from a fair, market, or religious pilgrimage in a cart drawn by a camel. The men and older boys walk; the women and older girls are careful to cover their faces most of the time (particularly in the presence of strangers). In the largest cities, meanwhile, cable television has arrived, bringing with it satellite broadcasts from Hong Kong that include Hindi movies, as well as MTV from the United States. Those with access to this new technology, including more than 200 million people who make up the consumer middle classes in India, are continually confronted with political news. If a particular event is not reported on the state-controlled radio or television stations, they can find out about it by watching the British Broadcasting Corporation (BBC) channel.

The importance of mass communications and the difference between urban and rural peoples cannot be overestimated, for the literacy rate in India is still relatively low. Moreover, despite the rise in literacy in recent decades, the absolute number of illiterates continues to increase—another example of the problems associated with India's continually growing population. The literacy rate has increased from roughly 16 percent in 1951 (the first census after India's independence from Great Britain) to 42 percent in 1991; but in the decade between 1981 and 1991 alone, more than 67 million people joined the illiterate population.

## Gender

Discussion about literacy leads into issues that pertain not just to the size or density of India's population but to its composition and diversity as

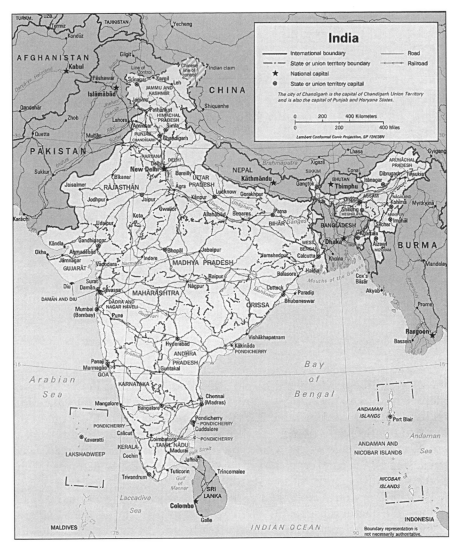

*Figure 2.1   Map of India*

well. In the case of literacy, for example, there are differences among the populations of literates and illiterates that are significant for politics in both the short and long run. The most important differences are related to gender and to geographic regions. As an example, the southwestern state of Kerala, with its combined male-female literacy rate of 90 percent and female literacy rate of 87 percent, is known for giving higher status to women than other Indian states.[2] Four major states in the northern half of

*Photo 2.1    Camel-drawn cart, Rajasthan. Photo courtesy of James W. Boyd.*

the country (Bihar, Madhya Pradesh, Rajasthan, and Uttar Pradesh) have literacy rates well under 50 percent. More striking is the gap in male-female literacy, as seen in Table 2.1: About three-fourths of the women in these four large states (which constitute 40 percent of India's population) are illiterate. Women's roles tend to be very traditional in these areas, as is suggested by the rural scene just discussed in Photo 2.1, which was taken in Rajasthan.

When literacy rates are linked to another characteristic of India's population—the **declining sex ratio**—we can start to answer questions that are relevant to every comparative politics study, such as who participates in political life and why. The declining sex ratio characterizes several other countries in Asia as well. The sex ratio is the proportion of females to males in a population. In most of the world's populations, females outnumber males, even though more males are born. The higher male birth rate is neutralized by a higher male mortality rate. The declining sex ratio in India means the proportion of females to males is declining, thereby raising questions about increasing mortality rates for girls and women. Table 2.2 illustrates this point more clearly: An equal sex ratio would be 1,000; that is, there would be 1,000 females for every 1,000 males. In 1901, the sex ratio in India was 972; it had dropped to 929 by 1991.

TABLE 2.1   Male and Female Literacy in Five Indian States (1991 census)

| State | Percent Male | Percent Female | Total Percent of Literates[a] |
|---|---|---|---|
| Kerala | 94.45 | 86.93 | 90.59 |
| Bihar | 52.63 | 23.10 | 38.54 |
| Madhya Pradesh | 57.43 | 28.39 | 43.45 |
| Rajasthan | 55.07 | 20.84 | 38.81 |
| Uttar Pradesh | 55.35 | 26.02 | 41.71 |

[a]Percentage of literates to estimated population, age 7 years and older.
*Source:* Adapted from Mahendra K. Premi, *India's Population: Heading Towards a Billion (An Analysis of 1991 Census Provisional Results)* (Delhi: B. R. Publishing Corporation, 1991), p. 69.

Three central questions are raised by this trend: (1) Is there greater underenumeration of females in the census? (2) Have living conditions for women deteriorated in comparison to those for men? (3) Has the sex ratio at birth become more favorable to men? The answers to these questions are fragmentary but suggest that census enumerators (who are generally male) tend to undercount females. Additionally, conditions for girls and women are not improving to the degree that one would expect with socioeconomic development, and the male sex ratio at birth is becoming more favorable, in part due to medical technology.[3] The evidence regarding the impact of technology on the sex ratio indicates that in India, as in China, the availability of fetal sex-determination tests, when combined with the traditional cultural preference for boys and the acceptability of abortion, results in a startling statistic: In over 95 percent of the cases in which abortion is chosen after a sex-determination test such as amniocentesis, the aborted fetus is female. In cases where abortion is not possible, neglect of female infants and girls, especially among the poor, results in high mortality rates, and sometimes female infanticide is practiced.[4]

Thus the declining sex ratio is just the tip of the iceberg where issues of gender are concerned. The advantages accorded Indian men begin at birth and cut across all aspects of life, affecting health, access to education, employment, and, of course, politics. It is not surprising, therefore, that formal political positions (in the government bureaucracy, legislatures, and courts) are overwhelmingly held by men. In the mid-1990s, less than 10 percent of the national bicameral legislature was female, less than 5 percent of national cabinet positions were held by women, there were no women on the Indian Supreme Court, and only one of the state-level chief ministers was a woman. At the same time, we cannot forget that one of Asia's most powerful political leaders in the past half century was **Indira Gandhi**, India's prime minister from 1966 to 1977 and again from 1980 to 1984.

TABLE 2.2   India's Declining Sex Ratio (females per thousand males)

| Selected Census Years | Sex Ratio |
|:---:|:---:|
| 1901 | 972 |
| 1921 | 955 |
| 1951 | 946 |
| 1971 | 930 |
| 1991 | 929 |

*Source:* Adapted from Mahendra K. Premi, *India's Population: Heading Towards a Billion (An Analysis of 1991 Census Provisional Results)* (Delhi: B. R. Publishing Corporation, 1991), p. 69.

The issues of gender and politics go beyond formal political roles, however. One of the oldest and most diverse women's movements in the world is found in India.[5] Self-styled women's rights activists and feminists today range from upper-class matrons active in social welfare causes to poor rural and urban women who have assumed leadership roles in grassroots political groups committed to radical change. Women's groups have taken the lead in debating and changing conditions of employment in urban slums and have addressed such diverse issues as environmental damage caused by large-scale development projects and the physical abuse of women. These activities represent a higher level of political influence and commitment than is found among women's groups in either China or Japan.

## Caste and Class

Caste is intrinsic to **Hinduism**, the principal religion in India. Even communities whose origins stem from a different worldview, such as Christian communities, are marked by caste divisions. In the dominant Hindu view, caste is inherent in the nature of human society: Relations between human beings are and should be defined by the behavioral norms and roles that are ascribed to one's caste. Caste, like gender, marks people at birth; only with great difficulty can individuals escape the attributes and roles of their caste.[6]

For non-Indians, caste and class are probably the hardest qualities of Indian society to understand.[7] Our English word "caste" is derived from the word that the seventeenth-century Portuguese used to describe the Hindu social groups they found in India. They called these groups *castas*, meaning tribes, clans, or families. The term *caste* has come to include two kinds of social divisions that, though different, are closely related. The larger of these divisions is known by its **Sanskrit** name *varna*, or "color," and has been loosely translated as both class and caste, which adds to the confusion.

Scholars believe that *varna* came to India when Aryan tribes began invading the subcontinent from the northwest around 4,000 years ago, a period about which historians know comparatively little.[8] Much of what is known about the origins of caste in *varna* is actually extrapolated from literary texts, the most famous of which is the *Rig Veda*, one of the world's great historical documents. The *Rig Veda* was originally a collection of hymns to be sung in praise of the gods of the early tribes that entered India as part of the Aryan invasion. The memorization and recitation of these and other Vedic hymns was the exclusive prerogative of the priestly class of these tribes. The most important of these tribes, the Bharatas, gave its name to India: **Bharat** (both in Sanskrit, the original Indo-European language of the Aryans, and Hindi, its most important modern derivative). This root word appears in other contexts in this book. It is found, for example, in the name of India's most controversial political party, the **Bharatiya Janata Party** (BJP), or Indian People's Party.

The original priestly class of the Bharatas and other tribes became the highest *varna* in the social order that was gradually created in what we now call India. Three additional *varna* gradually crystallized during the period of the *Rig Veda* and have survived to the present era. Beneath the priestly *varna* (the *brahmana*, or **Brahmins**), were the warriors, rulers, and administrators (Kshatriyas); traders, merchants, and farmers (Vaishyas); and at the bottom, peasants, serfs, or servants (Shudras).

As the Aryans settled among the darker-skinned peoples who were the original inhabitants of India, the meaning of color seems to have become more important, and the Aryans laid more stress on purity of blood.[9] Gradually, the indigenous groups sank in the social scale, class divisions hardened, and the system of *varna* was given religious sanction. The people most disadvantaged by this system were actually outside the *varna*, or outside the caste system, and were called by the pejorative term "**outcastes**." Constituting about 15 percent of the population of modern India, these people were also known as "**untouchables**," because they were viewed as so inferior that it would be ritually polluting for people in higher castes to touch them.[10]

*Varna* is one kind of social division included in the term caste. The other is known also by its Sanskrit name, *jati*. Generally, when the term "caste" is used here (as in "caste politics"), it means *jati*. India has several thousand *jati*, and *jati* is the social group that matters the most in the day-to-day lives of Indian women and men. Historically, *jati* may have emerged from the intermingling of all kinds of tribal groups, and historical evidence suggests that early *jati* were associated with different village trades or crafts, such as pottery. This would help account for the fact that in contemporary village India, caste (*jati*) often continues to be an occupational grouping. In urban areas, trades and occupations as a defining characteristic of caste tend to break down more rapidly, as do customs of ritual purification and pollution.[11]

Castes are historically endogamous; that is, their members marry within their own group. That this feature is very much alive can be seen in one of the most interesting features of modern Indian newspapers, the matrimonial ads. Families in search of appropriate marriage partners for their sons and daughters place an ad in the matrimonial classifieds and often specify the caste of the family, making it clear they are looking for a potential bride or groom of the same caste. The following illustration, which is a composite of several classifieds, includes caste and educational references and also makes clear the preference for fair-skinned marriage candidates: "Alliance invited for tall, handsome Brahmin engineer, seeking well-qualified, vegetarian, fair-skinned girl up to 30. Will love/care for life. Full details, photograph (returnable). Write to Box X."

Caste is also very much alive in politics. Many people thought that the importance of caste, particularly its most negative features such as discrimination against lower caste groups and "untouchables," would decline after India received its independence from Great Britain. One reason for this assumption was that one of India's great nationalist leaders during the first half of the twentieth century, **Mohandas K. Gandhi**, rejected the discriminatory features of the traditional caste system. The Mahatma (or "the Great Soul"), as Gandhi has become known, insisted that his followers, no matter what their caste, share such tasks as cleaning latrines. This would be viewed as polluting, and therefore repugnant, to all but the lowliest Hindus. Mahatma Gandhi also used the word "**harijans**" ("children of God") for untouchables, thereby indicating their special importance in his view of the ideal society to be created after the British were driven from India. It should be noted that Gandhi was partially responding to pressure from another brilliant Indian leader, **Dr. B. R. Ambedkar**. Like Gandhi, Ambedkar was a British-trained lawyer. Unlike Gandhi, he was an untouchable who had experienced firsthand the discrimination against "outcastes."

Gandhi succeeded in forcing many to rethink the role of caste in Indian society. He was a committed Hindu who believed that untouchability was an abhorrent corruption of Hinduism and should be eliminated. In contrast, Ambedkar called for the destruction of the entire caste system and attacked Hinduism itself, which he argued was the foundation of caste.[12] The Indian Constitution represents a compromise between these positions. For example, Article 17 proclaims that untouchability is abolished "and its practice in any form is forbidden." Caste, however, is not abolished, although Article 15 prohibits discrimination against any citizen on the basis of caste (as well as on the basis of race, sex, or religion). It may be argued, in fact, that the Constitution actually sanctified caste and ensured its enduring impact on Indian politics. The First Amendment to the Constitution in 1951 added to Article 15 the provision that nothing in the article prohibiting discrimination "shall prevent the State from making any special provision for the advancement of any socially and educationally backward classes or for the Scheduled Castes and the Scheduled Tribes." The castes and tribes in question are the former untouchable *jati* and indigenous tribes, whose names were first placed on a schedule or list by the British rulers in 1935 and 1936. The special provisions called for in the Constitution included, for example, the reservation of legislative seats and university positions for the **Scheduled Castes and Tribes**.[13] Such provisions created a precedent for Indian-style "affirmative action" measures to help the most disadvantaged citizens, and these measures are today the subject of intense political debate and conflict.

Caste has become politically salient for other reasons. It provides one of the most important organizational bases in India's intense, combative elections. So-called vote banks (groups of voters mobilized for a particular candidate) are often organized along caste lines, and prominent politicians, especially at the state and local levels, are often identified by their association with a particular caste. Caste has also become more important in recent decades because the lowest castes, consisting primarily of those formerly considered untouchables, have increasingly mobilized in order to press their political demands and combat discrimination. They have chosen to call themselves by the name *dalit*, meaning "oppressed" or "downtrodden," to signify their commitment to political activism.[14]

In view of the long-term social and cultural importance of both *varna* and *jati*, it is not surprising that *class* as conventionally understood in Western democracies (as a group of people marked by socioeconomic status) cannot be understood in isolation from caste. Particularly in Indian villages, class *is jati*. Even though most Indians still live in villages, urbanization persistently changes the country's socioeconomic landscape. In some cities, industrialization has created an urban proletariat, or working class. Long-standing problems of underemployment and unemployment radicalize men, in particular (including many from traditionally high-status castes), against policies they see as favoring lower castes. At the same time, there is a huge middle class whose tastes and lifestyles fuel an expanding consumer economy. Caste and class are interdependent, and both are in a state of flux.

Finally, one additional social category must be introduced here—the **Backward Classes** (BCs). The word "backward," as used in the Indian context, is distinctive and refers to a large, mixed category of people who are economically and socially disadvantaged in the Indian hierarchy. The Backward Classes are not classes in the Western sense but rather are a combination of caste and class, although the precise mixture of criteria for establishing the category is controversial. Together, the Backward Classes include the Scheduled Castes and Tribes, along with the "Other Backward Classes" (OBCs). The OBCs are a residual category, and the question of establishing the boundaries of this group for purposes of determining government benefits has become one of the most hotly contested political issues in India today.[15] We will return to the BCs and OBCs in Chapter 13.

## Language

Indians routinely identify themselves as northerners or southerners. One major reason for this distinction is that the northern and southern parts of the country are dominated by different families of spoken and written languages. There are five major language families in India, but the most important are the **Dravidian** languages in the South and the Indo-European or Sanskrit-based languages in the North.[16] The Dravidian peoples inhabited North India before the Aryan invasions, and as the Aryan tribes came in, it is thought that many Dravidians moved south. Today, Dravidian-based languages dominate four southern states: Andhra Pradesh, Karnataka, Kerala, and Tamilnadu. Photo 2.2, which was taken in Tamilnadu, shows a sign in two Dravidian languages (Tamil and Malayalam) and is also a good example of Indian English.

Although there are important differences among these four languages, the fact that they are part of the same linguistic family contributes to a sense of regional identity in the South. This sense of identity has taken on clear political importance in the individual states as political parties have formed to assert the distinctiveness of regional culture and problems. The Dravida Munnetra Kazhagam (DMK, Dravidian Progressive Federation) is a good example of this development. Originally, the DMK urged the secession of the Dravidian South from India, arguing that the South is racially and culturally distinctive and that it has been dominated economically and politically by the North. The DMK and its offshoot, the AIADMK (the All-India Anna DMK) have dominated politics in the state of Tamilnadu since Independence.

When the Aryans first came to India, they brought their own language, Sanskrit, with them. Sanskrit, which belongs to the Indo-European family of languages, is no longer commonly spoken, but it remains the basis for the languages that dominate North India, much as numerous West European languages are rooted in Latin. The most important of the Sanskrit-based languages, Hindi, is widespread in North India (hence southerners often refer to the "Hindi North").

When the Muslims began to occupy India in the thirteenth century, their rulers and administrators spoke Persian and Arabic (Persian was

*Photo 2.2 "Mocking of Ladies Is Punishable."*
*Photo courtesy of John M. Riley.*

used for official purposes until the nineteenth century). Ultimately, a new language called **Urdu** emerged from the combination of Hindi, Persian, and Arabic. Urdu subsequently became the court language of the Mughals, who ruled India from the sixteenth to the nineteenth centuries.[17] Today it is spoken principally in North India and is especially important in Kashmir.

Like the Sanskrit languages and Urdu, English is also historically associated with an "invasion" or conquest—that of the British. English was introduced into the Indian school system in the early nineteenth century by the British colonial rulers and for most of the past two centuries has been associated with India's educated elite. Although only about 2 percent of Indians are fluent in English, the language retains an importance far beyond what is suggested by this low percentage. As a language of the elite, English is spoken by national-level politicians, administrators, and businesspeople. Because many of the Indian languages are not mutually intelligible, English is the only language spoken throughout India. Far from disappearing, as most Independence leaders assumed it would, English has been "Indianized": It has taken on its own accents and idioms, reflecting the cultural context in which it evolved. The uniqueness of Indian English is perpetuated not only in oral communication but also in the country's huge number of newspapers, magazines, and books published in English.

In all, there are over one dozen major languages in India, each spoken by millions of people. There are many more languages with smaller numbers of speakers and still more regional dialects. The multiple scripts of these languages add further confusion. The Sanskrit-based and Dravidian-based languages have different scripts, and there are even different scripts, grammar, and pronunciation rules within these families. Urdu, which is Arabic-based, has another script and is read from right to left. The influence of English is seen not only in its widespread use as a spoken and written language but in the occasional romanization of other Indian languages.

Part 17 of the Indian Constitution is devoted to the issue of language. It declares Hindi in Devanagari script (the script in which Sanskrit is written) to be the country's official language and includes the provision that English would also be an official national language for fifteen years after the Constitution went into effect in 1950 (Article 343). All laws, court, and legislative proceedings, until otherwise determined by Parliament, would also be in English (Article 348). The Constitution further provides for the establishment of official state languages. All of India's major languages, including Hindi but not English, are recognized in a list appended to the Constitution. This list, the Eighth Schedule of the Constitution, serves to legitimize the importance of these languages, even as the Constitution tries to give special prominence to Hindi. Article 351, for example, declares:

> It shall be the duty of the Union to promote the spread of the Hindi language, to develop it so that it may serve as a medium of expression for all the elements of the composite culture of India and to secure its enrichment by assimilating without interfering with its genius, the forms, style and expressions used in Hindustani and in the other languages of India specified in the Eighth Schedule, and by drawing, wherever necessary or desirable, for its vocabulary, primarily on Sanskrit and secondarily on other languages.

Hindustani combines Hindi and Urdu; it was favored by British educators and also by Gandhi as a way of unifying Hindi-speaking Hindus and Urdu-speaking Muslims. But later, Indian leaders lost interest in Hindustani and emphasized Hindi as a way of developing national identity. One-fourth to one-third of Indians speak Hindi—and that is a large minority of the population, but far from a majority. This is one reason that Hindi has never become a national language. Another reason is the strong resistance to Hindi by the southern states, where most people do not read, speak, or understand Hindi. Consequently, alongside Hindi, English continues to be the second official language.

As a practical matter, Indian elites are generally at least bilingual, if not trilingual. High-level administrators and politicians who come from a state outside the northern "Hindi belt" speak their own regional language (Bengali, Kannada, Tamil, and so on), along with Hindi and English. In many states, migration from the countryside creates communities of people who speak one language in the middle of cities dominated by another language. These migrants will pick up some of the dominant languages in their new home, but seldom do they become linguistically integrated into their new region. Thus, urbanization has only partly eroded the divisions of language in India.

# Religion

Every major religion in the world has its adherents in India, and religion is central to many of India's most enduring political conflicts. The most recent of these was a conflict that resulted in the destruction, in 1992, of an old Muslim mosque called the Babri Masjid, in the North Indian town of **Ayodhya**. The mosque's destruction was followed by Hindu-Muslim riots in numerous cities, recalling the persistent tensions between the two largest and most important religious communities in India. The events surrounding Ayodhya will be discussed in more detail in Chapter 5 because they illustrate the confluence of so many contemporary political issues in India, including the recent politicization of Hinduism.

Religion is important not just because of the political conflicts it generates but also because of its impact throughout history on cultural norms and practices that, in turn, influence people's orientations toward government and politics. For example, Chapter 5 includes a discussion of the traditional Hindu concept of **dharma**, which embraces a number of English concepts, including duty, law, principle, and right, all of which have implications for politics.

For Westerners, religion is defined primarily as a set of beliefs that are accompanied by an institutionalized authority and recognizable ritual practices. Religion may be an important part of people's lives, but for most individuals in our secularized societies, it is just one part of a much larger whole. In contrast, for most Indians, religion is much more: It is an all-embracing worldview and "attitude of mind that helps individuals order their universe and their place in it."[18] Religion is *the* source of meaning for life, not a distinguishable "part" of it. This is especially true of Hinduism, the dominant religion in India both in terms of numbers of identifiable Hindus and in terms of its impact on Indian society and culture. Gandhi and Ambedkar, it will be recalled, had to confront the central place of Hinduism in India when they sought to reform (Gandhi) or eliminate (Ambedkar) the caste system, for Hinduism and caste are inextricably intertwined. Put differently, Hinduism and India's fundamental social structure are inseparable.

Hinduism is more easily understood as a worldview and social system than as a single religion in the conventional sense used by most Westerners.[19] The belief in an all-pervasive, absolute, formless Reality coexists with the belief in one or more superhuman manifestations of this absolute One. These manifestations constitute a plurality that expresses the richness of the One, and they are anthropomorphized, meaning that they take human shapes and display human characteristics. Although these gods and goddesses take different forms and are called by different names, they are accepted and recognized across the regions and languages of India. They become real to children through symbols, pictures, and stories; they are celebrated in temples and homes; and their representations are found everywhere: in stores, taxis, and even political cartoons. Much of the language and symbolism of politics draws from the tradition of this popularized Hinduism.

Philosophical Hinduism focuses on understanding and realizing an individual's oneness with the essence of life—the ultimate Reality, usually called **Brahman** (not to be confused with the priestly caste called Brahmin[20]). Much of the diversity of Hinduism stems from the acceptance of many ways of reaching oneness with Brahman. A commonly held belief, however, is that the soul must be reborn through countless lives, as one struggles to be reborn at higher levels of both caste and spiritual purity. As a practical matter, this process means that all individuals are expected to observe the norms and rituals prescribed by caste, as adapted for gender and age. The highest caste groupings (*varna*) are called "twice-born" castes, and their members rank higher in spiritual and social attainment than low castes and untouchables. They constitute the traditional religious, social, and political elites of India.

At the family and village level, most Hindus practice popular, devotional, *bhakti* Hinduism. The *bhakti* traditions are as diverse as the people of India and include many colorful practices that Westerners may find peculiar: They range from protecting cows and decorating them for festivals to slaughtering goats; from circumambulating rocks that represent the planets to dressing and undressing temple "gods" when waking them in the morning and putting them to bed at night. But behind this diversity are profound assumptions and beliefs that provide cohesion for the Hindu worldview. For example, Hindus generally accept the superiority of spiritual insight and intuition over the linear, scientific, and secular thought that has come to dominate Western culture. As we shall see in Chapter 5, much of the current debate over what it means to be a Hindu and an Indian revolves around these different views regarding the essence and purpose of life. At the heart of this debate lie fundamental

questions about the validity of India's secular constitution and the continued viability of the country's political institutions.

Approximately 84 percent of Indians are Hindus and 11 percent are
Muslim, or followers of Islam. Islam means submission to God's command, the Moral Law. God's message was revealed to his prophet,
Muhammad ibn Abdullah (the son of Abd Allah), who was born in Ara-
bia in C.E. 570.[21] The divine revelations continued for over more than two
decades in the early seventh century, when they were collected and written down in the Qur'an (*The Recitation*).[22] Thus Islam, like Christianity, is
a revealed religion whose truth is found in its Book.

The first Muslims arriving in India were Arabs, who came soon after
Muhammad's death in C.E. 632. But it was only three centuries later that
the invasions and migrations from the northwest set the stage for a long
period of Muslim political and military dominance. The sultanate of
Delhi, established in 1206, inaugurated a period of Muslim control in
North India, and in the sixteenth century, the **Mughal Empire** expanded
this control to most of the subcontinent. It was during this period that
Delhi became one of the three great capitals of Islam, along with Istanbul
(Ottoman Turkish) and Isfahan (in present-day Iran). Under the Mughal
Empire, some Hindu temples were destroyed and replaced by Muslim
mosques. One such mosque at Ayodhya, as noted earlier, was torn down
in 1992 by a crowd of Hindus who claimed that it had been built on the
site of an older Hindu temple.

The total number of Arab, Persian, Afghan, Turkish, and Mongol Muslim invaders who resided in India was never more than 1 or 2 percent of
the subcontinent's population, but through intermarriage with Hindus
and conversions, Muslims came to constitute one-fourth of India's population by the nineteenth century.[23] After **Partition,** the division of the Indian subcontinent into the independent states of Pakistan and India in
1947, and the migration of millions of Muslims to Pakistan, the proportion of Indian Muslims declined dramatically, although the number has
continued to grow and now stands at over 85 million, making India the
fourth-largest Muslim country in the world.

The importance of Islam in India is established not only by the size of
this minority and by its history as the religion of the Mughal Empire but
also, more recently, by its being the religion of India's neighbors, Pakistan
and Bangladesh. Seen from the perspective of some Hindus, in fact, India
stands in the middle of an Islamic belt that stretches from North Africa to
Indonesia and the southern Philippines. In this geographical context,
there is pressure to define the Indian nation as a *Hindu* nation. For Muslims also, the question of community identity is at stake in the conflict
with Hindus. One of Islam's central tenets holds that a power or state exalted above God is a corrupt wasteland.[24] Hence, the political ideal for an

Islamic community is an Islamic state. An Indian Muslim community that cannot fulfill itself in statehood (as Pakistan has done) risks assimilation with Hinduism or accommodation with a secular order that ultimately enfeebles the essence of Islamic will.[25]

In short, both Hindus and Muslims can and do lay claim to the greatness of Indian civilization; both feel threatened by "minority" status, either in Asia as a whole or in India; and both communities are seeking to redefine themselves vis-à-vis the other and in distinction to Western values and influences.

After Muslims, Christians and **Sikhs** constitute the largest religious minorities in India, with each group representing about 2 percent of the country's population. Christianity in India dates back 1,500 years and includes some of the earliest Christian communities established anywhere in the world. Originally, the Christian church was rooted in the southwest state of Kerala, and today about 25 percent of Kerala's population is Christian. To this early Christian community have been added the later Indian converts of Portuguese and French Catholics, British Anglicans, and American and European Protestants.

Christianity has influenced Indian politics in selected and often indirect ways. For example, missionaries were critical to the introduction of Western education in India under British rule. Western-educated men and women were responsible for a number of social reforms, including some that were especially important for women, such as the suppression of **sati** (the self-immolation of Hindu widows on their husbands' funeral pyres). Nineteenth-century Hindu social reformers like **Ram Mohan Roy** drew a great deal of inspiration from Christian social ethics.

The history of Sikhs in India is very different from that of Christians, partly because of their indigenous roots and partly because of their geographic concentration in the northwest state of Punjab. Sikhism was founded in the sixteenth century by Nanak, who became the first guru (teacher) of the Sikhs. Guru Nanak sought to create a synthesis of Hinduism and Islam in order to reform both. In the seventeenth century, after the fifth guru was executed by the Mughal emperor, the Sikhs became increasingly militant in order to protect their faith from Muslim demands to convert to Islam. Sikh followers were required to adhere to certain symbolic distinctions; for example, the vast majority of Sikh boys and men keep their beards and hair unshorn, and the men wear a distinctive turban that is easily recognizable not only in India but also in the many cities around the world where Sikhs have settled.

Gradually, the Sikhs established an independent state and were only conquered by the British in the 1840s. Under the British **Raj** (rule), the Sikh's military skills were put to the service of the empire, and Sikh men became prominent in the army. This tradition carried over into the post-

Independence period, and today the Sikhs number about 12 percent of the enlisted troops and 20 percent of the officer corps.[26]

Unlike the situation for Christians today, the importance of Sikhs in Indian politics far outstrips the small proportion of the population they represent. Not only are Sikhs prominent in the military (and civil) services, but they stand out in a number of urban occupations and have been successful farmers in their home state of Punjab. A nationalist Sikh movement with roots in the nineteenth century has developed, leading both to the creation of a separatist political party in Punjab and to a terrorist movement. One of the most important consequences of rising Sikh nationalism after Independence and Partition was the demand for a separate Punjabi-speaking Sikh state within India. The demand was finally accepted in the mid-1960s, and the large Punjab state was divided into two smaller states, one called Punjab, where Sikhs are in the bare majority, and another, Haryana, where Hindi-speaking Hindus dominate.[27]

The religions in India with the smallest number of adherents, **Zoroastrianism**, **Jainism**, and Buddhism, each compose well under 1 percent of India's population. The **Parsis**, or followers of the ancient Zoroastrian religion, are descendants of Persians who fled to India in the tenth century to escape Muslim invasions. Settling on the western coast, the Parsis are now important in India mainly as an economic force. They constitute one of the leading business communities and are especially important in the city of Mumbai (Bombay), India's primary financial and commercial metropolis.

Jainism and Buddhism, like Sikhism, are indigenous to India and grew out of movements seeking, in part, to reform Hinduism. Both date back about 2,500 years and are credited as important sources of the ethical model of *ahimsa* (nonviolence), a theme in Indian political and social thought. Mahatma Gandhi, who used fasting as a technique of *ahimsa* and who was a committed vegetarian, grew up around Jains and was clearly influenced by these Jain principles.[28]

As a philosophy of life and religion as well as a political force, Buddhism is far more significant today outside India than in the land of its birth. Its primary political importance in recent decades has been as a refuge for untouchables seeking to escape their inferior status within Hinduism. In 1956, not long before his death, B. R. Ambedkar and thousands of his followers denounced Hinduism and embraced Buddhism as a faith standing for equality and unity.

## Summary

India's population is not only the second largest in the world, but it is arguably the most diverse. The difference between rural and urban peoples and the gaps between men and women make India similar to many other countries; but in other ways, the differences among Indian citizens are unique. Caste structures society and the day-to-day contacts among people. Caste has also been the subject of intense political debate since the Independence movement. India's Constitution sets out the legal and philosophical context for government policies designed to improve the status and well-being of those most disadvantaged by the caste system. We will also see in future chapters that caste is an important basis for political mobilization and participation.

Caste is intrinsic to Hinduism, the dominant religion or worldview in India. But both caste and Hinduism influence India's other religions, such as Islam and Christianity. The conflict between Hindus and Muslims is a central theme in national Indian politics, and religion also plays a role in regional conflicts such as that in Punjab, where the Sikhs are the largest religious group.

Cutting across the differences of religion is the diversity of language and, along with it, ethnicity. One of the most difficult hurdles to national unity in India is the absence of any truly national language that is used and understood by a majority of people in every part of the country. Consequently, language issues, along with caste and religion, have been critical in India: Communication between groups and across regions is hindered, and the question of promoting Hindi (largely a northern language) exacerbates differences between North and South. As we will see in Chapter 11, language differences also account for the organization of the states in India's federal system.

This overwhelming diversity undergirds modern Indian politics and affects almost every political institution and public policy. Yet we must be cautious about prejudging this impact, for two reasons. First, so much diversity suggests that Indian politics must be anarchic, but this is clearly not the case. Systems and structures have been put in place over the last half century to accommodate, but also transcend, the differences among Indians, and these also constitute part of the political picture. Second, the traditional cultural divisions among Indians should not blind us to the role of socioeconomic and political changes in altering the boundaries between communities and, in particular, in creating new social groups and political movements. These groups may benefit from or be disadvantaged by both the changes and the government policies that accompany them.

## Notes

1. For general information on India's population, see Mahendra K. Premi, *India's Population: Heading Towards a Billion (An Analysis of 1991 Census Provisional Results)* (Delhi: B. R. Publishing Corporation, 1991).

2. Pravin Visaria and Leela Visaria, "India's Population: Second and Growing," *Population Bulletin* 36, no. 4 (1981), pp. 9, 13–14, 26; K. C. Zachariah, *The Anomaly of the Fertility Decline in India's Kerala State: A Field Investigation* (Washington, D.C.: World Bank, 1984).

3. Government of India, Department of Social Welfare, Ministry of Education and Social Welfare, *Towards Equality, Report of the Committee on the Status of Women in India* (New Delhi: Ministry of Education and Social Welfare, Government of India, 1974); Barbara D. Miller, *The Endangered Sex: Neglect of Female Children in Rural North India* (Ithaca: Cornell University Press, 1981).

4. Miller, *The Endangered Sex;* Elizabeth Moen, "Sex-Selective Eugenic Abortion: Prospects in China and India," *Issues in Reproductive and Genetic Engineering* 4, no. 3 (1991), pp. 231–249.

5. Jana M. Everett, *Women and Social Change in India* (New Delhi: Heritage Publishers and New York: St. Martin's Press, 1979); Radha Kumar, *The History of Doing: An Illustrated Account of Movements for Women's Rights and Feminism in India, 1800–1990* (London and New York: Verso, 1993).

6. The relative status of a caste may improve over time. See the writings of the Indian social anthropologist M. N. Srinivas, for example, his *Caste in Modern India* (Bombay: Asian Publishing House, 1962).

7. There are many descriptions of caste. Among the most useful are A. L. Basham, *The Wonder That Was India: A Survey of the Culture of the Indian Sub-Continent Before the Coming of the Muslims* (New York: Grove Press, 1954), chaps. 2, 5; Morton Klass, *Caste: The Emergence of the South Asian Social System* (Philadelphia: ISHI Publishers, 1980); Gerald D. Berreman, "The Concept of Caste," and Adrian C. Mayer, "The Indian Caste System," in the *International Encyclopedia of the Social Sciences,* vol. 2 (New York: Macmillan and Free Press, 1968), pp. 333–339 and 339–344, respectively; Dilip Hiro and the Minority Rights Group, *The Untouchables of India,* 2d ed. (London: Minority Rights Group, 1982); and the works of M. N. Srinivas (see n. 6).

8. There continues to be scholarly debate about events during this early historical period and about the origins of caste. Contrast, for example, the discussions by Basham and Klass (see n. 7).

9. This is Basham's interpretation, *The Wonder That Was India,* p. 35. Skin color is still important in India, despite centuries of ethnic intermixing: Matrimonial classifieds advertise prospective brides and grooms as "fair," marketing of consumer products relies on lighter-skinned models, and so on.

10. For insights on the life of untouchables, see Barbara R. Joshi, ed., *Untouchable: Voices of the Dalit Liberation Movement* (Highlands, N.J.: Zed Books, 1986).

11. An important feature of caste that developed through the centuries was proper observance of rituals connected to eating, cleansing, contacts with people of other *jati,* and so on. The physical closeness of urban life often makes it impossible to observe these rituals.

12. For a flavor of the debate between Gandhi and Ambedkar see M. K. Gandhi, *The Removal of Untouchability,* comp. and ed. Bharatan Kumarappa (Ahmedabad, Gujarat: Navajivan Publishing House, 1954); and B. R. Ambedkar, *Annihilation of Caste, with a Reply to Mahatma Gandhi* (Jullundur City, Punjab: Bheem Patrika Publications, 1971).

13. For an insider's view of the operation of a university reserved-seat system, see Kancha Ilaiah, "India's Caste/Class Culture: An Andhra Pradesh Perspective," in Arthur Bonner et al., *Democracy in India: A Hollow Shell* (Washington, D.C.: American University Press, 1994), pp. 49–64.

14. See the historical summary of the *dalit* movement by Eleanor Zelliot featured in the first issue of the *Dalit International Newsletter* 1, no. 1 (February 1996).

15. Andre Beteille, *The Backward Classes in Contemporary India* (Delhi: Oxford University Press, 1992).

16. Ashok K. Dutt and M. Margaret Geib, *Atlas of South Asia* (Boulder and London: Westview Press, 1987), pp. 110ff.

17. The word "Mughal" (or "Moghul") is the Indianized version of Mongol. The founder of the Mughal dynasty was descended from the famous thirteenth-century Mongol, Genghis Khan. The Mughals were not the first Muslim rulers in India; their name is given only to the rule that began with Babur in 1526. Many of North India's architectural wonders date from the period of Mughal rule.

18. Subrata Kumar Mitra, "Desecularising the State: Religion and Politics in India After Independence," *Comparative Studies in Society and History* 33, no. 4 (October 1991), p. 775.

19. For good introductions to Hinduism, see Beatrice Pitney Lamb, *India: A World in Transition*, 4th ed. (New York: Praeger, 1975), chap. 7; Huston Smith, *The World's Religions* (New York: HarperCollins, 1991), chap. 2; and A. L. Herman, *A Brief Introduction to Hinduism* (Boulder: Westview Press, 1991).

20. The name for the priestly caste is sometimes transliterated as "Brahman." I have chosen to use "Brahmin" in order to clarify the distinction between that and the concept of Brahman. See also Diana L. Eck, *Banaras: The City of Light* (New York: Alfred A. Knopf, 1982), p. 370.

21. The abbreviations B.C.E. (before the common era) and C.E. (common era) are used in this book in preference to B.C. (before Christ) and A.D. (anno Domini, the year of the Lord), reflecting the recent scholarly effort to avoid emphasizing Christian tradition when a majority of the world's peoples are not Christian. Other calendars, such as the Jewish, Chinese, Japanese, and Islamic, derive from different traditions. Admittedly, the point of distinction is still the life of Jesus.

22. John L. Esposito, "Muhammad, Prophet of God," in Roger Eastman, ed., *The Ways of Religion: An Introduction to the Major Traditions* (New York: Oxford University Press, 1993), pp. 371–376. Other useful introductory sources include Smith, *The World's Religions*, chap. 6; Kenneth Cragg, *The House of Islam* (Belmont, Calif.: Dickenson Publishing Company, 1969); and Seyyed Hossein Nasr, *Ideals and Realities of Islam* (Boston: Beacon Press and George Allen and Unwin, 1975).

23. Stanley Wolpert, *India* (Berkeley: University of California Press, 1991), p. 99.

24. Cragg, *House of Islam*, p. 17.

25. Ibid., p. 96. See also Nasr, *Ideals and Realities of Islam*, p. 29, on the political implications of the Islamic idea of Unity.

26. Robert L. Hardgrave, Jr., and Stanley A. Kochanek, *India: Government and Politics in a Developing Nation*, 5th ed. (Fort Worth, Tex.: Harcourt, Brace, 1993), p. 7.

27. Ibid., p. 139. Spoken Punjabi and Hindi are similar, but Punjabi is written in Gurmukhi, the script of the Sikh holy books. Punjab's Hindus, whose mother

tongue is Punjabi, write in Urdu or Devanagari script. Thus, religion and written language together contribute to the Hindu-Sikh tension in Northwest India.

28. Gandhi came from the west-coast state of Gujarat, where Jain populations are concentrated. See Mohandas K. Gandhi, *Autobiography: The Story of My Experiments with Truth* (New York: Dover Publications, 1983), p. 18.

*three*

# China

## Population Size and Distribution

As India's population moves closer to 1 billion, China's continues to move well beyond the billion mark. By the early 1990s, the population of the People's Republic of China stood at approximately 1.2 billion, with an annual growth rate estimated at 1.5 percent (considerably less than India's).[1] With almost three times as much territory, China's average population density is much less than India's. This comparison, however, does not take into account the concentration of people in the eastern part of the country, where the population density may be as much as one hundred times greater than in the sparsely populated western and northwestern regions. The eastern region, traditionally called "Inner China," is the site of the origins of Chinese civilization in a settled agricultural economy. In recent times, the eastern part of the country has also become the home of the largest concentrations of industry.

As in India, much of the thinly populated area consists of mountains or desert that cannot support a large population. This "Outer China" is where most of China's ethnic minorities have lived for centuries in relative isolation from the ethnic Chinese, or **Han** people. Politically, much of this area has been organized into autonomous regions since the 1949 revolution. Figure 3.1 shows the administrative divisions of modern China. As a consequence of this uneven distribution of people and the limited amount of arable land, there is actually less cultivated land per person in China than in either India or Japan.[2] The diversity of climate and topography also means that China has many different farming systems, family structures, and regional cuisines.

*Figure 3.1   Map of China*

China is becoming more urbanized, as is India. Despite efforts to control urban growth, there are over one dozen cities with a population of more than 2 million and another three dozen with a population of more than 1 million, all located in the eastern half of the country. Many of these cities date from ancient times and retain some of the flavor that marked them as great centers of Chinese civilization. Some of the coastal cities, like those in India, have architectural remnants of the Western presence in the nineteenth and twentieth centuries—reminders that neither of these great Asian civilizations could insulate itself from the physical presence of Westerners. Other cities reflect the environmental and aesthetic costs of the push for modernization: They are "relentlessly growing, nondescript, drab industrial centers."[3]

These cities and the pace of their growth are important for several reasons. First, they represent the government's commitment to socioeconomic modernization and industrialization and all that these efforts entail, including, presumably, lower fertility rates. By the early 1990s, the cities were at the center of China's dynamic economic growth, and even casual visitors could not miss the evidence of grassroots entrepreneurial activity as they strolled through street markets. New buildings are seemingly everywhere. But the demonstrable improvement in urban and suburban standards of living mask much of the poverty and tradition that continue to dominate the rural areas, where over 900 million Chinese still live. Thus China, like India, is marked by the gap between urban and rural values and lifestyles.

There is also a long tradition of political rebellion rooted in the cities, a tradition that includes the famous **May Fourth Movement** of 1919 and the **Tiananmen Square** democracy movement of 1989.[4] Not surprisingly, this history reflects the concentration of students and other intellectuals in the cities, and these are the people who have been at the forefront of demands for political and social change in China. The potential for civil instability grows when migration from rural areas, along with unemployment, swells the ranks of the dissatisfied. In analyzing the 1989 movement, for example, one scholar noted that economic problems in the countryside were driving hundreds of thousands of young men to the cities, where they had difficulty finding jobs and where their presence made possible the linking of social disorder born of economic dissatisfaction and the students' protest movement.[5] And, indeed, when it became obvious that the students' call for an end to excessive bureaucracy and corruption had widespread support among average citizens in cities like Beijing, the specter of rebellion undoubtedly contributed to the government's decision to use overwhelming force to crush the movement.[6]

Urban growth, unemployment, and even political instability are all part of the much larger picture of concern with China's population—both its size and its growth rate. From the government's point of view, nearly every policy goal is affected (and often undermined) by the numbers of people whose lives are supposed to be improved through modernization. Even so, the government's vigorous commitment to birth control since the late 1970s represents a change in Chinese Communist thinking about the advantages and disadvantages of a large population. Because China's population policies have attracted so much attention, the issue warrants discussion.

## Population Policies

Policies designed to limit population growth go back several decades in both India and China, but the Chinese policies have generated far more political controversy.[7] Debates about the significance of the country's population size have also colored Western perceptions of China for at least two centuries.

As early as 1798, **Thomas Malthus** argued that the size of the Chinese population would make it impossible for the country to feed itself.[8] Although China's population had dropped precipitously in the seventeenth century, it had more than doubled between the 1740s and 1790s, the half century before Malthus wrote his famous book.[9] By the middle of the nineteenth century, the population was well over 400 million, putting additional pressure on increasingly scarce arable land. Some observers thought that the population then grew more slowly or even stagnated during the following century, but the first census taken after the founding of the People's Republic of China counted more than 580 million people in 1953.

This population surge did not raise much official alarm in the 1950s for two reasons. First, the enormous enthusiasm and optimism propelled by the successful revolution led Communist leaders to emphasize the advantages of a large population and to be confident about the ability of the new regime to take care of it.[10] Second, Malthusian thinking was associated with the West and Western assumptions about Chinese inferiority (that is, with Orientalist thinking). Shortly before the establishment of the PRC in 1949, for example, U.S. Secretary of State Dean Acheson echoed Malthus's bleak assessment of the size of China's population in the U.S. government's "China white paper." Acheson argued that China's population growth in the eighteenth and nineteenth centuries had created "an unbearable pressure upon the land."[11] **Mao Zedong**, China's revolutionary leader and chairman of the Communist Party, in turn rejected the notion of a demographic curse, saying: "It is a very good thing that China has a big population. Even if China's population multiplies many times, she is fully capable of finding a solution; the solution is production."[12]

Between the founding of the People's Republic and the late 1970s, however, China's population had nearly doubled, largely because of a decline in mortality rates, and was rapidly approaching the 1 billion threshold. Although some birth control activities had been undertaken during the early decades of the PRC, only in the 1970s were China's leaders able to reach a consensus on population planning. This change was signaled in the country's 1978 Constitution, which declared in Article 53: "The state advocates and encourages family planning." Central to the policies that emerged from this mandate was the goal of limiting family size to one child per couple in order to reach zero population growth by the year 2000.

Both inside and outside China, the one-child policy and the measures taken to implement the policy were subjected to debate and intense criticism. In the United States, for example, the timing of the policy coincided with the election of President Ronald Reagan, whose administration was opposed to abortion and whose supporters attacked any use of abortion as a population control measure. It was China's use of abortion, in particular, that led to the U.S. decision in 1985 to withhold contributions to the United Nations Fund for Population Activities (UNFPA), which provides technical support for population planning and census activities in China and elsewhere.[13]

China's population policy was criticized in the United States because of its coercive features: Couples needed permission to have a child, the regularity of women's menstrual periods was routinely checked, couples were verbally harassed and were subject to economic penalties (such as loss of housing or food ration cards) if they did not conform to birth control practices, and late-term abortions were common.[14] The policies were also controversial inside China, both for their coercive elements and for the way they clashed with one of the central norms of traditional Chinese culture: the high value placed on boys and the low value on girls. The next section, which examines the interrelationship of traditional culture, gender, population, and politics, helps clarify the significance of cultural norms for population policies.

## Gender

Traditional Chinese culture—like that of most of Asia—has assigned women to subordinate cultural, social, and political status. Even women from rich families traditionally had few life options. Although they might be literate, for example, they were prohibited from taking the state examination, success in which opened up lucrative and prestigious government careers. By contemporary standards, the most repressive practice was foot binding, in which the toes of young girls were forcibly folded under and bound tightly in order to create the tiny feet that were a symbol of feminine beauty and sexuality. Although originally an upper-class custom, foot binding spread to lower classes and the peasantry, where many sought to emulate the elite (much as the custom of veiling spread from higher to lower classes in South Asia).[15]

Most scholars believe that the subordinate position of women resulted from one of two factors or from a combination of these. One was the ordering of society according to Confucian norms. The political norms of Confucianism will be discussed further in Chapter 6, but we can note here that central to the Confucian value system is the belief that the ideal society is hierarchically ordered. The first requirement for good government is social harmony, and harmony, in turn, is realized by individuals performing the roles ascribed to them within the family and in the broader society.

One of the most important role relationships in this traditional social system is that of husband and wife. Although in principle this husband-wife relationship is one of mutual respect and reciprocity, it seems clear that the advocacy of a hierarchical social ordering contributed to the development of unequal relationships, in this case between husbands and wives—and between men and women generally.[16] Indeed, some scholars go further and lay most of the blame for women's secondary status and often miserable lives on Confucian values and practices. Even if these values and practices were not advocated by Confucius or cannot be traced to the classic Confucian texts, they came to be accepted as standard by the Confucianized elite that governed China and over time were fostered and mandated (through government policies and laws) for the rest of society.[17]

The importance of having a male heir in every family illustrates these values. Confucianism cultivated families that were both **patrilineal** (where descent and kinship operate through the male, or father's, line) and **patriarchal**. Under patriarchy, men controlled property; fathers had great legal authority over women and children, including the right to choose their daughters' marriage partners, sell their daughters, and dispose of their daughters' labor; and women were seen as morally and intellectually less capable than men.[18] Confucianism emphasized the importance of patrilineal ancestor worship, and without a male descendant, the proper rituals could not be carried out. Adoption of a boy or man, if there was no natural male heir, was thus preferable to having only a daughter.

Confucianism is one reason for the traditional inequality between Chinese men and women. In addition to this, scholars point to women's roles in economic production as historically contributing to their secondary status. To understand this factor, we need to distinguish between **reproductive activities** and **productive activities**. Reproductive activities are those that assure the survival and well-being of the family and household. These activities include not only biological reproduction but also socioeconomic tasks such as procuring and preparing food, caring for children and elderly parents, cleaning, and health care. This unpaid work is carried out in the household, or **private sphere**, and is almost always the responsibility of women. Productive labor or production for exchange (usually paid work in industrialized economies) occurs in the **public sphere**—in fields, factories, and offices. Until recently, this public sphere was regarded in most societies (including China and India) as a male preserve, even when women were involved in agricultural work, for example.

The concepts of the private-public dichotomy and of productive and reproductive work are important because they are linked to the argument that the greater the involvement of women in the public, nondomestic sphere, the greater their status within their culture and in political matters. Women's status, scholars have argued, is lowest when the domestic and public spheres of activity are strongly differentiated and when women are isolated from each other and placed under the authority of a man in the home.[19]

As a general rule, this public-private distinction and the strong differentiation in male and female spheres of activity characterized not only traditional China but also much of post-1949 Communist society, particularly in the rural areas. For example, as late as the 1980s, after more than three decades of policies designed to destroy old modes of production and campaigns to emancipate women, in part by drawing them into productive activities, the old structures that had been so oppressive to women persisted. The household and kin group relationships were still in place and, as Elizabeth Croll has argued, continued to "reproduce the subordination of women": "The birth of sons remained an important source of prestige to women and policies to control reproduction [birth control] were not likely to have full effect until the birth of at least one son per household."[20]

With some understanding of the connection between Confucian norms and the importance of productive and reproductive activities, we can return to the issue of the government's population control policy. There are three elements that link gender and population policy. First, it seems clear that women have assumed a disproportionate burden for implementing government birth control objectives. Second, the combination of government policy, cultural norms, and sometimes eugenics technology appears to contribute to an imbalance in the sex ratio. Third, the link between gender and population policy, when placed in the context of the government's aggressive commitment to modernization, illustrates in ironic and sometimes tragic ways the unintended consequences of government policy.

The differential burden assumed by women and men in implementing birth planning is seen in the means used to control fertility and prevent births. Using intrauterine devices (IUDs) is the dominant contraceptive method, followed by female and male sterilization (vasectomy). But induced abortion continues to play a large role in averting births—and in the late 1980s, it accounted for at least 30 percent of all birth preventions. As shown in Table 3.1, between 1987 and 1989, IUDs, tubal ligations, or abortions were used by 93–95 percent of all individuals preventing births. The physical and psychological burden of the population limitation policy thus falls overwhelmingly on women, as it does in most countries.

It will be recalled from the discussion in the previous chapter that the sex ratio is the proportion of females to males in a population: An equal sex ratio would be 100 females to 100 males. Although India and China report their demographic statistics differently, census reports in both countries show an imbalance in the sex ratio such that the proportion of females is lower than would be expected under normal circumstances of

TABLE 3.1    IUD Insertions, Sterilizations, and Abortions in China, 1987–1989 (percentage of total)[a]

| Year | IUDs | Sterilizations | | Abortions | Total Percent | Total No. (in thousands) |
|------|------|--------|------|-----------|---------------|--------------------------|
| | | *Female* | *Male* | | | |
| 1987 | 46 | 16 | 6 | 32 | 100 | 32,214 |
| 1988 | 43 | 15 | 5 | 38 | 101 | 33,754 |
| 1989 | 45 | 18 | 7 | 30 | 100 | 34,793 |

[a]As reported by the China Population Information and Research Center. Percentages may not total 100, due to rounding.

*Source:* Adapted from H. Yuan Tien, *China's Strategic Demographic Initiative* (New York: Praeger, 1991), p. 156.

birth and death. Judith Banister found after careful data analysis that there have been periods in China where a dearth of females in certain age cohorts suggests higher female than male mortality, indicating either selective neglect of female babies or female infanticide.[21]

In the early 1980s, public concern about female infanticide surfaced both inside and outside China. Premier Zhao Ziyang condemned the crime in his 1982 report to the **National People's Congress (NPC),** China's national legislature, and reaffirmed China's Marriage Law, which states: "Infanticide by drowning and similar criminal acts are strictly prohibited."[22] Laws and political condemnation, however, have not significantly altered the sex ratio, a fact that contributes to persistent assumptions that China's "missing" girls are victims of deliberate neglect in infancy or, in some cases, sex-selective abortion.[23] In the mid-1980s, in fact, the number of "missing" girls averaged nearly 500,000.[24] Although some scholars believe that adoptions, which often go unreported, account for the whereabouts of many of the girls, evidence from the late 1980s and early 1990s, including the 1990 census, suggest that differential treatment of girls and boys at birth and in infancy is a continuing problem in China.[25]

Why should there be such enduring disadvantages attached to being female in China, particularly when Communist Party and state policies have long targeted reform of the status of women? Part of the answer lies in the combination of traditional culture and the division of labor that persists, particularly in rural areas. Part of the answer lies also in the gap between rhetoric, policy, and practice that characterizes reform in any political system. Beyond this, however, is the factor of the unintended consequences of public policy: Policies designed to accomplish one goal produce an unanticipated outcome in another policy area. Two illustrations are relevant to our discussion here. First, evidence suggests that the implementation of the one-child policy reinforced the traditional prejudice

*Photo 3.1    Chinese Father and Son. Photo
courtesy of Marcia M. Allen.*

against girls. Many couples who could have only one child were determined that it be a son (see Photo 3.1). Thus, population control policy contradicted policies to improve the status of girls.

Second, the accelerated push for population limitation occurred in the context of an equally accelerated push for economic modernization; in fact, the latter provided much of the justification for the former. In the rural areas, however, the reforms often had contradictory effects. Changes in agricultural policy, for example, were designed to increase productivity by introducing a profit motive and decreasing state control in what became known as the "household responsibility system." The goal of increased production at the household level necessitated more labor for field work and for projects that would bring in money. This, in turn, created incentives for greater family control over the allocation of women's labor and often meant pulling girls out of school earlier than boys. Agricultural reform also created incentives for people to have more children, especially male children, in violation of the one-child campaign.[26]

There have been numerous other effects—both intended and not—of population and economic reform policies. Often, these have disadvantaged girls and women, though not always; and it is clear overall that the status of Chinese women *has* improved in the last half century. For example, female life expectancy has certainly increased, as has women's access to public life. To date, the primary political lessons that pertain to gender in the Chinese experience are two: Gender distinctions cut across all socioeconomic arenas and therefore affect and are affected by state policies in every arena; and the entry to public political power is connected to status and well-being in the private sphere. Thus, it is not surprising that in the highest levels of party and state institutions in China as recently as the 1990s, there were no women present.

## Regions, Religion, and Ethnic Minorities

We have already seen how India is fragmented by innumerable differences of language, caste, and religion. There is also great diversity among China's peoples, but the political implications of ethnic diversity in China and the policies that address the status of minorities are different from those in India. This section describes these minorities in terms of their regional distribution and numbers, then summarizes state policy toward them. Special attention is given to Tibet, a region that has both domestic and international significance.

There are fifty-six government-designated **national minorities** in China. The 1990 census put their numbers at 91.2 million, with the largest groups being the Zhuang, Miao, and Yi in the South, the Hui (Muslim), Uighur, and Tibetan in the West and Northwest, and the Mongolian and Manchu in the North (see Table 3.2). Because of their location, the minorities have political significance disproportional to their numbers: The largest groups are concentrated in the border regions adjacent to Russia, India, and Vietnam, as well as bordering the recently independent Muslim republics of Central Asia, including Tajikistan. Any instability in these regions thus raises security concerns for the central government. In addition, some minority areas possess rich natural resources, including oil, coal, gold, and other minerals.

In India, the majority group is defined by Hinduism, but Hindus are divided by dozens of languages and dialects, as well as by thousands of *jati*. In China, it is the ethnic Chinese, commonly called the Han people, who constitute a unifying majority of over 90 percent of the country's population.[27] The distinguishing feature of the Han is that their language belongs to the **Sinitic** language family, which uses the writing system of Chinese characters. Although they *speak* different Chinese languages and dialects, the Han and most Chinese people have been unified by a common written language and its great literary tradition.

TABLE 3.2   China's Largest Ethnic Minority Groups, 1982 and 1990

| | *Number (in thousands)* | | *Percent Increase* |
|---|---|---|---|
| *Ethnic Group* | *1982* | *1990* | *1982–1990* |
| Zhuang | 13,388 | 15,490 | 16 |
| Manchu | 4,304 | 9,821 | 128 |
| Hui (Moslem) | 7,227 | 8,603 | 19 |
| Miao | 5,036 | 7,398 | 47 |
| Uighur | 5,963 | 7,214 | 21 |
| Yi | 5,457 | 6,572 | 20 |
| Tujia | 2,835 | 5,704 | 101 |
| Mongolian | 3,417 | 4,807 | 41 |
| Tibetan | 3,874 | 4,593 | 19 |

*Source:* Adapted from H. Yuan Tien et al., "China's Demographic Dilemmas," *Population Bulletin* 47, no. 1 (June 1992), p. 23.

It is primarily language and culture (including customs and religion) that distinguish the Han from other ethnic groups. In most cases, the groups recognized as national minorities by the Chinese government speak their own language, but there are exceptions. The Hui, for example, are part of the Han language group, but are Muslim.[28] There are also groups that speak a Sinitic sublanguage or dialect and regard themselves (and have been regarded) historically as a distinct people, but for a variety of reasons, they are *not* recognized as national minorities by the government.[29] An interesting illustration is the Hakka of southern China. The Hakka have long been viewed as a migratory people; they were central to the **Taiping Rebellion** in the nineteenth century; Hakka women did not bind their feet; and the Hakka are one of the important groups making up the population of the island of Taiwan.[30]

The recognition of the Han-speaking Muslims as an official minority raises questions about the intertwining of religion, ethnicity, and political status in China. For traditional Chinese deeply influenced by a Confucian worldview, religion as understood in the West is just one doctrine among others. Western religion, particularly Christianity, is also associated with nineteenth- and twentieth-century colonial intrusions. Further complicating the historical experience of religion in China is a legacy of Muslim revolts against Chinese rule and conflicts between Muslims and Chinese. In the mid-nineteenth century, for example, both the southern province of Yunnan and the northwest provinces of Gansu and Shaanxi experienced Muslim rebellion, and in the 1990s, there were Muslim protests over a variety of government policies.[31]

The **Cultural Revolution** of the 1960s and 1970s (see Chapters 8 and 10) brought direct suppression of religion in China. Religion was ridiculed as superstitious, places of worship or prayer were closed, religious texts and artworks destroyed. Only after the late 1970s did official policy permit renewed religious activity. The 1982 Constitution proclaims "freedom of religious belief" (Article 36):

> No state organ, public organization or individual may compel citizens to believe in, or not to believe in, any religion. . . .
> The state protects normal religious activities. No one may make use of religion to engage in activities that disrupt public order, impair the health of citizens or interfere with the educational system of the state.
> Religious bodies and religious affairs are not subject to any foreign domination.

In general, religion does not present the political problems in China that it does in India. However, there are exceptions, notably in cases where religious groups attempt to expand their influence against the interests of the state. If conflicts involving religion persist or grow in the future, they will likely reflect the convergence of several factors: Religion (like language) is part of the national identity of some minorities; transnational contacts, such as those between Muslims in western China and in the new Central Asian republics, nourish (both spiritually and financially) religious practice and institutions; and the numbers of ethnic minorities, including those distinguished particularly by religion, are growing at a rapid rate.

The 1990 census showed that the minority populations had increased by almost 24 million—or 36 percent—since the 1982 census. During this same eight-year period, the Han majority grew by 11 percent. For reasons to be explained shortly, the minorities had been largely exempt from the government's fertility control measures from the late 1970s to the mid-1980s, although in the late 1980s, fertility limitations were promoted in areas with a heavy concentration of minorities (except Tibet). Even so, the target for the minorities was not one child, as for the Han, but two or three children.[32] Still, the 1990 census showed that many minority families were exceeding that limit, and in the early 1990s, there were signs that the population policy for the ethnic minorities would parallel that for the Han Chinese. In a 1993 population symposium cosponsored by several government bureaus, for example, officials argued that "minorities should also implement family planning programs."[33]

The shift in population policy toward the ethnic minorities reveals the larger dilemma of devising policies that, on the one hand, respond to the different cultures and standards of living that exist among the Han and the minorities and, on the other hand, reflect China's long-standing concerns with its outlying regions and the need to assure central control over the entire country. The concern with security is itself a reflection of the fact that the Chinese multiethnic state was formed by the territorial expansion of the largest ethnic group, the Han, much as the former Soviet Union was dominated by the Russians. The commitment to centralized control is also consistent with the historical conviction among Han leaders about the superiority of their culture over that of "barbarian" outliers.[34]

In the 1970s, Chinese policy became more tolerant of diversity among minorities than it had been for many years. Restrictions on minority customs and languages were loosened after 1978, largely because political leaders wanted to maximize support for the new programs of economic and social modernization. It was in this context that the ethnic minorities were largely exempted from the requirements of the one-child population policies, a condition that lasted until well into the 1980s.

By the 1990s, the long-term goal of assimilation of the national minorities could claim notable successes, in large part through the force of economic modernization and its corrosive impact on traditional values and customs. At the same time, the breakup of the Soviet Union and the resurgence of ethnic identity in Central Asia, coupled with a revival of religion in many minority areas, suggested that the role of ethnic minorities in China, if not as contested as in India, would remain a central issue on the government's agenda. Within this broader picture, the case of Tibet illustrates many of the dilemmas still facing China.

### Tibet

Tibet is the best known of China's minority areas to outsiders, both because of the PRC's repression of the 1959 Tibetan rebellion and because of the widespread recognition of and admiration for Tibet's traditional spiritual and political leader, the **Dalai Lama** ("Grand Priest"). Tibet also demonstrates the enduring power of religion in a state where religious repression has often been official policy.

The history of Tibet is the history of the intermingling of Asian traditions. Known as one of the most inaccessible lands in the world, Tibet was populated originally by nomadic tribes, whose descendants are still found in the region. Although regular contact with surrounding cultures dates from the seventh century, earlier than that there had been intermittent contact along trade routes that linked China, India, and, further to the west, Persia.

Central to the Tibetan cultural identity is Buddhism, which entered from India in the form that we now know as Mahayana (the "Great Vehicle") Buddhism. By the twelfth century, when Buddhism had disappeared from most of South and Central Asia under Muslim pressure, it flourished in Tibet, with temples, monasteries, elaborate works of art, and an extensive set of sacred books. "The Tibetans became in effect the inheritors of the whole Indian Buddhist tradition,"[35] which they then developed in the unique ways that would distinguish the Tibetan culture from that of its Asian neighbors.

Chinese military intervention in the politics of Tibet began in the early eighteenth century when the emperor of the **Qing dynasty** sought to unify China under Manchu rule. At the height of its power, the dynasty had incorporated areas in eastern Tibet but had never imposed Chinese administrative forms on them. As the dynasty declined, so did its ability to control these areas.[36] By the end of the Qing period in the early twentieth century, a combination of local Tibetan rulers and British maneuvering from North India had reestablished a large measure of Tibetan autonomy.[37] But the Qing dynasty never relinquished its nominal control over the area, thus establishing the basis for the claim made by both the Nationalist and Communist governments that Tibet has always been part of China.

When Chinese Communist armies completed their conquest of Nationalist territory in 1949, the only areas not under their control were Tibet and Taiwan. The new government repeatedly stated its claim to both areas; in October 1950, Chinese troops entered Tibet, and in 1951, the Lhasa government signed an agreement that proclaimed Tibet an integral part of China but left the region with considerable local autonomy.

Tibet's shifting political status during the first years of the People's Republic was complicated by the early phases of the Cold War and U.S. hostility toward the new government in Beijing, as well as by the outbreak of the Korean War in 1950. Both the Indian and the American governments supported Tibetan resistance against the Chinese, contributing to the mutual suspicion among China, India, and the U.S.[38] Not surprisingly, external involvement also reinforced Communist China's preoccupation with the security of its territory and government.

Beijing's policy toward Tibet in the 1950s was conciliatory: It emphasized social and economic development, including medical facilities, road building, and the introduction of modern communications. Religion and the Dalai Lama's role as supreme spiritual ruler were left intact. But cultural misunderstandings and mutual distrust increased in proportion to the Chinese presence and the introduction of technological changes. Tibetan resistance grew, particularly after 1955.

In March 1959, protests against the Chinese broke into armed rebellion in Lhasa and the surrounding regions. The Chinese responded with military force, crushing the rebellion and declaring martial law throughout the Tibetan Autonomous Region. Beijing eliminated the surviving remnants of Tibetan autonomy and restructured the administration of the region in order to consolidate its control. The Dalai Lama fled to India, where he was given sanctuary and where he has maintained his residence up to the present time.[39]

In a portrait of his life and his country, the Dalai Lama, Tenzin Gyatso, stated: "Recently China has begun to take interest in the details of Tibetan history. This is good. Not a single *Tibetan* record states that Tibet has, at any time, been a part of China" [emphasis mine].[40] But from Beijing's point of view, Tibetan independence is unthinkable because it would mean breaking up the Chinese state. Therefore, in recent years, talk of compromise has focused on the return of the Dalai Lama and the granting of additional autonomy to Tibet. Were this to happen, Tibetans would have to confront the reality that the combined effects of Han migration, the centralizing policies of the state, and economic modernization have been eroding Tibetan distinctiveness—a dilemma that the region shares with other ethnic minority areas.

## Summary

Despite the enormous and obvious differences between China and India, there are some important similarities that stand out as we explore their respective political systems. Regional differences are important, notwithstanding the history of centralization in prerevolutionary and postrevolutionary China. The diversity of peoples living in China and India represents a political challenge for both states as they define the policies and political structures for accommodating or assimilating their minority populations. An equally obvious and critical difference between the two countries lies in the magnitude of the ethnic issues and the way these issues compete with other political questions on the government agendas. The size and relative cultural dominance of the Han majority in China guarantee that questions of national minorities will normally be subordinated to larger issues.

The special case of Tibet illustrates the convergence of some of our introductory themes. We cannot appreciate the recent history of Tibetans without recognizing that their homeland has been molded by the confluence of indigenous, intra-Asian, and non-Asian cultural and political forces. The Dalai Lama is powerful both because of his spiritual leadership and because he embodies for many the memory of, and hope for, a Tibetan nation-state. For the foreseeable future, however, Tibet will stay part of the Chinese state.

The discussion of China's population here includes an analysis of the role that population control policies play in Chinese politics. Like many other policies, those dealing with fertility have gone through different phases that reflect both ideological shifts and changes in state development priorities. The fact that these policies became especially controversial in the 1980s says as much about the lenses that Westerners use to scrutinize Chinese politics as it does about the reception of those policies internally.

Finally, it is clear that an important characteristic shared by China and India is the subordinate place assigned to women. The realization that the philosophical and cultural values of the two countries—and the resulting worldviews—are so obviously different leads us to ask why there are nonetheless similarities in gender roles. One hypothesis points to the importance of productive and reproductive roles. Whether these roles create cultural norms or primarily reflect them is still debated by scholars. Whatever the case, it is critical for our study of China and India to understand that as a result of all of these factors, politics is predominantly a male vocation.

# Notes

1. For analyses of Chinese demographic statistics and their reliability, see Judith Banister, *China's Changing Population* (Stanford: Stanford University Press, 1987), chap. 2; H. Yuan Tien, *China's Strategic Demographic Initiative* (New York: Praeger, 1991); and H. Yuan Tien et al., "China's Demographic Dilemma," *Population Bulletin* 47, no. 1 (June 1992).

2. Lucian W. Pye, *China: An Introduction*, 4th ed. (New York: HarperCollins, 1991), pp. 15–16.

3. Ibid., p. 19.

4. The May Fourth Movement began as mass protests in Beijing, when news from the post–World War I peace conference at Versailles, France, reached China. The Japanese had successfully pressed their right to take over Germany's prewar claims in Shandong Province, including the right to establish a military garrison in the city of Jinan. The May Fourth events gave rise to a new nationalist generation of political activists and intellectuals (see Chapter 6).

5. Frederic E. Wakeman, Jr., "The June Fourth Movement in China," *Items* (Social Science Research Council) 43, no. 3 (September 1989), pp. 57–58.

6. Ibid. The Tiananmen events are discussed further in Chapter 6.

7. The most controversial period in the history of India's population policy was the Emergency (1975–1977), when the government of Indira Gandhi pursued an aggressive program that included forced sterilization. Opposition to the program helped defeat her government in the 1977 elections.

8. Thomas Malthus's *An Essay on the Principle of Population* was first published in 1798. See his discussion of China in the 1803 edition, ed. Patricia James, for the Royal Economic Society (Reprint, Cambridge: Cambridge University Press, 1989, vol. 1, pp. 121–133). Malthus emphasized the role of infanticide in checking population (pp. 126, 129–130).

9. Jonathan D. Spence, *The Search for Modern China* (New York: W. W. Norton, 1990), pp. 93–95.

10. Tien, *China's Strategic Demographic Initiative*, pp. 20, 81–82.

11. United States, Department of State, *United States Relations with China with Special Reference to the Period 1944–1949* (Washington, D.C.: Government Printing Office, 1949), p. iv. The primary purpose of this document, referred to as the "China white paper," was to explain the impending victory of the Communist forces over the Nationalist forces in the Chinese civil war and, by implication, to justify the failure of U.S. policy in China.

12. Mao Tse-tung (Mao Zedong), *On the U.S. White Paper* (Peking: Foreign Languages Press, 1967), pp. 34–35.

13. Barbara B. Crane and Jason Finkle, "The United States, China, and the United Nations Population Fund: Dynamics of U.S. Policymaking," *Population and Development Review* 15, no. 1 (March 1989), pp. 23–59.

14. Both Banister, *China's Changing Population*, and Tien, *China's Strategic Demographic Initiative*, discuss the specific mechanisms of the one-child policy.

15. Lower-class families might bind a daughter's feet in order to make her more marriageable to a man of higher class and status. Judith Stacey, *Patriarchy and Socialist Revolution in China* (Berkeley: University of California Press, 1983), pp. 41–42.

16. Wei-ming Tu, *Confucian Thought: Selfhood as Creative Transformation* (Albany: State University of New York Press, 1985), pp. 141–145.

17. Patricia Ebrey, "The Chinese Family and the Spread of Confucian Values," in Gilbert Rozman, ed., *The East Asian Region: Confucian Heritage and Its Modern Adaptation* (Princeton: Princeton University Press, 1991), pp. 50–52; Tu, *Confucian Thought*, pp. 144–145; Stacey, *Patriarchy and Socialist Revolution*, chap. 2.

18. Ebrey, "The Chinese Family," pp. 48–49.

19. Michelle Zimbalist Rosaldo, "Woman, Culture, and Society: A Theoretical Overview," in Rosaldo and Louise Lamphere, eds., *Woman, Culture, and Society* (Stanford: Stanford University Press, 1974), p. 36; and Sue Ellen M. Charlton, *Women in Third World Development* (Boulder: Westview Press, 1984), pp. 25–26.

20. Elizabeth Croll, *Women and Rural Development in China* (Geneva: International Labour Office, 1985), p. 65.

21. Banister, *China's Changing Population*, p. 26. See also Banister's discussion and tables, pp. 21–25.

22. *Beijing Review* 26, no. 17 (April 25, 1983), p. 9. For the text of the 1950 Marriage Law (as revised in 1980), see Kay Ann Johnson, *Women, the Family and Peasant Revolution in China* (Chicago: University of Chicago Press, 1983), pp. 235–239.

23. Although the technologies that enable the determination of a fetus's sex (amniocentesis, ultrasound, and chorionic biopsy) are not yet widespread in China, they are linked to the voluntary abortions of female fetuses. In 1989, the Chinese Ministry of Public Health acknowledged the practice and called on medical personnel to stop checking the sex of unborn babies. "Stop Sex Checks of Fetuses," *Beijing Review* 32, no. 28 (July 10–16, 1989), pp. 12–13. See also Elizabeth Moen, "Sex-Selective Eugenic Abortion: Prospects in China and India," *Issues in Reproductive and Genetic Engineering* 4, no. 3 (1991), pp. 231–249.

24. Sten Johansson and Ola Nygren, "The Missing Girls of China: A New Demographic Account, "*Population and Development Review* 17, no. 1 (March 1991), p. 42. See also Terence H. Hull, "Recent Trends in Sex Ratios at Birth in China," *Population and Development Review* 16, no. 1 (March 1990), pp. 63–83.

25. In "The Missing Girls of China," Johansson and Nygren analyzed the data on adoptions. On the 1990 census, see Tien et al., "China's Demographic Dilemma," pp. 15–17.

26. Banister, *China's Changing Population*, pp. 189–190; Chengrui Li, *A Study of China's Population* (Beijing: Foreign Languages Press, 1992), p. 235.

27. The name Han derives from the Han dynasty (206 B.C.E.–C.E. 222), the period when Chinese imperial rule was consolidated and the territory of the Chinese state was expanded. Confucianism became the state ideology during this period.

28. The Hui presence throughout China is a good example of the intermingling of Asian traditions and thought systems. See the detailed study by Dru C. Gladney, *Muslim Chinese: Ethnic Nationalism in the People's Republic* (Cambridge: Harvard University Press, Council on East Asian Studies, 1996).

29. On the problem of defining ethnic or "national" minorities in China, see Thomas Heberer, *China and Its National Minorities: Autonomy or Assimilation?* (Armonk, N.Y., and London: M. E. Sharpe, 1989), chap. 1. Numerous groups have applied to be recognized as "official" minorities in the past forty years, but they have not succeeded. On the politics of recognition, see Dru C. Gladney, "Ethnic Identity in China: The New Politics of Difference," in William A. Joseph, ed., *China Briefing, 1994* (Boulder: Westview Press, with the Asia Society, 1994), pp. 175–177.

30. Leo J. Moser, *The Chinese Mosaic: The Peoples and Provinces of China* (Boulder: Westview Press, 1985), chap. 15. The Taiping Rebellion (1850–1864) took its name from Taiping Tianguo ("heavenly kingdom of great peace"), a movement that organized economically distressed peasants against the Qing (Manchu) dynasty. The movement was inspired partly by Christian ideas.

31. Spence, *Search for Modern China*, pp. 189–193; and Caroline Blunden and Mark Elvin, *Cultural Atlas of China* (New York: Facts on File, 1983), pp. 40–41. In 1997, Muslim separatists were held responsible for bomb explosions in Xinjiang Province and in Beijing.

32. Tien et al., "China's Demographic Dilemmas," pp. 22–23.

33. Chen Qiuping, "Progress Seen in Minority Population," *Beijing Review* 36, no. 29 (July 19–25, 1993), pp. 16–17.

34. Heberer, *China and Its National Minorities*, pp. 17–18; June Teufel Dreyer, *China's Forty Millions: Minority Nationalities and National Integration in the People's Republic of China* (Cambridge: Harvard University Press, 1976), chap. 1.

35. David Snellgrove and Hugh Richardson, *A Cultural History of Tibet* (Boston and London: Shambhala, 1986), p. 72.

36. Dreyer, *China's Forty Millions*, p. 34.

37. The British sought to use Tibet as a buffer state between the Tsarist Russian Empire and the British Empire in India. Seen from this perspective, Tibet's political history in the late nineteenth to early twentieth centuries was deeply influenced by competing imperial claims among Russia, China, and Britain. See the map entitled "Competing Imperialisms in Eurasia" in Blunden and Elvin, *Cultural Atlas of China*, pp. 34–35; the discussions in A. Tom Grunfeld, *The Making of Modern Tibet* (London: Zed Press and Armonk, N.Y.: M. E. Sharpe, 1987), chap. 3; and Melvyn C. Goldstein with Gelek Rimpoche, *A History of Modern Tibet, 1913–1951: The Demise of the Lamaist State* (Berkeley: University of California Press, 1989).

38. India, like Britain before it, was interested in seeing Tibet become a buffer state. But India was one of the first states to recognize the new PRC government in 1949 (and hence, Chinese claims to Tibet). Grunfeld, *Making of Modern Tibet*, chap. 5.

39. Analyses of these events are found in Grunfeld, *Making of Modern Tibet*, pp. 122–126 and chap. 7; and George Ginsburgs and Michael Mathos, *Communist China and Tibet: The First Dozen Years* (The Hague: Martinus Nijhoff, 1964), chap. 4.

40. Dalai Lama of Tibet, with Galen Rowell, *My Tibet* (Berkeley: University of California Press, for Mountain Light Press, 1990), p. 15.

# *four*

⤳

# Japan

## Population Size and Distribution

In contrast to China and India, where the majority of people still live in rural areas, Japan is predominantly urban. The Japanese urban-rural ratio, in fact, is roughly the reverse of the ratio in India and China. As Table 4.1 shows, approximately three-fourths of Japanese citizens live in areas designated as urban; in India and China, approximately three-fourths of the people live in rural areas.

Japan has a long history of urban centers, but migration to the cities during the twentieth century permanently transformed the nation. As recently as one century ago, Japan was still an agricultural nation whose population was distributed relatively equally across the country.

One of the important political consequences of urbanization since World War II has been controversy over the size and shape of the nation's electoral districts. By the 1980s, electoral reform had become a contentious issue among both Japanese politicians and the public. One reason for the controversy has been the overrepresentation of rural interests due to delayed redistricting: Rural-to-urban migration has left rural districts with a much smaller voter-to-representative ratio in the **Diet** (the Japanese parliament) than is found in the cities.

The great population concentrations of Japan lie in the southeastern plains called Kanto (to the east, the greater Tokyo metropolitan area) and Kansai (to the west, centering on the Osaka, Kyoto, and Kobe areas) (see Figure 4.1). The train trip between the two regions is a good introduction both to Japan's population distribution and to the country's topography. At both ends of the trip, cities stretch almost endlessly. In between, one glimpses a few small farms and forests, as well as suburban homes and

TABLE 4.1   Population Size and Distribution in Japan, China, and India

|         | Estimated Population[a] | Percent Urban | Percent Rural |
|---------|-------------------------|---------------|---------------|
| Japan   | 124.4                   | 77            | 23            |
| China   | 1,165.8                 | 26            | 74            |
| India   | 882.6                   | 26            | 74            |

[a]In millions, 1992

*Source:* Adapted from *1992 World Population Data Sheet* (Washington, D.C.: Population Reference Bureau, 1992).

gardens. The train passes Mt. Fuji to the north, and the coastline of the Pacific Ocean to the south—a reminder of the dominance of sea and mountains in Japan's topography and culture (see Photo 4.1).

Japan is, in fact, a mountainous archipelago, with a total land mass of about the same size as the state of Montana. The population density is higher than in China or India and even higher than the average density figure of 332 per square kilometer (0.386 square mile) suggests. Over two-thirds of Japan consists of mountainous terrain, and the population density per unit area under cultivation is the highest in the world.[1] Nearly one-quarter of the population lives in the greater Tokyo metropolitan area alone.

The size and distribution of the Japanese population raise several issues central to the discussions in this book pertaining to demographic changes, development policies, and the linkage between domestic and foreign policies. To begin with, Japan is arguably overpopulated. If we do not hear as much about overpopulation in Japan as in China and India, we may assume that it is due to the country's wealth. But this prosperity is relatively recent and, from a Japanese perspective, rests on a potentially fragile base. The physical vulnerability of the country to earthquakes, tidal waves, typhoons, and volcanic activity is well known. Likewise, the country's limited agricultural base and heavy dependence on imported resources contribute to real and perceived economic vulnerability.

It stands to reason that political leaders must be aware of this vulnerability as they formulate and implement domestic and foreign policies. By way of illustration, by the 1980s, Japan relied on imports (primarily oil, coal, and liquefied natural gas) for 90 percent of its energy supply. In order to counteract its increasing reliance on imports, the government began developing nuclear energy in the 1960s. By 1990, thirty-nine nuclear reactors provided about 10 percent of Japan's total energy supply. The government's nuclear energy policy in turn fueled the growth of a grass-roots antinuclear movement.[2]

This sense of vulnerability, when combined with an understanding of the **Liberal Democratic Party**'s (LDP) political base in rural areas, helps explain the long tradition of government policies of import protection in

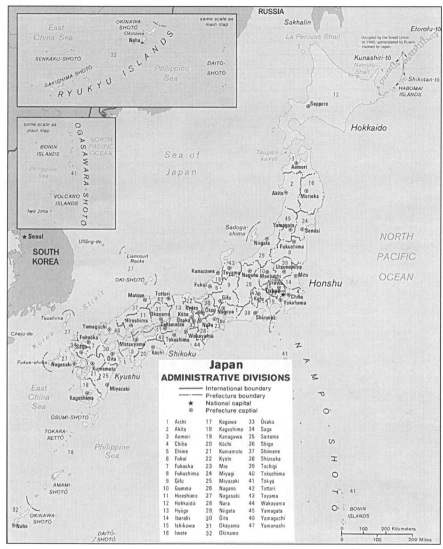

*Figure 4.1   Map of Japan*

trade, including restrictions on food imports such as rice. Trade protection and price supports were originally part of the post–World War II agricultural and land reforms designed to modernize farming and increase food production, as well as to foster rural support for democracy. These policies contributed to the creation of a relatively affluent farming population that, in turn, supported the LDP, which has dominated Japanese politics since the 1950s.

*Photo 4.1    Mount Fuji. Photo courtesy of James Boyd.*

## An Aging Population

The age structure is another aspect of the Japanese population that, like urbanization, is gradually altering the political scene. Over the next twenty-five years, 25 percent of the population will be elderly, with the result that Japan will have the largest population of elderly citizens in the world.[3] This trend reflects a number of demographic changes that reinforce each other: increased longevity, low birth rates, and low immigration rates. The increase in average life expectancy is tangible evidence of the improved standard of living of the average Japanese during the past half century. Until the mid-1940s, life expectancy for both men and women was less than 50 years. By the late 1980s, it was 82 years for women and 76 years for men.

These trends and their policy implications in Japan parallel widespread patterns in other industrialized societies. Demographic projections estimate that by 2020, there will be only three Japanese workers for each retiree. In the early 1980s, government policy began to shift in order to accommodate the increasing public service burden of a large nonworking population. In 1982, for example, existing provisions for a national system of free health care for the elderly were replaced by a requirement that made elderly persons subject to copayments for medical services. A 1986 amendment further increased the share of costs the elderly and their insurers (rather than the government) would bear for their health care. Even so, by the early 1990s, more than 25 percent of national health care expenditure was devoted to care of the elderly.[4]

The change in the age structure has had other consequences, including a shortage of workers in some areas and an increasing proportion of women in the population as a whole and specifically in the workforce. In the 1950s, for example, rapid economic growth stimulated the exodus of people from rural areas to the cities. The decline of the rural population has led to chronic farm labor shortages, an aging rural labor force, more part-time agricultural workers, and greater numbers of women in farm work. Over one-half the farm labor force is female.[5]

The combination of labor demands and economic prosperity has made Japan a magnet for immigrants, both legal and illegal, looking for jobs. The largest number of foreign workers come from other Asian countries, notably South Korea, Iran, and Malaysia. By the early 1990s, over 200,000 foreign workers were illegal immigrants.[6] This immigration pattern presents new political and social challenges for the Japanese. The foreigners are often caught up in cultural conflicts, and their presence sparks political debates over the status of ethnic minorities in a largely homogeneous society.

In the mid-1990s, Japan's worst recession since World War II altered the employment picture. Companies were slower to hire and hired fewer employees. Job competition among college graduates increased, and women, in particular, found it difficult to advance in the workplace despite policy changes in the 1980s and 1990s designed to assure equal opportunity. Some of the reasons for the particular disadvantages women faced are found in many countries; others are unique to Japan.

## Gender

As we have seen, the status of Indian and Chinese women has historically been subordinate to that of men in both public and private affairs. The same is true of Japan, although for historical reasons, there are important differences in the evolution of gender relations. Japan's history is marked by extensive borrowing of foreign values and practices at critical junctures. The combination of adopting from abroad and adapting to indigenous conditions has influenced gender patterns, as it has many other areas of Japanese society. Literature, which scholars have used to highlight the impressive cultural achievements of court women in Heian Japan (ca. 794–1185), provides apt early historical examples, the most famous of which is the early-eleventh-century novel *The Tale of Genji*, by Murasaki Shikibu.[7] The status of women changed, however, as the conservative influence of Chinese Confucianism, combined with the government's preoccupation with political and social stability, set the prevailing norms for royalty and commoner alike. The late feudal era, called the **Tokugawa,** or **Edo period** (1600–1868), in particular, was characterized by policies designed to reinforce stability and hierarchy through the application of Confucian norms. Ideal feminine behavior meant obedience and service to men—to father, husband, or son, depending on the woman's stage in life.

From the Tokugawa period through World War II, women were dependents of their male household heads and, by both law and custom, were completely subordinate to them. Even though the Meiji period, beginning in the 1860s, marked a dramatic opening to Western political, social, and cultural influences, there was little in these influences that would overturn earlier patterns, in part because gender segregation, the exclusion of women from public activities, and legal discrimination against women were all characteristic of Western societies themselves in the late nineteenth century. Lower-class women did work outside the home in Japanese fields and factories, but this work was considered an extension of their household positions. When they performed wage labor in mills and manufacturing plants, their wages were less than one-half those of men, and their status was exceedingly low.[8]

Postwar reforms instituted during the American occupation changed conditions for Japanese women. Their new legal status, at least, was comparable to that enjoyed by Western European and North American women in the 1940s. The 1947 Constitution affirmed:

> All of the people are equal under the law and there shall be no discrimination in political, economic or social relations because of race, creed, sex, social status or family origin. (Article 14)
>
> Marriage shall be based only on the mutual consent of both sexes and it shall be maintained through mutual co-operation with the equal rights of husband and wife as a basis.
>
> With regard to choice of spouse, property rights, inheritance, choice of domicile, divorce and other matters pertaining to marriage and the family, laws shall be enacted from the standpoint of individual dignity and the essential equality of the sexes. (Article 24)

The combination of postwar reform, demographic changes, and the transformation of the Japanese economy brought a freedom to women that would have been unimaginable in earlier decades. But it did not eliminate the traditional cultural assumptions of inequality or revolutionize either politics or public policy. The following discussion examines the degree of change in gender relations by focusing on four factors that help explain the paradoxes in women's status and the ambivalence that many Japanese women feel about changes in gender relations.[9] The four factors are traditional norms, legal precepts, demographic changes, and economic growth.

Formal legal and constitutional norms based on the ideology of democratic equality are important benchmarks of change. But they often conflict with traditional values that emphasize social harmony and hierarchical relations, both in the home and in the workplace. Susan J. Pharr's concept of "status politics" illuminates this tension and its implications for political behavior. In her analysis of the "tea pourers' revolt" of 1963, Pharr showed the persistence of women's secondary status in the workplace and the way in which cultural norms reinforce that status. The tea pourers, employees of the Kyoto municipal bureaucracy, protested job requirements that included custodial duties such as cleaning desktops and pouring tea for male office workers. Symbolically, the most flagrant challenge to the established cultural and bureaucratic order was the refusal of a small group of female civil servants to pour and carry cups of tea to the male employees of their section. The rebellious women were never formally reprimanded, yet within a few days they began to resume their tea-pouring duties.[10]

Pharr analyzed the tension that existed in the municipal office and that persists three decades later: the tension between the official ideology, which forbids discrimination on the basis of sex, and social norms that determine female work roles and opportunities. "As a ritual engaged in primarily by women, the serving of tea is a potent symbolic act expressing the asymmetry of the sexes. By pouring tea for men, women express their deference and inferiority to them."[11]

The contradictions between official and traditional ideologies continue to define women's roles in the Japanese workplace, even as the number of women working outside the home has changed dramatically. Fueling the movement of women from households and farms have been several complementary factors: high economic growth since the 1950s in the industrial and service (secondary and tertiary) sectors; changes in consumption patterns and the improvement in household living standards; and demographic changes, such as fewer births and deaths and the longer life spans noted in the previous section. Most directly affected by the demographic changes have been women's life cycles. For example, before World War II, the child-rearing period from the birth of the first child to the youngest child's entrance into primary school was 19.0 years. By the 1980s, the child-rearing period had dropped to less than 9 years—reflecting, of course, the decreasing number of children. As a result, the average woman has between 45 and 50 years to live after her children enter school.[12] This long life span, combined with high educational levels and reactions against traditional gender attitudes, help account for the increased grassroots female political activity discussed in Chapter 14.

## Ethnic Minorities

Minorities in Japan are not only immigrants, as suggested earlier, but indigenous. This section examines both types of minority groups, focusing first on the indigenous **Ainu** and *burakumin* and then on Koreans, who are historically an immigrant population.

The Ainu are the indigenous people of the northern island of Hokkaido. Their history is that of a people and culture confronting rapid erosion over the past one hundred and fifty years. During much of the Edo, or Tokugawa, period, Ainu peoples were more widely spread through northeastern Asia, ranging across the northern part of Honshu, the southern Kuril Islands, the lower reaches of the Amur River, and southern Kamchatka. The Ainu population in the early nineteenth century was about 24,000 but had dropped to less than 19,000 by midcentury.[13]

The Japanese treated the Ainu as aliens. As their population declined and the base of their traditional lifestyle in hunting, fishing and gathering disappeared, the Ainu absorbed more and more Japanese cultural characteristics. By the early twentieth century, Ainu-Japanese marriages began to increase, ultimately eliminating a large, culturally distinctive Ainu population. Today, for example, the Ainu language is no longer in daily use.[14] Despite signs of a cultural renaissance and efforts to organize politically in defense of Ainu interests, the Ainu have contemporary status similar to that of indigenous populations elsewhere whose traditional lifestyle has been destroyed or reduced to a curious reminder of the past for the majority, assimilating population.[15]

In contrast to the plight of the Ainu, issues pertaining to Japan's largest minority populations, the *burakumin* and the Koreans, today generate more political concern. The history, status, and problems of the *burakumin* resemble those of the former untouchables in India, with whom they are often compared. Unlike the *burakumin*, who are indigenous to Japan, the Koreans are immigrants whose presence in Japan and status were originally a result of twentieth-century Japanese colonialism. There are an estimated 3 million *burakumin* (about 2 percent of the Japanese population) and nearly 700,000 Koreans in Japan.[16]

## *Burakumin*

Over the course of a long period, Japan adopted (and adapted) the Chinese Confucian four-tiered class structure that imparted a hierarchical ordering to premodern Japanese society. The **samurai** (literally, "one who serves"), or warrior-administrators, ranked at the top, above the second level of primary producers or farmers. Artisans ranked third, and merchants were at the bottom. The subclasses of traditional Japanese society, the *hinin* (literally, "nonhumans") and *eta,* or *burakumin*, were outside this accepted order. The *hinin* were a heterogeneous group composed of beggars, fugitives from justice, prostitutes, and wanderers. Under the Tokugawa shogunate, they were compelled to undertake the worst jobs, such as caring for victims of contagious diseases, and to dress in specified ways that set them apart from the rest of the population.

The *burakumin* were hereditary outcastes originally called *eta*, a word commonly represented by the Chinese characters meaning "much filth." The *burakumin* have the same racial and ethnic characteristics as other Japanese, but they were traditionally thought to be subhuman because they performed tasks viewed as ritually polluting, including slaughtering animals and disposing of the dead. Historians and anthropologists are not certain about the origins of *eta* status but believe that the arrival and spread of Buddhism in Japan from the seventh century on reinforced pre-existing beliefs about pollution, especially as it related to blood and death. Because their pollution might defile others, government edicts forbade intermarriage between *eta* and non-*eta* and required residential segregation in specified hamlets, or *buraku*—hence the term "hamlet-people," or *buraku-min*.[17] Thus the term *burakumin* is a relatively modern euphemism for the traditional, more pejorative word, *eta*.

In 1871, the new Meiji government abolished the derogatory terms *eta* and *hinin* and legally emancipated the *burakumin*. However, the *burakumin* continued with their traditional occupations, and the persistence of the special hamlets, along with an official household-registration system, made them easy to identify. Up to the present time, *burakumin* tend to be associated with certain occupations, such as shoemaking and shoe sales or meat processing, and to be concentrated in identifiable neighborhoods even in major metropolitan areas such as Osaka. Families routinely conduct background checks on their children's prospective mates, in part to identify "inappropriate" spouses such as *burakumin*.[18]

In 1906, the novelist Toson Shimizaki movingly portrayed the situation of the *burakumin* in *The Broken Commandment*. The central character of the novel is a young *burakumin* schoolteacher named Ushimatsu Segawa, who has achieved his position by disguising his background—"passing"—as his father commanded him to do. Finally, friendship with an older *burakumin* who is openly campaigning against discrimination, along with the constant tension of keeping his secret, propels the schoolteacher to break his father's commandment and reveal his secret. In the following quoted passages, Ushimatsu wrestles with the consequences of revealing his secret, then does it.

> The deeper his thoughts probed, the darker they grew. Nothing could soften the horror of total rejection: of dismissal from the school, for instance. The humiliation would follow him to the grave. And how, afterwards, could he make a living? . . . Why should he be singled out as less than human, when all he wanted was to live as others lived? . . .
>
> [Later Ushimatsu reveals his secret to his class.] He bowed his head humbly before the class. "When you get home, tell your parents what I have

said. Tell them I confessed today, asking your forgiveness . . . *I am an eta, an outcast, an unclean being!"* [italics in original][19]

Ushimatsu's confession in this last scene provoked a debate many decades later about "political correctness" in the Japanese context. When *The Broken Commandment* was made into a movie, the Buraku Liberation League (BLL), an organization with roots dating back to the 1920s, called for the wording of Ushimatsu's final confession to be changed to: "I am a *burakumin*, but what's wrong with that?" The BLL's secretary-general denied that the organization was practicing censorship and defended both the BLL's position on the wording change for the movie and its demands that Japanese translations of several English-language books be altered to eliminate unacceptable references to *eta* and *burakumin*. Those disagreeing with the BLL position included some scholars whose works were changed in translation.[20]

At issue is the definition of appropriate policies in a number of related areas, ranging from official terminology referring to *burakumin* to social welfare programs designed to improve their status. Also at stake is the appropriate strategy to be followed by an advocacy organization such as the BLL, which is committed to equality for *burakumin*. The BLL's objection to the original portrayal of Ushimatsu was that he contributed to the humiliation of the *burakumin* by apologizing for a status that he should not have been ashamed of, since the battle for *burakumin* equality is far from won. Others argue that it is a distortion of both history and art to apply the political standards of the 1990s to situations from an earlier era and that the search for acceptable language has gone too far.

The critical point for the BLL is that the contemporary status of the *burakumin* resembles that of an underclass in other industrialized nations. Discrimination in the workplace and throughout society (including marriage) continues. Unemployment among *burakumin* is about ten times higher than that of other Japanese, and college admissions are one-half the national average. In 1990, some 7 percent of *burakumin* received public assistance—a figure six times the national average. *Burakumin* are subjected more to police repression as well.[21] The lack of other economic opportunities has tended to drive *burakumin* into illegal activities such as those conducted by the *yakuza*, Japan's underground mafia-type organization.[22] In short, although much has changed since Toson Shimizaki's novel first appeared, the *burakumin* still remain socially and economically apart.

## Koreans

When Japan annexed Korea in 1910, there were approximately 2,500 Koreans in Japan. This number increased dramatically during World War II, when the Japanese government brought Koreans to Japan as forced laborers. Although many of the more than 2 million Koreans were repatriated at the end of the war, others stayed in Japan and became the parents and grandparents of today's Korean minority. It is estimated, in fact, that 90 percent of the Koreans in Japan are Japanese-born and have few ties to Korea.[23] For example, many do not speak Korean, much as second- and third-generation Japanese-Americans speak no Japanese. However, birth in Japan itself does not give a person legal status as a Japanese citizen, so Korean-Japanese are overwhelmingly noncitizens in the country of their birth.

Discriminated against socially and economically, Koreans have struggled for several decades to improve their conditions. Gradually, their legal status has improved. The majority of Koreans are officially considered legal aliens, not Japanese citizens, and they compose about two-thirds of Japan's registered foreign national population. The amendment of Japan's Nationality Law in 1985 made more Korean residents of mixed parentage eligible to become Japanese citizens.[24] Between the early 1980s and early 1990s, the Japanese government granted permanent resident status to first-, second-, and third-generation Koreans in Japan. In 1993, permanent residents were no longer required to be fingerprinted.[25]

Still, controversy continues about the status of Koreans in Japan. They are discriminated against in jobs, cannot vote (but pay taxes), and are treated with contempt.[26] Their situation has complicated the history of conflict between Japan and Korea and the division of Korea into North and South. After World War II, for example, separate organizations were created to address the problems of the Korean-Japanese, one linked to North Korea and one to South Korea. These connections divided Koreans politically within Japan and undermined the effectiveness of the Korean community vis-à-vis the Japanese government.

A situation that further illustrates the connection between domestic and international factors in understanding the situation of Koreans (as well as other immigrant groups) is that of the **"comfort women."** "Comfort women" is a euphemism for Korean and other Asian women who were forced to provide sex for the Imperial Japanese Army during World War II. The shame of the Korean women imprisoned and exploited during the war had contributed to the lack of public discussion of their history until the 1990s. In 1991, several Korean women brought suit against the Japanese government in a Japanese court, asking for compensation for their wartime ordeal. Only in early 1992, shortly before the visit of Japan's prime minister to Korea, did the Japanese government reverse its long-standing denial of official involvement in abducting women for the army. Previously, the government had claimed that the "comfort stations" were simply private brothels.[27] Later the same year, the issue caught the attention of the Japanese Parliament when a female opposition member

*Photo 4.2   Korean Women's Protest. Photo by author.*

accused the government of stalling its investigation of the issue. The Diet-woman dismissed government statements that the case of the "comfort women" was just another bad chapter in the cruel history of the war. Instead, she argued that the army and government actions constituted a specific policy of discrimination against women *and* a particular ethnic group.[28] Ultimately, the government sponsored the creation of a private fund to pay former "comfort women," while continuing to reject making any formal apology or admission of legal responsibility.

The way in which the "comfort women" became part of the political process suggests some parallels for comparison with other countries and with the politicization of other issues in Japan. The issue linked disadvantaged groups—in this instance women and ethnic minorities. A handful of individuals chose the court system for redress of their grievances, even though Japan is widely viewed as a nonlitigious society. Private voluntary and professional organizations played important roles in providing facts and publicizing issues. Opposition Diet members acted as catalysts in prompting government action. The issue then took on international dimensions as nongovernmental organizations (NGOs) in Japan, Korea, and other East Asian countries joined the protest against Japanese government policy. Photo 4.2 shows one such protest staged by Korean women at the NGO Forum on Women at Beijing in 1995.

# Religion

It is conventional wisdom among visitors to Japan that the society they are introduced to is secular and materialistic, especially in comparison to a country such as India. Keen observers will also note, however, that there are shrines and temples everywhere. Some are large and celebrated architectural monuments; others are tiny, tucked into back streets and alleys. Moreover, anyone who has waited in line for hours on a cold New Year's Eve, squeezed into the midst of hundreds of thousands of Japanese—all to pay a brief visit to a famous shrine—must wonder if the connection with Japan's religious traditions is not more central to people's lives than is commonly assumed.

Japanese religions coexist in an intricate matrix created by a long and complex history.[29] Until the ancient Japanese came into contact with Chinese civilization and Buddhism, they assumed that the natural world as they knew it was the sacred, original world. The traditional lineage groups, or *uji*, were patriarchal and centered around a world of **kami** (sacred Shinto spirits). Approximately 2,000 years ago, a confederation of *uji* became known as the Yamato kingdom. As Japan and China came into contact, Yamato rulers paid tribute to Chinese courts, from which in turn they received kingly titles. Thus, rulers who were originally responsible for religious ceremonies (as well as for directing the agricultural life of the *uji*) became political rulers.[30]

In the sixth and seventh centuries, Yamato leaders sought to emulate China through political unification and the systemization of the old ceremonial and belief systems. The Sinicized term **"Shinto"** was adopted to signify "the way of the *kami*," and the Yamato created a legal and administrative structure, the Ritsuryo, that legitimized political rule in accordance with the *kami* belief system.[31] The Ritsuryo was an early predecessor of the imperial edict system that we will encounter again in the context of Japan's nineteenth-century modernization. The Ritsuryo synthesized indigenous and Chinese influences by anchoring the sovereign ruler's claims to legitimacy both in the way of the *kami* and also in monarchical systems of rule found in Chinese philosophies of governing. Japanese rulers were simultaneously the supreme political authority of the nation, the supreme priest, and the living or manifest *kami*, a genealogical descendant of their *uji* ancestor, **Amaterasu Omikami**, and thus they were entitled to rule the nation. This is the origin of what is commonly known in the West as the "myth" of the "divine emperor" and the source of "emperor worship," as it was cultivated from the late 1860s to the mid-1940s.

Another important historical theme is the impact of Buddhism and Confucianism on the Japanese court and state. The earliest formal document confirming the significance of Buddhism and Confucianism was the early-seventh-century "Constitution" of Prince Shotoku, who endeavored to devise a written code of government for Japan. The prince was influenced by the traditions of both Buddhism and Confucianism, which were part of the strands of Chinese culture imported from the sixth century on. Shotoku's document introduced several principles that are important for understanding the relationship between religion and government later in Japan. The Constitution affirmed the importance of obeying the ruler. The norm of obedience was articulated within the context of the Confucian goal of harmony. Harmony and obedience, in turn, were to be tempered by the Buddhist values of compassion, as well as by ethical behavior.[32]

The following sections describe those aspects of Shinto and Buddhism that are especially relevant to our study of politics. The section ends by introducing the role of Christianity in Japan. Confucianism, which was China's paramount ethical and political philosophy and also influenced Japan, is discussed later, in the context of the modern Japanese nation-state.

## Shinto

Because of the close association of Shinto with twentieth-century Japanese militarism, it is important to distinguish between the forms of Shinto that have historically been directly linked to the government and those forms that have broader cultural and religious significance.[33] **Imperial House Shinto** is observed at imperial institutions and "retains the most archaic styles of Shinto worship."[34] Many rituals of the imperial family are not open to the public, a fact brought home in recent years when televised coverage of special events involving the imperial family (such as the 1989 coronation of the present Emperor Akihito and the 1993 marriage of his son, Crown Prince Naruhito) omitted some Shinto rites performed only in the presence of a handful of individuals.

Shrine Shinto is practiced at the approximately one hundred thousand shrines that cover the Japanese landscape. The shrines are historically linked to a community grouping and today are organized under the Association of Shinto Shrines, which serves as a political pressure group. Rituals and ceremonial festivals, called *matsuri*, emphasize reverence for the various *kami* associated with the shrines. *Matsuri* mark important seasons and events, and for "outsiders" to Japanese culture, they represent one of the most accessible windows for observing modern customs that have ancient roots.[35]

**State Shinto** dates from the Meiji period and was a self-conscious government creation that combined Shrine Shinto and Imperial House Shinto. This amalgam was designed to build national identity and unity centering on devotion to the emperor, and it inculcated belief in the uniqueness and superiority of the Japanese people. During the period of

State Shinto, which lasted until the end of World War II (1945), Shinto was technically not a religion but a government institution whose priests were government officials (see Chapter 7).

Additional forms of Shinto have been identified and categorized, including "sect Shinto." Shinto sects are primarily characterized by their relatively recent origin and linkage to a charismatic personality. The earlier sects were founded in the nineteenth century and in many respects were a response to the massive changes wrought in Japanese society by modernization and urbanization.[36] These sects are increasingly grouped by scholars with Buddhist movements and organizations that are also of more recent origin and are offshoots of the old Buddhist traditions. Together, these "**new religions**," as they are called, have attracted millions of followers. One of the new religions with Buddhist roots, **Soka Gakkai**, is both the largest and the most politically significant in Japan. A different kind of new religion, the Aum Shinrikyo, was held responsible for the 1995 sarin nerve gas attack in a Tokyo subway.[37]

## Buddhism

It will be recalled that the earliest Shinto beliefs were institutionalized in the sixth century in response to the Chinese cultural and political influence that entered Japan during this period. Buddhism was one of these foreign imports. Although Buddhism is diffuse, its role in Japanese life since this period can hardly be overstated.

Japan was the geographical terminus in Asia of Buddhism; consequently, the nation inherited a variety of practices and beliefs that would hardly have been recognized in India, where Buddhism was born. In this regard, Buddhism is a prime exemplar of the intermingling and grafting of Asian traditions. Initially, Buddhism, like institutionalized Shinto, was predominantly a religion of the nobility and upper classes. Today, of course, the Buddhist legacy is ubiquitous, from its temples—which often stand next to Shinto shrines—to its death ceremonies, which are practiced by almost every household.

Prince Shotoku's patronage of Buddhism in the seventh century and an eighth-century imperial decision to build state-subsidized temples throughout Japan were testimonies to the early, close association between government and religion. In the centuries after its introduction, numerous schools of Buddhism appeared. For our purposes, the most important were Zen and Nichiren, both dating from the Kamakura period (1185–1333), sometimes referred to as Japan's "medieval" era. Zen, like earlier Buddhism, came from China and received official patronage. Soon Zen became associated with the ruling members of the emergent samurai class.[38] As samurai traditions and culture were woven into the fabric of

Japanese society, practices originally associated with Zen discipline, such as the tea ceremony, became widely accepted art forms. Today, these are often viewed as synonymous with Japanese culture.[39]

Unlike Zen, Nichiren, so named after its thirteenth-century founder, is indigenous to Japan. Nichiren believed that the social unrest of his day was due to decay in the practice of Buddhism, which he sought to reform. Much later, in the nineteenth century, Nichiren Buddhism fed into Japanese nationalism, in large part because of its emphasis on national revival. Nichiren also contributed to the creation of several new religions, including Soka Gakkai, mentioned earlier. Originally a lay organization affiliated with the Nichiren Shoshu sect, Soka Gakkai dates from the 1930s. In the early 1960s, its members took the lead in creating **Komeito** (the Clean Government Party). Aggressively proselytizing, Soka Gakkai enjoyed huge growth in the 1950s and 1960s. In recent years, it has severed its official links both with the Nichiren Shoshu hierarchy and with Komeito. Komeito, meanwhile, has seen its electoral support decline from its peak in the early 1970s, but it continued to play an active role in Japanese politics until the mid-1990s, when it merged with another party.

## Christianity

In terms of adherents, Christianity claims fewer than 1 percent of the Japanese population, despite roots that date back to Roman Catholic missionaries in the sixteenth century. For example, a government survey from 1970 showed fewer than 800,000 Christians of all denominations, when the Nichiren Shoshu sects (including Soka Gakkai) alone had well over 16 million followers.[40]

Still regarded as a foreign religion, Christianity bears mentioning here for two reasons that recall a parallel circumstance in India. Unlike other foreign imports such as Buddhism, Christianity has never received official patronage. In fact, its early history ended with a forceful and largely successful effort by the Tokugawa shogunate to stamp out the faith, which was viewed as an unwelcome vanguard of broader Western military and political influence. This move was part of the deliberate isolation of Japan from the West that is explained in Chapter 7.

Since the Meiji era and the reopening of Japan to Western influence, Christian organizations have been particularly important in contributing to education as part of broader modernization efforts in Japan. Notably, in the early twentieth century, when education was limited to a small number of government institutions, Western missionary efforts were central to the expansion of educational opportunity, especially for girls and women. Some of Japan's best-known universities, both women's and coeducational, were originally Christian. Along with education, Christians have been influential in the field of social work and in the early phases of the development of Socialist political movements. Today, like Marxism, the philosophical impact of Christianity is limited to a small group of intellectuals, among them the well-known writer Shusaku Endo.[41]

# Summary

The history of religion in Japan clearly reflects the themes that were introduced in Chapter 1. The indigenous tradition of Shinto—itself incorporating some ancient practices of folk religion—coexists with other Asian traditions that entered Japan from China and Korea, such as Buddhism and Confucianism. Western religions, notably Christianity, have been introduced to Japan as well, but with much less impact on the overall social fabric and, therefore, politics. Of all these traditions, Shinto has been the most closely associated with the modern development process because of the government's use of State Shinto for building and maintaining national cohesion. The intermingling of different forms of Shinto and Buddhism, along with ancient folk practices and the philosophical and social imprint of Confucianism, has created a cultural matrix in which it is difficult to isolate single features. This blending, in turn, helps account for the typically indirect relationship between Japanese religion and modern politics—in contrast to India, where religious communities and priorities are inseparable from the contemporary definition of politics.

The intertwining of religious and cultural traditions also makes it difficult to identify causal links between particular religious tenets and gender differences. In Japan, as in China and India, the history of female subordination is obvious, and it extends into the political realm. But this history is not without its complexities and contradictions. Sumiko Iwao, for example, has argued that women's relative absence from the public sphere, combined with the traditional importance of the family and women's role in the private sphere, gives women freedom and a certain kind of power.[42]

Just as changes in recent decades have altered relations between men and women, the Japanese people have confronted other changes that are directly and indirectly significant for our study of politics: Old minority communities continue to demand redress of grievances, whereas new immigrant groups puncture the homogeneity of Japanese society; rural communities that guaranteed stability and predictability for centuries have been replaced by the urban centers that now dominate the political and economic processes; an aging population strains the fabric of private lives and public policies. All of these trends suggest comparisons not only with China and India but also with North America.

# Notes

1. *Japan: An Illustrated Encyclopedia*, vol. 1 (Tokyo: Kodansha, 1993), p. 649. Hereafter cited as Kodansha, *Encyclopedia*.

2. Kodansha, *Encyclopedia*, vol. 1, p. 342; *Japan Times Weekly International Edition* (hereafter cited as *Japan Times WIE*), July 20–26, 1992.

3. Countries that will have comparable proportions of people over 60 in the next twenty-five years will be Sweden, Switzerland, and other advanced industrialized societies. Japan is unique in terms of the speed with which its population is aging. James H. Schulz, Allen Borowski, and William H. Crown, *Economics of Population Aging: The "Graying" of Australia, Japan, and the United States* (New York: Auburn House, 1991), pp. 9–12; John Creighton Campbell, *How Policies Change: The Japanese Government and the Aging Society* (Princeton: Princeton University Press, 1992), p. 6.

4. Kodansha, *Encyclopedia*, vol. 1, p. 14; Schulz, Borowski, and Crown, *Economics of Population Aging*, p. 50. The policy changes are analyzed in Campbell, *How Policies Change*, chap. 9. For a moving portrayal of the impact an elderly man has on his family, see Sawako Ariyoshi's novel, *The Twilight Years*, trans. Mildred Tahara (Tokyo: Kodansha, 1984). Eighty-six percent of caregivers for the elderly are female. *Japan Times WIE*, March 4–10, 1996.

5. Kodansha, *Encyclopedia*, vol. 1, p. 17; Prime Minister's Office (PMO), *Japanese Women Today* (Tokyo: PMO, 1990), pp. 18–19.

6. *Japan Times WIE*, July 13–19, 1992.

7. Murasaki Shikibu, *The Tale of Genji*, trans. Edward G. Seidensticker (New York: Alfred A. Knopf, 1976).

8. Susan J. Pharr, "Japan: Historical and Contemporary Perspectives," in *Women: Role and Status in Eight Countries*, ed. Janet Z. Giele and Audrey C. Smock (New York: John Wiley, 1977), pp. 219–255. See also the studies in pt. 1 of Gail Lee Berstein, ed., *Recreating Japanese Women, 1600–1945* (Berkeley: University of California Press, 1991).

9. See the interpretation of Sumiko Iwao, *The Japanese Woman: Traditional Image and Changing Reality* (New York: Free Press, 1993), chap. 10.

10. Susan J. Pharr, *Losing Face: Status Politics in Japan* (Berkeley: University of California Press, 1990), pp. 59–60.

11. Ibid., p. 67.

12. Japan Institute of Labor, *Problems of Working Women* (Tokyo: Japan Institute of Labor, 1986), pp. 5–6; PMO, *Japanese Women Today*, pp. 2–4.

13. Kodansha, *Encyclopedia*, vol. 1, p. 21.

14. Ibid., p. 22.

15. George A. De Vos and William O. Wetherall, *Japan's Minorities: Burakumin, Koreans, and Ainu* (London: Minority Rights Group, 1974), pp. 17–18; Oswald Iten, "Japan's Injustice to the Ainu," *Swiss Review of World Affairs*, no. 2 (February 1996), pp. 15–20. For a moving portrait, see Shigeru Kayano, *Our Land Was a Forest: An Ainu Memoir*, trans. Kyoko Selden and Lili Selden (Boulder: Westview Press, 1994).

16. Kodansha, *Encyclopedia*, vol. 1, pp. 146, 830.

17. De Vos and Wetherall, *Japan's Minorities*, pp. 6–7; Kodansha, *Encyclopedia*, vol. 1, p. 146. *Tokushu buraku* ("citizens of special communities") is another version of the euphemism.

18. Pharr, *Losing Face*, pp. 77–80.

19. Toson Shimizaki, *The Broken Commandment*, trans. Kenneth Strong (Tokyo: University of Tokyo Press, 1974), pp. 210, 229–230.

20. William Wetherall, "Status of 'Outcast' Group Changes with Wider Exposure," *Japan Times WIE*, March 16–22, 1992; Herman W. Smith, *The Myth of Japanese Homogeneity: Social-Ecological Diversity in Education and Socialization* (Commack, N.Y.: Nova Science Publications, 1995), p. 198.

21. Kodansha, *Encyclopedia*, vol. 1, p. 147; Smith, *Myth of Japanese Homogeneity*, pp. 199–204. Mikiso Hane has numerous examples of *burakumin* problems throughout the twentieth century in *Peasants, Rebels, and Outcastes: The Underside of Modern Japan* (New York: Pantheon Books, 1982), pp. 138–171.

22. David E. Kaplan and Alec Dubro, *Yakuza: The Explosive Account of Japan's Criminal Underworld* (Menlo Park, Calif.: Addison-Wesley, 1986), pp. 22–23, 145. Koreans also find in the *yakuza* opportunities for acceptance and upward mobility denied them in mainstream Japanese society. Changsoo Lee and George De Vos, *Koreans in Japan: Ethnic Conflict and Accommodation* (Berkeley: University of California Press, 1981), p. 364.

23. Kodansha, *Encyclopedia*, vol. 1, p. 830.

24. Ibid., p. 397.

25. This change was a response to prolonged protests against fingerprinting by permanent residents (including those married to Japanese nationals). For the story of an American who refused to be fingerprinted, see Michael Shapiro, *Japan: In the Land of the Brokenhearted* (New York: Henry Holt, 1989).

26. Louis D. Hayes, *Introduction to Japanese Politics* (New York: Paragon House, 1992), pp. 142–143.

27. *Japan Times WIE*, January 27–February 2 and February 3–9, 1992. For an extensive history of "comfort women" and the opening of the political debate, see George Hicks, *The Comfort Women: Japan's Brutal Regime of Enforced Prostitution in the Second World War* (New York: W. W. Norton, 1994), especially chaps. 8, 9.

28. *Japan Times WIE*, July 20–26 and August 3–9, 1992.

29. H. Byron Earhart, *Japanese Religion: Unity and Diversity*, 3d ed. (Belmont, Calif.: Wadsworth, 1982), chaps. 1, 2.

30. See Joseph M. Kitagawa's preface to Donald L. Philippi, *Norito: A Translation of the Ancient Japanese Ritual Prayers* (Princeton: Princeton University Press, 1990), pp. xx–xxii.

31. Ibid., p. xxii; Kodansha, *Encyclopedia*, vol. 2, pp. 1269–1271.

32. For the text of Shotoku's Constitution and an accompanying discussion, see Ian Reader, Esben Andreasen, and Finn Stefansson, *Japanese Religions: Past and Present* (Honolulu: University of Hawaii Press, 1993), pp. 163 and 167–169.

33. Various scholars have categorized Shinto forms differently. I have drawn on and synthesized the treatments found in the following: Earhart, *Japanese Religion*, chaps. 2–4; Agency for Cultural Affairs, *Japanese Religion: A Survey* (Tokyo: Kodansha, 1972), chaps. 2, 9; Reader, Andreasen, and Stefansson, *Japanese Religions*, chap.

4; and Joseph J. Spae, *Shinto Man* (Tokyo: Oriens Institute for Religious Research, 1972), chap. 1.

34. Agency for Cultural Affairs, *Japanese Religion*, p. 29.

35. The small travel book *Festivals of Japan* (Tokyo: Japan Travel Bureau, 1989) has numerous illustrations of *matsuri*.

36. Agency for Cultural Affairs, *Japanese Religion*, pp. 31, 91–92.

37. The definition of "new religions" varies among scholars; Aum Shinrikyo was usually called a "cult" by the press and might better be identified as a "'new' new religion." See Ian Reader, *Religion in Contemporary Japan* (Honolulu: University of Hawaii Press, 1991), p. 195.

38. H. Paul Varley, *Japanese Culture*, 3d ed. (Honolulu: University of Hawaii Press, 1984), p. 94.

39. Because of its popularity in the United States, the literature in English on Zen is extensive. See the introductions in Earhart, *Japanese Religion*, pp. 97–103, and Agency for Cultural Affairs, *Japanese Religion*, pp. 61–62.

40. Ibid., tables 5 (p. 254) and 6 (p. 257).

41. See, in particular, Shusaku Endo's novel *Silence*, the story of a seventeenth-century priest in Japan at the height of the persecution of Christians.

42. Iwao, *Japanese Woman*, chaps. 1, 3.

# Part Two

# The Foundation of Politics

Part One focused on those population characteristics that are especially significant for studying politics in India, China, and Japan. One of the goals of the chapters in Part One is to remind us that a country's population is not undifferentiated. That is, not all Indians or Chinese are ethnically the same, nor do they have the same history, the same socioeconomic status, or—by extension—the same political roles and access to the political process.

Part One also illustrated the book's comparative themes. The endurance of traditional culture and social organization helps account for the unique circumstances and issues in each of the countries, an illustration of this being caste in India. This national uniqueness, however, is muted by the intermingling and grafting of Asian traditions, which is the second broad theme. An obvious case of this grafting is the impact of Buddhism and Confucianism in Japan. An example of the third theme—the influence of Western values and institutions—is the small but occasionally important role of Christianity in India and Japan.

Part Two builds on these themes and deals more explicitly with the remaining themes of socioeconomic development, state, and nation. Development, which has become a political mandate for Asian governments, is largely a legacy of nineteenth- and twentieth-century political changes that swept Japan, China, and India. Although the causes of these changes were complex, they cannot be understood apart from Asia's encounter with Western power, ideologies, and technologies. A historical perspective is central to understanding these changes, and the chapters in Part Two emphasize patterns in the interplay between indigenous and external forces. To use one illustration of this interplay that picks up where

Chapter 4 left off: The role of Shinto in Japanese politics today can best be understood by seeing it as an indigenous religion that has been molded by its relationship to the Japanese state. This relationship was conditioned by preoccupations with development and national integrity, which, in turn, were deeply influenced by Japan's contacts with the West.

The example of Shinto recalls the fifth and sixth themes introduced in Chapter 1: the relationship between individuals and state institutions, and the formation of national identity. All six comparative themes are intertwined, but the last one, which highlights national identity and the historical movements of nationalism, is emphasized in Part Two. Readers should be aware at the outset that this selective focus is an analytical device: It is designed to provide coherence and some insight into rich and extremely complex historical developments. Put differently, the emphasis on nationalism and national identity is a lens that can magnify and clarify— and distort. With this caveat in mind, the remainder of this introduction expands on the significance of national identity and on the way it can help us understand the foundations of Indian, Chinese, and Japanese politics.

The terms "nationalism" and "national identity" as used in this book refer to a modern phenomenon that characterizes the past two centuries of Asian history. Nationalism inspires political movements that seek to foster a sense of identification with a territorially based state. It may reflect a persisting sense of national identity, particularly among intellectuals and government leaders. Typically, nationalism works to create a sense of national belonging among people whose previous political loyalty was owed to family, village, clan, caste, or lord. In its rawest and most negative forms, nationalism is linked to sentiments of ethnic and national superiority such as racism, imperialism, and militarism—all of which are amply illustrated in modern international relations. In its less pernicious forms and even creative aspects, nationalism may lead to liberation (for example, from imperial control), popular sovereignty, economic development, and a sense of self-worth, both individual and collective.

Asian nationalism, like nationalism elsewhere, has been both beneficial and destructive. It has made it possible to defend and enrich indigenous traditions, including the arts, from domination or destruction by foreign imports. It has also produced creative blends of native and foreign, of old and new. The destructive faces of Asian nationalism are equally obvious; some of these have already been hinted at in earlier chapters, notably with regard to discrimination against minority populations.

The purpose of the chapters that follow is not to catalog the pros and cons of nationalism but to use both the *idea* of the nation and the *process* of nation building as it has occurred in the past two centuries to illustrate two sets of interrelationships that are essential for understanding today's politics: the relationships between tradition and modernity and between the indigenous and the imported. Because we are primarily concerned here with the political dimensions of these relationships, the focus on the traditional and indigenous will emphasize political norms or ideologies and institutions. Chapter 5 summarizes the critical periods in Indian political history, including an analysis of the relative strength of classical and modern political ideas in the attempt to forge a common Indian national identity.

India is the only one of our Asian case studies subjected to outright Western colonialism. China's coastal areas felt the direct impact of Western imperialism, but much of its hinterland was left relatively unchanged. Nonetheless, in China, the nationalist reaction to the West was as virulent and (ultimately) as effective, if not more so, than the Indian reaction. It is ironic that in Asia, China stands out both for the endurance of its traditional culture and for the massiveness of its revolutionary experience.

One often-debated question about China is why its response to the "coming of the West" in the nineteenth century was so ineffective in contrast to Japan's. Turning the question around, we might ask: Why and how was Japan able to respond so quickly and effectively to the Western threat? What was the relationship between nationalism and development in this response? These are just some of the questions that the next three chapters will address.

# *five*

# Indian National Identity: Secular or Hindu?

Nowhere in Asia is the debate over the meaning of national identity or the effort to create and maintain national unity more vigorous and more pressing than in India. From the early stirrings of the nationalist movement in the nineteenth century to the end of the twentieth century, there have been deep cleavages over the question of what it means to be "Indian" and how the Indian nation should be defined. At the core of the debate is the issue of Hinduism and the question of whether it is the defining quality of Indianness or whether it is one faith among others in what has been a secular polity.

The roots of the debate are historical and philosophical. It is to the earliest history of India that this chapter first turns in order to understand the traditions of Indian political thought and organization. The chapter then looks at the way in which the Mughal Empire, followed by the British Empire, helped form the modern state of India. The Mughal and British periods are important for three reasons: They affected the political and legal norms that carried over to the twentieth century; they created a precedent for certain institutions of government; and they planted the seeds of modern communalism in India. The term "**communalism**" is used here in the Indian sense to mean loyalties to and tensions among the communities of faith that characterize the various religious groups, especially Hindus and Muslims.

The third and fourth sections focus on the nationalist movement, which culminated in the partition of British India into India and Pakistan. The chapter closes with a question that, though nearly buried for the first decades of the new republic, reemerged in the 1980s. The question is whether India is, and should be, a secular republic, and no issue better illustrates this dilemma than the Ayodhya crisis.

## Early India: Empire and Village[1]

The Mughal and British Empires were superimposed on a Hindu society that had been evolving for more than two thousand years when the first Muslim invasions in the tenth century began to undermine Hindu rule. Although there were vast differences across the subcontinent during this early period, the consolidation of Hindu values and practices, including caste, created a relatively high degree of cultural unity. A variety of political orders came and went, and the richest and most powerful kingdoms created architectural and literary monuments that contributed to the legendary greatness of classical India.

One of the most important of these ancient kingdoms was the Maurya (322–185 B.C.E.), which arose in North India in what is now the state of Bihar. The Mauryan Empire developed extensive civil and military bureaucracies, elaborate irrigation and road systems, and, of course, a taxation system. Although the first Mauryan king, Chandragupta, was the architect of India's greatest ancient empire, his chief minister was the de facto ruler of the state. To this minister, known to us today as **Kautilya**, is attributed the *Arthashastra*, meaning "treatise on polity," one of the most complex political documents to survive from an ancient civilization. As a source of information on state administration, the *Arthashastra* is fascinating, covering the details of topics such as the operation of council meetings, spying, and the king's personal safety.

Chandragupta's grandson was Ashoka, one of the greatest rulers of the ancient world (269–232 B.C.E.). Deeply influenced by Buddhism, Ashoka claimed to rule and expand his empire by humane and enlightened government rather than war. Under his missionaries, Buddhism started its long migration outside India, beginning with the island today known as Sri Lanka.

Central to Ashoka's government philosophy was the principle of "dharma," a word that has a variety of meanings. Dharma refers simultaneously to the sacred law that governs the universe and to the codes of conduct governing relations between social groups and also between individuals.[2] For individuals, dharma denotes a series of duties: personal, social, moral, and religious. It describes the way one is expected to behave in specific situations, and to offend this expectation is to make one

Photo 5.1    *Indian Rupee Note. Photo by author.*

liable to various sanctions.[3] Under Ashoka, the Hindu inspiration of dharma was colored by Buddhism and had the effect of relaxing the king's autocratic rule, moderating, for example, the extremes of punishment found under his predecessors. Observing the principle of *ahimsa* (nonviolence to all living things), Ashoka gave up the royal sport of hunting, and his reign helped establish the vegetarianism that today is integral to Indian culture and cuisine. In order to propagate and popularize Buddhist moral principles, Ashoka had pillars erected in different parts of his empire. Proclamations engraved on these pillars preached religious tolerance and warned against envy, impatience, and other human frailties that deviated from Buddhist ideals. The capital, or top, of the pillar at Sarnath, where the Buddha first preached, had four lions, the lion symbolizing royalty. This capital symbolizes the modern Indian state, as it appears on all Indian currency and serves as a daily reminder of the link between the India of 2,300 years ago and today. Photo 5.1 shows the capital of Ashoka's Sarnath pillar (the capital is still in the museum at Sarnath) on a one-hundred-rupee note. (Note also the multiple language scripts.)

One other ancient empire should be mentioned here for its contributions to the history of classical Indian, and specifically Hindu, greatness. The **Gupta** period (C.E. fourth to sixth century) was India's "golden age," in which the arts and sciences flourished. By the fifth century, Indian surgeons were performing plastic surgery to repair mutilated faces. The decimal and digit systems, which the West learned from the Arabs, originated in India during the Gupta era. Gupta scientists further developed the principles of astronomy learned from the Greeks.

As the West learned the decimal system from India via the Arabs, so it also learned much about the greatness of the Gupta period from Chinese Buddhist monks on pilgrimage to India. According to one of these pilgrims, Fa-Hsien, the empire was remarkable for its peacefulness, the rarity of serious crime, and the mildness of its administration. "At this time India was perhaps the happiest and most civilized region of the world, for the effete Roman Empire was nearing its destruction, and China was passing through a time of troubles between the two great periods of the Hans and the Tangs."[4]

As is suggested by this description, India was in the crosscurrents of the movement of ideas and peoples for hundreds of years. Invasions from the west brought Persian and Greek influence; Buddhism, born in India, moved south and east, inspiring pilgrims, who, fifteen hundred years ago (as today), returned to the subcontinent for the roots of their faith. Over the course of these same centuries, Hinduism, whose structure and worldview are distinctly Indian, evolved. Although influenced by the movements of Buddhism and Jainism,[5] Hinduism came to dominate India largely in the form in which we see it in the twentieth century, and the principles, popular deities, and caste system of the Hindu spiritual and social orders consolidated their hold over the worldview of the average Indian.

For these average Indians, the world that mattered was the world of the village, where self-government and caste combined to maintain predictability and order. Contact with law and punishment generally occurred within the context of the caste *pancha*, a traditional council of five or more leaders that heard civil cases and decided outcomes for caste members, and the **panchayat**, an organization of male village elders. In theory, the village was administered by the *panchayat*; it was taxed (in the form of produce, as were villages in China) but generally untouched by changes of rule from one kingdom to another. The principles of dharma operated within the village caste system, and acceptance of the obligations of one's caste came to mean the realization and fulfillment of dharma. Thus caste, *panchayat*, and dharma—all of which survived into the modern period—assured relative peace and social harmony, as well as a sense of order and belonging for most villagers.

The Muslim invasions ended the dominance of Hindu rulers, but they did not end the dominance of Hindu village life and values for most Indians. Nor did the invasions erase the memory of Hindu greatness that linked Indians to the period of the early empires.

> The memory of a great past and its reinterpretation strengthened the awakening of modern India, and in that lies the political significance of the long Hindu period. Its real achievements, however, are in directions other than strictly political—in the perfecting of a remarkable social order, and in the development of traditions and values that have had a lasting effect on all subsequent periods.[6]

# Creating the Indian State:
# The Mughal and the British Empires

*The Mughal Empire*

The first Muslim raids and invasions started as early as the eighth century in northwestern India, becoming more persistent and extensive in the tenth and eleventh centuries. The first major Muslim state, the Delhi sultanate, was founded in the early thirteenth century. The most powerful and longest-ruling Muslim state, the Mughal dynasty, was established in 1526 and was not formally terminated until 1862, although in reality its control over the subcontinent began to decline after the death of the last great Mughal emperor, Aurangzeb, in 1707. Beginning in the sixteenth century, the first sweep of European expansion into Asia brought English, Dutch, French, and Portuguese explorers, traders, missionaries, and conquerors. As the Mughal Empire declined in the eighteenth century, the Europeans moved in, taking one territory after another. Gradually, the British, whose effective rule was exercised by the **British East India Company**, eliminated their competitors, notably the French.

Political scientist Rajni Kothari has summarized the importance of the Mughal period for modern politics by pointing to four main characteristics of Muslim rule.[7] First, at the core of Muslim administration lay a strong military emphasis, necessitated by the long periods of fighting accompanying the Muslim incursions, defeat of indigenous kingdoms, and empire building.

Second, the Muslims confronted Hindus with completely different social and religious systems. Despite important instances of accommodation and periods of harmony, the two communities, with their respective worldviews and social organizations, remained largely separate. The Mughals were initially conquerors, and Islam was a proselytizing faith; and Muslim mosques often replaced Hindu temples—a point later emphasized by Hindu nationalists. The roots of the Ayodhya crisis examined at the end of this chapter spring from this reality.

The third characteristic of the Mughal state that was significant for India's subsequent political evolution was the creation of a clear center of political authority, located in the northern and most of the central subcontinent. The Mughal state was backed by an efficient administration responsible for law enforcement and tax collection. The British inherited this administrative structure and continued many of its forms, while changing others.

The fourth attribute of Mughal rule was its relative failure to alter local institutions and village affairs.[8] At the local level, public issues continued to be settled through customary channels such as the *panchayat*, and where Muslims came to live next to Hindus in the rural areas, the former typically accommodated to the social (if not the religious) system of the latter. And in one critical way, Muslim and Hindu values reinforced each other. "Among all classes . . . the preference for a son underlined the inferior position of women."[9] Muslim upper-class and court women were kept secluded in **purdah** (literally, "curtain"), confined to a separate section of the house or palace and veiled when outside. Lower classes and castes aspired to the practice of purdah, and it spread throughout India, complementing the indigenous Hindu norms that confined women to private affairs, and is still practiced today in various forms and degrees.

Directly and indirectly, the long periods of Muslim rule established the conditions for twentieth-century communalism. When the Mughal state dissolved, it left a huge Muslim population in North India that was a permanent, integral part of Indian society. Hindus and Muslims learned to live together for the most part, but when political tensions and cleavages rose at the national level—as they did with the nationalist movement— the impact was increasingly felt at the local level. The policies of the British Empire set the context for the nationalist period.

## The British Empire in India

The British story in India begins with the founding of the British East India Company in London in 1600. The purpose of the company, a Crown corporation, was to explore and exploit the opportunities for commerce in India, and within a few years, it had secured trading privileges from the Mughals. By the end of the seventeenth century, the company had established commercial enclaves in the coastal cities of Bombay, Madras, and Calcutta—cities that even today are known for their remnants of British architecture. Over the course of the eighteenth century, the company expanded, taking advantage of Mughal weaknesses and playing non-Mughal rulers against each other. By the mid-nineteenth century, the company, which employed both civil and military officials, controlled nearly two-thirds of the Indian subcontinent. This expansion was facilitated by centrifugal tendencies in the Mughal Empire and growing challenges to Mughal rule.[10]

Since the primary objective of the British East India Company was profit, its policies were designed to create the kind of political authority, social and economic order, and physical infrastructure (such as roads and railroads) to make this possible. Until the early nineteenth century, the company interfered little in local affairs or in the religious and social lives of most Indians. But changes in England itself soon made themselves felt in India, when British reformers demanded the elimination of visible and offensive Hindu customs (such as sati, the self-immolation of a widow on her husband's funeral pyre) that conflicted with Western, Christian values. Supported by Hindu reformers, the British sponsored limited social change in India. At the same time, the introduction of Western education and the English language as the medium of instruction in Indian high schools and colleges spread British liberal ideas.

Education was to influence profoundly the Indian nationalist movement that developed later in the nineteenth century. For some Hindus, the new learning complemented learning in the Sanskrit tradition, traditionally monopolized by Brahmins. For others, Western education and values largely supplanted the indigenous tradition. By the end of the nineteenth century, a growing class of educated men emerged to form the core of the nationalist movement. It included both Brahmins, who dominated India's religious and literary heritage, and non-Brahmins such as the young Mohandas Gandhi, who at age eighteen sailed to England to study law. The nationalist movement also included those who sought to apply the highest ideals of British liberalism to India, as well as those primarily seeking sinecures in the growing bureaucracy. The bureaucracy was a place where upwardly mobile young Indians could put their English to gain, and it was their stymied access to the bureaucracy that led to the creation of the **Indian National Congress** in the 1880s.

The collapse of the Mughal Empire and, with it, the replacement of Persian with English as the official language of government contributed to the alienation of Muslims in India. Traditionally educated in their own schools, where classical Arabic (the language of the Qur'an) joined Persian, the Muslims "failed to take advantage of English education and were soon displaced in the civil services by the rising Hindu middle class."[11]

The importance of the new Indian middle class is hard to overestimate, both because it was overwhelmingly Hindu and because through it, the British ruled India.

> Through this class new ideas of individualism and constitutionalism gained currency. This class manned the new professions. And from this class, political leadership emerged to challenge the might of the British Empire. The overall effect was profound. The new middle class, created by English education and drawn by the concepts of liberty, democracy, and socialism, was indeed the greatest legacy of the British Raj.[12]

To this, one might add that the new leadership ultimately created a predominantly secular vision of independent India. How this came to happen, despite the deep concern for revitalizing Hinduism that motivated important segments of the nationalist leadership, is the subject of the next section.

## Defining the Indian Nation-State

The 1840s and 1850s brought growing political and military instability to the Indian subcontinent, largely as a result of British efforts to expand control to the northwest, first into Afghanistan, later into Punjab. India lost twenty thousand lives (mostly Indian troops trained and led by British officers) in a futile effort to conquer Afghanistan—foreshadowing a similarly disastrous effort by the Soviet Union 140 years later. In the mid-1840s, British efforts to capture the still-independent Sikh kingdom of Punjab provoked the first of two bloody Sikh wars. Defeated, the Sikhs disbanded their armies and surrendered fertile agricultural lands to the British, along with strategic mountain areas, including Kashmir. Kashmir, whose population was and is still overwhelmingly Muslim, was in turn given to a Hindu ruler in exchange for his loyalty, thus establishing the claims made by the newly independent India in the 1940s that Kashmir belonged to India. At the end of the twentieth century, the struggle between the Indian government and autonomous Muslim movements in Kashmir—a struggle that also engages Pakistan—continues to be one of the greatest threats to peace and stability in South Asia.

The philosophy of government that resulted from these wars of conquest on the northwest frontier produced one face of British rule in India, a face that helps us understand the massacre at Amritsar, described later in the chapter. This was the "Punjab school" of British administration, "where men were men and things got done swiftly; where officials shot first and asked for evidence later; where higher officials always closed ranks behind subordinates, for that was how you survived in a seething sea of native sycophants, conspirators and rebels."[13]

British rule in India thus combined the ruthlessness and pragmatism of military conquest with the "enlightened" government of educational opportunity and public works projects, both of which were designed to render more effective imperial control and the extraction of wealth. Ironically, it was the combination of these policies that led to the so-called **Sepoy Mutiny**, the Anglo-Indian War of 1857. Both real and imagined British policy convinced the sepoys, the Indian soldiers who enabled some 38,000 British troops to control 200 million Indians, that their rulers were conspiring to convert them—Hindu and Muslim alike—to Christianity. One policy, for example, required Indian soldiers to accept service "anywhere," and it was rumored that Christian missionaries were conspiring with officials to send high-caste Hindus overseas, where they would be permanently polluted and would be easier targets for conversion.

Finally, in 1857, the British introduced a new breech-loading Enfield rifle, whose cartridges were smeared with cow and pig grease. Soldiers were instructed to bite the tip off the cartridge before inserting it into the breech, an act that violated the sensibilities of both Hindus, to whom the cow was sacred, and Muslims, to whom the pig was unclean. The troops began by refusing to load the rifles, then by rebelling at one post after another. The revolts remained largely isolated, with no leadership sufficiently strong or united to seriously threaten British rule. But the murder of British civilians spread panic. Fear and racial hatred exploded on both sides. The British reasserted military control in 1858, and that same year, the British Parliament in London transferred all rights of the old East India Company directly to the British Crown. The Raj was now officially a British government affair.

Although the revolt of 1857–1858 has been viewed by some Indian nationalists as an early war of independence, it was largely a conservative reaction to the multifaceted changes in early-nineteenth-century Indian society.[14] Ultimately, however, the revolt and the reaction to it contributed to the growth of both nationalism and communalism in India: to nationalism, by widening the gap between ruler and ruled, and to communalism, by deepening the suspicion between Hindus and Muslims as an independence movement began to take shape. To understand how this happened, we turn to the development of the nationalist movement.

## *Reviving and Reforming the Hindu Tradition*

Contact with Western philosophies, literatures, and institutions generated a variety of responses among Indian intellectuals. Central to these responses was the question of the relative merits of Hindu and Western traditions. The introduction of English education expanded familiarity with the West among Indians and broadened the debate to the new middle classes. Ultimately, the debate fused with the political awakening of the 1870s and 1880s.

Called by many the "Father of Modern India," Ram Mohan Roy stands out among the early Indian intellectuals. Born of devout Hindu parents in 1772, he mastered Persian and Arabic, then Sanskrit, and later English, out of an insatiable curiosity and a desire to read and also in order to qualify for government employment. He rose as high as a non-Britisher could in the Bengal Civil Service, retired early, and devoted his life to educating himself as well as the many Indians and Britishers with whom he came in contact. Deeply interested in Christianity, Ram Mohan Roy nonetheless defended Hinduism against the attacks of missionaries, whose judgments about Indian traditions were often colored by ignorance and the assumptions of inferiority that characterized Orientalist thinking.

Roy is important not only for his individual accomplishments but also because he represents a contributing strain to the development of modern nationalism that insists on the enduring essence of Hindu philosophy while demanding the reform of repressive social practices associated with the status of women and low-caste or outcaste Hindus. Decades later, nationalists such as G. K. Gokhale (1866–1915) and Mohandas K. Gandhi would seek simultaneously to revive and reform Hinduism as a basis for Indian identity.

In contrast to Roy, a religious reform movement developed in the 1870s that was both less influenced by contact with the West and also more insistent on the uniqueness and superiority of the truth found in the *Vedas*, including the *Rig Veda* mentioned in Chapter 2. The **Arya Samaj**, a nationalist group founded in Bombay in 1875, sought to restore an ideal Hindu Aryan past and criticized the influence of Islam and Christianity on India. The Arya Samaj's proselytizing fundamentalism contributed to the rise of enmity against Muslims in some areas and to a lineage of Hindu nationalism that can be seen today in the Bharatiya Janata Party, the political party most closely identified with the demand for a Hindu India.

Complementing the perspectives of people as diverse as Ram Mohan Roy, on the one hand, and the leaders of the Arya Samaj, on the other, were a wide variety of views regarding the nature of indigenous Indian traditions, the impact of the West in general, and, more particularly, the nature of British rule and how Indians should respond to it. The growing numbers of the educated elite came from different regions, different economic circumstances, and increasingly from different castes. Their views about their own traditions as well as about the British reflected these different circumstances, and their opinions also shifted as British policy itself shifted. British rule was not static: It responded to political mandates from home as well as to local pressures, such as the views of individual officials, social and economic conditions, and the activities of the Indian nationalists. The intermingling of all of these factors may be seen in the evolution of the Indian National Congress (conventionally called "Congress"), which, after its establishment in 1885, became the driving organization of the nationalist movement. The politics of the Congress reveal the ongoing effort to reformulate an Indian identity in terms of Hinduism, the growing challenge of politically articulate Muslims, and, ultimately, the conviction among key Congress leaders that an independent India must be secular.

## The Indian National Congress

Despite the fact that Britain's viceroy (or governor) in India in the early 1880s sought to introduce a measure of self-administration to Indian men, his liberal intentions were largely thwarted by resistant bureaucrats in the Indian Civil Service (ICS), the administrative "glue" that held British India together. The effective opening of the ICS to Indians, in fact, was one of the primary goals of the seventy-two men who met in Bombay in 1885 to call for a "new India" to respond to the aspirations of these educated Indians, now imbued with the ideals of British liberalism. Most of the representatives to the first annual meeting of the Indian National Congress were high-caste Hindus and Parsis, but several Englishmen also played active roles. Muslims were present at this first meeting, as well as at subsequent meetings, but never in proportion to the strength of their numbers in the Indian population—a factor that contributed to the perception that the Congress was primarily a Hindu organization.

The overarching objective of the Congress during its early years was to persuade the British to establish and expand representative institutions for Indians. Gradually, however, a second generation of Congressmen, impatient with British resistance and desiring more influence within the Congress, advocated more militant policies and extremist tactics. To this newer generation belonged the most successful early efforts to mobilize popular support beyond the educated elite by drawing on Hindu traditions and symbols. **Bal Gangadhar Tilak**, a Marathi-speaking journalist from western India, is the best known today of these nationalists who called not for reform of British rule but for elimination of it. Tilak became known as a defender of religious customs against both Hindu reformers and the imperial government, when it intervened in social and cultural practices by passing legislation to which conservative Hindus objected. In one such instance, Tilak's popularity soared when he attacked the government's Age of Consent Act, adopted after a young girl died following her husband's intercourse with her. The act raised the age of consent from ten to twelve; any intercourse that took place when the wife was under twelve would subsequently be classified as rape. A storm of protest followed the act, with Orthodox Hindus claiming that it violated the religious injunction that girls marry before puberty. In allying himself with the opposition to the Age of Consent Act, Tilak helped join two political strands that came to dominate important currents of the nationalist movement: direct opposition to government measures and defense of religious values as a way of mobilizing public support.

By the early twentieth century, the Congress was divided between two dominant factions: the "moderates," such as Gokhale, Gandhi's mentor in the Congress, who argued that the British could be persuaded to rule India by liberal political principles and grant Indians greater self-determination; and the "extremists," led by Tilak, who distrusted the British, were impatient, and sought methods that would force the British to leave India. Although some partisans of extremism advocated violence, within the Congress the extremists focused on boycotts as the method that would succeed where argument and negotiation had failed. They thought a political boycott of government institutions with an economic boycott of British goods would force British compliance with Congress demands. From these arguments came the conceptualization that real *swaraj*, or self-rule, meant not just political independence from imperial control but rejection of dependence on the state. This independence could be achieved only by renewed village self-sufficiency.

It would be inaccurate to call Tilak or most of the other extremist leaders Hindu communalists in the modern sense. Nonetheless, the "Hindu tinge" of the boycott movement and other elements of the nationalist movement in the early twentieth century "simultaneously generated unease and apprehension in the minds of the educated and politically conscious Muslims who were suspicious of a movement whose nationalist message was couched in religious terms, and who, therefore, saw the Nationalist Congress as representing a Hindu movement."[15] In 1906, those Muslims who shared this unease and opposition to Congress formed the **All-India Muslim League**. For many years, the membership of the league remained small and elite. Not until 1913 did **Muhammad Ali Jinnah**, later the founder of Pakistan, join the league, and not until the 1930s did the league seriously challenge the Congress's view of a united India that would replace the British Raj in the subcontinent. It is to this next phase in the building of the Indian nation-state that we now turn.

## Congress and the Politics of Gandhi, Nehru, and Jinnah

Four interrelated developments stand out from the twists and turns of the complex elements of the independence movement that gathered momentum after the turn of the century: (1) British policies of reaction and reform; (2) Gandhi's role in transforming the Congress into a mass movement; (3) the growing Muslim demand for a separate nation-state; and (4) Nehru's impact on the independence movement and on the newly independent state of India.

As suggested earlier, the British imperial government in India responded to a variety of pressures in devising and implementing its policies. This often meant that those policies bore unforeseen (and unintended) consequences. For example, in 1906, the same year the All-India Muslim League was founded, the British viceroy in India, Lord Minto, agreed to Muslim demands that the interests of the Muslim community be safeguarded in the reforms for India's government initiated in London by the new secretary of state for India, Lord Morley. When the **Morley-Minto Reforms** became law three years later, they included a provision for separate Muslim electorates in any subsequent elections. "The rights of the Muslims as a distinct community were hence recognized and guaranteed and were in the following decades to prove the major stumbling block between separatist Muslims and the Congress."[16] The British, seeing the utility of blunting the effectiveness of Congress nationalists by calling attention to the distinct needs of the Muslim community, were to resurrect this strategy in the 1930s and again contribute to Muslim-Hindu division.

The year 1919 marked a turning point in the life of the Indian National Congress and imperial rule in India. Mohandas Gandhi had returned to India from South Africa a few years earlier. In South Africa, he had practiced law and also developed his philosophy of *satyagraha*, or nonviolent resistance, which he translated as "soul force." Both law and *satyagraha* became cornerstones of Gandhi's leadership of the nationalist movement. Using law, he reasoned with and confronted the British on their own terms; with *satyagraha*, he mobilized India's masses for the nationalist cause while eschewing the violence found in most independence movements. In one of the earliest tests of his approach, he called for a general strike in protest against new laws extending the emergency powers that the government had assumed during World War I. In several North Indian cities, the strike turned into riots. In the Punjab city of Amritsar, martial law was declared. Defying the ban on meetings, twenty thousand people gathered in the central public area of Amritsar, the Jallianwala Bagh, to celebrate a festival. In a display of the "Punjab mentality" described earlier, the local British troop commander sealed off the only exit to the Jallianwala Bagh. After a quick order to disperse, he ordered his 150 men to fire on the crowd. Nearly 400 Indians were killed outright, and over 1,200 were wounded.

Although Gandhi was dismayed by the violence in the Punjab and felt that he shared responsibility for the disastrous outcome of the strikes, Amritsar also marked the beginning of Gandhi's leadership in the movement of noncooperation and civil disobedience that became the centerpiece of Congress policy after 1920. In the early 1920s, as it would later, the civil disobedience campaign brought violence, including communal violence, in its wake. In 1924, Gandhi undertook a twenty-one-day fast for Hindu-Muslim solidarity but failed to breach the gap.

Despite his commitment to Muslim-Hindu unity, Gandhi's philosophical roots, his style, and his language carried enough of the "Hindu tinge" that his politics, however secular, raised suspicions among those Muslims already insecure in the Congress. Gandhi worked for improvement in the miserable conditions of untouchables, the harijans, but as noted in Chapter 2, he never rejected caste. His belief in *ahimsa* and *satyagraha*, his resort to fasting, and his commitment to village self-reliance—symbolized by the spinning he did at his ashram (a retreat near Ahmedabad in his home state of Gujarat)—all reflected his Hindu inheritance. In the broadest sense, his insistence on obeying moral principles embodied dharma. Thus, even though he appealed to people on moral, not religious, grounds, "his political thought was couched in the language of religiosity."[17]

More than Gandhi, **Jawaharlal Nehru** (1889–1964) stands out as representing the commitment to a secular India. Trained, like Gandhi, with a law degree from London, Nehru returned to India in 1912 to practice law with his father. The young Nehru also followed his father into politics, where the elder Nehru was a leading moderate in the Indian National Congress. Devoted to Gandhi and seeing him as the inspiration of India's nationalist cause, Nehru nonetheless disagreed with him on many basic questions. Most important, their vision of independent India was poles apart. Gandhi's ideal was embodied in decentralized, agriculturally based, self-sufficient villages where dharma and *panchayat*s dominated. Nehru's views were influenced by European democratic socialism and emphasized a strong, modernized India with a centralized nation-state and planned industrial economy, a vision that Gandhi rejected.

Despite their differences, mutual respect and affection linked the two men, and they worked with other Congress leaders from the 1920s to the 1940s to end British rule. Another critical turning point in their efforts, comparable to Amritsar and the civil disobedience campaign of the early 1920s, came in the 1930s. By 1930, the Congress had unambiguously established its policy of complete independence, with another civil disobedience campaign declared to force the British to negotiate meaningful steps toward this end. To launch the campaign, Gandhi announced that he would violate the salt tax, which was a continuing burden on all Indians, but especially on the very poor.[18] Gandhi's approach to disobeying the tax law was calculated to mobilize grassroots support for independence by targeting one of the most hated aspects of the Raj and demonstrating that the Congress was not an elitist organization. In slightly more than three weeks, Gandhi and his supporters marched 240 miles from his ashram to the sea, where they took "free" salt. Other acts of civil disobedience, strikes, and mass demonstrations quickly followed throughout India. Within six months, some 60,000 people were arrested, and by 1933, more than 120,000 were imprisoned after another round of the civil disobedience campaign.

The mass arrests, along with indiscriminate beatings of both men and women, were one aspect of the British response. Along with the repression, though, came new efforts to negotiate with Congress leaders. Out of this counterpoint of reaction and reform emerged the 1935 **Government of India Act**, one of the landmarks of India's political history. The act sought to accommodate Congress demands by increasing responsible and representative government in India, expanding the electorate, and establishing a federal arrangement with a large measure of provincial autonomy. It was not independence, but it continued the movement toward self-rule; and although its provisions were criticized by Congress leaders as insufficient, many aspects of the act were carried over to India's Constitution.

The years of the early 1930s left other important political legacies. Through the civil disobedience campaigns, women were drawn into the independence movement for the first time in large numbers. Gandhi is thus credited with this important step in mobilizing women politically and moving them toward emancipation, although only upper-caste and foreign women worked closely with him at his ashram. In retrospect, scholars have analyzed Gandhi's views on gender as intrinsic to his unique conception of India's identity, although he did not support women's political, social, and economic equality in the same manner that women's rights advocates do in contemporary India. Gandhi encouraged women to picket liquor and foreign cloth shops but mainly prized their role as repositories of purity and goodness in the home, the private sphere. Thus, he shared the traditional gender attitude of most Congress leaders. But he went further in creating a national identity that was as androgynous as it was indigenous. Nonviolence and his use of the spinning wheel (a domestic tool), for example, combined Hindu and Buddhist ideals, feminine attributes, and village life. Thus "women appear as a collective representation by means of which the superiority and inviolability of the indigenous social tradition is demonstrated against the modern."[19]

Consolidation of the Hindu-Muslim division also dates from this same period. The constitutional discussions of the early 1930s quickened Muslims' concern to protect their position in the coming devolution of power to Indians. The preoccupation with safeguards led some Muslim leaders, including Muhammad Ali Jinnah, who undertook reorganization of the Muslim League in 1934, to renew their insistence on communal representation. Within a decade, Jinnah would unite Muslim leaders first behind the demand for a separate state within the Indian federation and then for complete independence. As the political stakes grew—as elections were conducted, the power of elected officials became meaningful, and independence loomed—compromise was rejected in favor of dividing the Hindu and Muslim communities into India and Pakistan.

Finally, the 1930s was a turning point for one other group that is critical to our understanding of modern Indian politics: the untouchables, Gandhi's harijans, labeled by the British as Scheduled Castes and Tribes in the 1935 Government of India Act. Chapter 2 pointed out the different positions taken by Gandhi and B. R. Ambedkar, leader of the untouchables. Gandhi insisted on the inclusion of harijans within the Hindu fold and fought for the abolition of untouchability, whereas Ambedkar maintained that equality was impossible within Hinduism. Ambedkar wanted separate communal electorates for untouchables, but Gandhi protested with a vow to fast to death, arguing that separate electorates premised on the assumption of separate communities violated his principle of reforming Hinduism by admitting untouchables within its fold. A few days into

Gandhi's fast, Ambedkar agreed to abandon separate electorates in exchange for reserving larger numbers of seats for untouchables in provincial councils and the central assembly.

The principles established as a result of the controversy carried over to the 1950 Constitution and into post-Independence politics: schedules (lists) appended to the Constitution to identify depressed castes; abolition of untouchability (but not caste) and guaranteed access to wells, water tanks, and other public areas for all Indians; and the initiation of "reservation" policies for the most disadvantaged Indians. Thus, though different in origin, the moral stances of Gandhi and Ambedkar converged to illuminate the untouchables' plight and laid the basis for the political mobilization of the most deprived and despised members of Indian society.

## *Swaraj* and Partition

The years from 1946 to 1948 were years of political promise and tragedy for the new Indian nation-state. At the end of World War II, as part of its new commitment to decolonize in Asia, the British government moved quickly to negotiate independence for India. The chief question was no longer "if" or even "when." The questions were, rather, "what" and "who." What would the physical boundaries of this new India be? Who would be its citizens? By 1946, the Muslim League had developed a following among Muslims that made its vision of separate states in South Asia impossible to ignore. The British government, which earlier had played its part in cultivating communal differences, now sought to preserve a united India, which of course was Gandhi's dream. But the communal lines were drawn: the Congress claimed to represent all of India; the Muslim League claimed to represent all Muslims.

The 1946 elections created an assembly that served two functions: The **Constituent Assembly** was charged with drafting India's Constitution; and the Provisional Parliament would govern when India actually became independent. Although Muslims had participated in the elections that created the assembly, the Muslim League boycotted its early sessions. Meanwhile, Jinnah had brought the league into India's interim government, headed by Nehru, without abandoning his goal of a separate state of Pakistan. Negotiations over the future lines of independent India reached an impasse; in early 1947, the British government declared that it would quit India and transfer power to "Indian" hands, whatever that might mean. Despite Gandhi's opposition, the majority of the Congress leaders had come to accept the inevitability of two separate states, and a plan for partitioning the subcontinent was drawn up.

Independent Pakistan would include two predominantly Muslim territories, one to the east and one to the west of India. The "vivisection" of the Indian subcontinent[20] may have been politically inevitable, but it had brutal consequences. India and Pakistan became independent in August 1947, but Partition overwhelmed the promise of the new nation-states. Millions of Hindus were left in Pakistan, millions of Muslims in India. The boundary in Punjab had been drawn in a manner that divided the Sikhs. "Here, in mounting hysteria, violence, and atrocity, Muslims fell upon Sikhs and Hindus in the West, and Sikhs and Hindus upon Muslims in the East. Before the end of the year half a million people had been killed."[21] In the chaos of Partition, 4.5 million Hindus and Sikhs left West Pakistan for India and 6 million Muslims moved in the other direction.

At the other side of India, Gandhi pledged to fast unto death in order to halt the viciousness. His dedication to intercommunal harmony partially succeeded, with the leaders of all the communities pledging to help protect Muslims. But Gandhi's efforts had alienated many Hindus, and shortly after he had ended his fast and returned to New Delhi, he was shot to death by a young Hindu associated with the militant Hindu organization, the Rashtriya Swayamsevak Sangh (RSS, or National Volunteer Organization).[22]

It may be argued that at his death, Gandhi had indeed failed in his vision of a unified, moral political community. Possibly, India would have received its independence by the postwar period even without Gandhi's mass mobilization campaigns. But it is certain that he made the Congress a more representative organization by demanding that it address the problems of India's dispossessed. He provided a model for political leaders that was rooted in Indian tradition rather than in the Western experience. And he left a moral legacy that fifty years later inspires alternative visions of human fulfillment, community, and development both in India and throughout the world.

With Gandhi's death, Jawaharlal Nehru emerged as the dominant figure in the Congress, now called the **Congress Party** of independent India. It was Nehru's vision of a secular, modern, centralized India that prevailed in the Constituent Assembly and set the tone for India's constitutional order. And it was Nehru who, as India's first and longest-tenured prime minister, set the new nation-state on its course in the middle of the twentieth century, a course that seemed promising until the 1970s. But the divisions born of empires and the nationalist movement persisted, as the following synopsis of the Ayodhya crisis illustrates.

## The Ayodhya Dispute

Ayodhya is a small town in the eastern part of India's most populous state, Uttar Pradesh, and is the legendary birthplace of the Hindu god **Ram**. The story of Ram is told in the traditional Indian epic the *Ramayana*, historically passed down by storytellers and performed in thousands of versions in a multitude of village dramas. In modern times, Hindu revivalists increasingly focused on Ram and the *Ramayana* as vehicles for a renaissance in Hindu identity. Modern technology accelerated this process, as the epic became available on audiocassettes, television, and videocassettes. In 1987, India's state-run television commenced an eighteen-month serial dramatization of the *Ramayana*. The episodes quickly became the most popular program ever shown: "On Sundays streets were deserted throughout India. Everyone was watching, even knots of cycle rickshaw drivers crowded in front of the T.V. store windows."[23]

The growth of Ram's popularity, as symbolized by the phenomenal interest in the *Ramayana*, is important to modern Indian politics and especially to the Ayodhya story for several reasons. It illustrates the degree to which popular culture continues to be infused with traditional cultural-religious images, language, and values, hinting at the persistent gap between the secular nation-state ideology of India's post-Independence Nehruvian leadership, and the worldviews of average Indians—a gap that only Gandhi (temporarily) bridged.[24] The Ram epic also demonstrates the power of modern communication media to create and sustain mass-based ideologies of nationalism. And the "capture" of Ram by Hindu nationalist organizations shows the dynamics of building support in a competitive electoral democracy.

Legend maintains that Ram was born about 1500 B.C.E. at Ayodhya, but not until the eleventh century, according to Hindu nationalists, was a temple in his honor built in the town. Muslim invaders first arrived in the twelfth century, and in the early sixteenth century, the Babri Mosque (Babri Masjid) was built by a nobleman from the court of Babur, the first Mughal emperor. Long before modern nationalism emerged, Hindus claimed that the mosque was built on the earlier Ram temple site. Hindu-Muslim clashes over the site date to the Mughal Empire, and shortly after the 1857–1858 mutiny, the British built a wall to separate the mosque and the adjoining area where Hindus continued to worship. Thus, conflict over the Babri Masjid has deep historical roots.

In the 1980s, the dispute was revived by the Bharatiya Janata Party and the Vishwa Hindu Parishad (VHP, World Hindu Council), the latter linked to the RSS (one of whose members assassinated Gandhi). Dedicated to the establishment of **Hindutva**, meaning a Hindu India, the VHP announced a fund-raising drive to build a temple to Ram at Ayodhya and called on devout Hindus to make bricks inscribed with Ram's name. Thousands of volunteers joined processions to Ayodhya to deliver bricks, demolish the mosque, and build a temple. By December 1992, after a long period of government indecision over the growing tension, some 300,000 faithful Hindus—overwhelmingly young men—had gathered at Ayod-

*Photo 5.2 Hindu Militant. Photo courtesy of* The Pioneer, *New Delhi.*

hya. The central government had amassed a large troop force in anticipation of violence but in fact did not intervene when thousands of the volunteers stormed and destroyed the mosque. Within a few days, over one thousand Indians lost their lives in the ensuing communal clashes throughout the country.

Photo 5.2 shows a wall drawing of Ram and a Hindu militant. The Ayodhya crisis is a good example of the way history (and historical memory) weighs on the contemporary Indian national identity.

## Summary

The Indian National Congress took the lead in defining a national identity for India in the half century before Independence, but the Congress was frequently not united and was never the sole "player" in the process of defining an independent India. From the early nineteenth century, Indian intellectual thought was deeply influenced by European ideas and thought systems, including science, law, Christianity, liberalism, and social democracy. It was within the framework of these influences and the realities of British imperialism that Hindu, Muslim, and truly secular nationalists (such as Nehru) wrestled with the meaning of Indian traditions—historical, spiritual, and cultural—and the strategies that would best serve the goal of moving the British out of India. The sad irony of *swaraj* was that it happened when and how it did largely as a result of Gandhi's determined moral and political leadership. This leadership, however, contributed to the Hindu tone of Indian nationalism during its formative stages, thus also fueling Muslim anxiety, even as Gandhi risked his life to foster Hindu-Muslim amity. Ultimately, he lost his life to a young Hindu man who believed that Gandhi was pro-Muslim.

Partition was the real tragedy of *swaraj*: It both resulted from and contributed to the spread of communalism in the twentieth century. And as a consequence of Partition, there was less of the subcontinent under the direct control of the Indian state in 1947 than had been controlled by the British Raj at its peak or by the Mauryan Empire of Ashoka over two thousand years earlier.

India's politics, both domestic and foreign, remain colored by the issues that were left unresolved at Independence. The chief external threat is from Muslim Pakistan, and the regions closest to Pakistan (Punjab and Kashmir) have been badly torn by political and religious strife. Although often isolated, communal violence continues to flare up, with no Gandhi fasting in order to stop it. Ayodhya is the most recent crisis, but not the only one. Moreover, the very successes of independent India in introducing and sustaining democratic processes, particularly through elections, have, like the British reforms of the 1930s, increased the political stakes by mobilizing new participants in the political process and thereby sharpening the temptation to appeal to communal loyalties as a way of mustering political support.

# Notes

1. The material in this section was compiled from A. L. Basham, *The Wonder That Was India* (New York: Grove Press, 1959), chap. 3; H. G. Rawlinson, *India: A Short Cultural History* (New York: Praeger, 1952), chaps. 5–8; Romila Thapar, *A History of India*, vol. 1 (Baltimore: Penguin Books, 1966); Stanley Wolpert, *A New History of India*, 2d ed. (New York: Oxford University Press, 1982); Beatrice Pitney Lamb, *India: A World in Transition*, 4th ed. (New York: Praeger, 1975), chap. 3.

2. The term "dharma" illustrates the many problems of translation discussed in Chapter 1. There is no single word in English that expresses the numerous meanings the word has in its various Indian contexts. Dharma changes through time and through contexts and may be explained by different English words such as righteousness, nature, law (in two senses: natural law or legislated law), duty, justice, right, religious merit, and religion. See the discussion in Wendy Doniger's introduction to *The Laws of Manu*, trans. Wendy Doniger with Brian K. Smith (New Delhi and London: Penguin Books, 1991), pp. liv–lviii, lxxvi–lxxvii.

3. Rajni Kothari, *Politics in India* (Boston: Little, Brown, 1970), p. 27. Kothari added that because the principal emphasis is on "duties to" not "rights against," the ideal was to limit one's wants, to be content and tolerant of one's lot in life.

4. Basham, *Wonder*, p. 66.

5. Both Jainism and Buddhism emerged in the sixth century B.C.E., when their founders sought to reform the rigid Hinduism and tyranny of the Brahmin priests that characterized the period.

6. Kothari, *India*, pp. 22–23.

7. Ibid., pp. 31–35.

8. It should be noted that there were parts of the subcontinent, primarily in the South and West, that remained under the Hindu rule of different kingdoms and princely states.

9. Thapar, *History of India*, p. 301.

10. For the details of British expansion, see Percival Spear, *The Oxford History of Modern India, 1740–1947* (Oxford: Clarendon Press, 1965), chaps. 1–11.

11. Robert L. Hardgrave, Jr., and Stanley A. Kochanek, *India: Government and Politics in a Developing Nation*, 5th ed. (Fort Worth, Tex.: Harcourt Brace College Publishers, 1993), p. 34.

12. Kothari, *India*, p. 40.

13. Wolpert, *New History*, p. 224.

14. Jim Masselos, *Indian Nationalism: A History*, 2d ed. rev. (New Delhi: Sterling Publishers, 1991), chap. 2.

15. Bipan Chandra, *Communalism in Modern India* (New Delhi: Vani Educational Books/Vikas Publishing, 1984), p. 144.

16. Masselos, *Indian Nationalism*, p. 134.

17. Chandra, *Communalism*, p. 146.

18. Spear, *Oxford History*, pp. 261–262, 347. The Raj, like the British East India Company before it, relied on a tax on salt—an essential commodity for all Indians—as a chief source of revenue.

19. Amrit Srinivasan, "Women and Reform of Indian Tradition: Gandhian Alternative to Liberalism," *Economic and Political Weekly* (December 19, 1987), p. 2226, quoted in Arthur Bonner et al., *Democracy in India: A Hollow Shell* (Washington, D.C.: American University Press, 1994), p. 200.

20. Granville Austin's term, used in his "The Constitution, Society, and Law," in Philip Oldenburg, ed., *India Briefing, 1993* (Boulder, Westview Press, 1993, with the Asia Society), p. 111.

21. Hardgrave and Kochanek, *India*, p. 52.

22. The RSS dates from the 1920s; a paramilitary organization, it was opposed to Gandhi's efforts on behalf of Hindu-Muslim unity. The RSS still exists and was implicated in the Ayodhya events of 1992.

23. Susanne Hoeber Rudolph and Lloyd I. Rudolph, "Modern Hate," *New Republic* (March 22, 1993), p. 26.

24. See the analysis by Sudipta Kaviraj, "On State, Society and Discourse in India," in James Manor, ed., *Rethinking Third World Politics* (London, N.Y.: Longman, 1992), pp. 72–99.

# *six*

# Ethics, Power, and Unity: Recreating the Chinese Nation

China has the oldest continuous civilization in the world. Its written language, its traditional system of government and ethical norms—to say nothing of Chinese technological and artistic accomplishments—came to define not just the Sinitic world[1] but much of East Asia. Over the course of 3,500 years, the chief features of Chinese civilization developed and with this civilization came a sense of what we would today call national identity. The Chinese defined themselves as the "central country" (the **Middle Kingdom**, or Zhongguo) and believed they were surrounded by inferior peoples and cultures. The traditions and longevity of the Middle Kingdom bred feelings of confidence, security, and superiority.

Why, with this legacy of a unique, advanced civilization, was China's self-confidence and territorial integrity so badly shaken in the nineteenth century? What has the combination of historical greatness and social, economic, and political demoralization in the modern period meant for the construction of a modern nation-state and a new, or recreated, national identity in the twentieth century? These are the types of questions this chapter begins to answer by first providing a background in China's traditional system of political and social order, Confucianism. The second major section of the chapter reviews the nineteenth- and twentieth-century challenges to this order, in the form of socioeconomic changes, Western imperialism, and revolution. The chapter then returns to the initial questions posed here and examines two case studies representing the kinds of challenges the Chinese nation-state faces: the reunification of Hong Kong and Taiwan with China and the political upheaval at Tiananmen Square in 1989.

## Confucianism: Social Harmony and Virtuous Rule

About 2,500 years ago, there occurred in China a vigorous debate about the nature of government and society. Different philosophical schools proposed alternative answers to questions that are still central to our thinking about politics: the nature of a well-ordered society, the role of force or law in maintaining that order, the desired qualities for rulers, and the ideal relationship between ruler and ruled.

The debate over these questions was generated by the political and social instability marking the decline of one of China's ancient dynasties. Regional kingdoms and their rulers competed for power; the scale and intensity of military conflict grew. But instability and conflict also generated social mobility and intellectual curiosity. Classical Chinese philosophy flourished under these conditions, and not surprisingly, most schools of thought focused more on the problems of this world than on the nature of divinity or deities. As a result, Chinese philosophy took on a predominantly secular and humanistic quality.[2] This secular emphasis is an important source of difference between Chinese and Indian worldviews.

Confucianism, the social and political philosophy that later came to dominate the Chinese government, emerged during this early period. Named after and in honor of the man Confucius ("Master Kung," 551–479 B.C.E.), the doctrines of what we understand today as Confucianism reflect centuries of accretions and reworkings. The disciples of Confucius summarized his life and teachings and, more than Master Kung himself, assured that the master's philosophy would endure. Two centuries after Confucius, for example, Mencius elaborated on Confucius's views regarding human nature, good government, and filial piety.

In addition to the writings of the great teachers and philosophers, government edicts were important in institutionalizing and spreading Confucian ideals, thus transforming Confucius's norms for elite behavior into guidelines and rituals for commoners. In this way, for example, the value placed on patrilineal descent among the ruling houses of early dynasties was embellished by rites for ancestors carried out by sons and grandsons. "Ancestor worship" and filial piety predated Confucius and Mencius, but the emphasis of the scholars on family relationships reinforced preexisting practices. Subsequently, government policies in areas such as population registration, taxation, landownership, and the legal authority of the head of the family (fathers) ensured that these norms would spread across class and geographical lines. After the seventh century, the development of a civil service examination system, which emphasized memorization of the Confucian classics and the concomitant emphasis on education as the road to government success served also to entrench Confucian ideals and practices.[3]

These Confucian values have played a formative role not just in Chinese civilization but throughout East Asia. Unlike most Western political philosophy, Confucian thought assumes that individuals exist in a web of social relationships whose maintenance requires conduct characterized by courtesy, proper decorum, compassion, and loyalty. Human beings should strive to perfect their innate qualities of goodness through virtuous and ethical behavior—which means practicing the norms of courtesy, for example, in a manner that sustains and improves social relationships.[4] Thus, there is a logical and inescapable linkage between innate humanness, social context, and public behavior. Social relations ideally mirror family relations, and social (and hence political) order is maintained by the cultivation of proper relationships. Put differently, private and public morality should reflect each other. The goal of the virtuous person—one who reflects both personal and public morality—is government service, a position of great responsibility. In principle, therefore, Confucian norms suggest that modern politicians should be judged as fit or not fit for public roles depending on their personal conduct. Adultery or bad management of family finances or dishonor of one's parents would thus be relevant to the judgments voters make as to a candidate's fitness for public leadership. This perspective is emphasized in succinct comic format found in a book that forms part of a widely distributed series used for teaching Chinese classics in Southeast Asia (see Figure 6.1).

As a practical matter, the measure of human perfectibility was best seen in the correct performance of one's social roles. Harmony in family and society alike depended on people knowing what was expected of them in their roles and behaving accordingly. This is the origin of the role relationships discussed in Chapter 3 in connection with Chinese patriarchy. In addition to the husband-wife relationship, four others were critical: those between ruler and subject, father and son, brother and brother, neighbor and neighbor. From the emphasis on social relationships, in turn, came other characteristics of traditional Chinese society: its hierarchical nature, the diminished significance of individual autonomy, and the stress on correct behavior. Both family socialization and formal education would guarantee that people understood their roles and behaved accordingly.

It is worth noting at this point that although there are many important differences between the Confucian and the Hindu worldviews, there are

Figure 6.1   *Confucian Comic. Excerpted from* The Analects of Confucius, *by Jeffrey Seow. Reproduced by permission of ASIAPAC Books Ltd., Singapore.*

two similarities here: the correct performance of social roles and a ranking of those roles within a social context viewed as naturally hierarchical. Thus, all humans are not "created equal" in the sense commonly understood in North America. This does not mean, however, that individuals do not have intrinsic worth but rather that their worth is defined by social context—whether that context is family, clan, caste, village, or a combination of these.

One of the important differences between these two great traditions is that Confucianism has always been explicitly political in its intent and its consequences. In theory, governing was viewed largely as a matter of ethical conduct, and political power resulted from virtuous conduct. The emperor was the living representative of the natural hierarchical order of the universe and in his person were joined heaven, earth, and humanity, as represented in the Chinese character for king (see Figure 6.2). Influential Han dynasty thinkers argued that the emperor occupied the center of heaven but was only the "executor of Heaven."[5] This argument contributed to the idea that the emperor's rule reflected the **Mandate of Heaven**, the loss of which was generally determined after the fact, when a dynasty fell. The Mandate of Heaven and the accompanying theory of **dynastic cycles** thus injected the potential for dramatic change of rule in an otherwise conservative, increasingly rigid set of governing norms. Dynastic cycles typically reflected the following sequence: Social and political disorder signaled dynastic decline and was followed by military conflict; restored peace brought economic and social well-being; but then growing resource scarcity was followed by repression and exploitation, rebellion, and finally the fall of another dynasty. Dynastic collapse was interpreted as meaning that the ruler had lost his mandate to govern.

Thus, Confucianism contains both conservative and radical elements. Its conceptualization of the good society stresses order, reciprocal relationships, and an ethical hierarchy in which some are more virtuous than others. Confucius and his followers expressed reverence for the past and the study of history, and their system has always been profoundly patriarchal and elitist. At the same time, at its best Confucianism "has been critical philosophy, one that saw a great gap between the possibilities of humanity and the reality of any given era. In this sense it is very radical and progressive."[6] Its emphasis on the educability of human beings offers the potential for both individual and social change. And for all their emphasis on social stability, Confucian philosophers recognized that human misery is incompatible with goodness: Those who are desperate for food or other basic necessities cannot be expected to fulfill human potential.

It is important to note here that despite the emphasis on ethical behavior, law and bureaucracy were hardly absent from traditional Chinese government. Han thinkers, in elaborating Confucian norms, were in large part legitimizing their own dynastic rule against that of the preceding

*Figure 6.2    Chinese Character for "King." Calligraphy courtesy of Kai-ho Mah.*

Qin dynasty, which had governed briefly and ruthlessly in the third century B.C.E. The Qin rulers were influenced by the so-called Legalist school, one of the numerous philosophies that competed with Confucianism in ancient China. The Legalists' prescription for government exalted state authority, military rule, and absolute, centralized administration, all legitimized through detailed, comprehensive laws. Even though the Qin dynasty was short-lived and Legalist thought gave way to Confucian norms, the emphasis on both bureaucracy and laws would be grafted onto and coexist with Confucian values in politics. The value placed on proper behavior and virtue, on the one hand, and on centralized, hierarchical institutions, on the other, means that Chinese political philosophy and government practice were both more complex and flexible than is sometimes thought and that in China (as elsewhere) there was often a considerable gap between the ideal society and the political reality.

## Opium, Humility, and Failed Reform

The **Opium War** (1839–1942) between China and Britain is central to our story of national identity for two reasons. First, it inaugurated the pattern of foreign imperialism and Chinese weakness that lasted until the twentieth century. Second, because of this pattern, the Opium War became the symbol of Chinese humiliation and prompted a century-long struggle to free China from foreign control and influence. This legacy is with us today, as we see in the People's Republic of China's policies on human rights, Hong Kong, trade, Tibet, and other matters on which the PRC resists foreign pressure.

Western pressure coincided with a period of growing domestic difficulty in China. The late eighteenth and early nineteenth centuries saw the Qing dynasty in economic and political decline, with opposition to Qing rule increasing both at the lowest and highest levels of Chinese society.[7] Although the decline and the corresponding opposition undermined the ability of the Chinese government to resist Western pressure later in the nineteenth century, the government was by no means enfeebled enough to acquiesce in foreign demands at the outset of the century.

The confrontation between Britain and China was caused initially by trade and balance of payments problems. European countries, as well as the United States, found it difficult to balance the cost of their imports of consumer goods from China, notably tea, silk, and porcelain, with sales of Western products. The difference was made up by shipments of silver bullion. By the 1820s, foreigners discovered that opium (produced in British India) commanded high prices in China and that its sale quickly redressed their balance of payments problem (and created one for China). Meanwhile, the conviction that China and the Chinese did not have to be treated as equals and the desire to eliminate all restrictions on foreign trade with China accelerated. Economics and culture—the latter colored by Orientalist thinking in Europe—thus merged to produce contempt for Chinese vulnerability. When a Chinese official tried to confiscate all the opium in Canton, the British, who had been at the forefront of the opium trade and whose efforts to establish diplomatic relations with China had been frustrated for decades, sent warships and troops to the China coast in 1839 and 1840. The fighting that followed was limited, in large part due to China's decidedly inferior military forces.

The **Treaty of Nanjing** (1842) ended the Opium War and set the standard for the unequal treaties that followed for the rest of the century. China ceded the island of Hong Kong to Britain, and British traders were given the right to reside and conduct business in five cities ("treaty ports") on China's coast. Not to be left out, the United States negotiated a treaty in 1844 that, in addition to securing trading privileges, established the principle of **extraterritorial jurisdiction**, which meant that foreign residents would be governed by the laws of their own countries, not China's. Belgium, Sweden, Norway, France, Russia, and, ultimately, Germany and Japan followed with more demands and more treaties.

In this fashion, Western imperialism and the unequal treaties provoked a sense in China of national humility, which in turn became the focus of a growing nationalist movement. As noted earlier, Western contact coincided with rising discontent within China. The nineteenth century, in fact, was bracketed by two major rebellions, and there was a third in midcentury: the White Lotus Rebellion (1796–1804), the great Taiping Rebellion of the 1850s that was mentioned earlier, and, at the end of the century, the **Boxer Uprising** (1899–1900).[8] To these were added a growing number of smaller peasant rebellions from the 1840s on, major Muslim revolts in the Northwest and the Southwest, and social disorder sparked by bandit gangs.[9] Both economic and political factors precipitated the revolts. For example, the population pressures that have generated concern in the PRC in the last two decades had already produced declining standards of living by the beginning of the nineteenth century as arable land, in particular, became scarce.

In retrospect, we know that the decline of the Qing dynasty both reflected and exacerbated the economic problems. The corruption of government officials that accompanied the opium trade undermined the dynasty's effectiveness and legitimacy. As the quality of the government's services waned and the quality of its officials diminished, so did its ability to maintain order. The spiral foreseen in the theory of dynastic cycles was set in motion, with the rebellions of the century punctuating the last phases of the cycle.

Whereas some of the revolts targeted local officials, the Taiping rebels challenged the legitimacy of the Qing dynasty itself. Borrowing extensively from Western ideas, particularly Christianity, the Taiping resembled the twentieth-century Communists in their rejection of the old order (both Confucianism and Manchu rule), their organizational and ideological discipline, and their missionary zeal.[10] The Taiping were also notable for their apparent commitment to women's rights: foot binding in areas under Taiping control was forbidden; women received land under the same conditions as men, could sit for government examinations, and could hold official posts. Women even fought in Taiping armies.

The failure of the Taiping Rebellion was complete by the mid-1860s, and by the end of the 1860s, all the other important rebellions that threatened the Qing had been stilled. For a short time thereafter, a reform movement known as the **Tongzhi Restoration,** so named after the reign title of the young emperor who ascended the throne in 1861, promised revival of Qing rule. Viewed broadly, the Tongzhi Restoration was a conservative restoration whose purpose was to reestablish peace and well-being by using Confucian practices to reverse, at least for a time, the course of dynastic decline. The restoration did not seek massive change legitimized in the name of an emperor "restored" to authority (as in Meiji Japan) but sought rather to restore virtue and stability to public life through the reaffirmation of Confucian values.[11] Hence, the Tongzhi Restoration never became for China what the Meiji Restoration was for Japan during the same period, that is, a period of dramatic modernization and nation building (see Chapter 7). Its failure can be attributed to a variety of factors, including corruption, divided leadership, and the overwhelming nature of the problems China faced in the mid-nineteenth century.

The events of the mid-nineteenth century, including Western encroachment, the Taiping Rebellion, and the Tongzhi Restoration, are all relevant to China's twentieth-century nation building. For late-nineteenth- and early-twentieth-century reformers, the "foreign calamity" of the Opium War and unequal treaties spurred debates about the relative merits of, and relationship between, Chinese culture and Western technology. Many reformers adopted the slogan "Chinese learning for the essence [*ti*]; Western learning for practical use [*yong*]." Putting the *ti-yong* **ideology** into practice, however, was impossible without undermining the assumptions of the Confucian Chinese worldview.

Although designed to secure social and political stability, Confucian philosophy had always admitted the necessity of change, for change provided the flexibility that ensured maintenance of the overall system. Even the most massive of changes, those in the dynastic cycle, were accommodated by Confucian political theory. The type of change that could hardly be accommodated was that which challenged the universality and the validity of the assumptions undergirding the Confucian worldview. China might learn from the West certain techniques and accept certain kinds of technology, but behind Western technology lay the assumptions and worldview of Science, including the primacy of human control over nature and a linear concept of progress. These differed from the core of traditional Confucianism, in which history was viewed as cyclical and thinkers concentrated on the problems of human relationships rather than on human mastery over the material world. To abandon these core assumptions would, in the view of Tongzhi reformers, constitute a refutation of universal truth and a denial of the essence of Chinese greatness.

By the end of the nineteenth century, the gap between Confucian knowledge and institutions, on the one hand, and the reality of the challenge of Western civilization, on the other, was magnified. The temporary vigor instilled by the Tongzhi Restoration had waned. Many of the symptoms that had led to the Taiping Rebellion (overtaxation, high rent, loss of land, lack of protection from corrupt officials) by fueling discontent in rural areas resurfaced. Meanwhile, at the highest levels, lack of direction and corruption in government and the imperial court compounded the crisis. "As a result, there was no real example of honesty and integrity where Confucian theory said they were most essential, at the top."[12]

The nineteenth century ended and the twentieth century began with a series of events that symbolized China's failure to respond to the growing crises besetting the country. The turning point was the **Sino-Japanese War** of 1894–1895, in which Japan, historically the country that looked up to and borrowed from its more advanced neighbor, now demonstrated the abject weakness of the Chinese state by inflicting military defeat.[13] In 1898, reformers who advocated following Japan's example in the vigorous adoption of foreign knowledge and institutions demanded a constitutional monarchy and for a short time even controlled the government. Ambitious reform, however, provoked a conservative reaction from those who argued that Chinese civilization could not be adapted to Western science and technology, which would inevitably destroy Confucian values.

There was a new element in this late-century debate—nationalism— and it focused attention on a central question: Was it better to try to

"save" Confucian culture and Chinese civilization (as traditionally defined) in their mutual dependence or to save the Chinese nation-state
even if meant the (necessary) sacrifice of traditional culture? The reformers argued for the nation-state, the conservatives for cultural integrity.[14]
The implications of the question can hardly be overstated. The Chinese
had defined themselves for centuries as the Middle Kingdom, superior
and central in the scheme of the universe. Now "barbarians" and borrow-
ers (the Japanese had begun their long history of borrowing religion, language, and government institutions from China in the seventh century)
alike had gone from imposing unequal treaties to securing territorial concessions along China's coast.[15] The implications for the radical reformers
were clear: China's universe no longer existed, having been replaced by a
world of cutthroat competition among nation-states.

The Boxer Uprising of 1898–1900 was sparked by a convergence of developments that exemplified the problems China faced at the turn of the
century. The Boxers, so-named because of the gestures that accompanied
their ritualistic dancing, were centered in Shandong Province, for some
years a target of Christian missionaries and the base for German concessions. Beset by prolonged famine, massive flooding, and long-term economic decline, young Chinese men, most of whom faced bleak economic
prospects, were drawn to a series of organizations that attacked the growing foreign presence. If the Chinese state would not defend itself against
imperialism, gunboat diplomacy, and the expanding power of Christian
churches, the Boxers would.[16]

The Boxers attacked churches, missionaries, Chinese Christians, and,
ultimately, everything foreign. Support for the Boxers spread throughout
Northeast China, and in 1900, they cut rail communications between Beijing and Tientsin and laid siege to foreign legations in Beijing. Originally
supporting the Boxers, the government subsequently opposed them as it
became clear they were out of control. In the end, it took an international
contingent of troops to relieve the legations.

The ignominy of the Boxer Uprising and its repression added to the
conviction among many Chinese intellectuals that China's national humiliation was due specifically to the Qing rulers who were, after all,
Manchus by origin and therefore foreigners themselves (that is, not part
of the Han people). The most important of these reformers was **Sun Yat-
sen** (1866–1925), who, ironically, was a Christian and had been educated
at a mission school in Hawaii. Trained as a doctor, Sun practiced medicine
in Portuguese Macao; only semitrained in the Chinese classics, he was
never imbued with the full weight of Confucian ideology and this fact, together with his contacts with the Western world and Chinese ex-patriots,
undoubtedly made him more open to ideas of radical change.

In 1905, Sun played a leadership role in founding the **Tongmeng Hui**[17]
in Tokyo, where many Chinese students went to learn from the Japanese

experience with modernization. The manifesto of the Tongmeng Hui addressed specifically Chinese concerns while showing the influence of Western republican ideas on Sun's thinking. The manifesto laid out the league's objectives as driving out the "Tartars" (Manchus) and restoring "China of the Chinese," establishing a republic, and equalizing landownership. The manifesto also called for the elimination of "social evils" such as slavery, foot binding, and opium use.[18]

The last major efforts to reform the Qing dynasty came as the revolutionary movement represented by Sun Yat-sen was also building. The government reformers sought to learn both from Japan and from Western nations as they set about abolishing the old examination system (in place since the seventh century); creating new educational programs, a modern army, and legal and financial systems; and exploring the possibilities for constitutional government (see Chapter 8). Of these changes, the most important was probably education. But in order to have modern education, students had to leave China, which put them in contact with anti-Qing revolutionary groups such as the Tongmeng Hui. "By giving modern education to its prospective official class, the dynasty reared its own executioners, dug its own grave, and signed its own death warrant."[19] It was as the Confucian conservatives had foreseen.

## Republican and Communist Revolution

In 1911, the revolutionaries sparked revolts, including troop mutinies, in several cities. The Qing court turned to **Yuan Shikai**, the general who had overturned the 1898 reforms and had subsequently become one of the most powerful men in China, to crush the rebellion. Yuan had been dismissed from office two years earlier with the fear that he was becoming too powerful. Now he bargained with the court: Manchus were being massacred throughout China; to save the situation, Yuan would become premier of the new Republic of China (ROC). Within a few weeks, on Christmas Day 1911, Sun Yat-sen returned from Europe and was quickly elected provisional president of the Chinese republic by the delegates of sixteen provincial assemblies, meeting in Nanjing. "China now had both a republican president and a Manchu emperor,"[20] but after frantic negotiations, the last Manchu emperor abdicated in February 1912. Shortly thereafter, in order to consolidate and legitimize the new government, Sun urged the Nanjing assembly to elect Yuan Shikai as provisional president, which it did.

The 1911 Republican revolution was primarily political. It eliminated the imperial system, but in its place were Yuan Shikai, increasingly an autocratic ruler; Sun Yat-sen's fledgling **Kuomintang** (KMT), or Nationalist Party (the successor to the Tongmeng Hui);[21] and a variety of regional forces whose strength grew as the infrastructure of dynastic rule disintegrated. Within five years after the revolution, China entered a period of warlordism, in which regional military leaders competed for power. Not only did warlordism prevent the development of the strong nation-state that had been a central goal of the revolutionaries, but it contributed to China's economic problems by inhibiting the development of production and commerce.

Juxtaposed against this political confusion and economic dislocation was continued intellectual ferment, especially among the young students exposed to exciting ideas from Europe, the United States, and the newly founded Soviet Union. The appeal of Western liberalism for many of the new intelligentsia turned into disillusionment when the Versailles Conference, which met in 1919 to formally negotiate settlements to end the war, awarded Shandong to Japan, which had conquered the territory from the Germans in 1914. Japan, like China, had been on the victorious side of the war,[22] but the Chinese assumed that Shandong would be returned to China. When the Chinese delegate to Versailles acquiesced in the Japanese conquest, several thousand Chinese students demonstrated in Beijing at Tiananmen Square on May 4, 1919. The demonstrations set off a nation-wide strike, in which the students were joined by members of the new urban working and middle classes. The protesters' themes were anti-imperialism and nationalism; they called for a new society based on science and democracy. Japanese nationals were attacked, and thousands of students were jailed.

The May Fourth Movement that emerged after World War I was first and foremost an intellectual and political movement that attracted significant numbers of young women as well as men. Beijing University had become the preeminent center of nationalism and political activism in China. One can imagine the excitement of the period, with ideas ranging from those of the American pragmatist, John Dewey, to those of Soviet Marxists-Leninists informing the debates about China's future. It was in this atmosphere of the quest for ideas and pragmatic solutions to China's problems, a quest fueled by intense nationalism, that the Chinese Communist Party was formed. The first meeting of the party took place in Shanghai in 1921; present were two organizers from the Comintern, or Communist International, the organization established by the Russian Bolsheviks to foster Communist revolutions in Europe and elsewhere. Among the dozen Chinese present was Mao Zedong, who went on to play a central role in the growth of the Communist movement and dominated politics in China from the 1940s until his death in 1976.

## Political-Military Conflicts: The Chinese Civil War

In order to provide an overview of the chaotic period from the early 1920s to the Communist victory in 1949, the following discussion is divided into two sections, the first dealing with the general lines of the conflict between the Nationalists and Communist Chinese and the second with the organizational, social, and ideological programs of the Communists that defined their revolution from the 1930s to the early 1950s.

At the time of the creation of the Communist Party, the dominant political force in China was the Kuomintang, and Sun Yat-sen was the most influential political leader, already seen as father of the Republican revolution both in China and elsewhere. Partly because of the legitimacy of Sun and the KMT and partly because Soviet Communists believed that it would be many years before the Communist Party could lead China to the kind of revolution that Russia had experienced, Comintern advisors ordered the handful of Chinese Communists to join the KMT as individuals. While maintaining an individual membership in the Nationalist Party, they would continue their Communist Party membership and discipline and eventually be in a position to shape the KMT into a force to unify the country and lead a socialist revolution. The Comintern position thus established one of the most curious facets of the long and bitter competition between the Communist and Nationalist parties: Both were structured in the early 1920s according to the dictates of Leninist organization in order to create a centralized Chinese government allied to Moscow (see Chapter 10). But from the viewpoint of the Russian Communist advisers in China, in the early 1920s the KMT was far better placed than the Communist Party to serve as a vanguard.

One of the first initiatives of the reorganized KMT was to establish the Whampoa Military Academy in Canton (Guangzhou) in order to train the military leadership necessary to seize control from China's regional warlords and create a strong, central authority. The head of the Academy was Chiang Kai-shek, who assumed leadership of the KMT in 1925, after Sun died. Chiang became the most important non-Communist leader in China during the civil war period and, after 1949, was president of the Republic of China in Taiwan.

Soviet influence was felt not only in the organization of the KMT and the CCP and the mandate for their cooperation but also in the dominant direction of Communist ideology and strategy. Consistent with Marxist-Leninist thought, the Communist Party gave priority to organizing workers in the urban areas. In spite of the fact that this left Communist organizers vulnerable to party opponents, the CCP continued to be urban-based until the late 1920s. The Communists failed in several cities where they organized armed uprisings, but Moscow continued to control organizational and ideological matters at the top level of the CCP.

By the end of the 1920s, the CCP was split between those who still maintained the Moscow ties and gave priority to organizing urban workers, and those who, like Mao Zedong, had retreated to the rural areas to concentrate on organizing the peasantry. By the early 1930s, these rural-based organizers were developing actual governing power in the form of separate "soviets," whose governments were a blend of civilian and military rule, concentrated in the southeastern province of Jiangxi. During this same period, the "Red Army" (which later became the People's Liberation Army, or PLA) was established as the movement's military arm.

The period from the late 1920s to the beginning of China's full-scale war with Japan saw the peak of the Nationalists' power. Chiang succeeded in eliminating or co-opting most of the provincial warlords, establishing a new capital in Nanjing, and undertaking programs of modernization. He also turned his attention to eliminating the Jiangxi soviets through a series of "encirclement campaigns" in which troops were sent to exterminate the Communist bases. Finally, in 1934, this military pressure forced the Communists to abandon their soviets and undertake the **Long March**, which lasted one year and took the party members, the PLA, and their followers some six thousand miles to Northwest China. Here the Communists reestablished themselves in Shaanxi Province. During the Long March, in July 1935, the Communist leadership reorganized the party and conclusively ended the old Moscow-inspired line of urban-based revolution. It was during this same period that Mao Zedong became the dominant (though not undisputed) leader of the Communist Party, a position that he was to hold until his death forty-one years later.

Historians continue to debate the accomplishments of the Kuomintang and Chiang Kai-shek during the Nanjing period, when the Communists frequently seemed on the verge of extinction. Whether the KMT might have succeeded in implementing its nationalist revolution is now a moot point, for its efforts were challenged not only by the Chinese Communists, but, more important in the mid-1930s, by the Japanese. In 1931, Japanese militarists provoked a crisis that led to their annexation of resource-rich Manchuria and the creation of a state they called Manchukuo, headed by the last Manchu emperor. In 1937, close to Beijing, Japanese troops attacked Chinese units, an incident that led to all-out war in East Asia. The Japanese moved quickly to control China's principal cities and coastal regions, as well as the railroad system. The brutality of the Japanese, particularly in such incidents as the "rape of Nanjing,"[23] encouraged national unity for a time between the Communists and the Nationalists, as well as among some remaining regional forces.

In retrospect, it is hard to underestimate the importance of the Japanese invasion and occupation of China. The Japanese skillfully exploited political and regional divisions in China; and their demand for an East Asian coprosperity sphere played to the anti-Western strain in Chinese nationalism. But the lingering bitterness in China over Japanese imperialism colors relations between the two countries even today, particularly when issues relevant to the wartime period reemerge (such as the controversy over the way in which Japanese textbooks describe this era).

As the Nationalist government displayed its corruption and its ineffectiveness in dealing with the war effort, the political confusion and self-doubt that were temporarily covered by the heroism of the early war period began to reemerge. In contrast to the Nationalists, the Communists seemed unified, purposeful, determined, and responsive to the needs of ordinary Chinese. These were the advantages that they brought to the final years of the civil war, after the defeat of Japan in 1945.

## Building the Revolution

Those who survived the Long March, approximately ten thousand of the nearly one hundred thousand who had set out from Jiangxi, settled in the mountainous region of Yanan. Although the heroism of the Long March has become one of the epic stories of the Communist revolution, in late 1935 the potential for revolution looked far from promising. The party had lost its southern bases, massive numbers of troops, and its supporters. For several years, the Communists pursued a **"united front"** policy with the Nationalists against the Japanese. The Red Army, consisting of over thirty thousand combat troops (including battle-hardened survivors of the Long March), was placed under nominal Kuomintang control, although it was actually commanded by veteran Communist commanders. The CCP leadership worked hard to ensure that, at all levels, its troops did not exploit the local farming communities on which they depended for food and supplies. These practices, along with the education and indoctrination programs of the Communists, gradually widened their base of support.

The united front policy, as well as the need to maximize support in order to secure and expand their bases, encouraged the Communists to pursue moderate strategies during the war period. Their bases utilized a tripartite system of political power: the local governments were composed of one-third Communist Party members, one-third "progressive" (left-wing) elements, and one-third independents. Drawing on Mao Zedong's experience in Hunan Province during the 1920s and the experience of the Jiangxi soviets, the CCP concentrated on building support in rural areas by pursuing a reformist agricultural policy that emphasized reduction of rent and interest rates. In this fashion, both poor and middle-class peasants were attracted to the Communist Party program.

The extent of the Communist revolution as developed at Yanan (both its promise and its limitations) can be seen in its policy toward women. The area in northern China where the Communist armies settled in the mid-1930s was even more restrictive in terms of the traditional norms governing women's behavior than Jiangxi and certainly more conservative than the urban areas from which some of the revolutionaries came.

Foot binding was still practiced and the "big feet" of the women who moved into the region as part of the Communist settlements were strange and even to some (in the context of the times) shocking. In this atmosphere, issues pertaining to women's rights were avoided by CCP leaders as too sensitive and divisive: "Official policy toward family reform became more conservative. The low-priority support given to implementing women's rights and marriage reforms in Kiangsi [Jiangxi] narrowed further in the wartime base areas and eventually turned to active suppression of those who attempted to raise such issues within the Party."[24]

Despite the low priority accorded social issues such as marriage reform and physical abuse of women, there were periodic efforts to encourage women's political participation and, above all, participation in economic production. The emphasis on production was consistent with the Marxist emphasis on economic revolution as the avenue to sociopolitical revolution and gender equality. Even more important was the desperate economic and political situation in which the Communists found themselves in the early 1940s, when the Japanese accelerated their attacks on Communist areas and cut them off from virtually all outside supplies. Thousands of women were organized (and paid) to produce cloth to meet the army's continuous need for uniforms and blankets. Although the policy was born of necessity, not feminism, one result was to offer women an opportunity to earn some money and to work with other women outside the restrictions of the family.[25]

In retrospect, the Communist experiences of the 1930s and 1940s were important for the post-1949 period because these were years not just of ideological pronouncements but also of practice. Party and army cadres learned both the limits and the possibilities of moderate policies and learned who could be trusted and who not. It was thus a period of organizational consolidation, and it laid the groundwork for the daunting tasks of reconstruction and revolution that confronted China after 1949.

## The Historical Legacy:
## Hong Kong and Tiananmen Square

In closing this chapter on China's history, it is useful to turn to two events from the contemporary period that illustrate the worldview of China's leaders and the dynamic interplay between domestic and international politics. Hong Kong's return to Chinese control in 1997 leaves only Taiwan outside the nation of China as it has been defined since the Qing dynasty. Thus, 1997 is an important chapter in the long saga of Western imperialism in East Asia. In contrast, the 1989 student-worker demonstrations in Beijing and the government's repression of those demonstrations raise different issues about national unity and identity.

## Hong Kong

The British presence in Hong Kong dates from the late 1830s, when, in the growing tension that preceded the Opium War, the British community in Canton retreated to the island. At that time, the thirty-square-mile island was largely uninhabited, but it would later become the chief port for European ships coming to China. The area between the island of Hong Kong and the Kowloon Peninsula boasts one of the best deep-water harbors in the world, a fact that did not escape the British. The Treaty of Nanjing, signed after the Opium War, provided for the cession of Hong Kong to Britain "in perpetuity." In 1860, the southern part of the Kowloon Peninsula was ceded in perpetuity also, and in 1898, the New Territories were leased to Britain for ninety-nine years. With these acquisitions, the British controlled over 350 square miles of prime coastal territory by the turn of the century.

It was the impending end of the ninety-nine-year lease on the New Territories that prompted the opening of negotiations between the United Kingdom and the People's Republic of China on the status of all the territories taken in the nineteenth century. After two years of talks, the governments of the two countries issued a joint declaration in 1984 describing the procedures to be followed and the status agreed upon for Hong Kong as of July 1, 1997. The most important provision was the PRC's agreement to create a Hong Kong **"special administrative region"** (SAR) after resuming sovereignty over the area. The SAR would be given the right to maintain its laws and its social and economic systems for a period of fifty years after reunification.[26] Very quickly, the British government became concerned that its long tradition of autocratic rule should be replaced by some democratic rule before the Chinese took over. It immediately began to pressure China to acquiesce in greater measures of democracy, notably by increasing the number of directly elected seats on the Legislative Council, Hong Kong's legislative body. In 1988, the Basic Law for the Hong Kong SAR was issued by the National People's Congress of the PRC. In effect, the Basic Law is the Constitution for Hong Kong after 1997; as such, it incorporates many of the British proposals developed after the initial 1984 joint declaration. The Tiananmen events of 1989 prompted the British to ask for (and the Chinese to agree to) additional guarantees of democracy for Hong Kong after 1997.

Viewing the events of the 1990s from the Chinese perspective, the acrimonious relations between the United Kingdom and the PRC after the appointment of a new British governor, Chris Patten, in 1993 were largely the result of bad faith on the part of Britain. Shortly after his appointment, Patten introduced a package of constitutional amendments to accelerate the progress toward democracy that had been carefully negotiated over the previous

☆☆☆
中国政府
对香港恢复行使主权
倒 计 时
距1997年7月1日

Photo 6.1    *Hong Kong Countdown. Photo by author.*

decade. He did so without consulting Beijing, in effect issuing a public challenge to China. Not surprisingly, the Chinese government resisted Patten's initiatives, seeing them as part of a long period of European interference in China's domestic affairs.[27] Meanwhile, the huge digital sign in Tiananmen Square continued its countdown to July 1, 1997 (see Photo 6.1).

## Tiananmen Square, 1989

In April 1989, the former secretary-general of the Chinese Communist Party, Hu Yaobang, died. Hu had been dismissed from his party post two years earlier, in part because he was criticized for his failure to control earlier student unrest. Now students used Hu's death to mourn his passing and to demand government reforms. Thousands rallied at Tiananmen Square; protests spread to other cities. Government officials promised to consider the students' complaints after they returned to their studies, but the demonstrations persisted. The impending visit of Soviet Premier Mikhail Gorbachev in mid-May and the publicity that would surround the Sino-Soviet summit offered opportunities to publicize the students' concerns. Signs and T-shirts with English slogans spread the news of the student demands. Still, as the days passed, the government made no move to clear the square.

On May 13, around three thousand students began a mass hunger strike, and the following day, thousands of ordinary citizens converged on the square. The following week, more than 1 million people demonstrated in and around Tiananmen Square. Workers marched in support of the students and, on May 19, organized an independent union of workers in Beijing. The situation now threatened to get out of control, and on May 20, the government declared martial law and cut off live satellite broadcasts. But when martial law had no immediate effect and the troops waiting on the outskirts of the city did not move in, many Chinese were optimistic that Premier Li Peng, the government hard-liner, would resign.

Within the highest echelons of the Communist Party, however, decisions were being made that moved the party leaders from indecision to take action against the students. Zhao Ziyang, the CCP secretary-general and the strongest supporter of the students, was reported to have been called a traitor by **Deng Xiaoping**, China's primary political leader (and himself a veteran of the May Fourth Movement).[28] Finally, early on the morning of June 3, troops moved into the square from the east, the west, and the north, to be met by thousands of citizens and hastily assembled barricades. The troops moved back. But late that same day, they moved in with force, and by dawn on June 4, the square had been cleared—at the cost of some three thousand lives.

More will be said about the meaning of the Tiananmen Square events in future chapters. For now, it is sufficient to note that although outsiders have interpreted the 1989 student movement primarily in terms of the demands for increased democracy, from the standpoint of the government, it represented a threat not just to the stability but to the survival of the regime. Weighing the costs of immediate damage to their image in world opinion incurred by quick and ruthless repression against the long-term damage to China's party legitimacy and political cohesion, the CCP leaders determined to eliminate the challenge to the regime as thoroughly as possible. Thus, seventy years after the May Fourth Movement protested the Treaty of Versailles and sparked the imagination of the young revolutionaries who would build the Chinese Communist Party, the old men of the party buried China's most recent democracy movement.

## Summary

The reversion of Hong Kong and the 1989 Tiananmen movement recall themes central to Chinese history that are also critical to understanding contemporary politics. The political and intellectual turmoil generated by the simultaneous decay of the imperial system and Western imperialism convinced reformers and revolutionaries alike that centralized state power, territorial integrity, and socioeconomic change were all essential to recreating Chinese greatness. The Communist Party succeeded where late-nineteenth-century and early twentieth-century reformers and, later, the Kuomintang failed. Its success was due to a number of factors, the most important of which were the war with Japan, corruption and division within the KMT, and the cohesion and political-military skill, as well as ruthlessness, of the CCP.

The preoccupation with state and nation building, as well as with social revolution, characterized not only the CCP's drive for power in China but its rule after 1949. By the 1960s, it seemed that the Communists had largely succeeded in eradicating "feudal" structures and ways of thinking. In retrospect, we know that to be a hasty judgment: The preference for sons explained in Chapter 3 illustrates just one way in which old social patterns die slowly.

## Notes

1. Technically, the term "Sinitic" refers to a branch of the Sino-Tibetan languages that includes Chinese and its "dialects." As an adjective, Sinitic is also used to mean Chinese. On the Sinitic languages and the Chinese writing system, see Edwin O. Reischauer and John K. Fairbank, *East Asia: The Great Tradition* (Boston: Houghton Mifflin, 1960), pp. 15–19 and 39–44.

2. A secular emphasis does not mean that Chinese society (then or now) has been devoid of religious traditions or impulses. Animism, for example, has ancient roots in China; and Confucius, who was profoundly humanistic in his concerns, drew on religious sentiment by linking his proposed good order with Heaven, or the natural order of things. John E. Schrecker, *The Chinese Revolution in Historical Perspective* (New York: Praeger, 1991), pp. 10–11.

3. On this historical process, see Patricia Ebrey, "The Chinese Family and the Spread of Confucian Values," in Gilbert Rozman, ed., *The East Asian Region: Confucian Heritage and Its Modern Adaptation* (Princeton: Princeton University Press, 1991), pp. 45–83.

4. Early Confucian scholars debated whether human beings were inherently good. Mencius believed they were, but another third-century B.C.E. philosopher, Xunzi (Hsun Tzu), said that "man was evil" and "goodness is acquired." See his argument in Wm. Theodore de Bary, Wing-tsit Chan, and Burton Watson, *Sources of Chinese Tradition*, vol. 1 (New York: Columbia University Press, 1960), pp. 104–108.

5. See, for example, Dung Jung-shu (Tung Chung-shu) in ibid., p. 163.

6. Schrecker, *Chinese Revolution*, pp. 11–12.

7. The Qing (Ch'ing or "Manchu") dynasty lasted from 1644 to the Republican overthrow in 1911. Although the Manchu rulers were foreigners, they did not change the basic structures of Chinese government and society.

8. The White Lotus uprising occurred in the mountainous region of north-central China; it was sparked by growing poverty and resentment against tax collectors and took its name from an old Buddhist-inspired cult, the White Lotus Society. On the Taiping Rebellion, see Chapter 3, n. 30. The Boxer Uprising was specifically antiforeign.

9. For the geographical scope of these revolts, see Caroline Blunden and Mark Elvin, *Cultural Atlas of China* (New York: Facts on File, 1983), p. 149.

10. Jonathan D. Spence, *The Search for Modern China* (New York: W. W. Norton, 1990), pp. 170–178. For in-depth analyses, see Jen Yu-wen, *The Taiping Revolutionary Movement* (New Haven: Yale University Press, 1973); and Franz Michael, *The Taiping Rebellion: History and Documents*, vol. 1 (Seattle: University of Washington Press, 1966).

11. Mary Clabaugh Wright, *The Last Stand of Chinese Conservatism, The T'ung-Chih Restoration, 1862–1874* (New York: Atheneum, 1966), p. 45.

12. Schrecker, *Chinese Revolution*, p. 107.

13. The war was fought over Japan's push to dominate Korea, where China claimed historical suzerainty, or political control.

14. In his classic study, *Confucian China and Its Modern Fate: A Trilogy*, Joseph R. Levenson argued that the culture versus nation debate was part of a long tradition: "In large part the intellectual history of modern China has been the process of making *kuo-chia* [a nation-state] of *t'ien-hsia* [a universal empire]" (Berkeley and Los Angeles: University of California Press, 1968), vol. 1, p. 103.

15. As a result of the Sino-Japanese war, China ceded to Japan the island of Formosa (today's Taiwan). In 1896, China signed a defensive alliance with Russia, in turn granting Russia the right to build and operate a railroad across northern Manchuria. In 1897, Germany occupied a port on the Shandong Peninsula, and by 1898, Germany, Great Britain, Russia, France, and Japan had begun the scramble for additional territorial concessions in China.

16. For a detailed study of the origins and activities of the Boxers, see Joseph W. Esherick, *The Origins of the Boxer Uprising* (Berkeley and Los Angeles: University of California Press, 1987), especially chaps. 1, 7.

17. The Tongmeng Hui is variously translated as the Alliance Society, Revolutionary Society or Alliance, or United League.

18. For the complete text, see Ssu-Yu Teng and John K. Fairbank, *China's Response to the West: A Documentary Survey, 1839–1923* (New York: Atheneum, 1967), pp. 227–229.

19. Ibid., p. 196.

20. Spence, *Search*, p. 267.

21. In the Pinyin system, Kuomintang is transliterated Guomindang (GMD). I have chosen to use the older spelling, which is still preferred in Taiwan, where the KMT ruled after 1949.

22. China never officially declared war but contributed to the war effort by sending workers to France to work in factories. They were never formally recognized for their efforts. I am grateful to Professor Bernard Olivier for clarifying the history of this period.

23. The phrase "rape of Nanjing" is used both literally and figuratively. The female rape victims, many of whom died, numbered around 20,000; an estimated

30,000 fugitive Chinese soldiers and 12,000 civilians were murdered. Wanton destruction and arson left much of the city in ruins. Spence, *Search*, p. 448.

24. Kay Ann Johnson, *Women, the Family, and Peasant Revolution in China* (Chicago: University of Chicago Press, 1983), p. 63. See also the discussion by Delia Davin, *Woman-Work: Women and the Party in Revolutionary China* (Oxford: Clarendon Press, 1976), chap. 1.

25. Johnson, *Women*, pp. 69–72.

26. "A Draft Agreement Between the Government of the United Kingdom of Great Britain and Northern Ireland and the Government of the People's Republic of China on the Future of Hong Kong" (London: Her Majesty's Stationery Office, September 1984), pp. 11–13.

27. See the analysis of Neville Maxwell, "The Conflict over Hong Kong," *Swiss Review of World Affairs* (April 1995), pp. 27–28.

28. "The Shattered Dream," *Los Angeles Times*, June 25, 1989, p. 7.

*seven*

# Japan:
# Tension
# in Tradition

In the early 1990s, the Japanese debated whether the government should contribute troops from its **Self Defense Forces** (SDF) to international peacekeeping activities. The governing Liberal Democratic Party (LDP) took the position that peacekeeping contributions would help fulfill Japan's international obligations and troops would be used in noncombatant roles. The opposition Socialist Party attacked the plan as a violation of Japan's Constitution, which, in Article 9, commits the country to "forever renounce . . . the threat or use of force as a means of settling international disputes."

By the mid-1990s, members of the Japanese SDF were being welcomed upon their return from peacekeeping operations in Cambodia and Rwanda and being prepared for other missions. There was no sign of constitutional revision, although some conservatives did favor it. Meanwhile, the Socialist Party had accepted SDF peacekeeping missions, and the political party system that had defined Japanese politics since the 1950s was a shambles, with some parties voting themselves out of existence and others fragmenting or combining.

The importance of these changes is understandable only when placed in a broader historical context. This chapter provides this context by focusing on the key periods in Japan's struggle with national unity and identity over the past four centuries. Parts of the analysis expand on the introductory material in Chapter 4, for example, explaining the significance of a unique Japanese theory of the state that drew its inspiration from Shinto. The chapter reviews the post–World War II occupation period, then returns to the SDF-peacekeeping debate as an illustration of Japan's ongoing effort to define a new identity in the international community.

## The Tokugawa Shogunate

The Tokugawa shogunate, or Edo period (1600–1867),[1] is of interest here for its role in setting the stage for the central theme in this chapter: tension in tradition. Through their ideology, institutions, and policies, the Tokugawa rulers sought stability and hierarchy in a country that had been racked by civil war in the sixteenth century. Thus, it is from this period that much of what we today think of as "traditional" in Japan has survived. At the same time, however, the period (unintentionally) laid the foundation for the socioeconomic transformation that occurred during the Meiji period—and hence for tension between modernity and tradition.

The Tokugawa period takes its name from the last of the feudal lords who sought to unify Japan in the late sixteenth century, Tokugawa Ieyasu, who received the title of shogun from the emperor in 1603.[2] Shoguns were the de facto military rulers of Japan between the late twelfth and mid-nineteenth centuries. The origins of their rule lay in military conquest, but all shoguns, including Ieyasu and his successors, stressed the imperial court as the source of legitimacy, prestige, and authority.[3]

From the perspective of modern politics, the most important aspects of the Tokugawa, or Edo, period are those that contributed to the creation of a united, stable state based on Confucian political norms and a clearly delineated social hierarchy. To understand the significance of the nineteenth-century events associated with the Meiji period, it is also important to see the way in which the Tokugawa rulers endeavored to isolate Japan from external, primarily European, influences.

Chapter 4 noted that as early as the sixth century, Japanese rulers had begun a process of borrowing from the Chinese. In addition to Buddhism and the Chinese system of writing, which migrated east from China and Korea, Confucian political and ethical ideas also entered Japan. In Japan, as in China, the Confucian concept of human and social order was fundamentally conservative: It was designed to conserve harmony in society and politics and to provide a set of ethical precepts for social order. It emphasized the obligations of ruler and subject on the basis of rigid relationships of superiority and inferiority. Gradually, the Confucian worldview and political-ethical values were grafted onto Japanese feudal society, both reinforcing and reflecting that feudal order.

A legal and hereditary class system consisting—in theory—of four basic social divisions characterized Tokugawa society. At the apex, of course, were the imperial family and household, the shogun, feudal lords, and priests. Next, the first of the four basic divisions was the samurai class, or *bushi* ("military gentry"), both warriors and administrators. Beneath the samurai ranked classes valued according to their economic contributions: peasants (primary producers), artisans (secondary producers), then merchants. In addition, there were people who, for a variety of reasons, fell outside the system and thus were both degraded and dishonored. The *burakumin* were chief among these. It should also be noted that there were gradations within the various social classes, including the samurai. This helps explain how the lower samurai took the initiative in attacking Tokugawa rule in the mid-nineteenth century.

The chief political value of the period was loyalty—loyalty of a particularistic nature. That is, people gave their loyalty primarily to the collectivity to which they belonged: the family, the village, the feudal realm (*han*), and, ultimately, Japan itself. The head of the collectivity held enormous symbolic importance, for he embodied the group and loyalty to it. Whether he was the family head, feudal lord, or emperor, he commanded and received absolute loyalty. Loyalty meant more than passive devotion; it meant active service and performance.[4] In large part because Tokugawa Japan was still feudal, loyalty was not, therefore, focused solely on the national government or its representatives. But the norm of compliance with higher authority, which characterized both the political and social systems, was entrenched in the behavior of every individual. This accounted for the high degree of public order, as well as for individual acts such as the willingness of samurai to commit seppuku (ritual suicide, or hara-kiri).

In these values and structures of loyalty are rooted two seemingly contradictory features of twentieth-century Japanese politics. On the one hand, the norms and practices of hierarchical loyalty could be, and were, transformed into a cohesive movement of nationalism. On the other hand, Japanese politics in the eighteenth century, as well as the twentieth, were filled with factionalism, reflecting the reality that loyalty was historically identified first and foremost with a specific subnational group (before there was any "nation" in the modern sense) and with the head of that group. Thus, identification with subgroups often superseded loyalty to the larger organization (such as a political party) or to the wider society.

Another important dimension of Tokugawa rule was the policy of deliberate isolation after 1600. The policy was facilitated by relative geographical isolation and by Japan's having escaped Chinese military and political domination (unlike Korea). Myths of divine protection linked isolation with a strong belief in Japan's invulnerability. In the thirteenth century, for example, the Mongols had attempted two invasions of Japan, the second one amassing about 140,000 men. The invaders were held at bay for almost two months until a typhoon struck, destroying much of the invading fleet. Those who survived returned home in defeat. The Japanese success was attributed to the country's uniqueness, manifest in the kamikaze ("divine wind") that had helped to destroy the enemy. The kamikaze was seen as intervention by the gods of Ise Shrine, one of Japan's most important Shinto centers, and thus reinforced the Japanese belief that their land was protected by the gods.[5]

Part of the policy of isolation was the elimination of Christianity mentioned in Chapter 4. Another element was restricting contacts with Europeans only to the Dutch at the port of Nagasaki. The persecution of Christians and the restriction of trade were also signs of the hardening of the feudal system, which was based on agriculture, and the diminished importance of international trade as part of Japan's economic system. The primary source of revenue for the government was taxes on agricultural production rather than, for example, manufacturing. The priority given to agriculture in both fiscal and social matters and the downgrading of commercial activities contributed to the prosperity merchants enjoyed by the eighteenth century because they were left largely unregulated and untaxed. The growth of the commercial classes, urban centers, internal trade, and a monetary system led to a unified national market—even though all of these trends violated the theory of an agrarian-based, feudal, rigid socioeconomic structure.

The last feature of the Edo period to examine here is the development of the idea of *kokutai*, usually translated as "national polity," "national essence," or "essence of the state." *Kokutai* was a new theory in which familistic, political, and religious ideas were merged and the state was conceptualized as a large family. The hierarchical loyalties mentioned earlier were gradually fused into a system of thought in which the emperor became the center of national unity. The relationship between the emperor and his subjects was like that between a father and his children; and the obligations of loyalty and service to the emperor would take precedence over all other obligations. This family concept of the state rested in turn on the belief that Japan's uniqueness lay in the direct descent of the imperial line from Amaterasu Omikami, the Sun Goddess. This myth, it may be recalled, had its origins in the Ritsuryo, which predated the Edo period by nearly one thousand years.

The ideas that characterized *kokutai* developed from a variety of writings that were part of the intellectual debates of the Edo period. *Kokutai* was also part of the reaction against foreign influence; but in this instance, the antiforeign sentiment was directed against China, not Europe. The best-known representative of *kokutai* was Motori Norinaga (1730–1801), who devoted his life to identifying, studying, and publicizing Japanese classics, including *The Tale of Genji*. Rejecting both Confucianism and Buddhism because of their Chinese origins, Motori drew on Shinto tradition to define Japanese uniqueness and in doing so helped to consolidate the underlying rationale of *kokutai*: the role of Amaterasu Omikami, the "Heaven-Shining Goddess." One of Motori's central themes was the way in which China had lost sight of the truth of the Sun Goddess, and he noted that only in "our Imperial Land" had the tradition been correctly and clearly transmitted. "Thus our country is the source and fountainhead of all other countries, and in all matters it excels all the others."[6]

In Motori's writings, one sees the core ideas that defined Japanese nationalism one century later. The clearest legacy of the *kokutai* scholars was to resurrect Shinto, recraft its political meanings, and thus define a unique Japan connected to its literature, history, and the Imperial Way (the special role of the emperor in the country's history and culture). In this manner it was an indispensable link in the chain of ideas and events that created a modernizing Japan in the nineteenth century.

## The Meiji Period

The Meiji period dates from 1868, when the young emperor Mutsuhito chose the name Meiji, or "Enlightened Rule," for his reign. It lasted until his death in 1912, and the emperor himself is known posthumously as Meiji. The era is sometimes referred to as the **Meiji Restoration** because early in 1868, samurai opposed to Tokugawa rule undertook what was in effect a coup d'état. They seized the Imperial Palace in Kyoto and announced that political power would revert to, hence be restored to, the emperor. The emperor had never been deposed, of course; but after eight centuries of military, or shogunal, rule, the idea of restoring the emperor signaled fundamental changes in norms of authority and legitimacy, as well as changes in domestic and foreign policies.

There were two general reasons for the collapse of Tokugawa rule: domestic economic and social problems and the growing threat from Western powers in East Asia. Despite the fact that the lives of peasants were minutely regulated, worsening economic conditions resulted in increasing numbers of revolts. In the mid-1830s, for example, a major famine led to the deaths of hundreds of thousands of people; destitute peasants flocked to the cities, and there were uprisings throughout Japan.[7] Nor were the peasants alone in protesting their declining living conditions. As both the government and feudal lords ran short of money, the stipends of samurai were often reduced. Hard-pressed even to support their families, some samurai actually crossed classes in order to be free to pursue commercial pursuits. Indigence brewed discontent among many samurai, as it did among the peasants.

The shogunate responded with a variety of reforms. These did little to stop the decline in the end, though as attempts to improve the efficiency of some government activities, such as taxation, the reforms contributed to the central authority of the national government over feudal domains, efforts that later received the full attention of the Meiji reformers.

The external threat was even less successfully resolved. The news of China's defeat by Britain in the Opium War brought home to the shogunate's rulers the truth about Western power *and* intentions. One decade after the British victory, the arrival of the American flotilla under Commodore Matthew C. Perry set off a chain of events that culminated in the Meiji Restoration. In the course of Perry's visits in 1853 and 1854, negotiations produced a treaty that opened two ports to American trade and provided for American consular representation in Japan. The shogunate's concessions divided both the feudal lords and the imperial court. By the end of the 1850s, the influx of foreigners sparked latent xenophobia, exemplified by the slogan *sonno joi:* "Revere (or honor) the emperor; expel the barbarians." Not surprisingly, the concepts of both *sonno* (imperial rule) and *joi* (repelling foreigners) had been developed by the *kokutai* schools of thought.

This background to the Meiji period helps us understand the various policies pursued after 1868, policies that otherwise seem contradictory. For example, Meiji rulers disestablished both the feudal domains and the traditional role of the samurai, while extolling the virtues represented by the old order, such as veneration of the martial arts and absolute loyalty to one's superior. Out of the Meiji period would come both nascent democratic institutions and the trappings of modern authoritarianism, both aggressive borrowing from other countries and aggressive xenophobia.

The restoration events of 1868 were followed by a brief period of civil war, between supporters of the new Meiji government and defenders of the old Tokugawa rule. During this period, **Edo** was renamed Tokyo and designated as the national capital. The new government was composed of samurai from the southwestern domains that had led the assault on the shogunate. It moved immediately to reunify the country and establish a strong central administration. Inspired by Western models, the government also drew up the **Charter Oath** to placate (or co-opt) potential opposition to the new regime. Issued by the emperor, the oath introduced ideas of assemblies, national unity, rejecting the past, and embracing the new:

> By this oath we set up as our aim the establishment of the national weal on a broad basis and the framing of a constitution and laws.
> 1. Deliberative assemblies shall be widely established and all matters decided by public discussion.
> 2. All classes, high and low, shall unite in vigorously carrying out the administration of affairs of state.

3. The common people, no less than the civil and military officials, shall each be allowed to pursue his own calling so that there may be no discontent.
4. Evil customs of the past shall be broken off and everything based upon the just laws of Nature.
5. Knowledge shall be sought throughout the world so as to strengthen the foundations of imperial rule.[8]

The assemblies and public discussion mentioned in the Charter Oath came to very little in the early years of the Meiji period, as the reformers emphasized the norm of unity found in the oath. The restoration leaders, increasingly younger samurai who had replaced the older, high-ranking nobles in imperial offices, moved quickly to abolish feudal structures and to launch Japan on a rapid course of modernization that touched every aspect of the country, including finances, government bureaucracy (both civilian and military), industrial technology, culture, and even dress and food.

The restoration successes do not mean that there were no divisions among the government leaders or that there were no crises. There were both: One of the most important crises was in fact an armed rebellion against the government in 1877 by impoverished and disestablished samurai; the problems of the samurai were linked also to divisions among the ruling oligarchy. One of the Meiji reforms that abolished the old feudal structures took from the samurai their old class privileges, just as the feudal realms or *han* were themselves eliminated. These changes left thousands of samurai unemployed; originally, they were given pensions, and later, lump sums, but both were insufficient to accommodate their economic needs. Some government leaders sought an expedition to Korea to recreate the old martial role for the samurai. The debate about Korea divided the Meiji oligarchs and led to the resignation of the militant faction that demanded action in Korea; the leader of this faction eventually headed the rebellion against the government in 1877.

The unity of the restoration leaders was broken, and factionalism soon became an acknowledged feature of national politics. Although the 1877 rebellion was the last military challenge to the Meiji government, members of the oligarchy began to reach beyond the government for support of their views. The political societies they created to build support were the precursors of today's political parties. One of the most notable leaders of the period, Itagaki Taisuke, created the Society of Patriots, whose original aim was to help the samurai. Support for Itagaki's society spread from samurai to rural aristocracy and, ultimately, to lower rural classes—all those hurt by the government's heavy reliance on rural taxation.

Itagaki had been a member of the restoration oligarchy, and his initiatives to pressure the government by creating nongovernmental associations illustrated the early, tentative roots of democracy in Japan, as well as the persistence of factionalism in a ruling coalition. In 1881, Itagaki reorganized his forces into the Liberal Party (Jiyuto), Japan's first political party. The Jiyuto went through several major reorganizations over the course of subsequent decades, but it reemerged after World War II and became one of the two core parties that merged to establish the Liberal Democratic Party.[9]

Neither the Jiyuto nor the other political parties established in the 1880s was mass based or tightly organized. Typically, they reflected personalism or a leader-follower relationship, and they were often permeated by cliques, a pattern that has persisted throughout the twentieth century in most Japanese parties. Likewise, none of the parties represented the growing classes of urban workers, the poor, or women. In this regard, they were not unlike parties that emerged in Europe during the nineteenth century, from which Japan's restoration leaders took much of their inspiration.

Perhaps inevitably, the movement for people's rights that Itagaki represented and the rapid permeation of Japanese society and politics by Western influences provoked a conservative reaction as the century drew to a close. The combination of rural outbreaks—a sign of persistent economic problems and social instability—and the increasing demands for political rights led the government to restrain political activity in the mid-1880s through laws that regulated the press and freedom of assembly. The government also sought to institutionalize Japan's new political system, while co-opting dissidents through the creation of a parliamentary assembly, the Diet. The **Meiji Constitution** of 1889 thus represented the two political traditions that were in tension as a result of the changes of the Meiji period: liberalization and conservative reaction. The creation of a bicameral Diet formally recognized the principle of popular participation in government. The electorate responsible for choosing the members of the lower house, the House of Representatives, was relatively small (it excluded all women, as well as men who did not meet certain tax qualifications), and the upper House of Peers (patterned after the British House of Lords) was not elected. But the Diet did have some real power; for example, its approval was necessary to pass the government budget.

The Meiji Constitution also created the institutions of prime minister and Cabinet. The key element of parliamentary responsibility of the Cabinet to the Diet—which characterized true parliamentary systems in Europe—was not present, but the Constitution did set the precedent for the parliamentary structures that were incorporated in Japan's post–World War II Constitution.

The ultimate source of sovereignty under the 1889 Constitution was the emperor, whose authority was "sacred and inviolable." The Constitution, in fact, had been presented to the people as a gift from the emperor. In no way were any of the new government institutions structured so as to interfere, or appear to conflict, with imperial prerogative. Thus, the core norm of the Constitution was compatible with the *kokutai* theory of the state.

Despite the affirmation of imperial sovereignty, the emperor continued to reign rather than rule. The Cabinet and the Diet shared power with the Imperial Household Ministry (responsible for the personal and official affairs of the emperor and his family), the bureaucracy of the various ministries (which in effect prepared most of the legislation passed by the Diet), and the general staffs of the army and navy, which had direct access to the emperor. These institutions would assure the continuation and, ultimately, the supremacy, of the most conservative elements of Japanese political values well into the twentieth century.

In 1890, the conservative backlash found one of its most eloquent and effective embodiments in the **Imperial Rescript on Education**. More than any other document of the Meiji period, the rescript illustrated the fusion of the *kokutai* principles with Confucianism, whose supporters had successfully argued that the rapid pace of modernization needed to be counteracted by reaffirming the legitimacy of the imperial order.[10] The rescript remained in place until the end of World War II and was a critical source of political indoctrination, as this extracted passage illustrates:

> Know ye, Our subjects:
> Our Imperial Ancestors have founded Our Empire on a basis broad and everlasting, and have deeply and firmly implanted virtue; Our subjects ever united in loyalty and filial piety have from generation to generation illustrated the beauty thereof. This is the glory of the fundamental character of Our Empire, and herein also lies the source of Our education. Ye, Our subjects, be filial to your parents, affectionate to your brothers and sisters; as husbands and wives be harmonious, as friends true; . . . should emergency arise, offer yourselves courageously to the State; and thus guard and maintain the prosperity of Our Imperial Throne coeval with heaven and earth. . . .
> The Way here set forth is indeed the teaching bequeathed by Our Imperial Ancestors, to be observed alike by Their Descendants and the subjects, infallible for all ages and true in all places.[11]

Copies of the Imperial Rescript on Education were distributed to every school in Japan and all students were required to memorize the text as part of their moral education. Ceremonial readings of the rescript developed into elaborate rituals, and Shinto priests were mobilized to distribute the document; they in turn standardized the rites conducted around it.[12] This intertwining of public education and Shinto ritual helps to explain the importance of State Shinto during the formative period of modern Japanese nationalism.

Readers may recall from Chapter 4 that State Shinto was a government-fostered ideology that combined the stories and myths of the origin of the imperial house with a belief in the superiority and uniqueness of the Japanese people. Shinto shrines and priests served to transmit the Imperial Way and to invoke loyalty to state and emperor alike. Viewed in this way, the rites of the shrines helped popularize the doctrine of *kokutai*, the special concept of the national polity. It was for these reasons that disestablishment of Shinto as a state doctrine was a high priority for American reformers during the post–World War II occupation of Japan.

The Meiji period ended in 1912, with the death of the emperor. By this time—that is, after less than a half century—Japan had undergone a massive economic transformation, catapulting itself to the threshold of the industrial age. The international implications of this transformation were perhaps inescapable, given the Meiji emphasis on national unity, securing Japan from aggression, and winning equality with the West. Two external wars in the space of ten years showed just how quickly economic prowess had been translated into military prowess. The first war, between China and Japan (the Sino-Japanese War), was fought over control of Korea, where China claimed suzerainty. The Japanese victory in 1895 was quick and decisive, and as a consequence, China ceded Formosa (today's Taiwan) and some other territories to Japan.[13] The Chinese government was also forced to recognize Korea's independence and negotiate a commercial treaty that gave Japan the privileges in China that the Western powers had secured. Thus, Japan began its long march to domination of East Asia, and the seeds of political discord between China, Japan, and Korea were further spread.

It was during this same period that Japan secured revision of its unequal treaties with Western nations, thus realizing a foreign policy goal that had become "a national obsession."[14] As has so often happened in modern history, once the liberal goals of nationalism, such as freedom and equality, are secured, nationalism moves into an aggressive, even xenophobic, phase. So it was with Japan. One of the immediate consequences of the Sino-Japanese war was to exacerbate the international competition for land and influence in Northeast Asia. One of the implications of this competition was the near-destruction of China's territorial integrity, as was discussed in the previous chapter. Another consequence was the growing tension between Russia and Japan: Japan was now the dominant power in Korea and was challenging Russia's economic and military presence in Manchuria. War broke out when the Japanese surprised the Russian fleet at Port Arthur with a night attack in 1904. The ensuing military battles confirmed Japan's stature as a modern nation, and the 1905 treaty that marked the end of the **Russo-Japanese War** confirmed Japan's paramount role in Korea and its expanding interests in

Manchuria. It is perhaps a sad irony that just at the point that Korea itself was enjoying a nationalist awakening, the country was annexed outright (in 1910) by Japan.[15] Japan's colonization of Korea produced the Japanese-Korean minority discussed in Chapter 4. Control over Korea was also viewed by many Japanese as further evidence of their country's cultural and historical superiority.

# The Twentieth Century: Pluralistic and Authoritarian Legacies

The key political issue after the death of the Meiji emperor in 1912 was the competition between authoritarian and liberal democratic political forces in defining the meaning of modern Japan. Was the surge of militarism in the 1930s and 1940s a logical consequence of the process of nation building as it occurred in Japan? Central to the conditions that led to militarism were the social and economic changes resulting from the policies of the Meiji leaders. These changes brought new groups into the political process, and at the same time, the old consensus about the basic goals of modernization was replaced by deep political cleavages among the leaders who gradually supplanted the nineteenth-century Meiji oligarchs. Ultimately, those who adhered to the interpretation of *kokutai*, State Shinto, and emperor worship, which represented the most conservative vision of Japan, prevailed.

The most important social and economic changes of the early twentieth century were the increasing integration of the Japanese economy into the world economy and uneven modernization throughout the country. Internationalization made the Japanese economy more susceptible to the business and financial cycles that affected other industrializing countries. Trade came to play a larger role in the structure of economic production, both in terms of defining markets and assuring raw materials. Industrial output rose, so it became necessary to import more raw materials, which in turn had to be paid for by selling exports. This resulted in the preoccupation with dependence on external resources that spurred Japanese territorial expansion in the 1930s and 1940s.

Both inflation and deflation accompanied the growth of the Japanese economy during the first three decades of the twentieth century, and not all sectors benefited equally from the economic changes. Silk, for example, was the chief export from Japan in the 1920s, and although the industry enjoyed price increases during the early part of the decade, the price of silk fell by more than two-thirds between 1925 and 1929.[16] By the end of World War I, over 300,000 workers, mostly girls, were employed in silk filatures, the establishments where silk from cocoons was spun into threads. Most of the workers came from impoverished rural families, and their wages, although very low, helped sustain their families.[17] But declining prices, increased competition from synthetic fabrics, and the Great Depression of 1929 meant falling wages and unemployment. Industrialization thus provided opportunities but also left some social groups especially vulnerable to the economic cycles that were exacerbated by the opening of Japan's economy to international influences. Women in particular assumed the role that would later define much of their economic participation after World War II—as a flexible source of labor moving in and out of the formal workforce, fueling economic growth with low wages and yielding jobs to male workers in times of economic downturn.

Industries such as silk and, later, cotton slowly changed the traditional social structures. The migration of young women to work in urban textile mills, for example, stimulated the urbanization process and linked the urban and rural areas in an era of rapid economic change.[18] An urban proletariat gradually developed, spawning labor unions, workers' strikes, and the establishment of leftist parties. Small Socialist "parties," drawing on the ideas of both Christian Socialists and early Marxists, were created (and banned) before World War I. The greatest surge of interest came during the 1920s, when leftists of various stripes gained followers in parts of the labor movement and especially in universities. The Japan Communist Party, formally organized in 1922, dates from this period.

For one dozen years, from the end of World War I to the early 1930s, political parties enjoyed considerable growth in their popular following and in their government influence. **Taisho democracy**, as the period of the 1920s came to be called,[19] was tentative and fragile, at best. The parties that existed had roots that were neither deep nor wide. The structure of political leadership was still oligarchic, not pluralistic. Social mobility and the growth of new urban classes had led to greater pressure for political participation, and universal male suffrage was adopted in 1925. But traditional social structures and loyalties were only partially eroded, and the erosion that had occurred made militant nationalism appealing for those who were especially vulnerable to socioeconomic changes. At the same time, state institutions, including the military and police bureaucracies, had become larger, centralized, and more efficient, their efficiency enhanced by the development of mass transportation and communication. By the early 1930s, state-created and state-administered mass organizations, which sought to organize people by social category, were more important than political parties. For example, there were three such organizations for women, each seeking to promote women's support for government policies.[20]

In the late 1920s, a combination of international and domestic developments stimulated demands for a new phase of national reconstruction. The rise of Chinese nationalism threatened Japanese interests in Manchuria, and depression at home raised calls from a variety of right-wing groups, both inside and outside the military, for new leadership. In 1931, Japanese army officers stationed in Manchuria plotted a complete takeover of Manchuria. Japanese railway tracks near the city of Mukden were bombed; army leaders blamed the Chinese and launched an attack against Chinese troops in Mukden. In Tokyo, the civilian government, divided over how to respond, was unable to stop the Japanese aggression in Manchuria. The following year, a new prime minister sought to terminate the conflict and reassert civilian control over the army. His assassination in 1932 ended these efforts and also ended the last party-led government until the end of World War II.

The historical line between the events of 1931–1932 and the full outbreak of war with China in 1937 was not without twists and turns. But the cumulative effect of the period was to consolidate the military's hold (in cooperation with high-ranking civilian bureaucrats) on the government, to "clarify" a nationalist line, and to silence all political and intellectual voices opposed to that line. Much like the Imperial Rescript on Education before it, the 1937 Fundamentals of Our National Polity, published by the Education Ministry, was distributed throughout Japan as a guide for national unity. The text criticized the assumptions and impact of imported Western ideologies that, by emphasizing individualism and human beings more generally, lacked "historical views." The text also stated that these ideologies had led to social confusion and were antithetical to Japan's history, which was grounded in the lineage running between Amaterasu Omikami and the emperor: "to serve the emperor and to receive the emperor's great august Will as one's own is the rationale of making our historical 'life' live in the present; and on this is based the morality of the people."

From this restatement of the core doctrine of *kokutai*, the "Fundamentals" asserted the importance of "Oriental morals," including loyalty, patriotism, filial piety, the martial spirit as exemplified in *bushido* (the "way of the warrior"), and national harmony. The concluding section of the text contrasted the Imperial Way with Occidental theories of the state that stressed the state as existing for the benefit of individuals. Japanese uniqueness lay in its history of assimilating imported ideologies and producing a new, original synthesis, including a view of the state as the "nuclear existence that gives birth to individual beings, which it transcends."[21]

Whereas the notion of the superhuman quality of the Japanese emperor disappeared with the postwar occupation and the new Constitution, other themes found in the Fundamentals of Our National Polity have periodically reappeared: the importance of distinguishing between Western and Eastern views of humans and society, the special assimilative qualities of Japanese culture, the enduring value of "Oriental" (Confucian) mores, and the transcendent nature of the state. Some Japanese politicians have reasserted these positions, as have leaders from other East Asian states.[22] It would not be implausible to suggest that these themes will become more prominent in the coming years as Asian governments promote their distinctive views in international relations.

## A New Constitutional Order

In the wake of the American nuclear bombings at Hiroshima and Nagasaki, World War II ended disastrously for Japan. The revulsion most Japanese felt against the war and the old leadership opened the way to radical changes. In the words of historian Edwin Reischauer:

> In the early postwar months, most Japanese were absorbed in the struggle to keep body and soul together, but underneath these immediate concerns there was a great longing for peace and a determination to avoid any repetition of this great catastrophe. People wanted something new and better than the old Japan that had come to grief. They were confused but open to change in a way they had never been before.[23]

Responsibility for the occupation (1945–1952) was nominally shared by the victorious allies of World War II, but in reality it was largely an American affair, conducted under the determined leadership of General Douglas MacArthur, **Supreme Commander for the Allied Powers**, or SCAP (as both MacArthur and his headquarters were known). SCAP policies set the tone for an occupation that would be both radical and conservative: radical in the scope of some of the changes demanded of Japanese society, conservative in the preservation of important institutions such as the emperor and the bureaucracy. The continuity provided by the bureaucracy accounted for much of the smoothness of the occupation, while also diluting its impact, because all occupation orders were issued to and executed by the Japanese government. The occupation sought wide-ranging changes, from demilitarization and purging those deemed responsible for the war to social, economic, and political reforms designed to prevent a recurrence of Japanese militarism.[24] Land reform resulted in a dramatic decrease of tenant farmers and a concomitant increase in small landowners. Labor unions were legalized, women were enfranchised, and compulsory education for girls and boys was extended.

Some reforms had less success than others. For example, American authorities blamed the *zaibatsu*, industrial and financial conglomerates, for much of the drive behind Japanese economic and military expansion. Reformers also believed that breaking up the *zaibatsu* would, like land reform, further the goal of distributing wealth throughout Japanese society. The great clan-based *zaibatsu* were broken up, but the old economic elites survived (along with their personal ties), as did the names of their concerns, such as Mitsubishi and Sumitomo.

After the occupation, the *zaibatsu* were succeeded by **keiretsu**, company networks joined by common links to banks and trading companies. None of Japan's top business barons figured in the war crimes trials, and within four years after the end of the war, the policies aimed at deconcentration of the economy were shelved. An important reason for the ease with which the combines were reconstituted was a shift in American occupation policies in the late 1940s, during the early phases of the Cold War. Events in Europe and Asia, including the successes of the Communist movement in China, led to a "reverse course" in American policy that emphasized rapid economic reconstruction of Japan as part of a broader strategy to build an anti-Communist presence in East Asia.[25]

The political basis for a postwar democratic Japan was to rest on a new constitution that would replace the Meiji Constitution. As noted earlier, the 1889 Constitution had been drafted as part of the conservative reaction against Japan's lavish borrowing of Western practices. But that Constitution had also introduced institutions that, especially during the 1920s, laid a foundation for parliamentary democracy. Japan at the end of World War II thus had a democratic as well as an authoritarian constitutional heritage, albeit the latter had dominated for a generation. The SCAP authorities were determined to strengthen the former, and the Constitution of 1947, which is discussed further in Chapter 8, established a new concept of state power, replacing the *kokutai* theory with norms of popular sovereignty and parliamentary democracy. The new Constitution was unique for its inclusion of a provision, in Article 9, stating that Japan renounced war as a sovereign right and would not maintain "land, sea, and air forces." This article was central to the debate over the Self Defense Forces.

## The SDF Debate

The predecessor to the SDF was established in 1950 (pursuant to a SCAP order), after the beginning of the Korean War. The SDF itself was formally created in 1954, and its justification has always been the need for local defense. Since the late 1970s, the Defense Agency has defined the role of the Self Defense Forces to include the ability to respond to domestic insurgency, arms smuggling, or the covert use of force in Japan's seas and airspace; to rebuff limited, small-scale aggression; and to carry out disaster relief operations anywhere in the country.[26] None of these activities entails using SDF troops outside the territorial jurisdiction of Japan, and to emphasize their defensive purposes, none of the services (army, navy, air force) has developed or purchased weapons whose primary and obvious purposes are aggressive. This posture has included rejection of nuclear weapons, even though Japan has a sophisticated nuclear industry. Overall, however, Japan has a powerful military establishment: approximately 250,000 personnel, one of the largest military budgets in the world, and a sophisticated defense industry that produces 90 percent of the equipment needed by the Self Defense Forces.[27]

There are a number of reasons for the expansion of the Japanese military, but one has been American pressure on Japan to assume a more active role in international relations. The Bush administration reasserted this pressure during the Gulf War of 1991, and the post–Cold War expansion of United Nations activities also led to numerous calls for a more active Japanese role in peacekeeping. During the same period, Japanese interest in a permanent seat on the U.N. Security Council grew, and the government believed that a peacekeeping role for the SDF would improve Japan's chances to gain the seat.

The legislation passed by the Diet in 1992 to permit the use of SDF personnel in U.N. operations was carefully crafted to win support from a majority of Diet members. The peacekeeping cooperation law permits up to two thousand troops to be sent overseas in response to a U.N. request and allows the SDF to engage in such activities as disarming rival factions that have agreed to a truce and monitoring elections and cease-fires. SDF personnel may carry light weapons for self-defense purposes only and may not participate in operations that involve military action.[28]

In fact, the new legislation is a landmark. It terminates the postwar tradition of no Japanese military personnel on foreign soil. It advances the cause of those in the foreign affairs and defense bureaucracies who have long campaigned for a more active Japanese role in international relations. And although it highlights the contradictions within the Japanese Constitution, the new SDF role also eliminates one of the outstanding anomalies in the nation's gradual redefinition of itself since World War II. Economic power, both the Japanese government and the international community seem to agree, must still be complemented by a military presence that projects national influence and earns the respect of other "great" powers.

## Summary

In modern centuries, Japan has never—not even at the height of Tokugawa isolation—been completely cut off from foreign influence. Yet ideas and institutions from elsewhere in Asia and from Europe and North America have often been in tension with indigenous traditions and values. Both rejection of the foreign and assimilation of it have marked Japanese national identity at various periods. Stated differently, the development of national identity contains uniquely Japanese elements, such as *kokutai* and Shinto, as well as adapted nonindigenous traditions, such as Confucianism and democratic parliamentarism. The role of the SDF in contemporary Japanese society is one chapter in a much longer and more complex story of building national pride and confidence without chauvinism, of creating national independence without militarism or xenophobia. In seeking this balance, of course, Japan resembles many other countries.

The tension in the evolution of Japanese nationalism provoked by the juxtaposition of indigenous and foreign has been reinforced by ambivalent attitudes toward the countries that have most directly influenced Japan: China and the United States. In the eighteenth century, for example, some intellectuals of the *kokutai* school sought to develop national learning through explicit rejection of Chinese influence. For others, admiration of Chinese civilization crumbled as China itself seemed to crumble before the West in the nineteenth century. By the 1930s, there were those who argued that efforts to establish Pan-Asianism or associations dubbed "Greater Asia" or the "New Order in East Asia"—all to be led by Japan— would serve to rescue China from the pervasive Western threat.[29] Thus, a period viewed as unbridled Japanese aggression by most Chinese (and Americans) was seen by many Japanese nationalists as a necessary response to a much longer historical problem of East Asian regeneration and redefinition vis-à-vis the Western challenge.

Just as modern Japan cannot be understood in isolation from East Asia, neither can it be understood without reference to the occupation and subsequent relations with the United States. Although many Americans are aware of our ambivalence toward Japan and even our alternating admiration and hostility, few of us understand the ways in which, grappling with their own history, many Japanese carry the same attitudes toward the United States and the West in general. These attitudes emerge in a variety of contexts, ranging from Japanese perceptions of their country's policies in the 1930s and 1940s to views about the social and cultural costs of economic modernization to the legitimacy of the 1947 Constitution.[30] Debates in Japan over defense and foreign trade, for example, illustrate the mixture of bilateral conflict and partnership that accompanies Japanese-American relations.

## Notes

1. Edo, modern Tokyo, was a coastal village in the late sixteenth to early seventeenth centuries. It became the capital of the shogunate and hence its name is used for the period.

2. Visitors to Japan may see Tokugawa Ieyasu's tomb today at Nikko, where the Toshogu Shrine contains Ieyasu's mausoleum. Ieyasu overcame his chief rival in

battle in 1600, so his rule is sometimes dated from that year, though he did not receive the title of shogun until 1603.

3. The shogunate is also referred to as the *bakufu* (literally, "tent government"), which recalls the military origins of the rule. The castle built by Ieyasu and his successors for the capital of the shogunate became the Imperial Palace in the nineteenth century.

4. Robert N. Bellah, *Tokugawa Religion: The Values of Pre-Industrial Japan* (Boston: Beacon Press, 1957), pp. 13–14.

5. *Japan: An Illustrated Encyclopedia* (Tokyo: Kodansha, 1993), vol. 1, pp. 727–728 (hereafter cited as Kodansha, *Encyclopedia*). During World War II, the word "kamikaze" was applied to pilots who flew suicide attacks on Allied ships.

6. Ryusaku Tsunoda, Wm. Theodore de Bary, and Donald Keene, comps., *Sources of Japanese Tradition* (New York: Columbia University Press, 1958), pp. 523.

7. Hundreds of thousands also died in the famine of the 1780s. In addition to causing starvation, famines forced peasant families to practice infanticide; many also sold daughters to brothels. Mikiso Hane, *Peasants, Rebels, and Outcastes: The Underside of Modern Japan* (New York: Pantheon Books, 1982), pp. 3–8.

8. Tsunoda, de Bary, and Keene, *Sources*, p. 644. For a discussion of the background and implications of the Charter Oath, see Nobutaka Ike, *The Beginnings of Political Democracy in Japan* (Baltimore: Johns Hopkins University Press, 1950).

9. The other major constituent party of the LDP was the Japan Democratic Party, whose roots can be traced to another party formed in the 1880s, the Constitutional Reform Party (Rikken Kaishinto).

10. Carol Gluck noted that the precise meaning of *kokutai* changed in the course of the nineteenth century, depending on the political goals of those invoking the supremacy of the national polity. *Japan's Modern Myths: Ideology in the Late Meiji Period* (Princeton: Princeton University Press, 1985), pp. 143–146. See also her discussion of the drafting of the rescript, pp. 120–124.

11. Tsunoda, de Bary, and Keene, *Sources*, p. 646.

12. Helen Hardacre, *Shinto and the State, 1868–1988* (Princeton: Princeton University Press, 1989), pp. 108–109, 122–123.

13. Also ceded were the Pescadores Islands and the Liaotung (South Manchuria) Peninsula. Under Russian-German-French diplomatic pressure, Japan then gave up Liaotung for an additional indemnity from China. John K. Fairbank, Edwin O. Reischauer, and Albert M. Craig, *East Asia: The Modern Transformation*, vol. 2 (Boston: Houghton Mifflin Co., 1965), pp. 382–384.

14. H. Paul Varley, *Japanese Culture*, 3d ed. (Honolulu: University of Hawaii Press, 1984), p. 238.

15. One sign of growing nationalism in Korea was a virtual rebellion against Japanese control in 1908–1910. The Japanese governor in Korea was assassinated in 1909 by a Korean patriot, and annexation followed the next year.

16. Fairbank, Reischauer, and Craig, *East Asia*, p. 498.

17. Hane, *Peasants*, pp. 172–204.

18. By the 1930s, cotton textile production had replaced silk as Japan's main export industry, accounting for one-fourth of all Japanese exports. Cotton-spinning firms employed over one-half of all industrial workers and over 80 percent of all female industrial workers. Barbara Molony, "Activism Among Women in the Taisho

Cotton Textile Industry," in Gail Lee Bernstein, ed. *Recreating Japanese Women, 1600–1945* (Berkeley: University of California Press, 1991), pp. 219–220, nn. 9, 14.

19. The Taisho emperor, Meiji's son, reigned from 1912 to 1925. On the politics of this period and the failure of democratic party government in the 1930s, see Robert A. Scalapino, *Democracy and the Party Movement in Prewar Japan: The Failure of the First Attempt* (Berkeley and Los Angeles: University of California Press, 1953); and Gordon Mark Berger, *Parties out of Power in Japan, 1931–1941* (Princeton: Princeton University Press, 1977).

20. Gregory J. Kasza, "The State and the Organization of Women in Prewar Japan," *Japan Foundation Newsletter* 18, no. 2 (October 1990), pp. 2–13.

21. For excerpts from the text, see Tsunoda, de Bary, and Keene, *Sources*, pp. 785–794. The complete text, with introduction, is in Robert King Hall, ed., and John Owen Gauntlett, trans., *Kokutai no hongi* (Cardinal principles of the national entity of Japan) (Newton, Mass.: Crofton, 1974).

22. Readers might see in these views a Japanese, or East Asian, version of the "stereotyping" found in the Orientalism discussed in Chapter 1 of this book. Might this be labeled "Occidentalism"?

23. Edwin O. Reischauer, *The Japanese* (Cambridge: Harvard University Press, 1978), p. 104.

24. Among the most interesting of the many sources on the occupation are Toshio Nishi, *Unconditional Democracy: Education and Politics in Occupied Japan, 1945–1952* (Stanford: Hoover Institution Press, Stanford University, 1982); Howard B. Schonberger, *Aftermath of War: Americans and the Remaking of Japan, 1945–1952* (Kent, Ohio: Kent State University Press, 1989); and Richard B. Finn, *Winners in Peace: MacArthur, Yoshida, and Postwar Japan* (Berkeley: University of California Press, 1992). In emphasizing the role of Shigeru Yoshida, Japan's prime minister for two-thirds of the occupation, Finn's study explains the way in which SCAP policies were tempered and filtered by the Japanese upon whom the occupation depended.

25. Schonberger, *Aftermath of War*, chap. 6; Michael Schaller, *The American Occupation of Japan: The Origins of the Cold War in Asia* (London: Oxford University Press, 1985).

26. Lewis D. Hayes, *Introduction to Japanese Politics* (New York: Paragon House, 1992), p. 248.

27. Ibid., pp. 249–254. For example, Japan has the world's largest military shipbuilding industry. Stockholm International Peace Research Institute, *SIPRI Yearbook 1994* (New York: Oxford Press, 1994), pp. 552, 554.

28. *Japan Times Weekly International Edition*, June 22–28, 1992.

29. Miwa Kimitada, "Japanese Policies and Concepts for a Regional Order in Asia, 1938–1940," in James W. White, Michio Umegaki, and Thomas R. H. Havens, eds., *The Ambivalence of Nationalism: Modern Japan Between East and West* (Lanham, Md.: University Press of America, 1990), pp. 133–156.

30. For two different insights into the relationships among modernization, Western influence, and national identity, see Norma Field, *In the Realm of a Dying Emperor* (New York: Pantheon Books, 1991); and Lawrence Olson, *Ambivalent Moderns: Portraits of Japanese Cultural Identity* (Savage, Md.: Rowman and Littlefield, 1992).

# Part Three

# *Government Structures: Form and Substance*

Part One described the demographic and cultural realities that underlie politics in India, China, and Japan. Part Two provided historical background, emphasizing the development of nationalism and the building of modern nation-states. Chapters 1–7 also introduced some public policy issues that illustrate the significance of history and culture in contemporary politics, including the Ayodhya crisis in India, Chinese views on Tibet and Hong Kong, and the "comfort women" and SDF issues in Japan.

Part Three describes government structures, the formal decisionmaking framework within which public policy unfolds. Chapter 8 provides a constitutional overview of the three countries. Chapter 9 then compares the parliamentary systems of India and Japan. Chapter 10 focuses on China, which developed a distinctive governing system after the 1949 revolution. The outstanding characteristic of this system has been the intertwining of Communist Party and state structures that has produced interlocking decisionmaking bodies at the highest levels.

Both Chapters 9 and 10 concentrate on government structures at the national level, whereas Chapter 11 examines the hierarchy of rule from the local levels to the regional and national levels. The phrase "hierarchy of rule" suggests a top-down system of government decisions and enforcement, which is often the case in Asia. But throughout the continent, the dynamics of politics are changing rapidly, in large part as a result of socioeconomic changes that exacerbate the pressures on governments at every level. Popular demands stimulate the creation of new groups and new political ideas. Chapter 11 emphasizes the implications of these new political dynamics for levels of government in India and China, two large states with very different political and cultural histories. Despite their differences, there are some similarities in the pressures for decentralization felt in both countries. The concluding section of Chapter 11 discusses Japan, where the pressures on subnational governments are less dramatic but where important changes are also taking place.

Socioeconomic changes have stimulated greater political participation throughout Asia, raising both old and new questions about the endurance of traditional cultures. The preceding chapters have already shown some of the ways in which indigenous cultural values are reshaped or reinforced in the contemporary era. The Bharatiya Janata Party emphasizes Hindu-Muslim distinctions in its nationalist ideology in India. China's population policy unintentionally reinforces the centuries-old preference for male offspring. The fate of other norms is more complex. Are the strictures of dharma dead as a consequence of urbanization and new forms of grassroots political participation? Or has democracy reinforced caste identity and, with it, dharma? What remains of Confucianism in China and Japan besides patriarchy and bureaucracy? The remainder of the book is intended to provide additional insight into these questions by examining the substance as well as the form of government institutions.

Chapters 8–11 also raise questions about the resilience of the government institutions that have been in place for the last half century. The Japanese government appears the most stable, but even in Japan, the political party system underwent major change in 1993, and the electoral system for the lower house of Parliament was reformed. Meanwhile, China watchers speculated about the viability of the party-state system in the wake of Deng Xiaoping's death and the demise of the Soviet Union, the political pressures symbolized by the events in Tiananmen Square, and the massive impact of rapid economic growth in the 1980s and 1990s. And India? For India, the burning question by the late 1990s seemed to be the survival of the Union itself.

Chapter 1 explained that different approaches to comparison are used in this book. Whereas Chapters 2–7 were essentially separate country studies, Chapter 8 on constitutions compares the three countries sequentially. The structure of Chapter 9 is again a little different: It is divided into a discussion of the primary government institutions in parliamentary systems, the legislatures and dual executives (heads of state and government). After a comparative introduction to each institution, a description of India and Japan follows. Chapter 10, in contrast, includes some diachronic comparison, that is, comparison of changes over time in China's political institutions. The organization of Chapter 11 resembles that of Chapter 8, with a sequential comparison of India, China, and Japan.

# *eight*

 ✎

# Constitutions

Constitutions provide a useful starting point for understanding government structures and procedures, and the evolution of constitutions over time tells us much about political values and behavior. The following sections explain the background of the Indian, Chinese, and Japanese constitutions, then investigate the relationship between the constitutions and politics in the three countries. Each section places the constitution within the historical framework introduced in earlier chapters and summarizes the structure of the document. Short cases illustrate the relevance of the documents to contemporary politics, for it is the political context that over time gives meaning to a constitution.

Constitutions are both descriptions and prescriptions. Their purpose is to describe the institutions of government, as well as the basic norms of governing. They usually include a statement of aspirations that, when understood in historical context, illuminate the circumstances producing the constitution and establish the norms and boundaries for political action. Thus, constitutions link the politics of the present with the past and the future by including citizen rights and duties, government structures and procedures, and amending procedures. All of these are found in the 1950 Indian Constitution, which continues in effect to the present.

## India

The drafting of the Indian Constitution was heavily influenced by the experience of British colonialism and by the nationalist movement, particularly the Indian National Congress, as well as by the interests and background of the delegates to the Constituent Assembly. The assembly served simultaneously as a provisional parliament and a constitutional drafting body. Elected in summer 1946, its members met from December 1946 to December 1949. The Indian National Congress won the over- whelming majority of assembly seats, with the result that the constitu- tional debates were dominated by Congress values and leaders, particu- larly Jawaharlal Nehru.

## Building Constitutionalism in India[1]

Two characteristics of the Constituent Assembly's deliberations explain both the nature of the document that emerged in 1949 and its evolution since. First, the deliberations were generally noncontroversial, largely be- cause much of the constitutional development begun under British rule was continued after Independence. Second, Congress's domination of the assembly insured that when potentially controversial issues did arise, the Congress position would usually prevail. But as the period of post-Inde- pendence unity waned, new political forces brought pressures for consti- tutional amendments. At its drafting, the Indian Constitution was already one of the longest and most complicated constitutions in the world, and these changes made it even more complex.

By the 1990s, the official version of the Indian Constitution was nearly two hundred pages long and contained approximately four hundred arti- cles, ten schedules, and several appendices. It had been amended more than sixty-five times, under a procedure that requires only a two-thirds majority of members present and voting in both houses of Parliament to alter most provisions.[2] Over one-half of the articles, most dealing with In- dia's administrative framework, were taken with generally minor changes from the 1935 Government of India Act passed by the British Par- liament. Thus, the continuity of a parliamentary form of government was guaranteed for independent India.

For students of Indian politics, the most interesting—and typically the most controversial—sections of the Constitution are those pertaining to fundamental rights and directive principles, government emergency powers, and relations between the central and state governments. Part Three of the Constitution contains an extensive list of fundamental rights that define constitutional government in democracies, including the right to freedom of speech, assembly and association, and religion. Also in- cluded are social provisions, such as the "right against exploitation," which prohibits traffic in human beings, forced labor, and child labor. In general, the political rights have been both more controversial and more honored than the social guarantees, reflecting the difficulties of changing long-entrenched widespread practices.

Part Four of the Constitution, entitled "**Directive Principles of State Policy**," is the counterpart to Part Three. The directive principles are not enforceable by any court but were viewed by the framers as principles to be followed in developing and implementing government policy. Whereas Part Three details provisions essential to the spirit of democracy, Part Four contains the vision of social revolution. For example, Article 39 lists "certain principles of policy to be followed by the State," to secure

A. that the citizen[s], men and women equally, have the right to an adequate means of livelihood;
B. that the ownership and control of the material resources of the community are so distributed as best to subserve the common good;
C. that the operation of the economic system does not result in the concentration of wealth and means of production to the common detriment;
D. that there is equal pay for equal work for both men and women.

Part Four also calls on the state in Article 46 to promote the "educational and economic interests of Scheduled Castes, Scheduled Tribes and other weaker sections" to protect them from social injustice and all forms of exploitation. This and related constitutional provisions giving the state a policy mandate to act on behalf of "weaker sections" undergird some of the most controversial government policies undertaken since Independence.

The following discussion briefly reviews the debate over the role of religion in India. The provisions regarding religion reveal some of the ambiguities and contradictions of the Indian Constitution, especially in the sections called Fundamental Rights and Directive Principles of State Policy. Discussion of other controversial areas in the Constitution, notably emergency powers and relations between the Union and state governments, is deferred to later chapters.

## Religion and "Secularism" in the Indian Constitution

Chapter 2 explained the way in which the diversity of the Indian population is grounded in religion, caste, gender, and language. Because religion and caste are historically intertwined in India, the constitutional provisions regarding religion are found both in the elaboration of the fundamental rights that are central to Indian democracy and in articles furthering the goal of social revolution. Part Three established freedom of religion as a fundamental right of Indian citizens. Article 25 (1) states: "Subject to public order, morality and health . . . all persons are equally entitled to freedom of conscience and the right freely to profess, practice and propagate religion." But Article 25 (2) qualifies this further by adding that the state may regulate any secular activity (economic, financial, political) associated with religious practice; and the state may also provide "for social welfare and reform or the throwing open of Hindu religious institutions of a public character to all classes and sections of Hindus." This last provision has the effect of removing, in principle, caste restrictions on access to Hindu institutions such as temples. Similarly, although the completely free exercise of Hindu traditions would continue the practice of untouchability, Article 17 abolishes "Untouchability" (but not caste) and forbids its practice "in any form."

Largely through the campaigns of the Bharatiya Janata Party, the question of whether India is and should be a secular democracy reemerged in the political debates of the 1980s and 1990s. Acutely aware of the implications of religion for national unity, India's independence leaders were committed to establishing a secular, democratic republic. For a variety of reasons, the word "secular" was not included in the Constitution until 1976, when it was added by amendment to the preamble (it is not found elsewhere in the document). Yet it is clear that the Constituent Assembly presumed that India would have a secular democracy without, obviously, being a secular society. This distinction between a secular polity and secular society is worth emphasizing as an important part of the puzzle of contemporary Indian politics. Stated simply: Can—and should—a society in which the overwhelming majority of people share the fundamentals of a Hindu worldview and make no distinction between secular and sacred aspire to a government that does not reflect this *Hindu* reality? The answers are multiple, as we will see throughout this book, and they all bear on the continued viability of the Constitution and the goal of national unity.

Scholars point out the inherent problems in using the English word "secular" for India, and they imply that these difficulties help account for the word's absence from the original version of the Constitution. Secularism is inextricably linked to the European experience of conflict and distinction between church and state. Thus imbued with historical and cultural meaning, secularism implies a distancing from religion that is ill-suited to the Indian context. In contrast, the Indian Constitution assumes state neutrality and even-handedness toward different religions, modified by the social goals noted earlier.[3] Executing the principle of even-handedness, however, has been extremely difficult. Nowhere is this better illustrated than in the widely publicized **Shah Bano case**, which inflamed political passions and raised questions about constitutional principle and legal intent. The broader philosophical issue raised by the case is how minority rights are to be protected in a liberal democracy.

**Shah Bano.**   The Shah Bano case began in the late 1970s, when Shah Bano's husband of forty-three years divorced her. He returned her *mehr*, or marriage settlement, a sum of about US$300, as required by Islamic law. She then sued for maintenance under the Criminal Procedure Code of India. A regional court awarded her maintenance, but her former husband appealed the judgment to the Supreme Court of India on the grounds that as a Muslim he had to obey the Sharia (the body of Islamic law), which required that he pay maintenance for three months only. The Supreme Court ruled that under the criminal code, a husband was required to pay maintenance to a wife without means of support. In his written opinion, however, the chief justice went further in his comments to call for a common civil code for all Indians.

The justice's argument epitomized a secular definition of the ideal nation-state, but it was viewed as an imminent threat to Muslims whose rights to community identity have been protected by the Indian legal system, which provides for state guarantees of Muslim and Christian (but not Hindu) laws in "private" matters of marriage, divorce, and inheritance. Although there have been many demands over the years for a common civil code,[4] communal tensions between Muslims and Hindus have generally guaranteed that Muslims who feel threatened by the Hindu majority will resist any policies seen as encroachments on their community laws and practices.

The Supreme Court ruling, combined with the chief justice's statements, generated more Muslim-Hindu conflict throughout India. Muslim religious leaders denounced the decision as interference in the rights of the Muslim community, and thousands of Muslims protested in the streets. Initially, the government, headed by Prime Minister Rajiv Gandhi, defended the court ruling and the secular authority of the state. Ultimately, however, the government backed down over fear of the political implications of its position: In dozens of hotly contested parliamentary constituencies, Gandhi's Congress Party depended on Muslim votes. Even though the overwhelming majority of Hindus—many of whom doubtless viewed Muslims as a legally privileged community—supported the court ruling, the government proposed legislation exempting Muslims from the provisions of the criminal procedure code that required husbands to support divorced wives. The Muslim Women (Protection of Rights on Divorce) Bill was passed despite widespread opposition, leaving unresolved the meaning of religious freedom in the Constitution and adding to the store of questions about the viability of secular democracy in India. The Shah Bano case also raised an important question about the relationship between *individual* and *group* rights. As Aimslee Embree observed:

> There [appears] to be some confusion in India, as in other liberal democracies, between the concept of religious freedom, one of the most cherished rights that has emerged in the long struggle of the individual against the state, and the concept of group rights. Religious freedom, in . . . the Indian constitution, means the right to practice and propagate one's faith without hindrance from the state, but increasingly this has been interpreted to mean

that the government should, in effect, support through law the customs that a community claims are basic to its internal life.

The assertion that groups have rights that cannot be challenged by the majority decision of voters as expressed through the legislature is based on the argument that the nation is an aggregate of groups, not of individuals.[5]

The tension among individuals, groups, and the state in India raises questions not only about the future of secular democracy but also about national unity and integrity. For now, it is important to stress that the Indian Constitution, the philosophies behind it, and the debates it generates are central to the dynamics of Indian politics.

# Japan

Chapter 7 concluded with a summary of the 1947 Japanese Constitution, which was adopted early in the postwar occupation of Japan. The status and role of the Self Defense Forces illustrates the way in which a constitutional question became the focus of public debate. More than any other section of the Constitution, of course, Article 9 raises the broader issue of the legitimacy of the entire document. To what extent can one expect that a constitution adopted under foreign tutelage, a document that deliberately curtailed a critical attribute of national sovereignty, would be accepted as legitimate by Japanese citizens? The answer to this question lies both in the origins of the Japanese Constitution and in its political and legal life since 1947.

## *The Occupation and the Japanese Constitution*[6]

Within two weeks of his arrival in Japan, General MacArthur stated that Japan's Constitution should be revised, and the following month, he issued a "bill of rights" directive ordering the Japanese government to free all political prisoners and remove all restrictions on political, civil, and religious liberties. The Japanese government was already working on election reform and by mid-December 1945, had passed a law giving all citizens over the age of twenty the right to vote. Meanwhile, three dozen political parties had formed (or reformed), and the forces that would come to dominate postwar Japanese politics were taking shape.

The importance of these activities is that in the space of four months, the movement for major political reform was well underway on both the Japanese and the occupation sides. SCAP was not operating in a vacuum or without the knowledge of Japanese leaders. The rebirth of Japan's political parties, in turn, brought a surge of debate about reform, particularly among those on the Left whose voices had been silenced by political repression in the 1930s and early 1940s. The tone of this momentous period was set at the end of 1945, when the emperor issued a New Year's rescript restating the Charter Oath of 1868 and renouncing the beliefs that the emperor was "divine" and that the Japanese people were superior. With this rescript and the other changes of the early occupation, essential constitutional principles were in place before any new document was drawn up.

In early 1946, MacArthur made the decision to draft a new Constitution without consulting either U.S. allies, the U.S. government in Washington, D.C., or the Japanese government. By moving so quickly, he planned to affirm the new position of the emperor (thus stilling demands for elimination of the imperial institution) and to link Japan's future to pacifism. SCAP officials, who took barely one week to produce a draft in February 1946, became, in effect, Japan's "constitutional convention."

When the American draft was presented to Japanese leaders responsible for implementing occupation policy, the officials were shocked by the Americans' sudden and direct pressure. MacArthur's argument that the SCAP Constitution offered the best way to preserve the imperial institution, however truncated, ultimately persuaded the Japanese government, but not without opposition in the Cabinet, and not without the emperor's intervention.[7] Even at this point, Japanese leaders were concerned about the implications of the no-war clause demanded by the Americans. Japanese negotiators subsequently succeeded in making some changes in the draft, but its essence was not altered, and on March 6, 1946, an imperial rescript approved the constitutional proposal.

From late spring to early fall 1946, the draft Constitution was debated in the wider political arena. Elections for the first postwar House of Representatives, the lower house of the Diet, were held in April 1946. Over the course of the late spring and summer, special Diet committees examined the proposed Constitution and the Diet amended the draft numerous times. Some of the amendments were minor and others were relatively significant, but none altered the basic structure or intent of the original SCAP draft.

Not surprisingly, the no-war clause was again scrutinized, with numerous questions raised about Japan's eventual ability to defend itself. One of the Diet committees studying the draft proposed a wording change to Article 9 that, however subtle, was significant because it established the basis for justifying the Self Defense Forces. The change (shown here in italics) was the addition of introductory phrases to each of the two paragraphs in the article: "*Aspiring sincerely to an international peace based on justice and order*, the Japanese people forever renounce war as a sovereign right"; and "*In order to accomplish the aim of the preceding paragraph*, land, sea, and air forces . . . will never be maintained." As interpreted by successive Japanese governments, this wording linked the "renunciation of war" to the existence of a peaceful international order and rejected the maintenance of war potential for the purpose of settling disputes but did not exclude self-defense.[8]

Both houses of the Diet overwhelmingly approved the new Constitution in October 1946, technically as an amendment to the 1889 Constitution. The emperor promulgated the Constitution in November, and it went into effect in May 1947. Despite lingering dissatisfaction over the existence of Article 9 and support for revision among conservative politicians, the Constitution has never been revised.[9]

## Constitutional Evolution and Legitimacy

The Japanese Constitution is much shorter than its Indian and Chinese counterparts. Approximately one dozen pages long, it begins with a lengthy preamble that introduces popular sovereignty in language in which the American imprint is unmistakable.

> We, the Japanese people, acting through our duly elected representatives . . . do proclaim that sovereign power resides with the people and do firmly establish this Constitution. Government is a sacred trust of the people, the authority for which is derived from the people, the powers of which are exercised by the representatives of the people, and the benefits of which are enjoyed by the people. This is a universal principle of mankind upon which this Constitution is founded.

The Constitution contains 103 articles divided into twenty-one chapters, including Chapter 2 (Article 9), "Renunciation of War." In sequence, the document defines the role of the emperor, the rights and duties of the people, and the functions of the Diet, Cabinet, and judiciary. Additional chapters address finance, local government, and the amending process. Chapter 10 reiterates the underlying philosophy of American constitutionalism that basic rights are not created by a constitutional document (where they might be removed through amendment or legislation) but are recognized and safeguarded by the Constitution. This is an important distinction for any constitutional order, but especially so for Japan, which historically had a different legal tradition than the United States. The 1889 Constitution *had* defined *subjects'* rights and duties but had qualified them with the statement that they existed "within the limits of the law." It was, in fact, the Diet that had passed the laws suppressing freedom from the end of the nineteenth century through World War II.

Chapter 3, "Rights and Duties of the People," is the longest chapter, with thirty-one articles addressing a wide range of civil and social rights. Some provisions recall familiar civil rights and liberties, such as the "right to life, liberty, and the pursuit of happiness," freedom of religion, freedom of assembly and association, and the right to be secure in the home against unwarranted searches and seizures. Other provisions reflect twentieth-century thinking about social and economic concerns on the list of citizen rights. Article 14, providing for equality under the law and specifying no discrimination in political, economic, or social relations "because of race, creed, sex, social status or family origin" is one example. The Constitution also states that "children shall not be exploited" (Article 27) and guarantees the availability of compulsory and free education to both boys and girls.

What has been the fate of these and other key provisions of the Constitution? For example, Article 81 establishes the principle of what Americans know as judicial review: "The Supreme Court is the court of last resort with power to determine the constitutionality of any law, order, regulation or official act." Yet judicial review and the Supreme Court in general have shown few signs of assuming the prominence in Japan that they have in the United States (see Chapter 13). The reasons for this are both political and cultural, and they explain the wide-ranging acceptance of, but relative disinterest in, the Constitution as a whole. In one study, for example, legal scholar Frank Upham has examined the way in which an elite Japanese bureaucracy strives to limit recourse to litigation in favor of administrative intervention in disputes, all as part of a broader effort to control social change. Upham stressed that this has not prevented the courts from playing an important role in some political and social conflicts but it *has* privileged government bureaucrats.[10] Clearly, this pattern is consistent with a history of government initiative and leadership in socioeconomic matters that dates to the Tokugawa period. Thus, what some see as a cultural preference for "informal" solutions to conflict (such as mediation) may also be seen as another illustration of elite, state-managed efforts to maintain social stability and control change. This pattern helps explain why Japanese courts often defer to administrators or politicians for dispute resolution and, more particularly, explains why the Supreme Court has not asserted its constitutional prerogatives in judicial review.

Article 9 of the Japanese Constitution *has* generated cases for judicial review of the SDF's constitutionality, but both the lower courts and the Supreme Court have resolved the technical questions in the cases without ruling on the constitutional question of the SDF's status, viewing the issue as outside the scope of their jurisdiction.[11] Although from one perspective this response seems like an excessively narrow definition of judicial prerogative, from another, it is true that the SDF is only one part of a much broader debate about Japanese foreign policy, relations with other countries (especially the United States), and, therefore, national identity and self-determination.[12]

# China

China's history of constitutionalism is both checkered and disjointed. The essence of European and American constitutions—that the power of the state is defined and restrained by basic law—is absent from the Chinese political tradition. True, as Chapter 6 explained, the Confucian emphasis on moral principles coexisted with a Legalist tradition dating to the third century B.C.E. The early Legalists argued that all, including emperor and ministers, should be equally obedient to the law. The rationale for this position, however, lay in the desire to strengthen the state in an era of war and cutthroat political competition. The Legalist school of political philosophy ultimately gave way to the Confucianist. Although Emperor Qin Shi Huangdi used Legalist doctrines to unite China, crush his opponents, and create an effective, centralized bureaucratic rule, his son rejected Legalism. Succeeding rulers also abandoned the comprehensive Legalist recipe for governing, in large part out of repugnance for the authoritarianism of the Qin state. Neither bureaucratic rule nor Legalist principles disappeared, of course, and their endurance reinforced China's long history of privileging the authority of the state, of rulers over subjects. Thus, law has traditionally been viewed as a tool at the service of the state; it never evolved as part of a broader constitutional philosophy of limiting the scope or powers of government for the benefit of the individual.

## *The Search for Constitutional Government*

Modern ideas of constitutionalism were introduced into China in the early twentieth century. It will be recalled from Chapter 6 that by the nineteenth century, the Qing dynasty was disintegrating. Qing rule ended shortly after the first decade of the twentieth century, a period of rapid political change and government reform efforts. Japan's successful modernization inspired Chinese reformers to look to constitutionalism as one way to unite rulers and ruled in the new era of the nation-state. In 1908, the empress dowager proclaimed a set of principles for a nine-year program to prepare China for constitutional self-government. But both she and the emperor died before the year was over and political turmoil soon derailed the program.[13]

As leader of the Republican movement, Sun Yat-sen also proposed a nine-year transition to constitutional government, but his plans were overtaken by the events of the early Republican period. China's first Constitution, drafted and promulgated in 1912 by a national council of provincial delegates supporting the Republican cause, was never implemented. A second provisional Constitution was written in the early 1930s, but it too fell victim to political chaos, and not until 1947 was another

Constitution promulgated. This Constitution had a short life in mainland China, but when the Nationalists moved their government to Taiwan in 1949, they took with them the Constitution that is still found in the Republic of China.[14]

## Constitutional Change in the PRC

The People's Republic of China has had four different state constitutions since it came to power in 1949, each indicating a different phase of China's political evolution. The 1954 Constitution signaled the consolidation of the new revolutionary regime that came to power in late 1949; the 1975 Constitution marked the transition from the Cultural Revolution to a period of normalization but was followed by a new document in 1978 that reflected the priorities of the leaders who rose to prominence after the death of Mao Zedong in 1976. The 1982 Constitution, which is still in force, signaled the ascendancy of Deng Xiaoping. In addition to these four documents, the Chinese Communist Party, China's ruling party, adopted five different constitutions during this same period. The first was in 1956, two years after the state Constitution, and the last was adopted in 1982, the same year in which the most recent state Constitution was adopted. In view of the preeminent role of the CCP, studying the role of constitutions in Chinese politics necessarily includes both the state and the party documents—a total of nine between 1954 and 1982.

The procedures for drafting and issuing both state and party constitutions have been similar: deliberation and writing by a committee of high-ranking leaders under the direction of preeminent leaders such as Mao Zedong or Deng Xiaoping and approval by either the National People's Congress (state) or the CCP National Party Congress. This ratification process has helped legitimize both the constitutional document and the political changes it marked. Only the 1954 state Constitution appears to have been subjected to widespread public deliberation prior to legislative ratification. The following historical overview shows the rhythm of constitutional change and the role of constitutions in reestablishing legitimacy after major political shifts.

## The Early Constitutions

Between 1949 and 1954, the PRC operated under the legitimacy and authority created by the successful revolutionary leadership of the Communist Party and a series of basic laws that established the structure of the central government and outlined programmatic goals. Although the Communist Party was the dominant political force in the PRC, these early years were characterized by efforts to build support for the new government among other "democratic" (non-Communist, anti-Kuomintang) groups. Coalition building and legitimizing the regime were made all the more urgent by China's engagement in the Korean War in late 1950. The combination of external threats and domestic consolidation delayed drafting of a state Constitution until 1953.

When the new leaders were confident that the revolution was secure, they submitted a constitutional draft, prepared by a government committee chaired by Mao Zedong, to public discussion. In spring 1954, over 150 million people reportedly participated in discussion meetings that produced over one hundred thousand proposed amendments, some of which eventually were adopted.[15] This exercise was less important for the content of proposed or actual changes than for the way in which it contributed to the legitimacy of the new regime.

Both consolidation and experimentation prompted the adoption of a Constitution in 1956 for the Communist Party as well. This party Constitution remained in force until 1969, when the radical phase of the Cultural Revolution subsided. The events of the Cultural Revolution, however, had rendered both the party and state constitutions irrelevant to the dynamics of politics.

From 1969 to 1978, three party and two state constitutions were issued. Taken together, they reflected the turbulence of the Cultural Revolution and the struggle over succession to Mao Zedong that are described in Chapter 10. One of the Cultural Revolution's immediate effects was to elevate the military's role in politics when the People's Liberation Army became the only institution capable of restoring public order. The Ninth Party Congress of the CCP (April 1969) signaled the phase of stabilization after the Cultural Revolution. Forty percent of those present at the Congress were army officers and the newly adopted Communist Party Constitution identified **Lin Biao**, China's defense minister, as the "heir apparent" to Mao Zedong. The following year, party leaders secretly drafted a new state Constitution, but the looming succession struggle intercepted its publication and ratification.[16]

The elevation of Lin Biao as constitutionally designated successor to Mao heralded the expanded power of the military in China's politics. But the growth of military influence produced a counterreaction among civilian leaders of the party. A new party Constitution in 1973 and a state Constitution in 1975 marked another shift in power. Premier **Zhou Enlai**, China's number two leader, and Mao Zedong both died in 1976. Immediately after Mao's death, maneuvering to replace him reached a peak. The Central Committee of the Communist Party announced in October 1976 that Hua Guofeng would succeed Mao as party chairman. A new CCP Constitution in 1977, followed by a third state Constitution in 1978, legitimized the new coalition that emerged after Mao's death and presumably marked the end of nearly two decades of struggle over leadership.

TABLE 8.1   State and Party Constitutions in the People's Republic of China

|  | *Political Event* | *Constitutions of the PRC* | *Constitutions of the CCP* |
|---|---|---|---|
| 1949 | PRC founded | — | — |
| 1950–1953 | Korean War | — | — |
| 1954 |  | yes | — |
| 1956 |  | — | yes |
| 1966 | Cultural Revolution begins | — | — |
| 1969 |  | — | yes |
| 1971 | Lin Biao dies | — | — |
| 1973 |  | — | yes |
| 1975 |  | yes | — |
| 1976 | Death of Mao Zedong; Hua Guofeng becomes party-state leader | — | — |
| 1977 |  | — | yes |
| 1978 |  | yes | — |
| 1979–1980 | Hua loses positions; rise of Deng Xiaoping | — | — |
| 1982 |  | yes | yes |
| 1987 |  | — | amended |
| 1988 |  | amended | — |
| 1992 |  | — | amended |
| 1993 |  | amended | — |
| 1997 | Death of Deng Xiaoping | — | — |

In fact, however, Hua Guofeng himself turned out to be a transition leader. Deng Xiaoping, twice purged in earlier conflicts among leadership factions, skillfully rebuilt his party support in the late 1970s. His supporters came to control the Central Committee and Politburo, the top CCP organs, and by 1980 were secure enough to begin the process of drafting new constitutions for the party and the state. Two years later, the CCP and the PRC both had new constitutions, documents that have remained in place into the late 1990s. Table 8.1 summarizes these key events in China's post-1949 political history and shows the dates of the nine state and party constitutions adopted from the 1950s to the 1980s.

This checkered history of constitutional change illustrates the different roles that Chinese constitutions play, in contrast to the role of the constitution in India and Japan. Constitutions become fictive when they are overtaken by events that leave them outdated. Nonetheless, Chinese leaders obviously view these documents as an important part of the process of legitimizing new leaders and new policies. The documents also explain the formal structures of power and tell us much about official ideology and policy goals.

## *The 1982 Constitutions*

One of the distinguishing features of both state and party Chinese constitutions is a lengthy introduction or preamble that seeks to legitimize the political system through reminders of China's historical greatness and the revolutionary missions of the PRC and the CCP. Statements of broad policy goals are also woven into the preambles. In general, these preambles serve the same purpose as the much shorter introductions to the Japanese and American constitutions: They link the past, present, and future through idealistic visions and ideological assertions. The following excerpts from the 1982 state Constitution of the PRC illustrate this linkage.

> China is a country with one of the longest histories in the world. The people of all of China's nationalities have jointly created a culture of grandeur and have a glorious revolutionary tradition.
>
> After 1840, feudal China was gradually turned into a semi-colonial and semi-feudal country. The Chinese people waged many successive heroic struggles for national independence and liberation and for democracy and freedom. . . .
>
> After waging protracted and arduous struggles, armed and otherwise . . . the Chinese people of all nationalities led by the Communist Party of China with Chairman Mao Zedong as its leader ultimately, in 1949, overthrew the rule of imperialism, feudalism and bureaucrat-capitalism . . . and founded the People's Republic of China.

Comparing the introductions with specific constitutional provisions further illuminates the rationale for important Chinese policies, both domestic and foreign. For example, the preamble and various articles of the PRC Constitution state the official policy on national minorities discussed earlier in Chapter 3. The section quoted above refers to "the Chinese people of all nationalities," acknowledging the diversity that is reemphasized in a later paragraph that warns against "Han chauvinism." This same paragraph, however, affirms that the People's Republic of China is a *"unitary* multinational state" [emphasis added] and cautions that it is also necessary to "combat local national chauvinism." Local national chauvinism would include activities by any ethnic groups seen as a threat to national unity. Article 4 of the Constitution suggests both the supportive and the limiting nature of the policies toward minorities:

> All nationalities in the People's Republic of China are equal. . . . The state assists areas inhabited by minority nationalities in accelerating their economic and cultural development according to the characteristics and needs of the various minority nationalities.
>
> Regional autonomy is practiced in areas where people of minority nationalities live in concentrated communities . . . All national autonomous areas are integral parts of the People's Republic of China.

By extending the logic of the central historical goal of modern China—national unity and independence—the Constitution also signals the official policy toward Taiwan: "Taiwan is part of the sacred territory of the People's Republic of China. It is the inviolable duty of all Chinese people, including our compatriots in Taiwan, to accomplish the great task of reunifying the motherland."

The CCP Constitution includes the same themes found in the state Constitution. Its introduction discusses at greater length the nature of "socialist democracy" in China, as well as the role of the Communist Party in nation building and economic development. Whereas the PRC Constitution explains the organization of the state, including the role of the National People's Congress, the president, and the State Council, the CCP Constitution lays out the criteria for party membership and describes party organization.

Taken together, the constitutions serve as a guide to the chief ideological tenets that drive Chinese politics. They also explain, in broad terms, the organizational framework for both the state and the Communist Party. They are not reliable guides to the daily operations of the government, party, or other important political organs, such as the military—but of course this is true of constitutions in general. The party-state leadership clearly views constitutions as important for marking and legitimizing change, hence the frequency with which the documents are redrafted or amended. The 1993 amendments to the state Constitution illustrate these roles and also shed light on the dynamics of party-state relations in the constitutional change process.

The 1993 National People's Congress, like the 1992 National Party Congress, was a bridge to the post-Deng era. The new leadership, like new policy mandates, came from the central organs of the Communist Party, the Central Committee, the Politburo, and its Standing Committee. The revisions to the PRC Constitution were formally proposed by the Central Committee to mark China's economic and political changes since the late 1970s. All of these revisions were foreshadowed by amendments to the party Constitution ratified at the 1992 Party Congress. The amendments introduced the language of a "socialist market economy" into the Constitution, replacing the emphasis on a state-run, centrally planned economy. A number of changes throughout the Constitution thus brought the document into line with the evolution of Chinese national development in the post-Mao Zedong period.[17]

## Summary

For all three countries, the idea of constitutionalism was a late-nineteenth-century import from the West, and one of the outstanding characteristics of the Indian and Japanese constitutions is the degree to which they still bear the imprint of Britain and the United States, respectively. In contrast to China, India and Japan continue to operate under the norms and institutions laid out in their post–World War II constitutions, documents that have established, in large part, the fundamental legitimacy of the two democracies (whereas in China fundamental legitimacy has been created and recreated by the Communist Party). In Japan and India, as in most countries, constitutional provisions may be ignored or bypassed. This is becoming a greater problem in India, and one may speculate that if the Indian Constitution is becoming more fictive, it is due to the weight of the political problems and conflicts confronting the country. These conflicts, in turn, guarantee that constitutional issues play a greater role in the vigorous debate about India's future than they do for either Japan or China.

# Notes

1. On the origin and structure of the Constitution, see Granville Austin, *The Indian Constitution: Cornerstone of a Nation* (Oxford: Clarendon Press, 1966) and "The Constitution, Society, and Law," in Philip Oldenburg, ed., *India Briefing—1993* (Boulder: Westview Press, with the Asia Society, 1993), pp. 103–129.

2. The exceptions are provisions pertaining to the election of the president, the structure and functions of the Supreme Court, the high courts in the states, legislative relations between the Union and state governments, and the distribution of functions between the Union and state governments as found in the Seventh Schedule. Amendments to these provisions require that at least one-half of the state legislatures also approve the change. For a discussion of the issues pertaining to the ease of constitutional amendment, see Ramesh Thakur, *The Government and Politics of India* (New York: St. Martin's Press, 1995), pp. 60–61.

3. For a discussion of these and related issues, see the essays in M. M. Sankhdher, ed., *Secularism in India: Dilemmas and Challenges* (New Delhi: Deep and Deep, 1992), and G. M. Banatwalla, *Religion and Politics in India* (Bombay: G. M. Banatwalla/India Book Distributors, 1992).

4. Article 44 of the Constitution (in Part Four, Directive Principles of State Policy) says that "the State shall endeavor to secure for the citizens a uniform civil code throughout the territory of India." In the nineteenth century, the British adopted a policy of permitting Hindus to be governed by Hindu laws and Muslims by Muslim laws in family matters, and this policy was carried over after independence, despite Article 44. The result is a patchwork of laws, practices, and state and Supreme Court decisions concerning such matters as marriage, divorce, maintenance, inheritance, and adoption throughout India.

5. Ainslie T. Embree, *Utopias in Conflict: Religion and Nationalism in Modern India* (Delhi: Oxford University Press, 1990), pp. 91–92.

6. The information in this section relies primarily on the following sources: Richard B. Finn, *Winners in Peace: MacArthur, Yoshida, and Postwar Japan* (Berkeley: University of California Press, 1992); Robert E. Ward, "Presurrender Planning:

Treatment of the Emperor and Constitutional Changes" and Theodore H. Mc-Nelly, "'Induced Revolution': The Policy and Process of Constitutional Reform in Occupied Japan," both to be found in Robert E. Ward and Sakamoto Yoshikazu, eds., *Democratizing Japan: The Allied Occupation* (Honolulu: University of Hawaii Press, 1987), pp. 1–41 and 76–106, respectively; Yoshida Shigeru, *The Yoshida Memoirs: The Story of Japan in Crisis* (Boston: Houghton Mifflin and Cambridge: Riverside Press, 1962), chap. 13; and Koichi Kishimoto, *Politics in Modern Japan: Development and Organization*, 3d ed. (Tokyo: Japan Echo, 1988), chap. 3.

7. Finn, *Winners in Peace*, pp. 99–100; Yoshida, *Memoirs*, p. 135.

8. Key SCAP officials also apparently understood the modifications as permitting defense forces. McNelly, "'Induced Revolution,'" pp. 92–93.

9. A commission on the Constitution explored revision from 1956 to 1964 and recommended amendments supported by conservative politicians. Lacking sufficient political support for revision, however, the amendments were never submitted to the Diet. Ibid., pp. 99–100.

10. Frank K. Upham, *Law and Social Change in Postwar Japan* (Cambridge: Harvard University Press, 1987).

11. Kishimoto, *Politics in Modern Japan*, pp. 46–47; James E. Auer, "Article Nine: Renunciation of War," in Percy R. Luney, Jr., and Kazuyuki Takahashi, *Japanese Constitutional Law* (Tokyo: University of Tokyo Press, 1993), pp. 80–81.

12. Ironically, challenges to SDF constitutionality came from left-wing groups opposed also to the Japan-U.S. 1951 Treaty of Mutual Cooperation and Security. However, ultranationalists opposed to the postwar U.S.-Japanese partnership sought to revise the Constitution to eliminate Article 9 or even to draft a new constitution. On balance, public opinion has supported the unrevised Constitution, mutual security with the United States, and continuation of the ambiguous (but changing) role of the SDF.

13. John K. Fairbank, Edwin O. Reischauer, and Albert M. Craig, *East Asia: The Modern Transformation* (Boston: Houghton Mifflin, 1965), pp. 625–631; Jonathan D. Spence, *The Search for Modern China* (New York: W. W. Norton, 1990), pp. 245–249.

14. Chi-tung Lin and Herbert H. P. Ma, "The Constitution and Government of the Republic of China," trans. John W. Garver and Herbert H. P. Ma, in Lawrence W. Beer, ed., *Constitutional Systems in Late Twentieth-Century Asia* (Seattle: University of Washington Press, 1992), pp. 88–127. The ROC Constitution was extensively amended in the 1990s to reflect changing circumstances.

15. Leslie Wolf-Phillips, ed., *Constitutions of Modern States: Selected Texts and Commentary* (New York: Praeger, 1968), p. 2.

16. For the text, see Winberg Chai, introduction and "Text of the 1970 Draft of the Revised Constitution of the People's Republic of China," *Studies in Comparative Communism* 4, no. 1 (January 1971), pp. 97–106.

17. Chen Qiuping, "Constitution Amended to Advance a Market Economy," *Beijing Review*, 36 (April 26–May 2, 1993), pp. 14–16.

# *nine*

# The Parliamentary System in Asia: India and Japan

The formal government structures in India, China, and Japan conform to what political scientists call a "parliamentary system," whose chief features are found in Great Britain (thus the term "Westminster system" is also used). This chapter first reviews the nature of parliamentary systems and then compares the way they operate in India and Japan. Discussion of China is deferred to Chapter 10 because, despite the resemblance to parliamentary structures found in the Chinese government, the preeminent role of the Communist Party has created a unique structure of power.

## Parliamentary Systems

In a parliamentary system, the legislature is theoretically the primary institution reflecting the will of the people. The political authority of the executive rests with the prime minister and the Cabinet, which together derive their mandate from and are responsible to the legislature, or Parliament. This cabinet government (the prime minister and Cabinet ministers) can govern only so long as Parliament grants its support or confidence. The head of government, generally called the prime minister, is usually the leader of the largest party in the legislature, and this party may hold a majority of seats by itself or, alternatively, may be the largest of several parties in a coalition government. Both situations have occurred in India and Japan in the last decade. The members of Parliament (MPs) are directly elected by the voters, and the Cabinet ministers usually retain their legislative seats while they serve in the government. In this manner, there is a **fusion of powers** in parliamentary systems that contrasts with the separation of powers found in presidential systems such as that of the United States.

In addition to the prime minister, who is the political executive, parliamentary systems also have a symbolic executive or head of state. The head of state represents the historical continuity, dignity, and ongoing legal authority of the nation-state that transcends the political majorities resulting from periodic elections. Although the head of state may be called the president (as in India), the coexistence of this position with a prime minister distinguishes the system as parliamentary, not presidential. The head of state formally appoints a prime minister, accepts the resignation of a government, and calls elections, but these functions are exercised only on the advice of the prime minister and under defined constitutional limits.

There are numerous variations on this basic parliamentary pattern. By way of illustration, heads of state may differ: some inherit their positions (monarchs), whereas others are indirectly elected, for example by an electoral college; legislatures may be bicameral or unicameral; and the ways in which the prime minister and Cabinet secure legislative support or confidence also vary. To appreciate this diversity and better understand the democratic rationale of parliamentary systems, let us turn to the Indian and Japanese cases.

## Legislative Framework

Both India and Japan have bicameral legislatures, with the lower house in each case being the more powerful of the two bodies. The lower houses are directly elected by the voters and have greater legislative power (especially in money matters), and the government is responsible to and must have the confidence of the lower house. It is in this relationship between the government and the lower house of Parliament that the Westminster model has left its stamp on the political institutions of the two countries.

### The Indian Parliament

The Indian national Parliament consists of the lower house, the **Lok Sabha** (House of the People), and the upper house, the **Rajya Sabha** (Council of States), and the president of India.[1] All but two of the Lok

Sabha members are elected from single-member constituencies through-out India's states and Union Territories; two representatives of the Anglo-Indian community may be appointed by the president if, in the words of the Constitution, "he is of the opinion that the Anglo-Indian community is not adequately represented" (Article 331). The term of the Lok Sabha, like that of the British House of Commons, is five years, unless it is dis-solved sooner. Under a proclamation of emergency, however, the presi-dent of India may extend the life of the Lok Sabha by one year at a time, although not for longer than six months after the term of the emergency proclamation expires.

The Rajya Sabha is less than one-half the size of the 545-member Lok Sabha; the Constitution limits it to 250 members, twelve of whom are nominated by the president in recognition of their "special knowledge or practical experience" in literature, science, art, or social service (Article 80). The remainder are elected by the state legislative assemblies accord-ing to a formula that allocates seats to the states in approximate propor-tion to the size of their population. The primary purpose of the Rajya Sabha, as this system of indirect election suggests, is to emphasize the role of the states in India's federal system (see Chapter 11). Unlike the Lok Sabha, the Rajya Sabha may not be dissolved. Its terms are staggered so that (as in the case of the U.S. Senate), one-third of the membership is elected every two years.

With the exception of "money bills" dealing with taxation, borrowing, or spending, legislation may be introduced in either house. Not only must money bills originate in the Lok Sabha, but the Rajya Sabha may only delay—not stop—passage of a money bill approved by the Lok Sabha. Other legislation, however, must be approved by both houses.

## *The Japanese Diet*[2]

There are numerous similarities between the houses of the Japanese Diet and those of the Indian Parliament. The lower house, the larger of the two, is the House of Representatives. Its five hundred members are all elected for four-year terms, although the House (like the Lok Sabha) may be dis-solved sooner if the Cabinet so decides.[3] Early dissolution in Japan, like In-dia, Britain, and other parliamentary systems, may occur either when the government loses the confidence of the lower house or when the prime minister seeks to increase his or her party's strength in Parliament. Al-though the Japanese Constitution makes it clear that the Cabinet must maintain the confidence of the House of Representatives in order to gov-ern, the Constitution also states that the Cabinet is collectively responsible "to the Diet," meaning both the upper and lower houses, for its policies. In contrast, the Indian Cabinet is responsible only to the Lok Sabha.

The powers of the House of Representatives are superior to those of the upper house, the House of Councillors, in two important areas. The Constitution directs that the prime minister must be chosen from the members of the Diet and that a majority of the Cabinet ministers must also be Diet members. However, should the two houses of the Diet disagree on the choice of the prime minister and no agreement be reached through a joint committee, "the decision of the House of Representatives shall be the decision of the Diet" (Article 67).

The House of Representatives also has superior legislative authority, not just in budgetary matters but in all cases where there is disagreement between the two houses. A bill passed by the House of Representatives and on which the House of Councillors makes a different decision becomes a law when passed a second time by a two-thirds majority of the House of Representatives. Moreover, as in India, the budget must first be submitted to the lower house, and in case of disagreement between the two houses, the decision of the House of Representatives stands as the decision for the Diet as a whole.

The House of Councillors has 252 members chosen through an electoral formula designed to balance local and national constituencies. One-half of the councillors are elected from constituencies that are coterminous with the prefectures, the basic unit of local government in Japan. The remainder of the councillors are chosen from a single national constituency, using a system of proportional representation. Thus, the upper house is structured to represent voters in a different way from the lower house, which is also the case in India. Another similarity with India is that councillors' terms are staggered: the term of office for members of the House of Councillors is six years, with one-half elected every three years. Finally, like the Rajya Sabha, the House of Councillors may not be dissolved.

As this sketch of the Japanese and Indian legislatures suggests, the rationale behind the structures and functions of the two parliaments is the same. The differences that stand out—such as the fact that the Japanese Cabinet is collectively responsible to the Diet as a whole, not just the lower house—are less significant than the similarities. Ultimately, what distinguishes both systems as parliamentary is the fusion of legislative and executive roles and the constitutional requirement that the Cabinet (or Council of Ministers) maintain the confidence of the lower house of Parliament. This observation is not to diminish the differences that result from variations in culture, political party dynamics, and the internal rules of operation of the legislatures but rather serves to demonstrate that undergirding these variations is a fundamental logic about how government authority should be structured.

The next sections examine the executives in India and Japan, beginning with the symbolic executive, or head of state. Although the Indian president and the Japanese emperor share important constitutional similarities, there are also significant differences that can be traced to the countries' varied histories. After the head of state, the political executive or head of government is discussed. The prime minister and Cabinet serve the same constitutional function in India and Japan, as modified by historical and cultural contexts.

## Heads of State: Indian President and Japanese Emperor

Earlier chapters provided historical perspective on the decisions that led to one of the most obvious distinctions between India and Japan. Nationalist leaders in India emphasized their liberation from British colonialism by rejecting any continued role, however symbolic, for the British monarch in Indian politics. The framers of the Japanese Constitution, in contrast, chose to maintain an emperor, however apolitical, for symbolic continuity. Thus, India and Japan offer different models of parliamentary democracy: One is a republic, the other a constitutional monarchy. Both in terms of constitutional delegation of authority and in political reality, the Indian president is more powerful than the Japanese emperor as head of state, but even the Indian president is clearly subordinate to the prime minister.

### The Indian President: Leader or Lackey?

India has a president and a vice president, with the vice president charged primarily with executing the functions of the presidency during the president's illness or absence. The vice president becomes acting president in the event of the latter's death, resignation, or removal. He is also the ex officio chairman of the Rajya Sabha.

Both the president and the vice president are indirectly elected. The procedure for presidential election is the more complicated of the two, involving an electoral college composed of all elected members of the state legislative assemblies and the national Parliament. In contrast, the vice president is elected by the members of both houses of Parliament sitting in joint session.

The president and the vice president are elected for five-year terms and may be reelected. Although not required by the Constitution, most Indian presidents have previously served as vice president. In the earliest years of the republic, men of great stature who might be considered above the political fray were chosen as president, but in recent decades the most important criterion has been the presidential candidate's acceptability to the prime minister.[4]

As in most parliamentary systems, the president as head of state nominally has formidable powers that, however, are exercised on the advice of the Council of Ministers, or Cabinet. Since the Council of Ministers is dominated by the prime minister, it is the prime minister in effect who provides the advice on which the president acts. All executive actions of the government of India are expressed in the name of the president (Article 77). He (all Indian presidents have been men) summons both houses of Parliament and dissolves the lower house when necessary; he assents to legislation, appoints the governors of the states, the justices of the Supreme Court and state high courts, the attorney general, and the auditor general of India; he is the commander in chief of the armed forces and also has the power of pardon.

In the 1950s, when Rajendra Prasad was India's first president, the issue of presidential discretion emerged on several occasions. As early as 1951, Prasad expressed the desire to act solely on his own judgment, independently of the Council of Ministers, when assenting to parliamentary legislation and when sending messages to Parliament. Had Prasad's position prevailed, it would have undermined the conventions of cabinet government as they had developed in Britain and as had been intended by the Constituent Assembly. One wonders why a man who had presided over the Constituent Assembly before becoming president would take such a position, and the answer lies principally in a particular piece of legislation that the president was deeply opposed to, a bill that invalidated Hindu personal law.[5] The British precedent limiting action by the head of state to implementing the advice of the head of government and Cabinet ultimately prevailed, although the incident did leave open the question of what a president might do under circumstances of a hung (divided) Parliament.

The Forty-second Amendment to the Constitution, passed in 1976, was designed to eliminate ambiguity by clearly articulating the convention inherited from the British and reinforced in the 1950s. Article 74 states that there shall be a Council of Ministers headed by the prime minister "to aid and advise the President who *shall*, in the exercise of his functions, act in accordance with such advice" [emphasis added]. Under normal circumstances, the president thus represents and reflects the political will of the prime minister and Cabinet. In time of political instability, however, presidential discretion may come into play—as, indeed, the British monarch may have greater discretion when there is no parliamentary majority. What is the president's role when there is no clear, single prime ministerial candidate, that is, when there is no clear majority in Parliament? In the absence of a single-party majority, the president may either turn to the largest party or to a group of parties—whichever seems more likely to secure the greatest parliamentary support. In 1979, for example, when

Prime Minister Morarji Desai's government resigned in the face of a no-confidence motion, the president (under parliamentary convention) could have dissolved Parliament and called for elections. But he turned to a smaller opposition party that claimed wide support to see if it could form a government. It did, but the government lasted less than a month. The president might have continued to seek another leader who could form a coalition government, but instead, after the second government collapse, he called for elections.[6] After the 1996 Lok Sabha elections, President S. D. Sharma called on the largest party, the Bharatiya Janata Party to form a government, even though it was over seventy seats short of a majority. When, thirteen days later, the new prime minister-designate resigned after an unsuccessful effort to build a majority, the president turned to a multiparty opposition coalition that, had it been faster to organize itself, might have been the president's first choice.[7] By the 1990s, it seemed clear that India had entered a period of more coalition governments, with the result that presidential discretion was likely to increase.

**President's Rule.**   One of the most controversial developments in Indian politics has been the use and abuse of the emergency provisions specified in the Constitution, and the question arises as to the role of the president in implementing these provisions. Articles 352 to 360 anticipate three types of emergency: (1) a threat to India's security by war, external aggression, or internal disturbance; (2) a breakdown in the government of a state; or (3) a threat to financial stability. The first case, that of a national emergency, is discussed later in this chapter. The second of these situations entails what is commonly known as **President's Rule**. Although the authority for invoking President's Rule lies primarily with the prime minister, this emergency power is examined here because it sheds light on the issue of presidential discretion as it has evolved since the founding of the republic.

On the receipt of a report from the governor of a state that a situation has arisen in which state governance cannot be carried on in accordance with the provisions of the Constitution, the president may then (1) himself assume all or any of the state government's functions or vest these in any authority (such as the governor) in the state other than the state legislature, (2) declare that the powers normally exercised by the state legislature will be exercised by the national Parliament, or (3) make other provisions necessary to carry out the proclamation, including suspending the operation of the Indian Constitution or any body (*except* the judiciary) in the state.

Invoked infrequently until the late 1960s, President's Rule soon became a tool in the hands of the ruling Congress Party and was used both to deal with regional instability (as intended by the Constitution) and to eliminate state governments headed by opposition parties. Between 1966 and 1977 alone, India's presidents acquiesced in Prime Minister Indira Gandhi's demands to invoke President's Rule in thirty-nine instances. By the mid-1990s, President's Rule had been declared in approximately one hundred cases.

The increased use of President's Rule reflects a number of long-term developments in Indian politics: the preoccupation with threats to national unity, the efforts of a declining Congress Party to maintain control over both the national and state governments, and the erosion of the federal system established by the Constitution. In Punjab, for example, President's Rule was declared first in 1951, and subsequently in 1968, 1971, 1983, and 1987. Finally, in the early 1990s, the Constitution was amended to exempt Punjab from the three-year limit for successive proclamations of emergency (each of which is in effect for a maximum of six months if approved by Parliament). Supporters of invoking President's Rule in Punjab insist on the central government's legitimate concerns with national security in a highly volatile political climate on the border with Pakistan. Thoughtful critics, however, make an equally plausible case that excessive use of President's Rule has exacerbated an already difficult political situation by undermining the normal development of state government and regional political parties.[8]

At the core of the debate over President's Rule is the way in which it has been routinely used for clearly partisan purposes—that is, to suspend state executives (the chief minister and Councils of Ministers) and legislative assemblies that, though popularly elected, contravene the political wishes and priorities of the prime minister and Council of Ministers at the Union level. Prime Minister Indira Gandhi was especially criticized for expanding the partisan use of President's Rule, but even her father, Jawaharlal Nehru, recommended the imposition of President's Rule to eliminate non–Congress Party governments in some states.[9] More recently, in 1993, after the turmoil of Ayodhya, President S. D. Sharma, acting on the advice of Congress Prime Minister Narasimha Rao, dismissed governments headed by the opposition Bharatiya Janata Party in four states.

Could and should the president counsel prudence in the use of emergency powers? The president is clearly charged by the Constitution to act on the advice of the Council of Ministers and prime minister. But some presidents have weakened the stature of their office by acquiescing in the erosion of the Constitution's civil rights protections through excessive declarations of both President's Rule and national emergency.[10]

Despite these concerns, a weak president is consistent with constitutional intent, and a strong president might well provoke both a political and a constitutional crisis. The only way to remove a president is through impeachment, a procedure requiring a two-thirds majority of all members of both houses of Parliament. Conceivably, a strong prime minister backed by majorities in both houses could not force impeachment of a president determined to act independently of the government, and the result would be deadlock. The likely scenario in coming years, as suggested earlier, is an incremental enlargement of presidential discretion in an era of divided parties and unstable parliamentary majorities, and such a scenario may in fact encourage a more assertive presidency.[11]

## Imperial Controversy

We have already been introduced to the *kokutai* theory of state found in the Meiji Constitution of 1889. Under that Constitution, the emperor, who was "sacred and inviolable," possessed supreme authority. But the Constitution also provided that the emperor exercise his powers with the guidance of advisory bodies. The ambiguity here is that in principle the monarch was not answerable to any other source of authority or political institution, yet it was acknowledged simultaneously that the emperor did not act alone and that advisers shared responsibility.[12] Thus, the 1889 Constitution continued the traditional separation of power and authority with an emperor who reigned but did not rule—at least not in the meaningful day-to-day sense of a political executive. This ambiguity, in turn, helped explain how, in the 1940s, both those who blamed the emperor for the war and those who viewed him as buffeted by (if not captive to) his advisers, could claim historical support for their positions.[13]

The 1947 Constitution eliminated any ambiguity about the emperor's role at the outset. Rejecting the doctrine of *kokutai*, Article 1 states: "The Emperor shall be the symbol of the State and of the unity of the people, *deriving his position from the will of the people with whom resides sovereign power*" [emphasis added]. Article 3 states that the advice and approval of the Cabinet is required for all acts of the emperor "in matters of state," and Article 4 adds that the emperor shall not have any powers related to government. Nonetheless, the emperor's powers as described in the Constitution are typical of those accorded most heads of state. He appoints the prime minister ("as designated by the Diet") and also the chief judge of the Supreme Court ("as designated by the Cabinet"). He convokes and dissolves the Diet, with the advice and approval of the Cabinet and "on behalf of the people." To these essential functions are added other symbolic activities, such as receiving foreign ambassadors. All of these activities are carried out under the authority of the Cabinet, however.

In effect, the wording of the Japanese Constitution removed from the emperor the residual sovereign authority that still belongs to the British monarch, who, under certain circumstances, may indirectly influence

British politics through the exercise of judgment and advice. Why, then, should there be controversy over the emperor and his role in politics? Ultranationalists resent the narrowing of imperial authority to a sliver of its former scope, whereas those critical of the country's nationalist excesses (notably the leftist parties) believe that the cultural and institutional forces that could threaten Japanese democracy converge on the symbol of the imperial house. On both sides, it is the emperor's symbolic role in politics that fuels concern.

It is worth recalling here some historical features of Japan's imperial institution. The Japanese term for the emperor, *tenno*, literally means "heavenly sovereign." The ceremony of imperial accession is followed by a complex and ancient ritual called *daijosai*, in which the emperor offers specially prepared foods to the sun goddess, Amaterasu Omikami, and then enters a ceremony of spiritual communion with the Shinto spirits.[14] These rituals, preserved as part of Imperial House Shinto, last served to remind the Japanese people of their imperial traditions when Emperor Akihito succeeded his father, the Emperor Showa (Emperor Hirohito) in 1989.

The various ceremonies, both private and public, that marked the 1989–1990 imperial transition were surrounded by renewed controversy over the imperial system and the constitutionality of using public funds for religious rituals. The preparations for Emperor Akihito's *daijosai* in fall 1990, for example, were carried out in secrecy because of threats of terrorism by those opposed to the imperial system. Earlier, funeral preparations for Akihito's father, Hirohito, were complicated by the fact that so many of the traditional rites spring from Imperial House Shinto and are associated with State Shinto. Consequently, two funerals were held: Private Shinto rites were conducted by the Imperial Household Agency, whereas the public state funeral was secular but preceded by a ninety-minute Shinto ritual. Although the ritual was not technically part of the state funeral, it was held at the same place as the funeral and was observed by the official guests assembled for the state ceremony. In protest, Takako Doi, head of the Japan Socialist Party (JSP), arrived late in order to avoid the Shinto rites, and all invited members of the Japan Communist Party (JCP) boycotted both the public Shinto and the state ceremonies.[15]

In contrast to this, rightists protested against anyone who criticized their ultranationalist interpretation of the historical and symbolic roles of the emperor. Perhaps the most notorious case involved the mayor of Nagasaki, who was divested of his honorary functions in the local branch of the Liberal Democratic Party after he stated that Emperor Hirohito bore responsibility for the events of World War II. Then, in January 1990, as he left his office, the mayor was shot and wounded by a member of a right-wing group.[16]

Despite the controversy that reemerged during this transition period, everything points to the continued normalization of the emperor as a constitutional monarch. At the time of his accession, Emperor Akihito specifically affirmed his commitment to the 1947 Constitution and the role assigned to him by that Constitution. A public consensus clearly supports this new symbolic role. The debates over Shinto rites do not appear to interest most Japanese, because little is known about the details of the rites and what they symbolize. Moreover, "anything the emperor did, short of walking on water, would not have deified him in their eyes."[17]

In 1993, Crown Prince Naruhito followed the precedent set by his father and younger brother by marrying a commoner, career diplomat Masako Owada. In a manner familiar to observers of the British monarchy, the media exploited every opportunity to stimulate, then feed, public curiosity. Television cameras followed Owada's every move; all who knew her in college or at work were interviewed; her clothes and haircuts were scrutinized. In title, the *tenno* might be a "heavenly sovereign," but in practice, he and his family are clearly of this world.[18]

## Locus of Power: Cabinet and Prime Minister

This section first reviews prime ministers and cabinets in India and Japan before looking more closely at prime ministers as political executives. Variations among prime ministers result from constitutional prerogatives, historical circumstances, individual personalities, and political party systems. To illustrate these variations, the discussion of the Indian prime minister highlights the interplay of the Constitution, Indian history, and the prime minister's personality that resulted in the Emergency period. The discussion of the Japanese prime minister highlights the role of political parties.

### Comparative Overview

The constitutional provisions regarding the designation of the prime minister and Cabinet in both countries are characteristic of other parliamentary systems, and the differences between the two countries are consistent with variations in other parliamentary systems. In Japan, as noted earlier, the emperor formally appoints as prime minister the person previously chosen by the Diet. The prime minister then appoints Cabinet ministers, who must be civilians and a majority of whom must be Diet members. The prime minister may also remove ministers "as he chooses" (Article 68). Although ministers may be chosen from either house of the Diet, in practice, the great majority, as well as all of the prime ministers, have come from the lower house.

In India, the president chooses the prime minister, who in turn selects the members of the Council of Ministers to be officially appointed by the president.[19] All ministers must be members of either the upper or the lower house of Parliament, and following the British custom, it is presumed that the prime minister will be a member of the Lok Sabha. When Indira Gandhi first became prime minister in the 1960s, for example, she was a member of the Rajya Sabha, but subsequently she was elected to a seat in the Lok Sabha.

Cabinet ministers in both countries share **collective responsibility** for government policy and are expected to contribute to the crafting and co-ordination of that policy, as well as its defense before the legislature. In the event of a defeat of government policy entailing a loss of confidence, all Cabinet ministers, including the prime minister, are expected to resign. In addition to collective responsibility, the ministers are held individually responsible for the operations of the government departments they are charged with administering, as well as for their own professional conduct. Thus, when heavy public criticism is directed against a minister—because of a scandal, for example—he or she may resign (or be fired) from the Cabinet.

The most serious question regarding the cabinet system of government in a parliamentary system is the way in which and the degree to which the ministers are held accountable for their policies and activities. This question is neither new nor limited to India and Japan. Some observers of British politics, for example, suggest that the ability of a majority party to control legislative agendas, combined with the dominant role of the prime minister both in his or her party and in the government produces a concentration of power that erodes democratic accountability.[20] Although the increasing trend toward coalition governments in both countries raises the possibility that instability will become a more important issue than the overconcentration of authority, the long history of governments dominated by one party argues for a closer look at the prime minister's role and powers.

## Indira Gandhi and the Emergency

At the time the Constituent Assembly was meeting in India, the country was confronting the massive problems caused by Partition, severe economic dislocation, and communal violence. Newly independent India also fought its first international war (with Pakistan in 1948) during this period. The members of the assembly were preoccupied with national unity and security; consequently, the Indian Constitution contains provisions for dealing with emergencies both at the regional (state) level and at the national level. Whereas President's Rule has become a regular part of the prime minister's political agenda, declarations of national emergency have been far rarer. The most celebrated instance of emergency rule, which occurred under Prime Minister Indira Gandhi from 1975 to 1977, has come to be known simply as "the Emergency." More than any other period in the history of the Indian republic, the Emergency illustrated the degree to which power could be concentrated in the hands of the prime minister and Cabinet and democratic processes could be held hostage by a strong, determined leader.

**The Emergency.**   The origins of the Emergency lay in a combination of political and economic developments in the late 1960s and early 1970s. The ruling Congress Party had weakened and was split by factions. Indira Gandhi, prime minister since 1966, sought to free herself from the control of the party machine and a small group of powerful state leaders. Determined to build a broad base of support, she established a separate political party called the Congress (I) (for Indira) Party. Her strategy was one used by other leaders confronting resistance from entrenched interests, whether in party or government: Appeal directly to the people with populist images and policies, bypassing or undermining intermediary structures.[21]

In March 1971, Mrs. Gandhi dissolved the Lok Sabha and called new elections, which the Congress (I) won, taking 68 percent of the seats. It proved impossible, however, to implement the promises of economic and social transformation made during the elections. By 1973, severe economic problems, including food shortages and spiraling energy costs in the wake of the dramatic increase in world petroleum prices, encouraged widespread rioting and strikes. The antigovernment opposition gathered support in one state after another, and by 1975, demands for the prime minister's resignation were widespread. Finally, in mid-June, a state high court found Mrs. Gandhi guilty of election code violations in her constituency during the 1971 Lok Sabha election. The violations were relatively minor, but the court finding nonetheless meant that she would lose her parliamentary seat, forcing her resignation as prime minister. When a mass rally in New Delhi called for the government to resign, Indira Gandhi asked the president to proclaim a state of emergency as provided for by Article 352 of the Constitution.

Before most Indians knew of the proclamation, the principal opposition leaders had already been arrested and a news blackout imposed on New Delhi. During the twenty-one months that the proclamation was in force, over one hundred thousand people were detained without trial, two dozen organizations were banned, and rigorous press censorship was imposed. Parliament—dominated by the prime minister and Congress (I) since 1971—approved these measures as it had the original emergency

proclamation. Even more important for the evolution of the Indian Constitution and Indian politics, the Parliament approved wide-reaching
changes to the Constitution. The primary effect of these changes was to
secure parliamentary (or prime ministerial) supremacy and to diminish
the power of the courts and the constitutional guarantees to fundamental
rights.[22]

The Emergency ended in early 1977, when Prime Minister Gandhi, in
anticipation that her party would win, called for new Lok Sabha elections. The newly formed Janata Party, however, won a majority of seats,
sweeping the Congress (I) government out of power and officially ending
the Emergency.

The significance of this dramatic period for our discussion lies in the
way it illustrates the interplay of history and personality in defining the
role of the prime minister and executive-legislative relations in a parliamentary system. Would other Indian prime ministers have reacted the
way that Indira Gandhi did under the same circumstances? Although this
question is rhetorical, we can use it to explore two related factors relevant
to understanding executive power. It is clear that Mrs. Gandhi viewed
herself and her political survival as indispensable to India under the
threatening conditions the country faced in the early 1970s, including a
hostile international environment and domestic poverty and inequality.
"Her experiences in childhood [as the daughter of independence leader
Jawaharlal Nehru] and as a young adult revolved almost completely
around duty to the nation. . . . No wonder the boundaries between her
own interests and those of the nation were so blurred."[23] In this respect,
her autocratic leadership recalls the style of many nationalist leaders, especially in countries emerging from colonial rule and confronting seemingly overwhelming problems (see Photo 9.1).

Some scholars would add a gender factor to this consideration. Although Prime Minister Gandhi seldom identified herself in gender terms,
her style, career, and performance were all shaped by India's patriarchal
political system. Much of the hostility she encountered from politicians,
including those in her own party, was directed at her because she was a
woman. Central to her survival strategy, therefore, was to behave as
many successful (male) leaders might in India or elsewhere—acting aggressive, competitive, and, upon occasion, ruthless.[24]

In retrospect, the Emergency highlights a central dilemma in Indian
politics. In view of both the actual and expected threats to the Indian republic in the 1940s and since, was the Constituent Assembly not wise to
provide constitutionally sanctioned states of emergency? But is there not
also an inherent danger in the combination of sanctioned emergency procedures *and* a parliamentary system that, by definition, admits to the possibility of concentrated executive power, a danger exacerbated by com-

*Photo 9.1    Indira Gandhi Billboard. Photo courtesy of James Boyd.*

petitive elections that mobilize people for political participation and thus increase pressures on the government? More will be said about this dilemma, but for now it is necessary to turn to another determinant of prime ministers' roles, the political party system.

## Political Parties and the Japanese Prime Minister

The number, kind, and relative strength of political parties affects the degree of freedom a prime minister has to formulate and implement policy. A prime minister at the head of a party that is internally unified and has a strong parliamentary majority, especially in the lower house, is able to form a government with concentrated power rarely found in a presidential system, with its separation of powers. In contrast, a prime minister confronted with intraparty factionalism or indiscipline and perhaps a coalition government, is constrained by his or her own party organization, along with the need to negotiate with other parties.[25] Japan, both under LDP rule and more recently under coalition governments, provides numerous illustrations of these constraints.

Between 1945 and 1995, Japan had twenty-four prime ministers (India had ten during the same period), most of whose names have been forgotten by all but the specialist in Japanese politics. In contrast to the United States, Britain, or India, where political eras are marked by the name of a president ("the Reagan administration") or prime minister (politics "under Margaret Thatcher" or "under Rajiv Gandhi"), Japanese prime ministers seldom see their names used as the benchmark of an era. One obvious reason for this difference is the relatively high rate of turnover in Japanese prime ministers. However, unlike those European countries that also experience frequent turnover of the head of government, between 1955 and 1993, Japan was essentially ruled by one party that was unencumbered by coalition government except for a short period in the 1980s. The explanation for the lower profile of the Japanese prime minister during this period lies not in interparty politics, but in intraparty politics, that is, the political nature of the LDP itself.

Although it had roots in nineteenth century Meiji politics, the modern LDP dates officially from 1955, when it was created by a merger of the Liberal and Democratic parties. The LDP has always been structured around formal factions, and with rare exceptions, all LDP presidents have been faction heads (see Chapter 12). Kenji Hayao's study of Japanese prime ministers shows that in order to become a faction leader, party leader, and likely prime minister, a potential candidate must meet a number of criteria, including membership in the lower house, seniority (having served five or six terms), and relative youth.[26] Hayao does not list gender as a criterion because it is assumed that successful candidates will be male.[27]

These criteria, in turn, imply a number of others. Seniority, for example, requires a safe seat, which means that prospective candidates are more likely to come from Japan's rural areas, where voting patterns are more stable. Long tenure also means that candidates win their first races as young men and are career politicians.[28] During the years that it takes to move up the ranks, the would-be party presidents will become experts not only in policy matters and legislative politics but also (and perhaps more important) in factional and party affairs. And to do well within one's faction and party means helping others gain government and party appointments and raising money for election campaigns. Some of these qualities, such as fund-raising and organizational ability, characterize successful politicians nearly everywhere. In the LDP, the ability to rise both within a faction and across faction lines also requires a collaborative, even self-effacing, style of leadership, as illustrated in the aphorism of Noboru Takeshita, prime minister in the late 1980s: "Sweat it out yourself and give others the credit."[29]

Taken together, the experiences of LDP presidents and prime ministers show a pattern, condensed in this profile: men who have close ties to their district and throughout their party, who over the years have developed the ability to minimize conflict with their colleagues, and to whom many party members are obligated for influence and money. Although not required to manage interparty coalitions, LDP prime ministers are masters of the art of managing coalitions within their party. Nevertheless, they have never been able to take party support for granted; LDP presidents are elected for a two-year term with a maximum of two consecutive terms allowable, and a one-year extension is permissible only with the support of two-thirds of the LDP Diet members.

The consequence of these factors is that LDP prime ministers are inclined more toward a reactive than an initiating leadership role in policy matters. Moreover, events since 1993 promise to reinforce this reactive role. In summer 1993, the LDP government was defeated by a no-confidence motion in the House of Representatives, in which thirty-nine LDP members voted against the government.[30] The formation of two new conservative parties by LDP defectors led to a restructuring of Japanese parties that lasted several years. Japan's first non-LDP government in nearly forty years constituted itself in August 1993, with seven parties sharing power in a cabinet headed by rising star Morohiro Hosokawa. Hosokawa seemed to exemplify a new style for Japan's prime ministers: He entered the 1993 national election fray never having served in the Diet (he was prefectural governor) and had formed his own party only three months before the House election. Hosokawa headed a Cabinet that spanned Socialists (in government for the first time since 1948) and conservatives, including former LDP members.

Hosokawa's star fell as abruptly as it rose, when he resigned in 1994 after allegations of corruption. A new government coalition was formed, but it lasted only a few months. In July 1994, Japan's fourth government in one year was established under the carefully negotiated leadership of Socialist Prime Minister Tomichi Murayama. Feeding the cynicism of some observers of Japanese politics was the composition of the new government: Socialists, LDP (for years the committed political foes of the Socialists), and a small splinter party composed of former LDP members. Under the pressures of managing coalition politics, Murayama abandoned several long-held tenets of Socialist policy, such as opposition to the Self Defense Forces.[31] By 1996, the government was again led by an

LDP prime minister. Although Japan's parties were being restructured and governments reshuffled, the primacy placed on the prime minister's mediating ability had not changed.

# Summary

The parliamentary systems of India and Japan are similar in terms of their key features: bicameral legislatures, with a more powerful lower house; fusion of powers between the legislative and executive branches; and a dual executive with authority concentrated in the prime minister and secondarily in the Cabinet. Differences can be traced to historical and constitutional factors, both of which have shaped the role of the Indian president in times of emergency and the diminished political significance but continued symbolism of the Japanese emperor. Finally, in the Indian and Japanese prime ministers, it is clear that constitutional provisions, historical circumstances, political party dynamics, gender, and personality interact to produce differences among political executives who, in principle, play the same role in their governments.

# Notes

1. It is unusual for the head of state in a parliamentary system to also be designated as part of Parliament (the head of government almost always is). Presumably, India's Constituent Assembly chose to emphasize the interdependence of the legislative and executive branches in this fashion and may also have seen the provision as further assurance against uncontrolled executive authority. Granville Austin, *The Indian Constitution: Cornerstone of a Nation* (Oxford: Clarendon Press, 1966), pp. 126–128.

2. The Japanese name of the legislature is Kokkai, more literally translated as national "assembly" than Diet. However, its official English name is Diet or National Diet, which is also by convention more familiar. *Japan: An Illustrated Encyclopedia*, vol. 1 (Tokyo: Kodansha, 1993), pp. 282–283 (hereafter cited as Kodansha, *Encyclopedia*).

3. The number of House seats varies with redistricting, as in other parliamentary systems. For example, there were 512 seats at stake in the 1990 election, 511 in 1993. Under a new election system adopted in 1996, the number was reduced to 500. For a list of changes in the election system and the number of House seats from 1890–1990, see Daniel B. Ramsdell, *The Japanese Diet: Stability and Change in the Japanese House of Representatives, 1890–1990* (Lanham, Md.: University Press of America, 1992), pp. 7–8.

4. Sarla Malik, *The Prime Minister of India: Powers and Functions* (Pilani, Rajasthan: Chinta Prakashan, 1984), pp. 132–135; and James Manor, "The Prime Minister and the President," in Manor, ed., *Nehru to the Nineties: The Changing Office of Prime Minister in India* (Vancouver: University of British Columbia Press, 1994), pp. 123–125.

5. Austin, *Indian Constitution*, pp. 135–143. The legislation in question was the Hindu Code bill. Prasad, a conservative Hindu, found the bill distasteful. Relations between President Prasad and Prime Minister Nehru were generally tense because Nehru had opposed Prasad's selection as president. Malik, *Prime Minister of India*, pp. 130–142; Manor, "Prime Minister and President," p. 120.

6. Presidential discretion is also at issue when there is no clear leader of a majority party in Parliament. See the discussion in Malik, *Prime Minister*, pp. 18–30. For insight into the presidential decisions in the 1979 prime ministerial successions, see Manor, "Prime Minister and President," pp. 130–132.

7. Manoj Mitta, "The President: Walking a Tightrope," *India Today* (May 31, 1996), pp. 18–19.

8. See, for example, Robin Jeffrey, *What's Happening to India: Punjab, Ethnic Conflict, and the Test for Federalism*, 2d ed. (New York: Holmes and Meier), 1994.

9. B. D. Dua, "The Prime Minister and the Federal System," in Manor, *Nehru to the Nineties*, pp. 20–47, discusses in detail the use of president's rule by all of India's prime ministers up to the 1990s. On its early use, including the Nehru period, see Shriram Maheshwari, *President's Rule in India* (Delhi: Macmillan Company and Columbia, Missouri: South Asia Books, 1977), chaps. 2, 3.

10. Perhaps the best example of this was President Fakhruddin Ali Ahmed's role in the declaration of emergency that inaugurated the Emergency (1975–1977) when, in the middle of the night, he signed a proclamation of national emergency at the request of Prime Minister Indira Gandhi and one of her ministers, a proclamation that a majority of the Council of Ministers would likely have opposed. Manor, "Prime Minister and President," p. 124.

11. Ibid., pp. 136–137.

12. Koichi Kishimoto, *Politics in Modern Japan: Development and Organization*, 3d ed. (Tokyo: Japan Echo, 1988), p. 28.

13. Controversy over the emperor's role during the war influenced the debate over the role he should play in the postwar order. Robert E. Ward, "Presurrender Planning: Treatment of the Emperor and Constitutional Changes," in Robert E. Ward and Sakamoto Yoshikazu, eds., *Democratizing Japan: The Allied Occupation* (Honolulu: University of Hawaii Press, 1987), pp. 1–41.

14. On the imperial regalia and *daijosai*, see Kodansha, *Encyclopedia*, vol. 1, pp. 80 (Atsuta Shrine), 262–263, 596, 627–628 (Ise Shrine).

15. *Keesing's Record of World Events* (February 1989), p. 36, 462.

16. For a discussion of this and related incidents, see Yoichi Higuchi, "The Constitution and the Emperor System: Is Revisionism Alive?" in Percy R. Luney, Jr., and Kazuyuki Takahashi, eds., *Japanese Constitutional Law* (Tokyo: University of Tokyo Press, 1993), pp. 65–67.

17. Bruce Stronach, *Beyond the Rising Sun: Nationalism in Contemporary Japan* (Westport, Conn.: Praeger, 1995), p. 107.

18. Critics of the extensive media coverage of the engagement and wedding included Korean rights activists, who saw the event as reinforcing the imperial system under which Koreans (both in Japan and Korea) had suffered so much. *Japan Times Weekly International Edition* (hereafter cited as *Japan Times WIE*), April 5–11, 1993.

19. The Indian Council of Ministers has grown to approximately forty members, too large to be efficient. Consequently, a Cabinet has developed as the inner body of the council. Although not mentioned in the Constitution, the functions of the Cabinet are presumed to be those of the Council of Ministers.

20. See, for example, Jorgen S. Rasmussen, *The British Political Process: Concentrated Power Versus Accountability* (Belmont, Calif.: Wadsworth, 1993).

21. For an analysis of Mrs. Gandhi's "survival strategy" as it reflected her leadership style, see Jana Everett, "Indira Gandhi and the Exercise of Power," in Michael A. Genovese, ed., *Women as National Leaders* (Newbury Park, Calif.: Sage Publications, 1993), pp. 103–134.

22. The most sweeping and controversial of the amendments was the forty-second. For its background and text, see Rajeev Dhavan, *The Amendment: Conspiracy or Revolution?* (Allahabad, Uttar Pradesh: Wheeler Publishing, 1978).

23. Everett, "Indira Gandhi," p. 131. It is plausible that Mrs. Gandhi also shared the British view of a "loyal opposition," which in her view had been violated by her Indian opponents.

24. Ibid., pp. 126–128.

25. Patrick Weller noted: "The structure of the party outside parliament determines the number of independent centres of power that exist within the party and therefore the number of bodies with whom the prime minister may need to maintain a direct relationship." *First Among Equals: Prime Ministers in Westminster Systems* (Sydney and London: George Allen and Unwin, 1985), p. 19.

26. Kenji Hayao, *The Japanese Prime Minister and Public Policy* (Pittsburgh: University of Pittsburgh Press, 1993), pp. 97–105. The average age at which prime ministers assumed power through 1991 was 65, but in 1993, the relatively young Morohiro Hosokawa became prime minister at age 55.

27. Ramsdell, *Japanese Diet*, chap. 9, discussed the paucity of women (especially from the LDP) in the House of Representatives.

28. They often also inherit their seats from their fathers or fathers-in-law. Hayao, *Japanese Prime Minister*, p. 105.

29. Quoted in ibid., p. 107.

30. *Japan Times WIE*, June 28–July 4, 1993.

31. On the implications of the policy shifts, see Fukatsu Masumi, "The SDPJ's Astronomical Shift in Policy," *Japan Quarterly* 42, no. 1 (January–March 1995), pp. 76–82.

*ten*

China:
The Party-State
System

The most distinguishing characteristic of Chinese government and politics has been the mutual interpenetration of the Communist Party and government structures from the national to the local level. Although unique among the three countries compared in this book, this **party-state system** existed in the USSR until 1991, as well as in other Communist states, and also in Taiwan until the late 1980s.[1] Just as the parliamentary structures in India and Japan are illustrative cases of a general type of governing system, so the Chinese party-state system is one variant of a larger category of governing types. A question that fascinates China watchers now is this: How are party-state relations changing at the close of the twentieth century? Will they continue to evolve until China is no longer recognizable as a party-state system? Or will the system's basic features be reaffirmed as new leaders, with new agendas, take over?

The background needed to discuss such questions is presented in the following way. The chapter begins with a description of the formal decisionmaking and administrative structures of the People's Republic of China and the Chinese Communist Party and the relationship between these two institutions. This is followed by a discussion of the philosophy behind this dual system and what the Chinese call the "leading role" of the party. Next, a historical overview of the major political periods since 1949 is presented. The concluding section evaluates China's leadership in light of the dramatic shifts in political personalities and policy agendas.

184

# The Party-State System

The term "state" as used here encompasses all the formal governing structures, both civilian and military, from the national to the local levels, in China. The state structures are described in the 1982 PRC Constitution, and the formal party structures are outlined in the 1982 Chinese Communist Party Constitution.

## State Structures

As outlined in the PRC's Constitution, government at the national level is organized along the lines of a parliamentary system. The National People's Congress is "the highest organ of state power" (Article 57) and exercises the legislative power of the state. The NPC consists of approximately three thousand deputies from the provincial level, as well as deputies from the armed forces. Normally, it meets annually, and between plenary sessions, its business is conducted by its Standing Committee. In principle, the NPC chooses and may remove from office China's top political officials, including the president and vice president, the premier of the State Council, the chairman of the Central Military Commission, and the president of the Supreme People's Court. The president of the PRC serves as the symbolic head of state, and the premier of the State Council (the Cabinet) is the head of government.

Because of the NPC's size and its relatively short meetings, its real authority is exercised by the Standing Committee, whose term runs concurrently with the term of the Congress. The Standing Committee itself has over 130 members; its chairman is the head of the NPC. Until recent years, the NPC was viewed almost entirely as a "rubber-stamp" legislature, whose purpose was to add legitimacy (through unanimous approval) to policies determined elsewhere and to officials chosen elsewhere. In the 1980s, however, evidence began to accumulate that the Congress was asserting its constitutional mandate by demanding a role in policy deliberation, drafting major proposals, and even stalling initiatives sought by party officials. In the 1990s, the chairman of the Standing Committee and head of the NPC, Qiao Shi, took the position that some democratization should accompany economic modernization, and this led the NPC into greater prominence.[2]

Effective executive authority at the national level belongs to the State Council, headed by the premier. In the mid-1990s, the full State Council was composed of over eighty members, including the premier, four vice premiers, state councillors, ministers in charge of ministries and commissions, and heads of specialized agencies. Within the State Council is a Standing Committee that acts as an "inner cabinet" and comprises the most important members of the council. The State Council, like the Cabinets in India and Japan, is the chief policymaking and administrative organ of the national government. It is the real center of state power, responsible for drafting laws, the budget, and the administrative plan and for submitting these to the National People's Congress for approval. It also oversees the implementation of all state policy.

In addition to the National People's Congress and the State Council, with their respective standing committees and the vertical hierarchies of the various state ministries, the national government structures include the Military Affairs Commission and the highest echelon of the judiciary, the Supreme People's Court and Supreme People's Procuratorate (see Chapter 13). None of these governing bodies is static. In particular, the state ministries, like those in India and Japan, may be merged, divided, and combined in different ways to reflect changing State Council priorities or to improve administrative efficiency in China's vast bureaucracy.

## Party Structures

The highest organs of power in the Communist Party are the National Party Congress[3] and the Central Committee elected by it. The Party Congress has a membership of roughly two thousand delegates and, under the provisions of the 1982 Constitution, is held once every five years (Article 18). Its main political role is to applaud decisions made elsewhere. The sessions of the Party Congresses, which receive a great deal of media coverage, are numbered sequentially and legitimize major policy efforts or initiatives. The Twelfth Congress, for example, met for eleven days in September 1982 and symbolized Deng Xiaoping's ascent to political primacy and approved the 1982 party Constitution. The Fourteenth Congress (October 1992) reaffirmed the market-oriented changes that were underway and ratified new party leadership.

The executive bodies of the National Party Congress are more important than the Congress itself and in fact are the most important political bodies in China. The Central Committee members are nominally elected by the Party Congress and serve five-year terms. The Central Committee is itself large (more than three hundred full and alternate members were elected in 1992) and meets only once or twice a year in plenary session. Its importance derives both from its constitutional authority and from the fact that most of its members hold other important positions, thus membership on the Central Committee is a way of gauging political influence. As noted, the Central Committee is (according to the party Constitution) elected by the National Party Congress. In fact, the Politburo (Political Bureau), which is formally elected by the Central Committee, actually determines the list of nominees standing for election to the Central Committee.[4]

The Politburo and the Standing Committee of the Politburo constitute the core of the CCP's power. The Politburo's membership generally ranges from fifteen to twenty-five members, and its Standing Committee includes around six members. Although the 1982 party Constitution states that the Politburo and Standing Committee are elected by the Central Committee, the lists submitted for election appear to be the result of careful behind-the-scenes negotiation and co-optation by those already in power. The power struggles that have occurred among China's top leaders generally involve Politburo or Standing Committee members, with the members of the Standing Committee representing the apex of party power.

There are three other important party organizations at the national level: the Secretariat, the Military Affairs Commission, and the Central Commission for Discipline Inspection. The Secretariat provides administrative support for the Central Committee and Politburo and is headed by the general secretary of the Central Committee, who is a Politburo member and, as a result of having control over party organization, is one of China's two or three preeminent leaders. In the first two decades of the post–Mao Zedong period, only three men held this position: Hu Yaobang, Zhao Ziyang, and Jiang Zemin.

The Military Affairs Commission, whose membership is the same as the government Military Commission, reports directly to the Politburo, oversees the armed forces, and makes national defense policies. In one form or another, it has existed since the 1930s and represents the party's control over the military. This control is exercised through the General Political Department, which is responsible for the political education of the troops. This function, along with the Military Commission's power to appoint and remove military personnel, explains its critical importance in Chinese politics. Consequently, the head of the commission is also one of the country's most important national leaders.

The Discipline Inspection Commission is responsible for party discipline, performance, and morale. This is the body charged with maintaining the correctness of party policy and ideology, which it does through a hierarchical system of regional and local commissions for inspecting party discipline. The Discipline Inspection Commission assumes particular importance during periods of party campaigns, such as the "**rectification campaigns**" described later in this chapter, and in recent years, it has played a role in investigating charges of corruption among party officials.[5]

## Party-State Interpenetration

The state and party institutions described in the preceding two sections are interconnected at all levels. In theory and in practice, the Communist Party has been the more important of the two since before 1949: The party initiates policy and controls its implementation through the complex state machinery. This is accomplished through a system of **interlocking direc-torship**, in which party leaders simultaneously hold government positions. For example, Qiao Shi, the head of the National People's Congress, came up through the party ranks from his earliest participation in the Communist student movement. In 1985, he was named to the Politburo, then became a vice premier of the State Council. While holding both high party and government positions, in 1993 he assumed another important post in the state hierarchy, that of chairman of the Standing Committee of the NPC.[6]

Two other especially significant men, Jiang Zemin and Li Peng, illus-trate the pattern in which leaders gain experience first in party work and then in government management (often at the regional level) before mov-ing into national party prominence and high government positions. Like Qiao, Jiang first built his party connections in Shanghai, China's influential and dynamic eastern port city, and held high posts in the management of heavy industry. He became a full member of the CCP Central Committee in 1982 and within two years assumed important State Council positions. Then he returned to Shanghai, where by the late 1980s he was mayor of the powerful Shanghai municipality, then party secretary.[7] He became a Politburo member in 1987, and after the Tiananmen Square crisis in 1989, replaced Zhao Ziyang as general secretary of the party and joined the Politburo Standing Committee. He also heads the party's Military Com-mission. In 1993, he was elected by the National People's Congress to be China's head of state, president of the People's Republic of China.

As noted earlier, the president's role is largely symbolic, so the choice of Jiang was a confirmation of his previously acquired power and stature (which is generally the case even in true parliamentary systems). More significant is the premier's position at the top of the state hierarchy. Elected premier of the State Council in 1987, Li Peng (like Qiao and Jiang) joined the Communist Party in the 1940s. Li shares with Jiang a strong technical background (both men received training in the former Soviet Union), and since the 1960s, Li has worked in Beijing. By the early 1980s, he was both a vice minister of the State Council and the party secretary for a newly established Ministry of Water Resources and Electric Power, a ministry central to China's modernization efforts.[8] At the same time, he gained a seat on the Central Committee, and shortly thereafter, the Polit-buro. He became a member of the Politburo Standing Committee in 1987, the same year that he became premier.

These men are three examples of leaders who simultaneously hold top party and state positions; they are the norm, not the exception. Such posi-tions as these are also important because they designate the key players in the succession politics that are described in the last section of this chapter.

Interlocking directorates exist on every level of the party-state hierarchy. The most important provincial, municipal, and county government officials are trusted party members, presumably able to assure that party policy is correctly implemented. The higher the position, the tighter the party-state connection. Because the Politburo and its Standing Committee have small memberships, not every member of the State Council can simultaneously be a member of one of the highest party organs. Normally, they are members of the Central Committee. Similar patterns are found at lower levels of the party and state hierarchies, with the actual degree of overlap in dual memberships declining at the lower levels.

Deng Xiaoping, after his leadership was confirmed with the adoption of the CCP and PRC constitutions in 1982, pushed for a number of government reforms to accompany his strategy for economic modernization. One of his reform goals was the "regularization" of government administration to decrease the overlap in party and state personnel posts. Such regularization was intended to bring new blood into policymaking and administration at a time of aging leadership and also to help prevent the extreme concentration of power at the top that characterized China under Mao Zedong. Zhao Ziyang, who was premier of the State Council and also general secretary of the CCP until forced from power in 1989, sought to continue Deng's reforms by separating party and state positions. He admitted in 1987, however, that the lack of differentiation between party and government functions continued to be a problem.[9]

To put this in a larger comparative perspective, it can be noted that it is common for the top political party leaders in many countries to also head the government; this is, in fact, one of the characteristics of a parliamentary system. Moreover, national party organizations often establish a functional structure that parallels the government ministries in order to maintain party expertise and better direct government policy (for the party in power) or critique and hold the government accountable (for opposition parties). The party-state system that has characterized Communist countries, however, is distinctive due to the degree of overlap from the national to the local level. It differs also because of the underlying principle that the government should *not* be independent of the party. Both civilian and military authority are to be directed by and held accountable to the Communist Party, which, in theory, reflects the will of the people and the leadership of the revolution.

Viewed from a pluralistic perspective that assumes the desirability of autonomous organizations, competitive party politics and elections, and other procedural characteristics of liberal democracies, continued one-party control is a considerable roadblock to democratic development. However, recent research on China's legislative bodies, the People's Congresses, suggests a more subtle and complex picture. Overlapping leadership facilitates close contact with the party and enhances the likelihood of a legislative "presence" when important decisions are made. Over the long run, this presence is conducive to expanded legislative jurisdiction and capacity. As one scholar has observed, the "web of party control" over People's Congresses (from the NPC to the local level) is "pervasive and effective," but this control may facilitate legislative development.[10]

The philosophy behind one-party control is our next topic. Discussion will include Leninist theories of the **"vanguard of the proletariat"** and **"democratic centralism,"** which inspired the Communist Party of the Soviet Union and, after it, that of China. We will also examine the importance of "Marxism-Leninism and Mao Zedong Thought" as ideological principles that undergird the legitimacy of Communist rule in China.

## The Leading Role of the Party

Readers may recall from Chapter 6 that the Chinese Communist Party was founded shortly after World War I with the organizational assistance of the newly created Comintern (Communist International), which was controlled by the Soviet Union. The inspiration behind the Comintern was V. I. Lenin, best known as the leader of the 1917 Bolshevik Russian Revolution.[11] Karl Marx and Frederick Engels bequeathed to the Russian and Chinese revolutions their analysis of class structures and interrelationships as a way of explaining the nature of socioeconomic change and political power, but Lenin provided the tools to create change and mobilize power under circumstances that Marx and Engels never foresaw. Lenin's ideas, transported to the Chinese Communist Party through the Comintern, helped the fledgling party build support and seize the initiative from the Kuomintang and supporters of the Republican revolution.

### The Leninist Party

Lenin conceptualized a tightly knit political party as the hard-core group that would implement a revolution. Marx had argued that in capitalist societies the workers (or proletariat) would develop revolutionary potential because of their being exploited in the capitalist drive to maximize profit. Revolutionary potential would thus be greatest in the highly industrialized societies of advanced capitalism and would be expressed through spontaneous workers' strikes and demonstrations. But these signs of class struggle did not inevitably produce the conditions necessary for replacing the old order. Lenin understood that spontaneity would not build a new society, but he argued that organization, backed by theoretical understanding and education, would. Thus, his Communist Party was conceived as the leading edge, or "vanguard of the proletariat," whose primary purpose was to prepare the working masses for revolution by educating and organizing them.[12]

Lenin's model party had several key features, later adapted by the Chinese. The party served as a transmission belt, imparting the will of the leaders to the rank and file and others who supported the revolution's goals. Party leaders were expected to be professional revolutionaries possessing a Marxist understanding of social and political forces and prepared to commit their lives to the revolutionary cause. Another characteristic of the party was the insistence on discipline, both among the leaders and the followers. Discipline was essential in order to maintain secrecy and safety because the party was constantly threatened by government repression. Once a revolution was underway, this same discipline made it possible to maintain momentum and eliminate enemies of the revolution and eventually to build a new society.

Lenin's organizational principle is among his most famous legacies. This principle, called democratic centralism, encompasses both dissent and unanimity, free discussion and enforced discipline, in the life of the party. As a practical matter, "democracy" means consultation and free expression of views during the consultative period before a decision is taken; once taken, centralized direction in the implementation of the decision prevails. In the words of the 1982 CCP Constitution: "Within the Party, democracy is given full play, a high degree of centralism is practiced on the basis of democracy and a sense of organization and discipline is strengthened, so as to ensure unity of action throughout its ranks and the prompt and effective implementation of its decisions."[13]

As the vanguard of the proletariat, the Leninist party both reflected and *created* the will of the masses through education. Education or "propaganda" (meaning the teaching of party doctrine) became one of the most important activities of party leaders and, more generally, party members. The importance attributed to education also helps explain the primacy of ideological pronouncements and movements within the CCP to purify or "rectify" the party's ideological line. As explained below, "rectification campaigns" have been integral to CCP life since its early years.

The importance of education should not, however, blind one to the role of coercion throughout the revolutionary process. Overthrowing a government and even breaking up the apparatus of the old state are relatively easy tasks compared to transforming the social, cultural, and economic systems that undergird the state. In the language of the CCP Constitution, the party "represents the interests of the working class and the broadest masses of the people" and must lead the people in establishing a "people's democratic dictatorship."[14] This dictatorship is necessary to eliminate enemies of the revolution and deal with "contradictions" (conflicts) in Chinese society.[15] Justified by this necessity, Mao Zedong and other CCP leaders, like Lenin before them, could be—and often were—ruthless. Throughout the revolutionary process, including the period of the people's democratic dictatorship, the Communist Party thus maintains its "leading role," both in theory and in practice.

## Marxism-Leninism and Mao Zedong Thought

Most of what Mao Zedong and the other early Communist Chinese leaders wrote and said about the desirability and inevitability of China's revolution owes its inspiration to the Marx-Engels theory of the nature of historical evolution and the importance of class structures and relations of production in socioeconomic change. To bridge the gap between revolutionary potential and the will to create a socialist society in China, Mao Zedong drew on Lenin's ideas and developed his own mixture of theory and practice. Maoism—or what the Chinese Communist Party calls Mao Zedong Thought—has reinforced the leading role of the party and provides the ideological justification for the twists and turns of China's revolution. The introduction to the 1982 CCP Constitution explains Mao Zedong Thought in these words:

> The Chinese Communists, with Comrade Mao Zedong as their chief representative, created Mao Zedong Thought by integrating the universal principles of Marxism-Leninism with the concrete practice of the Chinese revolution. Mao Zedong Thought is Marxism-Leninism applied and developed in China; it consists of a body of theoretical principles concerning the revolution and construction in China and a summary of experience therein, both of which have been proved correct by practice; it represents the crystallized, collective wisdom of the Communist Party of China.

As China came to grips with the negative consequences of the Cultural Revolution and more generally with Mao's leadership, one of the greatest challenges confronting the party was to retain the legitimacy built up for the CCP and China's revolution by constant association with Mao Zedong. The problem was tackled in 1981, five years after Mao's death, when the party issued a lengthy document entitled "On Questions of Party History." After carefully sorting out Mao's history, the document concluded that he had made "gross mistakes," but that on balance "Comrade Mao Zedong was a great Marxist and a great proletarian revolutionary, strategist and theorist."[16] As was later explained, not every "word Mao uttered and every article he wrote, much less his personal mistakes, belong to Mao Zedong Thought." The party did not confuse all of Mao's personal acts with the sum of Mao Zedong Thought: "Mao Zedong Thought means the correct theoretical principles for the Chinese revolution and the summation of experiences" and the "crystallization of collective wisdom" of the party, as emphasized in the passage just quoted.[17]

The ability of the CCP to come to power and to maintain itself in power for the past half century has resulted not just from effective organization and ideological indoctrination of the masses but also from the practical consequences of its policies. Its continued legitimacy thus depends on developments in all three areas. The next section summarizes the major policy shifts from the 1950s to the 1980s, paying particular attention to the implications of these shifts for China's party-state system.

## The Evolution of Party-State Relations[18]

In surveying party-state relations from the 1950s to the 1980s, several questions stand out. Did the role of the Communist Party change as new political and legal institutions were put in place after the Communists captured power in 1949? What were the main conflicts inside and outside the party, including conflicts over the goals of the revolution, and how did the party leadership handle those conflicts? What role did the People's Liberation Army—the driving force behind the Communist victory—play in the implementation of these goals?

### Restoring Order and Implementing Reform

The first years after 1949 were consumed by the overwhelming tasks of stabilizing the country and putting into place the new government institutions. Some features of this period have already been discussed. For example, Tibet was brought under Beijing's control in 1950, but Taiwan "escaped." China's reunification with Taiwan was delayed by the Cold War, which had developed in Europe after World War II and spread to Asia with the Korean War. The PRC intervened in Korea in late 1950 in response to the fear that American troops, which were pushing the North Koreans back and marching toward the Yalu River (the boundary between Korea and China), would invade China. Chinese successes in the war further legitimized the new government as responsible for the survival of the nation.

The early 1950s were also a period of close relations with the Soviet Union, with Russian textbooks used in the schools and Soviet advisers helping to build the new institutions of the state. By 1952, China was stable enough for the leadership to turn its attention to economic development, drawing on the Soviet national planning approach. The First Five-Year Plan, introduced in late 1952, followed the Soviet model by emphasizing heavy industry at the expense of agriculture and consumer goods. The desire to emulate the Soviet Union also meant that promising young Communists such as Jiang Zemin and Li Peng studied and trained in the USSR.

Consolidation of party rule during the early years entailed both conciliation and repression, much as it had in the Yanan period of the 1930s and 1940s, when the CCP was building its organizational base. The party carried its strategy over into the early 1950s, encouraging "united front" groups and permitting the continuation of non-Communist "minority" and "democratic" political parties. At the same time, those who opposed the new order or were *presumed* to oppose it (such as landlords) were dealt with ruthlessly.

Within a month of promulgating the Agrarian Reform Law in 1950, the government also issued the Marriage Law. Both land and marriage reform characterized the "antifeudal" campaign of the CCP and were central to the goal of destroying the traditional culture and socioeconomic structures of prerevolutionary China. The dilemma over women's rights that had confronted party cadres during the Yanan period reemerged, however. The landless, poor, and middle-class peasants whom the party was attempting to unite were divided across class ranks by attempts at marriage reform. The Marriage Law gave women equal rights with men in matters of marriage, divorce, choice of work, inheritance, and child custody, and a poor male peasant might find himself losing to his wife or even daughter-in-law some of the gains realized from agrarian reform. Although the Marriage Law was a landmark in the CCP's goal to improve the status of women, it fell short of revolutionizing that status when it appeared to conflict with objectives that seemed more central to maintaining popular (male) support in the conservative rural areas.[19]

The confidence of the new leaders in the combined successes of foreign and domestic policy, the elimination of opposition, and the inauguration of a strategy of economic modernization was signaled by the promulgation of the two constitutions discussed in Chapter 8, the 1954 state Constitution and the 1956 party Constitution. This confidence also manifested itself in a new phase of apparent liberalism and toleration of dissent. In May 1956, Mao Zedong appealed for intellectuals, who had been forced for several years to undergo self-criticism sessions over their antirevolutionary sentiments, to come forth with their criticisms and concerns about the government. Mao's invitation was couched in the slogan "Let a hundred schools of thought contend; let a hundred flowers bloom."[20] In response, intellectuals gradually came forward to criticize both party and government, mostly for the failure to achieve their professed goals. By 1957, it was apparent that there was, indeed, widespread dissatisfaction and resentment.

Whether Mao's **Hundred Flowers Campaign** was really a plot to flush out dissent or whether he was genuinely shocked by the extent of the dissent is debatable. The consequence, however, was a new campaign to weed out "counterrevolutionaries," launched after Mao issued his essay "On the Correct Handling of Contradictions Among the People" in June 1957. The essay harked back to his 1930s theory on contradiction, in which he distinguished between "nonantagonistic" and "antagonistic" contradictions. The former were part of the normal course of revolutionary change and reflected inevitable differences of opinion. The latter, however, reflected class differences and threatened the revolution itself. The dissenting intellectuals clearly fell into the second category. Millions of individuals were subjected to police interrogation, forced to criticize themselves for counterrevolutionary views, and "sent down" to the countryside for "reeducation," to learn from the peasants.

The Anti-Rightist Campaign, as this policy was known, was one of numerous such mass campaigns since 1949 that have targeted specific groups in Chinese society, such as landlords, intellectuals, or Communist Party members themselves. As a method of control, these rectification campaigns were rooted in the experience of the Yanan period and are noteworthy both as instruments of political control and as techniques of maintaining ideological conformity and party discipline.[21] The Anti-Rightist Campaign is also significant as a precursor of the massive attacks on all those deemed guilty of antirevolutionary thoughts or lifestyles that characterized the Cultural Revolution a decade later.

## Reviving Revolution

The year after the Anti-Rightist Campaign, China embarked on a radical attempt to accelerate the revolutionary process. Abandoning the Soviet-inspired emphasis on centralization and heavy industry, the **Great Leap Forward** in 1958 called for extreme decentralization of industrial production at the same time that **communes** were introduced in the rural areas. Correct political thought, or "redness," became the motivation for greater economic productivity, while expertise was devalued as essential to the development process. Decentralization, communes, egalitarianism, and ideological motivation were the hallmarks of a new "Maoist model" of development. Although later discredited, this model captured the imagination of many outside China who saw it as an alternative to the Soviet and Western European capital- and technology-intensive approaches to modernization.

The communes merged the administrative unit at the township level with collectivized economic production. Large communes included as many as fifty thousand people, whereas small communes in remote areas might have five to six thousand. Communes were intended to be self-sufficient, providing education and health care as well as political and economic direction for all households under their control. Because they were to represent an advanced stage of socialism, peasants were not permitted to own any private plots or even farm animals.

The communes remained for many years, but the most radical policies of the Great Leap Forward were abandoned between 1960 and 1962. Now called the "Three Bad Years," the period between 1958 and 1961 was an economic disaster that opened the first major breach in the CCP leadership since the 1930s. Over 20 million Chinese died from starvation and illness stemming from malnutrition as a consequence of massive dislocations of agricultural production, failed crops, and accelerated work demands that undermined people's health. Meanwhile, in 1959, the USSR withdrew *all* of its aid, from blueprints to technical personnel to spare parts, in reaction to what Soviet leaders saw as irresponsible Chinese policies.

In 1959–1960, the CCP leadership divided over the Great Leap Forward and China's isolation in the wake of the Soviet withdrawal. For a decade, Mao Zedong, who had held both the top party and state positions, had dominated China's policy agenda. Now the Great Leap Forward had set China's modernization back years. Top CCP leaders who had been with Mao for two decades or more harshly criticized his policies, confirming Mao's growing suspicion that even veteran Communists could lose their revolutionary commitment. In his view, the establishment of China's socialist system had not yet eliminated "feudal" and antisocialist attitudes or behavior. Although some changes were made in the top leadership and for a time Mao's overwhelming domination of China's politics loosened, his conviction that too many in the party had been consumed by self-interest would lead him to unleash a massive attack against the CCP itself in a few years.

## The Great Proletarian Cultural Revolution

The Cultural Revolution, like the Great Leap Forward, was a watershed of post-1949 Chinese politics. Although it was both a leadership struggle and a conflict over the meaning of revolution, the Cultural Revolution appeared as political madness to outside observers. The end of the Cultural Revolution overlapped with the struggle over the succession to Mao Zedong, and only with the death of Mao and the arrest of the so-called **Gang of Four** in 1976 could China move on to the reform era associated with Deng Xiaoping.

There is still much that is not known about the decisions that lay behind the start of the Cultural Revolution, but it seems clear that its roots were in Mao's preoccupations with the direction of Chinese socialism that had earlier prompted the Great Leap Forward and the divisions among

Chinese leaders in the early 1960s. By 1965, there were four major groups of Chinese leaders.[22] Mao Zedong and those (including his wife, Jiang Qing) who shared his view of a revolution of ideological conviction ("reds") over technocrats ("experts"), pressed for another campaign to raise political consciousness. This group sustained the personality cult of Mao as the "Great Helmsman" of the Chinese revolution. A second group was dominated by CCP leaders such as Liu Shaoqi and Deng Xiaoping, who were Leninists in their commitment to party leadership and integrity. They were also pragmatists, believing in the importance of following socioeconomic strategies that would hasten China on the road to development. The third group, composed of government officials, shared with the party pragmatists the commitment to modernization. This group was headed by Premier Zhou Enlai, who ultimately chose to support Mao when the conflict between the radical Maoists and organizational pragmatists could no longer be avoided. The fourth group, the military, was itself divided between those who accepted the Maoist approach to development, notably Lin Biao, the defense minister and head of the People's Liberation Army, and those whose primary concern was political order and a professionalized military.

In late 1965, Mao engineered the arrest of several top military and party officials whom he apparently believed were conspiring against him and who, in any case, were ideologically unacceptable. The conflict among the CCP leaders grew, and in spring 1966, Zhou Enlai allied himself with Mao's demands for a protracted campaign to eliminate "bourgeois ideology" in every aspect of culture. In the name of the CCP Central Committee, Mao declared the official opening of the Great Proletarian Cultural Revolution. Mao and Mao Zedong Thought were elevated as the source of all wisdom on the new revolutionary culture that, in and of itself, would assure the future of Chinese socialism.

Mao's long-standing obsession with "revisionism" within the Communist Party itself prompted his call, in August 1966, to China's youth to root out "old" culture and all those who represented or supported it. High-ranking government and party officials, including Liu Shaoqi and Deng Xiaoping, were removed from their posts and, along with their families, subjected to mass criticism and humiliation.[23] Millions of teenagers, dubbed **Red Guards**, "poured over the land, shouting down distinguished leaders, destroying precious art objects, and extolling puritan virtues."[24] Party committees joined in the attacks on teachers and school administrators, only to see students turning on party leaders themselves. Moderate student leaders were replaced by more radical ones. Destroying the "four olds" (old ideas, old culture, old customs, and old habits) quickly became the excuse for attacks on anything and anyone deemed unrevolutionary by the Red Guards.

By mid-1967, the Red Guards had brought China to near anarchy. Marches, demonstrations, and study sessions gave way to mob violence and arbitrary, vicious attacks on anyone deviating from the Red Guards' unpredictable view of correct behavior. During the peak of the Cultural Revolution in 1966–1967, millions of young people poured into Beijing and other large cities, enjoying logistical support from the army. But by late 1967, the army gradually assumed control in an effort to restore order. With the party organization decimated, the PLA itself took over governing. By fall 1967, the PLA ruled directly in twenty-two of China's provinces.[25] This military prominence explains why Lin Biao, the leader of the pro-Maoist faction in the army, was designated Mao Zedong's "heir apparent" in the 1969 CCP Constitution described in Chapter 8.

For those who suffered during the Cultural Revolution, including the purged Deng Xiaoping and his son (who was thrown from an upper-story window and permanently crippled), the period from the beginning of the Cultural Revolution to Mao's death constitute the Ten Bad Years. The disasters of the decade, including the destruction of the party and state bureaucracies, the derailment of economic modernization, and China's loss of international esteem, inspired the reform strategies after Mao's death. But even with the success of reforms from the 1970s to the 1990s, legacies of the Cultural Revolution have persisted. Those who saw their lives disrupted for years, often with their families and homes destroyed, harbored bitterness and suspicion about politics in general and the CCP leadership, specifically.[26] Many who became party members during the 1960s were politically correct but technically incompetent and later acted as a drag on China's modernization efforts.

## Succession Politics: The Transition to Reform

From the late 1960s to the mid-1970s, the process of rebuilding both party and state structures proceeded slowly. Although a few ministries emerged relatively unscathed, many ceased to operate, as did the State Council itself. For a period, the integration and overlap of party and state structures was almost complete, as every government office was subjected to the control of a "revolutionary committee" whose leading member was also the party secretary.

In 1971, Lin Biao (Mao's "heir apparent") was killed in an airplane crash in Mongolia, apparently while trying to flee to the Soviet Union. Although the details surrounding this incident have never been verified, the party two years later charged that Lin had plotted to assassinate Mao Zedong and, with the help of other military leaders, to seize power in a coup d'état. Not surprisingly, the incident raised questions about the loyalty of the army and hastened the normalization process, in which party control over the military was reasserted.

The Lin Biao affair elevated Zhou Enlai as China's most important leader after Mao Zedong. By 1973, Zhou had moved to rehabilitate old party cadres purged during the Cultural Revolution, including his former protégé, Deng Xiaoping, who had been held under house arrest for seven years.[27] Deng moved quickly to assume key posts and place moderates in party positions in order to position himself for the coming succession battle. However, when Zhou died in early 1976, Deng was purged again almost immediately by Maoist "radicals" in the CCP leadership.

The death of Mao Zedong in September 1976 produced the next spasm in the succession struggle. At the center of the struggle was the Gang of Four, composed of Jiang Qing and her three colleagues from Shanghai. Jiang claimed that on his deathbed, her husband said she should be the new party chairman, but China's acting prime minister, Hua Guofeng, disputed the claim. One month after Mao's death, his wife and her colleagues were arrested, seemingly clearing the way for Hua, a compromise choice for the succession, to build his reputation as China's preeminent leader.[28] But in 1977, Hua acquiesced to Deng's return to leadership—a major strategic mistake, for within three years Hua had been maneuvered out of all top party posts by Deng. The stage had been cleared for the reform period.

## The Four Modernizations

Although associated with Deng Xiaoping, China's contemporary modernization strategy dates to Premier Zhou Enlai's 1975 proposal for comprehensive modernization in the four areas of agriculture, industry, defense, and science and technology by the year 2000.[29] The pragmatists' commitment to this program, known as the Four Modernizations, was opposed by those still wedded to the Maoist revolutionary model, but after the arrest of the Gang of Four, Hua Guofeng reintroduced Zhou's plan in 1978.[30] Although these plans went through numerous changes over the ensuing decade, they marked the beginning of China's reform period.

While Zhou was still alive and then again after his rehabilitation under Hua, Deng Xiaoping played a central role in the planning and implementation of the Four Modernizations. With the demotion of Hua and, in 1982, the adoption of the new party and state constitutions, Deng was secure in his position of preeminent leader. In the 1980s, he became known as the architect of China's "second revolution," and it was not until the Tiananmen events of 1989 that the issues of stable leadership and the direction of the revolution again moved to the forefront of Chinese politics. These questions will be taken up again in Chapter 12. For now, we turn to an assessment of the first three decades of China's revolution under the "leading role of the party."

## Assessing the Party-State System

Viewed retrospectively, the most important phases of China's revolution have been a reaction to, or "correction" of, what occurred in a previous phase. Mistakes were made, then admitted, leaders differed over what—or who—was responsible, and policies were changed. Throughout the period, though, the same political problems recur, albeit in new forms. These problems are both unique to China and shared with other developing nations, including India: maintenance of order, political legitimacy and stability, leadership succession, and tension between the central and regional governments. To these must be added the core issue that plagues countries that have endured massive revolution: When is the revolution judged complete, so that society can operate "normally"?

The road to normalization, however, is poorly marked. The twists and turns in Chinese politics from the 1950s to the 1980s will not be replicated, but they do suggest some long-standing, unresolved questions, such as how to address the tension between centralization and decentralization, how to regularize government institutions, including the development of laws and courts, and how to create a "civil society" strengthened by groups free from party or government control, all questions taken up in future chapters. The most provocative short-term question is what kind of leadership the post-Deng period will bring. This is the issue with which this chapter closes.

Five characteristics of China's leadership during the last two decades of the twentieth century stand out. First, top leaders, even at the regional level, have held both party and state positions, but the source of their influence has continued to be their rank in the Communist Party hierarchy. Although efforts were made in the 1980s to separate party and state institutions, the integration of the two hierarchies has persisted in the 1990s, and preserving the "leading role of the party" has remained a top priority.

Second, with the exception of the end of the Cultural Revolution and the Lin Biao period, China has been under civilian rule. Nonetheless, military support has continued to be essential for those who aspired to succeed Deng Xiaoping as China's preeminent leader. For example, in a move to consolidate his position at the Fourteenth Party Congress in 1992, CCP General Secretary Jiang Zemin succeeded in outmaneuvering one of Deng's chief supporters in the PLA, whom he presumably saw as a potential threat to his power. This move was followed by a general shakeup of the PLA's hierarchy, including the transfer of a number of regional military commanders.[31]

Jiang's jockeying to assume Deng's mantle and the long domination of Chinese politics by "strongmen," suggests a third characteristic of China's leadership: Not only personalism but factionalism as well play important roles. Personalism in China has entailed the elevation of pre-eminent leaders, and it is typical of personalist politics that even as the "cult" of Mao Zedong was criticized and Deng Xiaoping undertook to prevent overconcentration of power in the hands of a single individual, Deng himself was elevated as a preeminent leader. As in many nation-states lacking a strong tradition of regularized transfers of power, acquiring and maintaining power in China relies on building personal loyalty within the party and state hierarchies, both of which are factionalized. Factional politics and personalism are discussed further in Chapter 12.

Fourth, despite continuing differences over important issues in China's political and economic future, the backgrounds of the country's leaders has reflected the importance attributed to technical expertise. With the passing of the last survivors of the Long March of the 1930s went those who supported Mao Zedong's emphasis on "redness" over "expertise." Modernization calls for leadership that understands the complex problems of economic growth. Differences over the speed or priorities of that growth have still occurred, but the commitment to modernization has framed the debate and differences have surfaced within the context of this commitment.

Finally, one might ask how representative of the Chinese population as a whole China's leadership has been. The simple answer is "not very." Efforts have been made to recruit ethnic minorities into the CCP, but no members of non-Han ethnic groups were elected to the party elite (Politburo and Standing Committee) at either the Thirteenth or the Fourteenth National Party Congresses.[32] Minority CCP first secretaries in minority autonomous regions have been equally scarce.[33] Likewise, the top party posts have remained male preserves. The most important CCP organs, the Politburo, its Standing Committee, and the Secretariat, have had no female members. Out of the 319 full and alternate members of the Central Committee elected at the Fourteenth Party Congress in 1992, 10.3 percent were minority nationals (close to their proportion in China's population), but only 7.5 percent were women.[34] In short, the Chinese political system has shared with a preponderance of systems in the world the exclusion of women from top political leadership.

# Notes

1. The Kuomintang (KMT) adopted the same organization as the CCP shortly after World War I, when both were advised by Comintern representatives. The KMT used this structure to rule Taiwan after 1949 until democratic reforms were introduced in the late 1980s. On the reforms, see Tun-jen Cheng and Stephan Haggard, eds., *Political Change in Taiwan* (Boulder: Lynne Rienner, 1992), and Peter R.

Moody, Jr., *Political Change on Taiwan: A Study of Ruling Party Adaptability* (New York: Praeger, 1992).

2. Murray Scot Tanner, "The Erosion of Communist Party Control over Lawmaking in China," *China Quarterly*, no. 138 (June 1994), pp. 381–403.

3. In order to avoid confusion with the National People's Congress, the National Party Congress will not be abbreviated as NPC.

4. The Thirteenth Party Congress (1987) was the first at which the list of nominees for election to the Central Committee contained more names than the number of slots to be filled (but only five names more). Kenneth Lieberthal, *Governing China: From Revolution Through Reform* (New York: W. W. Norton, 1995), p. 160.

5. During the Fourteenth Party Congress (1992), it was stated that the commission had investigated more than 870,000 cases of corruption and that 154,000 party members had been expelled from 1987 to 1992. James C. F. Wang, *Contemporary Chinese Politics: An Introduction* (Englewood Cliffs, N.J.: Prentice-Hall, 1995), p. 80. See also Shan Wei and Peng Daxin, "Battle Against Corruption Still Raging," *Beijing Review* 39, no. 1 (January 1–7, 1996), pp. 21–24.

6. *Beijing Review* 35, no. 44 (November 2–8, 1992), pp. 14–15.

7. Ibid., p. 13.

8. Ibid., p. 14.

9. Zhao Ziyang, "On Separating Party from Government," *Beijing Review* 30, no. 50 (December 14–20, 1987), pp. 18–20.

10. Kevin J. O'Brien, "Chinese People's Congresses and Legislative Embeddedness: Understanding Early Organizational Development," *Comparative Political Studies* 27, no. 1 (April 1994), p. 91. O'Brien's research found that even reformers concerned with strengthening People's Congresses didn't necessarily advocate greater party-state separation.

11. See Alfred G. Meyer's classic study, *Leninism* (Cambridge: Harvard University Press, 1957); also Neil Harding, *Lenin's Political Thought*, 2 vols. (New York: St. Martin's Press, 1977).

12. See, in particular, pts. 2 and 3 of Lenin's classic work *What Is to Be Done?* (first published in 1902 and reissued in numerous editions).

13. From the "General Programme" of the Constitution. See *The Twelfth National Congress of the CPC* (Beijing: Foreign Languages Press, 1982), p. 97.

14. This terminology was derived from Marx, Engels, and Lenin, for whom the "dictatorship of the proletariat" referred to the form of state organization in which a newly victorious working class would use the coercive power of the state to put down the enemies of the revolution. Harding, *Lenin's Political Thought*, vol. 2, pp. 85–87, 134–140, and chap. 9.

15. The theoretical significance of the term "contradiction" is explained in the essay "On Contradiction," claimed to have been written by Mao Zedong in 1937 during the Yanan period but first published in 1952. The essay is reprinted in numerous anthologies.

16. *Beijing Review* 24, no. 27 (July 6, 1981), p. 29.

17. Zhang Bizhong, "Differentiations Are Necessary," *Beijing Review* 24, no. 38 (September 21, 1981), p. 17. When the party celebrated the one-hundredth anniversary of Mao's birth in 1993, Jiang Zemin stated: "Mao Zedong Thought will forever remain a theoretical treasure-house for Chinese Communists and a spiri-

tual pillar of the Chinese nation." "Mao Zedong's Historic Contributions," *Beijing Review* 37, no. 2 (January 10–16, 1994), p. 9.

18. There are many good sources that cover this period. The following are recommended: Roderick MacFarquhar, ed., *The Politics of China, 1949–1989* (Cambridge: Cambridge University Press, 1993); Lucian W. Pye, *China: An Introduction*, 4th ed. (New York: HarperCollins, 1991); and Jonathan D. Spence, *The Search for Modern China* (New York: W. W. Norton, 1990), chaps. 19–24. Essential documents of the period are compiled and annotated in Harold C. Hinton, ed., *The People's Republic of China, 1949–1979: A Documentary Survey*, 5 vols. (Wilmington, Del.: Scholarly Resources, 1980).

19. Kay Ann Johnson, *Women, the Family and Peasant Revolution in China* (Chicago: University of Chicago Press, 1983), chap. 8.

20. The slogan alluded to the ancient Zhou dynasty period of the twelfth to third centuries B.C.E., when "one hundred contending schools" of philosophy, including the Confucianist, Daoist, and Legalist, clashed. Pye, *China*, pp. 36, 244–246. For the text of Mao's original One Hundred Flowers speech, see Harding, *Documentary Survey*, vol. 2, pp. 341–349.

21. One of the most famous such movements was the 1942–1944 Rectification Campaign. See Mark Selden, *The Yenan Way in Revolutionary China* (Cambridge: Harvard University Press, 1971), pp. 188–200. The rectification method emphasized intensive education, small-group study, criticism and self-criticism, and thought reform. Suzanne Ogden discussed rectification as a managerial form in the 1980s in *China's Unresolved Issues: Politics, Development, and Culture*, 3d ed. (Englewood Cliffs, N.J.: Prentice-Hall, 1995), pp. 291–296.

22. See the discussion in Pye, *China*, pp. 294–295; and Spence, *Search for Modern China*, pp. 596–604. Tang Tsou analyzed intraparty factions (what he calls "informal groups") in *The Cultural Revolution and Post-Mao Reforms: A Historical Perspective* (Chicago: University of Chicago Press, 1986), chaps. 2, 3. The authors in MacFarquhar, *Politics of China*, also emphasize elite disunity.

23. Liu was head of state and a senior member of the Standing Committee of the Politburo. Deng was secretary general of the party and a vice premier under Zhou Enlai.

24. Pye, *China*, p. 298.

25. Ibid., p. 306.

26. Spence, *Search for Modern China*, pp. 617, 634–635. See, for example, the poignant stories in Chihua Wen, *The Red Mirror: Children of China's Cultural Revolution*, ed. Bruce Jones (Boulder: Westview Press, 1995).

27. Liu Shaoqi, who was purged (like Deng) in 1966, died in 1969.

28. Jiang and her three closest radical colleagues were dubbed the Gang of Four after their arrest, as part of the campaign to discredit them and the Maoist model. They were tried in 1980 and found guilty of a long list of counts related to their activities during the Cultural Revolution. Jiang Qing's death sentence was suspended in order to give her time to "repent." She committed suicide in 1991, while still under house arrest.

29. See Zhou's "Report on the Work of the Government," *Peking Review* (*Beijing Review*) 18, no. 4 (January 24, 1975), pp. 21–25.

30. Hua Guofeng, "Report on the Work of the Government," *Peking Review* 21, no. 10 (March 10, 1978), pp. 8–40.

31. Tony Saich, "The Fourteenth Party Congress: A Programme for Authoritarian Rule," *China Quarterly* 132 (December 1992), pp. 1149–1150; and "Quarterly Chronicle and Documentation," *China Quarterly* 133 (March 1993), p.199.

32. Saich, "Fourteenth Party Congress," pp. 1151–1152.

33. Until the early 1990s, at least, there appear to have been only two minority first party secretaries in autonomous regions. Dru C. Gladney, "Ethnic Identity in China: The New Politics of Difference," in William A. Joseph, ed., *China Briefing, 1994* (Boulder: Westview Press, with the Asia Society, 1994), p. 185.

34. "Quarterly Chronicle," p. 193.

# *eleven*

# Levels of Government and Regionalism

This chapter examines the importance of subnational levels of government in the relationship between citizens and governments in India, China, and Japan. The first section summarizes federal and unitary systems, and the second examines Indian federalism, which has been molded and cross-pressured by the forces of both centralization and decentralization over the past half century.

The third section of the chapter discusses China's local and regional governments, with particular attention given to the decentralization of power that altered Chinese politics in the 1980s and 1990s. Despite critical differences between India and China, these two Asian giants share many of the same problems that result when traditional societies undergo rapid change.

The last section of the chapter discusses Japan's levels of government. Japan has not experienced the kinds of pressures on local and regional governments that India and China have. Nonetheless, politics outside of Tokyo are far from static, as the case of the Okinawan dispute over American troops will illustrate.

## Federal and Unitary Systems

In a federal system, there are two levels of government with *constitutional* authority to make laws affecting citizens.[1] Every country has more than one level of government, but in unitary systems, the regional and local governments may be created, changed, and abolished at will by the national government, and the powers of the subnational governments are those granted by the national government, which monopolizes sovereignty.

In theory, the distinction between federal and unitary systems is clear. In practice, the distinction is often murky, even messy. Constitutions typically list powers belonging to the central government and regional governments and may also enumerate shared jurisdictions. But dynamic socioeconomic conditions, along with shifting political values and judicial interpretations, influence the evolution of these jurisdictions in ways unforeseen by the drafters of the constitutions. This has happened in Canada and the United States as well as in India.

Evolution in federal systems has been matched by changes in unitary systems, where contemporary history provides examples of national governments attempting to centralize control over their country during some periods but decentralizing at others; or they may centralize in some spheres of activity (such as economic policy) but decentralize in others (social policy). Political and economic conditions often breed as many stresses in unitary systems as they do in federal systems. Such stresses are evident in China, for example, where economic reform policies have included substantial decentralization of policymaking and the introduction of what some scholars have called "market-preserving federalism."[2]

Level-of-government relationships in India are especially complex. The national government, also known as the center or Union, has constitutional powers superior to those of the regional units, called states. The emergency powers and President's Rule examined in Chapter 9 are examples of the ultimate authority of the center. But states have become more important for a variety of reasons, creating tensions between the levels of government. It is to these dynamics that we turn next.

## (Dis)Unity in the Indian Federation

To better understand the countervailing tendencies in Indian federalism, we need to review how India's Constitution designates the division of powers between the center and the states. As noted earlier, the Constitution has undergone substantial amendment over the years, with implications for relations between the national and state governments. In addition, political parties, specifically, and political participation, more generally, have also changed the center-state relationship.

### Constitutional Provisions

Early in their deliberations, members of the Constituent Assembly concluded that a federal arrangement would best secure Indian unity and democracy. The country was too vast and too diverse and the regions had too many distinct histories, to imagine that a centralized unitary system would be able to meet the challenges facing the nationalist leaders.

A federal arrangement was also consistent with India's long history. Readers may recall from Chapter 5 that ancient India had numerous great empires, but none of these encompassed the entire subcontinent. The empires had strong power centers but allowed peripheries to have legitimate power and responsibility for implementing decisions in ways appropriate to local conditions. The durability of village government, the *panchayat*, reinforced local autonomy.[3]

Indian federalism, variously described as centralized, cooperative, or quasi-federal,[4] is distinguished by a number of features, some of which it shares with other federations and some of which are unique. First, the Constitution, in Article 1, characterizes India as a "Union of States"; nowhere does it describe the country as a federation or discuss federalism as such. Unlike the United States but like many other types of federal systems, Indian states do not have constitutions; there is only the national Constitution.[5] Part Four of the Union Constitution describes in considerable detail the structure of government to be found in each state.

Dividing government functions between the Union and the states, the Seventh Schedule of the Constitution contains detailed lists of the respective spheres of action of each level of government. Although the Union list is the longest and most comprehensive, the state list includes important and familiar (to North Americans) activities, such as the right to constitute and determine the powers of local government entities. A concurrent list details nearly fifty areas of shared jurisdiction. The national Parliament has **residuary power**, the power to make laws with respect to any matter not enumerated in the state or concurrent list.

Another important feature of Indian federalism is the distribution of financial power, an area of controversy in most federal systems. The Constitution gives the most significant taxing powers to the Union government, those of income taxes, excise taxes, and customs duties. States may levy sales taxes and taxes on agricultural income, alcoholic beverages (an important source of revenue for many states), certain mineral rights, luxuries (including entertainment, such as movie tickets), and a number of other items. Together, these revenues have accounted for less than one-half of state expenditures. The remainder comes from taxes that are collected by the central government but are turned over to the states. In addition, the central government distributes grants-in-aid to poorer states as a way of compensating for regional inequities.[6]

In summary, the historical concerns about national unity produced a constitution in India that instituted some measure of regional autonomy balanced with superior authority for the national government. Chapter 9 also noted that the Rajya Sabha, structured to represent state interests, is less powerful than the Lok Sabha. Only in a few instances that directly impinge on the states' authority does the upper house have the power to block lower-house action. The Constitution authorizes the national Parliament to make laws regarding matters on the state list if approved by two-thirds of the voting members present and voting in the Rajya Sabha. This provision, along with the provision that Parliament may legislate with respect to any state matter when a proclamation of emergency is in effect, holds the potential for dramatically expanding the Union government's residual power.

Finally, the constitutional amending process also tips the balance of Indian federalism toward the center. Most of the Constitution's provisions may be amended by the national Parliament alone, with the approval of the majority of both houses (including two-thirds of the members present and voting). This includes such important sections of the Constitution as the enumeration of fundamental rights. However, amendment of those sections of the Constitution pertaining specifically to the states, such as the Seventh Schedule lists, the representation of states in Parliament, and the relations between the Union and states laid out in Part Eleven, also require ratification by the legislatures of at least one-half of the states. Ironically, alteration of the boundaries of states or the formation of new states does not require formal approval of the states involved. These changes may be made solely under the authority of the national Parliament.

This discussion of the constitutional provisions pertinent to Indian federalism is essential to understanding how the government operates and what the political "ground rules" are. Neither the structures nor the ground rules are static, however. The next section examines the forces that demonstrate both the flexibility of India's federal system and the risks facing it.

## The Regionalization of Politics

When the Constituent Assembly was debating and drafting the Indian Constitution, its members were preoccupied with communal (Hindu-Muslim) conflict and the disastrous effects of Partition. But it was linguistic diversity that provided the first major challenge to the federal arrangement.

**States' Reorganization.**   Most of the British-created regional units were linguistically heterogeneous, and prior to Independence, the Indian National Congress had called for the formation of linguistically based provinces. But by the late 1940s, the most important Congress leaders were preoccupied with national unity and viewed the establishment of states along linguistic lines as threatening that unity by fostering subnational loyalties. Shortly after the Constitution went into effect in 1950, however, demands by linguistic groups—demands that had never disappeared—escalated. In 1953, the state of Andhra Pradesh, with a Telegu-speaking majority, was created from the old British unit of Madras. The other part of Madras became Tamilnadu (with a Tamil-speaking population).

Acquiescence to Telegu demands produced a clamor among other language groups for their own states. Reluctantly, Prime Minister Nehru appointed the States Reorganization Commission to examine the problem. The commission's 1955 report recommended that political boundaries be redrawn largely along linguistic lines, and the 1956 States Reorganization Act provided for fourteen states and six Union Territories (in contrast to the twenty-seven states that had existed in 1950). **States reorganization** in the 1950s, however, failed to appease all those making demands, and in the 1960s, the state of Bombay was divided into two new states (Gujarat and Maharashtra), as was Punjab (Punjab and Haryana).

**Punjab.** Nehru's fears that states reorganization would contribute to regionalism in Indian politics were probably well founded, although other factors that explain the growth of regionalism were and continue to be at work. The situation in Punjab, where there is pressure for a Sikh state, illustrates this complexity. A political party, the Akali Dal ("army of the faithful"), has argued for a separate nation-state since Independence and Partition. Originally, the Akali Dal couched its demand in linguistic, not communal (religious), terms, but it appealed primarily to Sikhs.[7] Their demands for recognition of Punjabi (that is, Sikh) identity, however, have been frustrated by their attempts to win an electoral majority in the state. Before the division of the old state of Punjab in 1966, Sikhs constituted only about one-third of the state population and not all Sikhs supported the Akali Dal. After the division, Sikhs formed a bare majority of the population, and the Akali Dal increasingly pushed for a dominant Sikh identity in Punjab. But the Akali Dal never had enough electoral support to form a majority government. Through the 1970s, this situation meant that Punjab's state politics were never polarized completely along either linguistic or communal lines, but it also meant that the aspirations of supporters of a truly Sikh state were frustrated.

In the 1980s, the situation turned violent, and Punjab quickly became one of the most dangerous threats to national unity and stability. The disintegration of the political situation resulted from the convergence of two independent developments.[8] The first was division between militants and moderates within the Akali Dal Party and within the Sikh community generally. A Sikh religious leader, Sant Jarnail Singh Bhindranwale, who saw as his mission the consolidation and purification of the Sikhs, emerged as an important militant leader.[9]

The second factor at work was the changed nature of center-state relations under Prime Minister Indira Gandhi. Prime Minister Gandhi's goal was to guarantee Congress preeminence in Punjabi politics by undermining the Akali Dal. To this end, her government encouraged Bhindranwale in the early 1980s as a way of dividing the Akali Dal. However, extremist Sikh attacks on Hindus began to threaten Congress support among Hindu voters, and President's Rule was imposed in Punjab in 1983. Bhindranwale and Sikh terrorists set up their armed headquarters in the Golden Temple, the symbolic center of the Sikh religion in the city of Amritsar. Ultimately, Mrs. Gandhi ordered the Indian army to flush out Bhindranwale's sanctuary in "**Operation Bluestar**" in June 1984. Bhindranwale was killed, along with hundreds of his supporters and hundreds of Indian troops. Even among those Sikhs who had never supported the extremists' cause, Operation Bluestar was viewed as an assault on the essence of Sikhism. Five months later, Mrs. Gandhi was assassinated by two Sikh bodyguards, an act that in turn led to the massacre of thousands of Sikhs by mobs in New Delhi and elsewhere.

The events of 1984 left a sordid legacy in Indian politics, both in center-state and in communal relations. President's Rule, as suggested in Chapter 9, stymied the normal development of competitive elections in Punjab, and communal hatred grew unchecked. The situation appeared to stabilize in the early 1990s, but in September 1995, Sikh terrorists assassinated the chief minister of Punjab, and the potential for long-term political accommodation in Punjab was again cast in doubt.

Although the example of the Akali Dal is extreme, the role it has played illustrates an important political trend influencing Indian federalism. This trend is the regionalization of politics, which in turn reflects other political developments such as the decline of the Congress Party and the mobilization of voters around regional issues. The increasing importance of state parties—that is, parties within a particular state that have little or no national prominence—is one of the most salient aspects of the regionalization process.

**State Party Systems.**    Paul R. Brass has categorized three types of Indian state party systems: those in which one party dominates, those in which one party dominates but there is institutionalized opposition, and those with competitive parties.[10] For many years, the first type was widespread, with a state-based Congress Party organization monopolizing power. Prime Minister Nehru's approach to center-state relations included negotiation with state party bosses in such a way as to maintain stability at the center and a measure of autonomy for the states. His daughter's efforts, when she was prime minister, to centralize control over state Congress machines ultimately undermined the party both nationally and regionally. By the 1990s, there were no longer any states where the Congress Party was predictably dominant.

In the one-party-dominant systems with institutionalized opposition, the dominant party is often still Congress, but opposition parties have been strong enough over time to alternate in power. As early as 1985, the BJP was the main opposition party in three Indian states and eventually formed governments there, as it did in Maharashtra in 1995. Thus, as the electorate changes, so may the party systems, often becoming more competitive.

The states with competitive party systems generally include Congress as one of the major parties, and Congress often forms the government. But alternation in power is a real possibility and, in some instances, frequent. The non-Congress parties illustrate the variety in Indian politics: they include longtime regional players like the Communist parties in West Bengal and Kerala, caste-based parties, and parties that have grown out of regional movements for cultural and linguistic identity (such as the DMK and AIADMK in Tamilnadu noted in Chapter 4).

State politics illustrate both the promises of and threats to Indian democracy. Politics at the state level, which is often the scene of political turmoil—enough so to warrant the imposition of President's Rule, as we have seen—also reflect the spread of political participation to many groups formerly excluded, such as the low castes. Caste conflict typically plays out at the local and state level and often results in violence as increasing numbers of groups vie for scarce resources. At the same time, traditional sources of authority have been eroded, the Congress Party has often seemed headed toward self-destruction, and although other political parties have successfully competed for the power to form governments, they have been unsuccessful in implementing reform policies in most states.

Despite this rather gloomy assessment, some analyses of Indian politics suggest that the development of strong regional polities offers the best hope for national unity and democracy. Dennis Austin, for example, has maintained "guarded optimism" about India's future because the nation's extreme diversity makes it possible to insulate some regions from the instability of others.[11] Arendt Lijphart has argued that India's survival as a deeply divided, multiethnic democracy is tied to the degree of consociationalism it displays. Consociational theory views democratic stability in divided societies as linked to the degree and kind of power-sharing arrangements available to minority linguistic and religious groups. Thus, greater state autonomy and control over matters important to minorities would contribute to national stability. Although Lijphart's theory sets other prerequisites for consociational democracy, his is an argument for strengthening regional power sharing, not for encouraging greater centralization.[12]

In this evaluation of Indian federalism, there emerges a picture of a highly centralized system as outlined in the Constitution and as reinforced by the central role that the Congress Party has played over the decades. Nonetheless, there are strong pressures for decentralization, and persuasive arguments that strengthening the states will contribute to stability and democracy in the Union. India, however, is not alone in experiencing pressures for decentralization. Regionalism in China is also a political reality, as the next section explains.

## Regions and Regionalism in China

The section that follows first summarizes the organization of provincial and local governments in China and then explores the growth of regionalism that has accompanied the socioeconomic changes of the past two decades.

China is organized into twenty-two provinces, five autonomous regions, and three municipalities (metropolitan areas administered directly by the central government). The most recent change in provincial boundaries was the separation of Hainan Island from Guangdong Province, creating a new province. The incorporation of Hong Kong in 1997 as a special administrative region also alters the administrative map. Beneath the provincial level are the local government entities: the cities, counties, and municipalities. The 1982 Constitution prescribes People's Congresses at each level as "local organs of state power" (Article 96). Executive authority is vested in provincial governors, municipal mayors, and chiefs in the townships. In general, the provincial and local government structures mirror those of the central government.[13]

The provinces reflect China's traditional geographical and cultural regions, and like India's states, they differ substantially in size, wealth, topography, and even language. The county, or *xian*, is the administrative subunit of the province, and there are approximately two thousand of them. Since the late 1980s, governance has grown in so-called village committees, which are designed to encourage limited democracy, autonomy, and cadre accountability in China's more than nine hundred thousand villages.[14] Both village committees and neighborhood committees in the municipalities have served to maintain state control at the grassroots level, but the committees are also potential targets of citizen pressures to address local concerns and thus serve as transmission belts to higher authority.

China is formally a unitary state, so the powers of all regional units are delegated by the national government, and the highest-ranking regional authorities are appointed by the central government. Despite this, China is not as centralized as once believed. Provinces are especially important political players, and their power has grown in the 1980s and 1990s, for several reasons. China's size and diversity contribute to regional forces that have always challenged national unity. The expanse and huge populations of some of the provinces have meant that the central government must rely on provincial governments to coordinate policy, as well as to deliver goods and services. The increased scope and complexity of the economy has added not only to the burdens but also to the leverage of regional officials responsible for implementing national policy.

Part of the post-Mao reform effort, in fact, was to shift, or devolve, power from the national to the regional bureaucracies.[15] This devolution of power accounted for the development of what some have argued is, in fact, Chinese-style federalism. Whereas Western federalism is typically rooted in an explicit system for protecting individual rights, has strong constitutional foundations, and is associated with democratization, these traditions have been absent in China. Instead, China's decentralization has been characterized by conditions that have required the allocation of responsibilities among different levels of government in order to implement the market reforms of the 1980s and 1990s.[16] For example, subnational governments were given primary authority over the economy within specified jurisdictions, including control of many state-owned industrial enterprises formerly controlled by the central government. Likewise, major construction or entrepreneurial undertakings have required provincial cooperation to organize resources, including people. For an economic system in which national planning still weighs heavily, therefore, cooperation has been essential for continued economic growth. This political reality, together with the role of the territorial units in collecting all taxes, has given these units substantial bargaining power.[17]

Decline in ideological discipline, along with the free-for-all competition for wealth—and the corruption that has come about in its wake—has also eroded the leverage of the central government over subnational governments. This erosion, in turn, has contributed to differences among national leaders and to the desire of so-called new conservatives, or neoconservatives, to reinforce the authority of the state by emphasizing themes of national unity and the need to tighten control over the provinces.[18]

Finally, we need to look more closely at why and how economic liberalization has encouraged decentralization. Crucial to the new development strategy after Mao was the decision to shift from national self-reliance to the international market. Earlier policies sought equalization of wealth between regions and classes, and capital investment was directed to underdeveloped inland provinces. But in the 1980s, the coastal regions, where commercial and industrial development had concentrated before 1949, were targeted for investment in order to expand China's export capacity. One result of this policy shift was obvious by the early 1990s, when the coastal provinces led by Guangdong, Zhejiang, and Fujian, experienced the highest rates of economic growth in the world.[19] Other results were not so obvious to outsiders. For example, wealth and corruption increased, but so did interregional and provincial competition and tension with the central government.

## SEZs and Regional Economies

As early as 1980, the central government designated "**special economic zones**" (SEZs) on the coast, with incentives to attract foreign investment. The SEZs are tax-free zones that provide customs exemptions and preferential treatment for foreign investors. Concentrated in coastal South China, the first four of the SEZs helped make Guangdong and Fujian Provinces the richest in China, with their growth rates around 20 percent in the early 1990s and per capita incomes four to five times higher than China's average. Along with coastal provinces further north and the large metropolises of Shanghai, Beijing, and Tianjin, China's eastern strip, which comprises 30 percent of China's population, became known as the "Gold Coast" and accounted for almost one-half of the country's gross domestic product (GDP) by the mid-1990s. This region also received approximately 80 percent of all foreign direct investment in China.[20]

There are two repercussions of this economic boom that are pertinent to the discussion of regionalism in China. The rapid growth severely exacerbated the disparity in wealth between coastal provinces and the remaining seventeen inland provinces, as well as the autonomous areas, where most of the minority nationalities live. For example, by 1994, the per capita GDP of Shanghai was more than ten times that of Guizhou, a province inhabited primarily by ethnic groups.[21] This regional economic disequilibrium increased pressures on the central government from the inland provinces for policy remedies and increased resistance to central interference from the richer provinces.

A second repercussion was the dramatic shift in employment and population migration patterns. These regional disparities drove millions of people to migrate to the richer provinces in search of opportunities. It was estimated that by 1995 the "floating population" of unemployed and underemployed approached 80 to 100 million people. This floating population was disproportionately made up of young males with modest educational levels (elementary to junior high school).[22]

The size of this population shift, like the problem of regional inequity, appears to have been an unintended consequence of central state policy. The post-Mao reform efforts of the late 1970s and early 1980s focused on a policy known as the rural responsibility system, which was designed to increase agricultural production and farm income. Central to the system were contracts issued to peasants that established quotas for agricultural production. Once the quotas were met, farms and households could retain any additional earnings. Specialization and commodity production increasingly replaced subsistence agriculture. Increased agricultural output, along with greater peasant mobility, work options, and rural wealth were among the benefits of the reform. But increased investment in production, including improved technology, also contributed to the growth of rural surplus labor, a source of the urban migrants. Moreover, by the mid-1980s, government investment in agriculture diminished in favor of the new emphasis on urban economies. In addition, peasants increasingly put their profits into new housing and consumer goods rather than investing in new technologies or other factors of agricultural production.[23] Meanwhile, the cost of agricultural inputs, such as fertilizer, increased faster than farm incomes. The decentralization of control that accompanied reform gave county and township officials the authority and incentive to manipulate for their own purposes local tax structures and allocations from the central government.[24] An old Chinese pattern of exploitation by local officials, accompanied by occasional peasant revolts, reemerged in the rural areas.[25]

## Special Cases: Tibet and Hong Kong Revisited

To conclude this section on China, we return to Tibet and Hong Kong and to issues that were introduced in earlier chapters. Tibet, under China's administrative hierarchy, is an autonomous region, whereas Hong Kong was accorded the unique status of special administrative region. Both regions illustrate the continuing tensions between centralization and decentralization in China.

According to the 1982 state Constitution, national autonomous regions, like the provinces, have local government structures consisting of People's Congresses and "people's governments." Following the model for national and provincial-level structures, the congresses are "local organs of state power" whose authority is concentrated in a standing committee headed by a chairman and vice chairman. Under the terms of the Law on Regional Autonomy of Minorities adopted in 1984, the administrative head of an autonomous region, prefecture, or county must be of the nationality exercising regional autonomy in the area concerned.[26] In keeping with more recent policies promoting recognition (rather than assimilation) of national minorities, the Constitution also provides that state laws and policies in the autonomous areas be implemented "in the light of the existing local situation" (Article 115). In theory, this provision, especially when accompanied by national policies that provide special benefits to minorities (such as state investments or exemption from stringent application of population control policies), encourages greater decentralization in the autonomous areas.

Tibet, although unique in many respects, illustrates the general dilemma facing any policies designed to enhance regional autonomy, especially in border areas. In the mid-1980s, the central government adopted several policies indicating support for preserving Tibetan culture and religion. The regional party secretary for the Tibetan Autonomous Region (TAR), Wu Jinghua, had built his career in bureaucracies dealing with minority affairs and was known to have some understanding of Tibetan culture. The TAR governor was a Tibetan (and a former prefectural party secretary), a man who believed that traditional Tibetan culture was not inconsistent with economic modernization. The Panchen Lama, Tibetan Buddhism's highest spiritual leader after the Dalai Lama, enjoyed more freedom of speech under this administration. Educational programs in Tibetan were allowed.[27]

But from late 1988 to early 1989, the central government changed courses. The top party and government leaders in the TAR were replaced, and in March 1989, martial law was declared in Lhasa in the wake of anti-Chinese rioting (two months before martial law was declared in Beijing at the time of the Tiananmen demonstrations). Martial law was terminated in 1990, but Beijing's policies during the 1990s reemphasized strong central control over the region. The policy of targeting Tibet for special development projects, begun in the mid-1980s, was resumed, but a 1992 white paper on Tibet implied renewed Han ethnocentrism in its emphasis on the backwardness of traditional Tibetan culture.[28] Meanwhile, international criticism of human rights violations in Tibet was unrelenting.[29] It is clear that granting greater autonomy to Tibet to safeguard its religion and culture would have improved the situation (from a Tibetan point of view), but it would also have undermined Beijing's confidence in its ability to control the region. Meanwhile, some one hundred thousand or more Chinese troops continued to be stationed in Tibet to reinforce the political controls as of the mid-1990s.[30]

The same question concerning the extent of autonomy also surrounds the Hong Kong situation. The Basic Law of the Hong Kong Special Administrative Region was approved by the Seventh National People's Congress in 1990. A central feature of the basic law was the stipulation that the principle of "one country, two systems" would apply to the Hong Kong SAR for fifty years. This provision promised that China's socialist system and policies would not be practiced in Hong Kong during this period. The basic law also anticipated a high degree of autonomy in the SAR, although the region comes directly under central government authority.[31]

The basic law provided for four local institutions in Hong Kong: the Legislative Council (referred to as LegCo); a chief executive chosen the first time by an electoral college and approved by the central government's State Council; a judiciary to enforce laws carried over from British-ruled Hong Kong as well as laws enacted by the Legislative Council; and local, or district, organizations. For several years after the approval of the basic law, the efforts of Britain's Hong Kong Governor, Chris Patten, to inject more democracy into Hong Kong politics was a near-constant irritant in Chinese-British relations. From China's point of view, Patten's initiatives violated the understandings that produced the basic law and raised suspicions that Britain was trying to thwart Chinese sovereignty by laying the groundwork for political autonomy in the former colony. For example, Britain passed a bill of rights for its colony and proposed to broaden representation in LegCo.

In 1996, China made clear its intent to dissolve the LegCo created under British rule, replacing it with a provisional legislative council elected by the Nomination Committee, whose four hundred members were chosen under procedures determined by the Preparatory Commission for the Hong Kong SAR. Because the Preparatory Commission itself was a subcommittee of the National People's Congress, it was clear that the central government was tightening its control over the transition period.[32]

Few presumed by the mid-1990s that Hong Kong would enjoy a great deal of political autonomy under the SAR arrangement. Yet it was also true that two factors, in particular, argued for a continuation of some self-determination—or at least local assertiveness—in the former colony. One was Hong Kong's role as the center of a powerful South China economic region. The second was the relative vitality of grassroots political organizations that, when seen in the broader context of growing democratization at the local level in much of China, warranted modification of an automatic "top-down" scenario for the SAR.

## Prefectures and Municipalities in Japan

Decentralization of the Japanese state after World War II was one of the U.S. occupation's top priorities. SCAP officials saw greater local autonomy as a means to strengthen Japanese democracy by breaking up concentrated bureaucratic authority revolving around the prewar Home Ministry, which had appointed and overseen the prefectural governors. The 1947 Japanese Constitution confirmed the "principle of local autonomy" (Article 92) and the Local Autonomy Act of 1947 defined a two-tiered structure of prefectures and municipalities, separating local from national administration. The act also established the competencies and provided for the election of assemblies and chief executives (governors and mayors).

Although the true local autonomy envisaged by SCAP was unrealized, postwar Japan did institutionalize the separation between levels of government, and over the decades, prefectural and municipal officials have become more responsive to local constituencies. Urbanization and rapid economic growth created a host of problems, ranging from spiraling land prices to air and water pollution. These problems sparked grassroots protests and citizen pressures for ameliorative policies from local governments. Meanwhile, local elections for governors, mayors, and assembly representatives focused attention both on the problems and on alternative solutions. Local politics became more competitive; progressive parties cut off from national influence won local races. For example, by the early 1970s, long before serious challenge to LDP hegemony at the national level, major cities in Japan, including Tokyo, Osaka, Kyoto, Nagoya, and Yokohama, had elected leftist governors or mayors.

Japan is now divided into forty-seven prefectures of varying sizes and types, including three municipal prefectures with large populations (Tokyo, Osaka, and Kyoto). There are over 3,200 municipalities (cities, towns, and villages). Despite the legal principle of local autonomy, it is generally agreed that the national government is in a superior position and that Japan is properly classified as a unitary system. Nevertheless, the reality of intergovernmental relations is more complex than this observation suggests. The Local Autonomy Law, amended over the years, delegates a wide range of functions to local entities, ranging from regional development and management of water and power supply, sewage treatment, and transportation facilities to preservation of the environment and cultural properties. These are administrative responsibilities delegated by the national government, and local entities may also enact ordinances applicable within their own boundaries.[33]

As noted earlier, urbanization and industrialization have exacerbated numerous problems that local entities are responsible for and that they are under public pressure to address. Consequently, the old model of top-down policymaking has been modified in recognition of pressures on local governments, bottom-up demands on the national government, and complex horizontal linkages between various prefectures and municipalities. It is now more accurate to say that although Japanese government is still comparatively centralized, decentralization has been growing for some years and seems likely to continue.[34] The next section discusses the unusual case of Okinawa Prefecture, which illustrates the maximum degree of political and legal authority that a prefectural governor may summon in a conflict with the central government. Although no other regional government has found itself in the same situation, the Okinawan case is important because of its international, as well as its national, implications.

## Okinawa

The islands of the Ryukyu Archipelago, of which the largest is Okinawa, constitute Japan's far-flung southwestern Okinawa Prefecture. Okinawa's prefectural capital, Naha, is in fact closer to the capital cities of Taiwan (Taipei) and Korea (Seoul) than it is to Tokyo. In view of this geographical location, it is not surprising that the Ryukyus developed a traditional culture, including indigenous dialects, distinct from the rest of Japan.

Okinawa's strategic location meant that it bore an enormous burden during the Allied ground assault on Japan that began in April 1945. The battle(s) for Okinawa lasted almost three months and were among the bloodiest of the war.[35] By August 1945, when the Ryukyu Islands were placed under U.S. military governance, 250,000 Japanese (including nearly 150,000 civilians on the islands) were dead; 12,500 Americans had been killed, and 37,000 had been wounded. Naha and other cities had been completely leveled; industry and agriculture had become nonexistent. All of this became part of the collective memory of Okinawans, influencing prefectural politics decades later.

The U.S. occupation of Japan lasted until 1952, but the Ryukyus remained under U.S. control until 1972. Military rule was a two-edged sword: The military authorities were responsible for rebuilding the islands' infrastructure and providing civilian jobs, but the redeveloped economy was heavily dependent on the American military presence. Homes were bulldozed and agricultural land confiscated to make room for expanding military bases and other facilities, especially as the strategic value of Okinawa was reaffirmed during the Korean and Vietnam Wars. By 1995, more than twenty years after the reversion of the Ryukyus, three-fourths of American bases in Japan and over 23,000 American troops were still located in Okinawa Prefecture.[36]

The right of the United States to occupy land in the prefecture dates from the postwar occupation period, but over the years, landowners increasingly protested the continued leasing of their property for American military facilities.[37] The landowners, along with many other Okinawans who resented both the American presence and the prefecture's treatment at the hands of a distant and often indifferent Japanese government, especially in negotiations over the future of the bases, pressured the provincial governor to represent their position more forcefully. In 1995, the base controversy exploded when three U.S. military men were arrested for abducting and raping a twelve-year-old Japanese girl. Over the course of the ensuing trial of the three men, tensions in the relations between Okinawa Prefecture and Tokyo were thrown into sharp relief, as were tensions in Japanese-U.S. relations.

In 1990, Washington and Tokyo had agreed to work toward returning many of the forty U.S. military sites in Okinawa to local control. Some of these sites were very small, but from the prefectural perspective, return would symbolize a good-faith effort by both national governments to give Okinawa more influence over its own future. In 1991, Okinawa's governor, Masahide Ota, threatened to withhold his signature from documents forcing local landowners to continue leasing land to the United States. He backed down when the central government agreed to secure base reductions from the United States. But in 1995, confronted, on the one hand, by a government slow or unwilling (from the Okinawan point of view) to defend the prefecture's position to the Americans and, on the other hand, by angry demands from his electors, Governor Ota was adamant in his refusal to sign similar documents again.

Ultimately, a prefectural governor's power is limited by both legal and political considerations. The prime minister of Japan is authorized by law to order the governor to sign the documents and if he refuses, to file a lawsuit against him. If the governor does not comply with a court order to sign, the prime minister can sign the papers himself. In 1995, both parties wanted to avoid such a deadlock and preferred negotiations. Governor Ota was strengthened in his position by popular outrage over the rape case and impatience over the central government's failure to move years earlier on the base issue. The central government, meanwhile, faced conflict with the United States over a number of issues and, like the U.S. government, had to balance multiple concerns while not appearing to capitulate to foreign pressure. Japan's prime minister at the time, Tomichi Murayama, found himself in the ironic position of a long-time Socialist who for years had opposed the U.S. military presence in Japan but who now headed a coalition government. Forced to abandon his earlier pacifism, Murayama nonetheless hoped to appease simultaneously his coalition partners, the U.S. negotiators, conservative central government bureaucrats, Okinawans, and Japanese public opinion.

Negotiations between the central, Okinawan, and U.S. governments dragged on, engaging a variety of agencies and courts from the local to the national level. When a regional court ordered Governor Ota to sign documents extending the leases, he appealed to the Supreme Court. In September 1996, the dispute was, at least for the time being, resolved in favor of the central government when the Supreme Court dismissed the governor's appeal and he agreed to sign the documents.

## Summary

Relations between levels of government have shown themselves to be dynamic and flexible in India, China, and Japan over the past half century.

Nominally, India is a federal system, whereas China and Japan are unitary states. But Indian federalism is cross-pressured by a Constitution that tilts the balance toward the central government and by regional developments, including cultural demands and the growth of regional parties, that push the country toward decentralization. China has a unitary system, and the Communist Party is structured to guarantee central control, but economic policies have promoted decentralization.

The trends in India and China are not irreversible, although once regional governments and (in India) political parties have developed a vested interest in controlling their own affairs with minimal interference from a higher level of government, reversing this course is likely to be as long and gradual a process as decentralization. In China, however, the maintenance of strong central control has been part of the agenda of the neoconservatives in the post-Deng era. In India, threats to national integrity, particularly in border regions such as Punjab and Jammu and Kashmir, have also preoccupied national leaders. One might even imagine that India's prime minister and China's premier would use much the same political vocabulary to describe their top worries: national unity and socioeconomic development.

In fundamental ways, however, the political structures and processes in India and China are so different as to make one very cautious about generalized comparisons. In particular, the level of political competition, including continual and widespread elections, is much greater in India, with the result that the implementation of cohesive, coherent policies through several layers of government is even harder to realize than in China.

By contrast, intergovernmental relations in Japan have seemed straightforward. But by setting up the mechanisms for some local autonomy in a country with strong traditions of centralization, the occupation authorities established the conditions for the increased responsibility and assertiveness of prefectures and municipalities. Although unique in many respects, the Okinawa case also illustrates how relations between a provincial government and the central government may become conflictual.

In all these countries, intergovernmental relations are influenced by bureaucracies, both civilian and military, in addition to the other sources of influence discussed in this chapter. Part Four, which follows, includes a discussion of these bureaucracies, as well as other structures and political developments that set the context for relations between individuals and the state.

## Notes

1. The following analyses of federalism are especially helpful: Ivo D. Duchacek, *Comparative Federalism: The Territorial Dimension of Politics* (New York: Holt, Rine-

hart, and Winston, 1970); Daniel J. Elazar, *Exploring Federalism* (Tuscaloosa: University of Alabama Press, 1987); and "Federalism," *International Encyclopedia of the Social Sciences*, 1968, vol. 5, pp. 353–367; Preston King, *Federalism and Federation* (Baltimore: Johns Hopkins University Press, 1982).

2. Gabriella Montinola, Yingyi Qian, and Barry R. Weingast, "Federalism, Chinese Style: The Political Basis for Economic Success in China," *World Politics* 48, no. 1 (October 1995), pp. 50–81.

3. Romila Thapar, *A History of India*, vol. 1 (Baltimore: Penguin Books, 1966), pp. 89–91, 144–145, and chap. 5.

4. Granville Austin, *The Indian Constitution: Cornerstone of a Nation* (Oxford: Clarendon Press, 1966), p. 187; Ramesh Thakur, *The Government and Politics of India* (New York: St. Martin's Press, 1995), pp. 71–72; Robert L. Hardgrave, Jr., and Stanley A. Kochanek, *India: Government and Politics in a Developing Nation*, 5th ed. (Fort Worth, Tex.: Harcourt Brace College Publishers), pp. 127, 131.

5. The exception is Jammu and Kashmir, a north-Indian state that theoretically has the right to determine its own constitution and that has a different status in the Indian Union.

6. Austin, *Indian Constitution*, chap. 9; Thakur, *Government . . . of India*, pp. 76–81.

7. The Punjabi language is the mother tongue of both Sikhs and Hindus (and before the nineteenth century, of Muslims as well), although Hindus increasingly have renounced Punjabi in favor of Hindi for political reasons. By Partition, only Sikhs *wrote* Punjabi, using the Gurmukhi script in which their scriptures are written. Therefore, to claim a separate Punjabi-speaking state was effectively a religious (Sikh) demand as well. But after the horrors of Partition, any explicit demand for a religion-based state was unacceptable to the Congress leaders who dominated Union politics. Robin Jeffrey, *What's Happening to India? Punjab, Ethnic Conflict, and the Test for Federalism*, 2d ed. (New York: Holmes and Meier, 1994), pp. 69, 101–105. On the historical and social roots of Sikh nationalism, see Peter van der Veer, *Religious Nationalism: Hindus and Muslims in India* (Berkeley: University of California Press, 1994), pp. 53–56, 73–77.

8. This analysis is derived primarily from Paul R. Brass, "The Punjab Crisis and the Unity of India," in Atul Kohli, ed., *India's Democracy: An Analysis of Changing State-Society Relations* (Princeton: Princeton University Press, 1988), pp. 169–213; Paul R. Brass, *The Politics of India Since Independence* (Cambridge: Cambridge University Press, 1990), pp. 170–178; Jeffrey, *What's Happening?* chaps. 6, 7; and Thakur, *Government . . . India*, pp. 21–27.

9. For an understanding of the socioeconomic and political conditions that encouraged support for Bhindranwale, see Joyce J. M. Pettigrew, *The Sikhs of the Punjab: Unheard Voices of State and Guerrilla Violence* (London and Atlantic Highlands, N.J.: Zed Books, 1995).

10. Brass, *Politics of India*, pp. 109–118.

11. *Democracy and Violence in India and Sri Lanka* (London: Royal Institute of International Affairs, 1994).

12. "The Puzzle of Indian Democracy: A Consociational Interpretation," *American Political Science Review* 90, no. 2 (June 1996), pp. 258–268.

13. Local government organizations are described in Chinese Academy of Social Sciences, *Information China*, vol. 1, comp. and trans. China Social Sciences Pub-

lishing House, ed. C. V. James (Oxford, New York, and Beijing: Pergamon Press, 1989), pp. 395–397.

14. Implementation of the Organic Law of Villagers' Committees, adopted in 1987, has been uneven, however. Kevin J. O'Brien, "Implementing Political Reform in China's Villages," *Australian Journal of Chinese Affairs* 32 (July 1994), pp. 33–59.

15. Suzanne Ogden, *China's Unresolved Issues: Politics, Development, and Culture,* 3d ed. (Englewood Cliffs, N.J.: Prentice-Hall, 1995), pp. 289–290. See also Susan L. Shirk's analysis of the political bargaining that accompanied reform policies and what she has called "playing to the provinces." *The Political Logic of Economic Reform in China* (Berkeley and Los Angeles: University of California Press, 1993).

16. In "Federalism, Chinese Style," Montinola, Qian, and Weingast analyzed the characteristics of China's "market-preserving federalism." See especially pp. 54–57, 60–73.

17. In late 1993, the Communist Party Central Committee issued a policy statement entitled "Concerning the Establishment of a Socialist Market Economic Structure." The new policies anticipated major tax reform as part of a revamped national revenue program. When (and if) fully implemented, the reform would strengthen national control over major taxation categories but would also establish separate central and local taxation systems. *Beijing Review* 36, no. 47 (November 22–28, 1993), pp. 12–31, especially item 18. Bargaining occurs not just between provinces but at the subprovincial level as well. See Kenneth G. Lieberthal and David M. Lampton, eds., *Bureaucracy, Politics, and Decision Making in Post-Mao China* (Berkeley: University of California Press, 1992), particularly pt. 4.

18. Joseph Fewsmith, "Jockeying for Position in the Post-Deng Era," and Merle Goldman, "Is Democracy Possible?" both in *Current History* 94, no. 593 (September 1995), pp. 253 and 263, respectively.

19. Overall, China averaged between 9 and 10 percent annual growth rate from 1979 through 1994, but its per capita GNP, at US$500, was still low. Li Lanqing, "China's Economic Reform and Opening," *Beijing Review* 39, no. 2 (January 8–14, 1996), p. 15.

20. Jan S. Prybyla, "All That Glitters? The Foreign Investment Boom," *Current History* 94, no. 593 (September 1995), p. 178.

21. Jiang Wandi, "Balance Reemphasized in Regional Development," *Beijing Review* 39, no. 4 (January 22–28, 1996), p. 20.

22. Margaret Maurer-Fazio, "Building a Labor Market in China," *Current History* 94, no. 593 (September 1995), p. 287; Prybyla, "All that Glitters?" p. 278. The removal of government restrictions on travel facilitated migration.

23. In 1995, the central government admitted that investment in agriculture had been inadequate and called for increased measures to stimulate production as well as to develop industries in rural areas, as part of the Ninth Five-Year Plan (1996–2000). Li, "China's Economic Reform," pp. 15–17; and Wu Naitar, "CPC Plans [for the Formulation of the Ninth Five-Year Plan] Attract Worldwide Attention," *Beijing Review* 39, no. 1 (January 1–7, 1996), pp. 14–17.

24. Kenneth Lieberthal, *Governing China: From Revolution Through Reform* (New York: W. W. Norton, 1995), pp. 273–274.

25. See, for example, the report in the newsletter, "China Focus," Princeton (New Jersey) China Initiative, 3, no. 12 (December 1995), p. 7. Outbreaks of rural

violence were the result of other factors as well. Elizabeth J. Perry, "Rural Collective Violence: The Fruits of Recent Reforms," in Perry and Christine Wong, *The Political Economy of Reform in Post-Mao China* (Cambridge: Council on East Asian Studies/Harvard University, 1985), pp. 175–192.

26. For a summary of this law, see *Beijing Review* 27, no. 26 (June 25, 1984), pp. 17–19.

27. Solomon M. Karmel, "Ethnic Tension and the Struggle for Order: China's Policies in Tibet," *Pacific Affairs* 68, no. 4 (winter 1995–1996), pp. 485–508.

28. For the text of the white paper, entitled "Tibet—Its Ownership and Human Rights Situation," see *Beijing Review*, 35, no. 39 (September 28–October 4, 1992), pp. 10–43.

29. See, for example, the annual reports of Amnesty International and the *World Report* of Human Rights Watch/Asia Watch. Security measures are generally tight, especially in Lhasa, and Tibetan monks and nuns make up a majority of the political prisoners in the TAR. *Amnesty International Report 1995* (London and New York: Amnesty International, 1995), p. 99.

30. James C. F. Wang, *Contemporary Chinese Politics: An Introduction*, 5th ed. (Englewood Cliffs, N.J.: Prentice-Hall, 1995), p. 168, uses the figure 100,000. In "Ethnic Tension," p. 501, Karmel cites estimates between 40,000 and 250,000.

31. "Basic Law of the Hong Kong Special Administrative Region of the People's Republic of China," *International Legal Materials* 29, no. 6 (November 1990), pp. 1519–1551.

32. For the details, see Yan Jiaqi, "Beijing's New Roll-Back on Hong Kong," *China Strategic Review* 1, no. 7 (October 5, 1996), pp. 9–13.

33. Koichi Kishimoto, *Politics in Modern Japan: Development and Organization*, 3d ed. (Tokyo: Japan Echo, 1988), pp. 144–145; and Charles F. Bingman, *Japanese Government Leadership and Management* (New York: St. Martin's Press, 1989), p. 53.

34. Ibid., pp. 56–58; Richard J. Samuels, *The Politics of Regional Policy in Japan: Localities Incorporated?* (Princeton: Princeton University Press, 1983); and Steven R. Reed, *Japanese Prefectures and Policymaking* (Pittsburgh: Pittsburgh University Press, 1986), chap. 7.

35. Armando Sanchez, *Okinawa: Past and Present* (Los Angeles: E.M.S. Glenny, 1993), p. 10. Sanchez has provided an American military and civilian perspective on Okinawa; for portraits especially sympathetic to the Okinawan view, see Norma Field, *In the Realm of a Dying Emperor* (New York: Pantheon, 1991), pt. 1; and Reiji Yoshida, "Okinawa's Bitter Legacy," *Japan Times Weekly International Edition* (hereafter cited as *Japan Times WIE*), November 27–December 3, 1995.

36. William R. Evinger, ed., *Directory of U.S. Military Bases Worldwide*, 2d ed. (Phoenix: Oryx Press, 1995), pp. 257–262.

37. During the first decade after reversion of the Ryukyus to Japan, the central government offered high rents to encourage landowners to sign leases permitting military use of their land. After 1982, an antimilitary campaign increased the number of antiwar landowners. By 1996, 2,937 landowners were refusing to sign lease contracts. *Japan Times WIE*, April 8–14, 1996.

# Part Four

# *The Individual and the State*

Parts One and Two of this book explored the foundations of politics and introduced both the people and the issues that color politics in India, China, and Japan. Part Three examined the governing institutions at the national and subnational levels. Part Four explains in greater detail the links between individuals and the institutions of the state. The word "state" in this context refers to the multiple institutions, both civilian and military, local and national, that represent the legitimate power and authority of governing.

It is tempting to see politics as largely a matter of political parties and elections, on the one hand, and government response and regulation, on the other. Despite ideologies that argue for such simplistic relationships, most of us understand that the connections between individuals and the processes of governing are far more complex. Part Four does not attempt to cover all aspects of these connections and processes. Rather, the purpose of discussing these relationships here is to emphasize patterns and raise questions. Since political leaders, government composition, and policy issues change frequently, even suddenly, Chapters 12–14 focus on patterns that—presumably—are interesting and will be important over the next decade. No attempt has been made to cover every aspect of the political processes for each of the three countries. Instead, comparisons have been structured in order to raise broad questions about politics, both in Asia and elsewhere.

Chapter 12, "The Decay of One-Party Rule," examines the ways in which the authority of the Congress and Liberal Democratic parties, on one side, and the Chinese Communist Party, on the other, has been challenged and eroded. Despite the obvious differences between India and

Japan, the comparison between Congress and the LDP is logical: Both dominated national elections and formed governments from the 1950s to the 1990s, even as both experienced factionalism, corruption, and other signs of the decay that undermined them. In contrast to India and Japan, China established a system of one-party rule that drew its inspiration from Lenin. By the 1980s, however, there were signs of challenges to the once-unquestioned monopoly of Chinese politics by the CCP, and CCP leaders addressed openly the problems of decay and corruption within their party. Despite the events of Tiananmen Square in 1989 and the collapse of one-party rule in the Soviet Union, few China watchers were predicting the imminent demise of CCP rule in the 1990s. Likewise, no China watchers precluded the possibility of a slow transformation of Chinese politics as new groups and issues wormed their way into the interstices of Chinese society.

Chapter 13 emphasizes the role of state institutions in controlling the territory and population of the nation-state. The first section examines the major issues pertaining to the civil bureaucracies in India, China, and Japan. The second focuses on the role of security forces in the context of the development challenges facing the three nations in the next century. The last section looks at the development of the judicial systems.

As noted early in this book, socioeconomic development has been a conscious government objective in all three countries, but development policies have created nearly as many problems as they have solved. We have already seen two illustrations of the unintended consequences of development policies in China: the contradiction between birth control and the value placed on girls, and the consequences of rapid economic growth on the eastern coast for the rest of the country. Chapter 14, "The Politics of Development and the Development of Politics," further illustrates the importance of socioeconomic development in politics by examining its cost for specific groups in society and for the physical environment. The first half of the chapter uses the cases of the construction of water management projects in Asia, particularly huge dams, as a way of illustrating the politics of development. The second half of the chapter then explores the way development policies have led to new modes of political participation.

# *twelve*

# The Decay of One-Party Rule

Political parties are only one of the institutions linking citizens and governments, and their historical development is relatively recent. Although many European parties trace their roots to the first half of the nineteenth century, the earliest Asian parties appeared toward the end of that century. The predecessors of the contemporary Congress and Liberal Democratic parties date to the 1880s; the Chinese Communist Party, in contrast, was established shortly after World War I, as were other Communist parties in Asia and Europe.

After World War II, national policymaking in India and Japan was dominated for long periods by the Congress and Liberal Democratic parties, respectively. The leaders of these parties controlled most of the governments and set the agendas for foreign and domestic policies. In the parliaments, of course, other parties held seats and, with varying degrees of success over the years, endeavored to hold their governments accountable. At the state level in India and at the local levels in both India and Japan, these alternative parties often won elections and formed governments. Thus, only at the national level may these two countries properly be classified as one-party-dominant systems. Moreover, even at the national level, the dominance of Congress and the LDP has been of a very different order from the dominance of the Communist Party in China, where real alternatives to the CCP have been philosophically and politically excluded.

Most of the discussion in this chapter focuses on the national party systems of India and Japan, exploring the reasons for their longevity as well as their decay. The Chinese case is included for comparison when it sheds light on a particular process or structure, such as intraparty factions. The first section compares the origins and structures of the Congress, Liberal Democratic, and Communist parties. The next section surveys the major opposition parties in India and Japan and the interparty relationships that determined the coalition governments in both countries in the mid- and late 1990s. The third section focuses on electoral systems. Contested elections are central to democratic competition, but electoral systems themselves influence the nature of that competition and tell us much about the values that structure party representation. This section also includes a short discussion of local-level elections in China.

## The Congress, Liberal Democratic, and Chinese Communist Parties

### *Origins and Structures*

The origins of the Congress Party in India and the Communist Party in China are similar in several striking ways. Both had roots in the dramatic changes occurring in the two countries as their nationalist movements sought to cope with Western imperialism and the inadequacies of traditional social and political structures. Both Congress and the CCP were, in fact, *the* nationalist movements during much of their history, yet both parties borrowed heavily from Western ideas. Both were led by courageous and charismatic figures who were able to mobilize millions of Indians and Chinese on behalf of their parties. Neither party was monolithic during the early decades, as different leaders, strategies, and ideologies vied for dominance. Yet by 1950, Congress and the CCP were indisputably the ruling parties of their respective countries, each with a preeminent leader who commanded enormous authority within his party: Jawaharlal Nehru in the Congress and Mao Zedong in the CCP.

The critical differences between Congress and the CCP are most notably in the philosophies that have informed the parties' internal organizations and external policies. An obvious difference is Congress's commitment to electoral competition and other elements of political democracy during all but two of the years that it dominated national politics—in contrast to the CCP's rejection of elections as a valid measure of either legitimacy or popular support. Most Congress leaders at the national level were deeply influenced by Western values of liberal democratic competition in political life. In contrast, the CCP operated under the Leninist norms of single-party monopoly of revolutionary momentum.

The history of the Liberal Democratic party is very different from that of either the Congress or the CCP. Although the LDP has its roots in the political societies formed during the Meiji period, it took its contemporary form only in the 1950s. Ideology has seldom played a major role in determining either its leadership or its policies, and its legitimacy derived from the success of its economic development strategy, not from its origins in a mass-based nationalist movement. Nonetheless, it shares with the Congress Party the extensive internal factionalism that has resulted in the periodic splitting off of new political groups.

**The Congress Party.**  Chapter 5 explained the evolution of the Indian National Congress from its founding in 1885 through the 1940s. Although often divided by philosophies, political strategies, and personalities during these decades, Congress outdistanced other parties established during the pre- and post-Independence periods in popular support. The other parties did not seriously begin to challenge Congress until the late 1960s. From *swaraj* in 1947 until 1967, Congress enjoyed such majorities in the national legislature and in nearly all of the state legislatures that India became known as a one-party-dominant system.

This dominance was partly due to the party's legitimacy as a national movement, but its organizational reach and successful performance of interest aggregation were as important as this heritage. The defining characteristic of a political party has long been considered by political scientists to be the ability to aggregate constituents' interests for the purpose of contesting elections and, if elected, to implement policies. Congress far surpassed its competitors in the performance of these functions. Drawing on the lessons learned during nationalist campaigns, Congress leaders at all levels became skilled at forging alliances among different social groups in order to win elections under the new constitutional rules.

The early Congress leaders constituted a small, largely homogeneous elite, mostly upper caste and English-educated. But despite their similar status, these leaders had frequent ideological disagreements over party and government priorities; later, however, the primary goal of party officials became almost exclusively holding office. Patronage and the delivery of services to constituents—both possible because of Congress's near monopoly of elected government positions—served further to maintain the party in power. Increasingly, the party attracted careerists who gained support by appealing to traditional, parochial loyalties, thus gradually building intraparty tension between the goals of modernization and change, on the one hand, and maintenance of the traditional order, on the other.

**The Chinese Communist Party.**  Like the Congress Party, the CCP has experienced internal tensions. China's size and diversity have contributed to regional pressures, and there have always been philosophical and policy differences within the party. In contrast to the Congress Party, however, the internal organization of the CCP is designed to maintain cohesion, at the price of diversity if necessary. Different concepts of party membership lie at the root of the differences between the two parties.

Membership in India's Congress Party (like the LDP), requires only payment of a small subscription sum. There are no ideological or other requirements. Membership in the Communist Party provides a striking contrast. The first chapter of the CCP Constitution details the ideological and procedural requirements of party membership. New members must both apply and be recommended by two full party members. The application must be accepted by a general membership meeting of the party branch concerned and by the next-higher party level. New members then undergo a probationary period of one year (Articles 5–7). Members at the lowest level of the party hierarchy are organized into units or cells established in every social and political organization in the country—in factories, neighborhoods, schools, villages, PLA companies, and anyplace else where there are at least three full party members.

Since 1949, CCP membership has been the most important prerequisite for power and influence in China. Although members are ideologically directed to "serve the people wholeheartedly" and "not seek personal gain or privileges" (Article 2), CCP membership has conferred elite status. During the early decades, this status derived from the presumed higher levels of political education and commitment to the revolution's goals, along with the inherent authority conferred on the party and its members by virtue of the leading role of the party in China's governing system. Status has also derived from the relatively small proportion of China's population admitted to party membership. The percentage has varied over the decades but is typically between 4 and 5 percent. In the mid-1990s, there were approximately 55 million CCP members.

Although the CCP was reorganized and consolidated after the Cultural Revolution, the reform period since the 1970s has brought a succession of new problems. One problem was the very rapid recruitment of new members after the Cultural Revolution and again in the mid-1970s by the Gang of Four. Many of the newer members were admitted using ideological standards that were subsequently rejected by the reform leaders during the late 1970s and after. With the emphasis on economic modernization came the concern that too many party members lacked the competence required by the new policies. In the late 1980s and early 1990s, party recruitment therefore focused on better educated, younger members.

Even more important problems have been lax discipline and an abuse of authority from the local levels to the top of the CCP hierarchy. In the 1987–1992 period alone, more than 150,000 members were expelled from the party for corruption.[1] Maintenance of the party's recruitment standards and appeal has been an even broader concern. By the mid-1990s, economic growth had not only generated corruption but had sprouted a new elite whose status derived from wealth rather than party membership (although membership frequently facilitated the accumulation of wealth). The party reportedly still recruited 1 million new members a year, but there were strong indications that fewer young people, especially those with higher education and skills and therefore other options, were attracted to joining the party.[2]

**The Liberal Democratic Party.** The Japanese party system from the 1950s to the 1990s resembles the Congress system in some ways, most notably in the ability of the LDP to aggregate diverse interests and co-opt opposition positions in order to sustain electoral dominance. In its origins, historical evolution, and policies, however, it is unique.

Unlike the Congress and Communist parties, the LDP is not rooted in a nationalist, revolutionary movement, although its predecessors can be traced back more than a century to Itagaki's Society of Patriots and the Liberal Party (Jiyuto) in the 1870s and early 1880s (see Chapter 7). Japan's political parties flourished in the 1920s but declined in the 1930s. In 1940, all parties were officially dissolved and replaced by the Imperial Rule Assistance Association. During the occupation period, parties were allowed to reestablish themselves almost immediately. By the end of 1945, three conservative parties (Liberal, Progressive, and Cooperative), as well as the Communist and Socialist parties, had been formed.

In the first decade after the war, both the conservative and leftist parties went through several organizational and name changes. The most important change was the merger in 1955 of the two largest conservative parties, the Liberals and the Democrats (the latter formed from the Progressive and Cooperative parties in 1947). However, from its inception, the Liberal Democratic Party has been a coalition of factions, as were its predecessors. Although there were and have continued to be some policy differences among individual LDP politicians, both ideology and policies have been fluid, usually characterized by general, middle-of-the-road positions permitting flexible, indeed multiple, interpretations. From the outset, the purpose of the LDP coalition was to assure conservative rule. In 1955, the clearest threat to this rule came from the imminent reunification of the Japan Socialist Party, which had split four years earlier. The move to consolidate conservative forces was strongly supported by business interests that then, as now, provided LDP financial support.[3]

*Intraparty Factionalism*

Factionalism is an important characteristic shared by the LDP, the Congress, and the CCP, although the nature of the factions differs in the three cases. Factions frequently are leader-follower, or patron-client, groups, and relations among members are often highly personalized. Factions play contradictory roles in party organizations: They make it possible to integrate divergent interests and groups, and they widen the base of political involvement; but well-organized factions may also pose a threat to party and government unity.[4]

There are several general characteristics of intraparty factionalism. First, factions often operate in ways that suggest the carryover of traditional political values (such as group loyalty) into contemporary political party competition. Second, the personal ties that frequently define factions provide an alternative to other links, such as ideology or ethnicity, as a way to organize and mobilize people for political participation. Third, factional ties often operate "behind the scenes" to determine political influence and policy decisions, making it difficult for those outside the system to understand the political process. Finally, as noted earlier, factions may threaten party unity when strong leaders in opposition to the party mainstream leave the party and join the opposition.

**LDP Factions.**   The structure of factions, including the importance of personal loyalty to a faction leader, suggests that this particular form of political organization is a good example of the way traditional values have carried over to late-twentieth-century politics in Asia. Readers may recall that loyalty was the central value of the Tokugawa system of social and political organization. Individuals were linked hierarchically through personal ties that provided group cohesion, but these same kinds of ties led to factional divisions among ruling elites. Thus, Japanese political parties originated in the disagreements among the oligarchs that arose shortly after the Meiji Restoration.

Some years ago, Japanese social anthropologist Chie Nakane analyzed the structure of groups throughout Japanese society.[5] She argued that the ranking of all members of the group in relation to each other and in accordance with the principle of seniority provides cohesion. Group leadership is restricted to one person, and all members of the group are linked in a relationship of superior-inferior status. Although the strength of this relationship varies among groups, in general the hierarchical ties contribute to group stability. These ties are an important example of the persistence of traditional social norms.

For most of its history, there have been at least five organized factions in the LDP. Originally, factions consisted of Diet members "bound by the ties of obligation and debt that have long played an important role in Japanese political custom."[6] Faction members commit to the leadership of a senior party member who has developed close ties with other politicians, the bureaucracy, and the business community and has demonstrated his ability to raise money and dispense patronage. At the top echelon, party and Diet posts are apportioned to reflect the relative strength of factions within the ruling party.

Factions serve as the campaign support organization from the grass-roots to the national level. At the local level, candidates are supported by personal *koenkai*, quasi-permanent organizations for cultivating the candidate's constituency. They represent the personal interest of the Diet member, not the LDP overall. There is no local LDP organization outside of the *koenkai*; rather, at the local level, the LDP has always been a confederation of *koenkai*. At the local, prefectural, and national levels, factions maintain their own office, budget, and staff and hold regular meetings. Factions thus operate as parties within parties.

Factions tend to be stable for long periods, changing mainly when a faction leader retires from politics or dies. Within the faction, individuals advance through seniority as well as by ability, and in the Diet, seniority is based on the number of times a politician has been elected as a member of a particular faction. To change factions means a loss of seniority, so ambitious politicians are generally discouraged from changing factions.

Other Japanese parties have been factionalized, but LDP factions are the best known because of the party's long governing role. LDP factions have been criticized for decades as contributing to the inordinate cost of Japanese elections, to influence peddling, and to other corruption-linked political practices. Some LDP defenders of factions argued that they were a "necessary evil," given the multimember constituency electoral system for the House of Representatives. It was, in fact, public criticism of the connection between the electoral system, factions, and money politics that led to the long, drawn-out effort to reform electoral districts described later in this chapter. Public criticism also contributed to the decision to formally dissolve the LDP's factions in December 1994, but the election of party president (and later prime minister) Ryutaro Hashimoto in 1995 and his choice of Cabinet members after the 1996 House of Representatives elections were both linked to faction politics.[7]

**Congress Party Factions.** The durability of Japanese factions suggests that they reflect both cultural habits and political necessity. The same is true of factions in India's Congress Party. Like the LDP, Congress has long been internally factionalized. Particularly during the first two decades after Independence, factions within the Congress interacted in a way that provided built-in opposition, as well as accommodation of different ideological and policy stances. Thus, factions organizationally helped Congress build the consensus that led to its dominance both before and after Independence.

Also like the LDP, factional competition within Congress determined the dynamics of the formal party structures that were described earlier:

Factions contested for control of the important committees at each level through formal elections preceded by membership drives in which competing faction leaders attempted to enroll, even if only on paper, as many member-supporters as possible. Although the factional conflicts which developed often became intense and bitter . . . they also served to keep the party organization alive and to compel party leaders to build support in the districts and localities throughout the country.[8]

The nature of these factional conflicts varied from the local to the national level, and their effect on the party changed over time. Until 1967, their integrative functions outweighed their disintegrative threat. By their very nature, factions have been personalistic, often led by local "notables" whose original following came from caste or religious groups or from their control of private or public institutions, especially those with resources to distribute. But since their primary goal was to acquire political power in competition with other factions and external parties, faction leaders have sought alliances across traditional group boundaries. Factional competition has ultimately contributed to the secular nature of Congress politics: "By drawing in new caste and religious groups . . . factions politicized them in secular terms."[9]

Until his death in 1964, Nehru and his closest confidants controlled national politics largely by mediating factional conflicts at both the state and national levels. Mediation was, in fact, central to the ability of the Congress to maintain control. After Nehru's death, the party was torn by a succession struggle that involved his daughter, Indira Gandhi, and men who were faction leaders, often at the state level. This struggle was an important part of the history of Mrs. Gandhi's populist approach to mobilizing support in the 1971 elections, which in turn contributed to the dynamics that produced the Emergency. The Congress Party had split first in 1969, and it divided again in 1977, after the Emergency and in response to Mrs. Gandhi's handling of it. After 1977, the Congress of Indira Gandhi was designated Congress (I)—the "I" standing for "Indira"—thus symbolizing her increasingly centralized, personal control of the party machinery.

Rather than using the mediating style of her father, Prime Minister Gandhi exerted control in a way that demanded loyalty to her personally. Factional conflict continued at the state and national levels, but the prime minister intervened by making decisions regarding matters such as the selection of state chief ministers on the basis of the degree of their loyalty to her. When Indira Gandhi was assassinated in 1984, her son Rajiv was automatically chosen as the new leader of Congress (I); despite early hopes that he would help revive Congress as a mass-based party, his approach to intraparty affairs largely duplicated that of his mother. Democratic processes within the party disappeared as elections to party posts were replaced by the appointment of Gandhi sycophants. Factions continued as part of the competition for favor, but they ceased to play a predominantly integrative role, contributing instead to the decline of the party.

In both the LDP and the Congress, intraparty factions have been responsible for much of the decisionmaking that occurs at both regional and national levels. Even when the two parties have dominated national politics to the extent that Japan and India were one-party-dominant systems, factional conflict decreed that party leaders had to take factional leaders and preferences into account when allocating posts and setting policy priorities. Both factional conflict and the necessity of accommodating faction preferences have been part of top-level decisionmaking in the Chinese Communist Party as well.

**CCP Factions.** By the time of the Cultural Revolution, it became increasingly evident to scholars of Chinese politics that elite factions were responsible for conflict at the central government level. Although the details were not known, the purges of rival leaders during the 1950s and 1960s, as suggested in Chapter 10, could be explained by mutually reinforcing personal and ideological rivalries that took the form of factions. Analyzing Chinese politics after Mao Zedong's death in 1976, Lowell Dittmer, for example, argued that a cycle of elite conflict defined Chinese politics through the 1980s, a period that culminated in the removal of Zhao Ziyang in the wake of the Tiananmen events of 1989.[10] The factional conflicts in the 1970s and 1980s that Dittmer analyzed were based more on personal relationships than ideological differences, although other scholars have linked factions to broader conflicts within Chinese society brought on by economic reform.[11]

Succession politics clearly exacerbated factional rivalry. The variety of scenarios regarding Deng Xiaoping's death and the dissolution of the ruling coalition that dominated top-level decisions for some fifteen years relied on assessments of the relative factional strength of the various contenders to succeed Deng. Underlying succession politics, as Dittmer suggested, is continued personal rivalry. Despite the efforts of Deng and other top leaders to "regularize" decisionmaking and diminish personalism, in the mid-1990s the chief operating principle of power among the CCP elites was still personalism. According to Kenneth Lieberthal:

> Organizations—committees, offices, and their rules—exist in abundance, even at the highest levels of the Chinese system. But in reality the top power elite . . . personally redefine the real rules of the game on an ongoing basis, and they are constrained only by the views and actions of others within this inner circle. . . . At all levels of the political system the PRC has been a highly personalized system embedded in a complex organizational matrix.[12]

In addition to those who hold formal positions in the party, the top elite includes the personal assistants to the top leaders, the most interesting of which is the mishu, the personal office secretary. These individuals are close to the top leaders and derive power from them; they are not part of any open bureaucratic structure. Each leader may have several *mishu*s, who can become important political players in their own right over time. Typically, a *mishu* has not come up through the bureaucratic ranks but is recruited personally by his patron. But because of his importance in representing his boss at official functions, he is assigned bureaucratic rank, which he carries with him when he leaves his *mishu* position.[13] "The *mishu* system thus provides a vehicle for factional politics."[14] After a period of personal service, a top leader will have his *mishu*s transferred to other political posts, which in turn enhances that leader's influence. Leaders also strengthen their ties with each other by employing as *mishu*s their colleagues' children, making it possible for the latter to bypass lower positions on their way up the political ladder.

The network of relationships found in the *mishu* system and more generally in factions is one example of the pervasiveness of *guanxi*, or connection, in China. Personal connections were important in prerevolutionary society, where they typically reflected family or clan ties. In modern China, *guanxi* includes a variety of interpersonal relationships and makes it possible to circumvent formal state or party strictures in order to acquire goods and services or just to get things done. *Guanxi* has contributed to corruption as colleagues and family members use their ties to profit from the economic opportunities that have opened up in the past twenty years, but connections also facilitate transactions in a society still marked by scarcity and bureaucratic encumbrances.

## Party Fragmentation and Decline

This discussion of intraparty factionalism closes with a review of the way in which factions have contributed to the fragmentation of the Congress and LDP. The two major, formal splits in the Congress (1969 and 1977) were linked to Indira Gandhi's leadership. Under her son and successor, Rajiv Gandhi, the Congress remained unified at the national level, although, as noted earlier, his centralizing leadership helped corrode the party's internal structures. Narasimha Rao, the prime minister from 1991 to 1996, succeeded in maintaining a Congress-led government in power through its full term, despite intraparty factions and frequent divisions among Congress leaders in the Council of Ministers. These divisions were both symptoms and causes of the weaknesses that in turn contributed to Congress's defeat in the 1996 Lok Sabha and state legislative elections.

In the 1996 Lok Sabha elections, the Congress share of the votes dropped over 8 percent from its 1991 total. Exit polls indicated that both intraparty factionalism and the proliferation of regional parties were contributing to the erosion of Congress support. These political shifts, in turn, reflected profound changes in the electorate. "The rainbow of social communities brought together by the Congress (I) in the era of one-party dominance has not disappeared from the political horizon, but its slices are beginning to fall apart."[15]

During the same period that factionalism was contributing to the crumbling electoral fortunes of the Congress Party, factionalism led to the first non-LDP government in Japan since the establishment of the party in 1955. In 1992, the largest LDP faction, controlled by Shin Kanemaru, began to unravel. Kanemaru admitted receiving an illegal political donation from a Tokyo trucking company and resigned as LDP vice president.

Kanemaru was the third major leader of his faction to be charged with large-scale corruption. His faction, more than any other, was linked to the kind of backroom political maneuvering, pork barrel politics, and outright illegal campaign practices that were building public cynicism and discontent. It was the accumulated effect of the LDP's "politics as usual," joined by the latest Kanemaru scandal and the factional split, that ultimately produced major change in the 1990s. Kanemaru ultimately resigned his Diet seat, but the LDP leaders were divided over how much reform to undertake in order to contain the political damage. After several twists and turns in strategy and further divisions within the Kanemaru faction, the faction itself broke up in 1992.

In June 1993, the government lost a vote of no-confidence and in the ensuing House of Representatives elections, the LDP lost its control of the lower house. In August 1993, the first non-LDP-led government in nearly forty years took office. This was to be the first of several coalition governments over the next several years, and in each coalition there were parties that were, in effect, either factional remnants of the pre-1993 LDP or the LDP itself.

## Opposition Parties

In addition to the factors already discussed, another important reason for the ability of the Congress and LDP to dominate for so long was the weakness and general disunity of the opposition parties.

### Japan: Socialists, Buddhists, and Communists

From the 1950s to the early 1990s, Japan had three types of opposition parties: those of the Left (Socialists and Communists), those in the floating center (the Democratic Socialist Party and Komeito, or Clean Government Party), and those in the conservative opposition, consisting largely of former LDP factions and dissidents. The leftist parties provided the most enduring ideological opposition to the LDP: They originated in the flowering of parties early in the century and expanded their support as the working class itself grew, though they spent much of their early history underground.

**Socialists.**  The Japan Socialist Party, created in 1945, has been marked by two kinds of divisions that have undermined its postwar promise to provide a progressive alternative to the LDP. The JSP, like its predecessors, was divided ideologically between left and right wings. The left and right wings of the party split in 1951 over the issue of the peace treaty with the United States, which the left wing rejected. It reunified in 1955, then divided again in 1960 when its right wing broke away to form the Democratic Socialist Party (DSP). The second division of the JSP was factional. In fact, the JSP most resembled the LDP in its internal organization. The factions reflected historical divisions among smaller prewar parties, as well as the ideological cleavages just noted.

Through the 1970s and into the 1980s, the JSP received about 20 percent of the vote in Diet elections, although it often did better in local elections. But in the late 1980s, when the LDP was torn by scandal and voters hated a new LDP-imposed national consumption tax, the JSP benefited. Under Takako Doi, the JSP made major gains in the 1989 House of Councillors elections, in which the LDP lost its majority. In the mid-1980s and again in 1990, the party modified its ideology to eliminate Marxist-Leninist references and to emphasize its social democratic nature. It changed the English version of its name in 1991, and in 1996, its Japanese name, to the Social Democratic Party in a bid to position itself as a more acceptable party in the post–Cold War era.

Despite these changes, the new Social Democrats failed to emulate their European social democratic colleagues, who had formed numerous governments since the 1960s. Only when the LDP fractured in 1993 did they join a governing coalition, and when Socialist Tomichi Murayama became prime minister in 1994, his eighteen months in office were marked by constant tension within his own party—including debate throughout most of his tenure over the proposed dissolution of his party! The party's identity, especially in foreign policy, was destroyed when, as noted in Chapter 9, Murayama abandoned all pretense of opposition to the SDF and again when he made the difficult decision to sue Okinawa's governor to force compliance with Tokyo's policy of renewing local land leases to the U.S. military (his party historically supported antimilitary activities in Okinawa). Although some important steps were taken during the Murayama administration to address problems that the LDP had long denied, notably compensation for atomic bomb victims and "comfort women," the legacy of this period in government seemed likely to be further marginalization of the party.[16]

Two other opposition parties in Japan are particularly interesting because their organization, ideologies, and constituencies differed from those of the LDP and the Socialists. Komeito and the Japan Communist Party were created as mass-based membership parties. Unlike the Liberal Democratic and Socialist parties, whose internal structures have long been factionalized and which do not have strong, cohesive membership bases, Komeito and the JCP are known for their grassroots organization.

**Buddhists.** Komeito was established in the mid-1960s as an offshoot of the Soka Gakkai, the lay organization of the Nichiren Shoshu Buddhist sect described in Chapter 4. Soka Gakkai is a proselytizing organization committed to infusing politics with its Buddhist values. Although formal Komeito-Soka Gakkai ties were severed in 1970, the original religious links made Komeito suspect for many Japanese even as they made it more appealing to others. The party's constituents included many alienated voters, including those who were low income, less educated, and female.[17] Ideologically, Komeito rejected both the extreme individualism of Western democracy and Marxist collectivism, instead supporting strong welfare measures, traditional values, and nationalist foreign policies.

Komeito's electoral fortunes rose and fell from the 1960s to the 1990s. Although considered an opposition party during the period of LDP dominance, it made its interest in a centrist-progressive alliance clear in order to govern.[18] It joined the 1993 Hosokawa coalition government, then formally disbanded in late 1994 to join with eight other parties and groups to form the Shinshinto (New Frontier Party).

Komeito's legacy is important in two respects. First, its grassroots organization was absorbed by the new conservative party, Shinshinto, which in turn relied heavily on the vote-mobilizing abilities of Soka Gakkai. Second, Soka Gakkai's strength raises questions about the role of religion in Japanese politics. The question of whether Soka Gakkai exerted improper influence in politics came to the fore in a 1995–1996 debate over revision of Japan's Religious Corporation Law, which provides tax benefits for officially recognized religious groups and generally limits government interference in their activities. In 1995, the government proposed amending the law by tightening registration and reporting requirements for religious groups. It argued that the proposed changes would have made it easier to track the activities of the religious cult, Aum Shinrikyo, that was held responsible for the terrorist sarin attacks, including one in a Tokyo subway, in 1994 and 1995. Shinshinto, by the mid-1990s the main opposition party, argued that the amendments constituted a thinly veiled attack on Soka Gakkai's support for Shinshinto in the 1995 House of Councillors election. Soka Gakkai's president rejected the suggestion that its voter turnout campaigns had ever infringed on the law.[19] Despite opposition by Shinshinto and a number of religious organizations, the amendments to the Religious Corporation Law passed the Diet in late 1995.

**Communists.**   Much older than Komeito, the JCP is rooted in the proletarian politics of the Taisho period following World War I. Established in 1922 (the year after the CCP's founding), the JCP enjoyed support from the USSR for most of its history. Like Komeito, the JCP is urban-based, and its strongest supporters have been those dissatisfied with the existing order. It has frequently criticized the close U.S.-Japan relationship and, along with the Socialists, has appealed to voters in the peace movement. Its showing in Diet elections has never surpassed 11 percent, although, like other leftist parties, it has often done better in municipal elections. There seemed little likelihood that this pattern would change: As the Social Democrats moved to the center and Komeito disappeared into the centrist Shinshinto, the Communists remained one of the few bellwethers of voter dissatisfaction with establishment parties.

## India: The BJP and the United Front

By the 1990s, Japan's confusing array of parties was more than matched by India's. Twenty-eight parties were represented in the Lok Sabha after the 1996 elections, although one-third of these held only one or two seats. Added to this was the array of parties in state-level politics; some of these regional parties, such as the DMK from Tamilnadu, won seats in the Lok Sabha, but many did not.

No introduction to these parties can capture all their richness, but two patterns stand out. First, parties have often drawn explicitly on traditional values for their voter appeal. By the mid-1990s, the Bharatiya Janata Party stood out for the way it built its appeal on a call for a *Hindu* India. Second, a number of smaller parties sought to challenge Congress dominance by constituting a national or leftist "front" alternative. Although the mix of parties changed, front coalitions held power in 1977–1979, 1989–1991, and after the 1996 elections.

**The BJP.**   All Indian parties, to a degree, try to enhance their electoral appeal by referring to traditional cultural or religious themes. The BJP, in particular, benefited from the reaction against secularism that has grown in much of India over the past two decades, and it has also successfully tapped nationalist sentiment. Nationalism marks the key elements of the BJP platform, including its vision of a Hindu nation and its opposition to preferential policies (especially for Muslims), as well as its taking a strong defense posture and rejecting some kinds of foreign investment. Its proposed approach to economic development anticipates revival of the *swadeshi* (self-reliance) movement developed in the early twentieth century by Indian nationalists. Originally tied to a boycott of British goods, *swadeshi* called for using indigenous goods and technology. Criticizing the Congress Party and four decades of a "Nehruvian model" of economic policies that resulted in socioeconomic dualism, the BJP attacked the Rao government's economic reforms of the early 1990s. In the BJP's analysis, these reforms benefited the consumer middle classes, while leaving three-fourths of the population in poverty, increasing the national debt, and further degrading India's national resources.[20]

From the date of its official establishment in 1984 onward, the BJP has systematically increased its percentage of votes in Lok Sabha elections from 7.4 (1984) to 23.5 (1996). In the 1990s, in the states where it was strongest, including most of northern, central, and southwestern India, its vote share was closer to 36 percent. Accounting for this growth was a combination of factors: the appeal of its clearly defined program (especially among younger, male, upper-caste voters frustrated with quotas for lower castes), the cohesiveness of its leadership and hierarchical party organization, its effective grassroots mobilization (including the use of disciplined RSS members during elections), and its willingness to exploit religious sentiments.[21] The last two factors have been especially controversial, fueling the fires of those who attack the BJP as a right-wing, antiminority, chauvinistic party. Critics hold it responsible for the 1992–1993 Ayodhya crisis, in which a nationwide BJP-inspired campaign to build a temple to the Hindu god Ram at his legendary birthplace resulted in mobs tearing down a mosque at the site, prompting Hindu-Muslim riots (see Chapter 5).

The BJP has succeeded in broadening both its geographical base and its appeal among voters. In addition to its improved showing in national elections, it has become a major player in state politics, particularly in the North. Despite some important limits on its appeal, which is much lower among women, lower castes, and southern (Dravidian-speaking) voters, the BJP emerged as the single-largest party in the Lok Sabha as a result of the 1996 elections. Over the course of fifteen years, it had become the only single-party, credible alternative to the Congress in national politics.

**The United Front.** The BJP effort to form a government in 1996 lasted less than two weeks. Its successor was the United Front, a coalition of thirteen left-of-center and regional parties. The most durable of these were two Communist parties, the Communist Party of India (CPI) and the CPI (Marxist), which split from the CPI in 1964; the regional culture-language parties such as the DMK (Tamilnadu); and the northern, centrist

Janata Party that had led the non-Congress government in 1977–1979 and formed the core of a National Front coalition government in 1989–1991. All of these parties had governing experience at the state or national level, and together they reflected widespread geographical support. Uniting them was their commitment to secularism and rejection of communalism (both part of their anti-BJP appeal) and attacks on the Congress government of Narasimha Rao. As with its coalition predecessors of 1977 and 1989, the inspiration for the United Front was opposition to Congress. Almost immediately, however, even this opposition was muted when the 178-seat United Front coalition accepted the support of 135 Congress MPs to form a government. Although not part of the government, Congress had become a coalition broker—much as the LDP had when Socialist Prime Minister Murayama took office in 1994 (although in the Japanese case, LDP ministers joined the government).

By the late 1990s, the era of minority governments and coalition politics had become part of the political landscape of India and Japan, and it seemed unlikely that either the Congress or the LDP could resuscitate itself sufficiently to turn the clock back to a time of former dominance, although the two parties remained central to coalition arithmetic. Before discussing the role of electoral systems in these changes, this section closes with a look at China's **"democratic parties."**

## China's "Democratic Parties"

The PRC's 1982 Constitution, like its predecessors, acknowledges in its preamble the existence of "democratic parties" that are part of "a broad patriotic united front" under the Communist Party's leadership. The Chinese People's Consultative Conference serves as an umbrella, or "united front," organization for these parties. When the Constitution was amended by the National People's Congress in 1993, the following sentence, which further acknowledges multiple parties, was added to the preamble: "Multi-party cooperation and the political consultation system under the leadership of the Communist Party of China shall continue and develop for the extended future."

There are eight recognized democratic parties in China, all dating to the pre-1949 period.[22] Since 1949, these parties have had no political freedom to deviate from "the leadership of the Communist Party," as stated explicitly in the Constitution; the party leaders, in fact, are CCP members. Their membership is small (ten to fifty thousand), especially in comparison to the CCP's.[23] Why, then, do they exist?

By providing nominal continuity to the prerevolutionary period, the continued existence of the parties arguably contributes, however marginally, to the legitimacy of Communist rule. In general, the parties are philanthropic or educational (for example, they perform such services as running schools) rather than explicitly political. Finally, before the 1980s, they were the only parties likely to accept intellectuals as members, as the CCP normally rejected intellectuals.

Despite the steps taken toward political reform, notably through the introduction of the elections described in the next section, the democratic parties are still incidental to China's political processes. Given their history, it seems highly unlikely that they could serve as a channel of discontent. Moreover, as Suzanne Ogden has pointed out, the persistence of a Confucian tradition that emphasizes harmony, along with the historical legacy of chaos associated with China's only effort (however superficial) to introduce European-style political democracy after the 1912 Republican revolution, "may mean that the majority of Chinese people do not find the Western practice of true multiparty competition appealing."[24]

## Election Dynamics

In liberal democracies, political parties and elections are inseparable. A core rationale for political parties is to aggregate voter preferences in order to contest, and *win*, elections. Electoral systems set the rules for these contests, advantaging some kinds of parties over others. As an example, parties that may not have majority support anywhere but that have widespread plurality support (for example, one-third of the votes cast) typically benefit from the "first-past-the-post" (FPTP), single-member constituency (SMC) system that is used in the United States, Canada, Britain, and India. Small parties, especially those not regionally concentrated, prefer some kind of proportional representation (PR) system because it guarantees them legislative representation in approximate proportion to the votes they receive in the elections.

### FPTP in India

Elections for the Lok Sabha are conducted under the FPTP system, first introduced by the British and maintained after Independence. Voters elect a single member of Parliament from each district. Like Britain and Canada, but unlike the United States, candidates need not be residents of the districts where they run. By-elections (interim elections) are relatively common, and party leaders typically choose a safe constituency to run in, even when it means forcing the resignation of a colleague who already holds the district's seat. When Deve Gowda was chosen to head the United Front government in 1996, for example, he was not an MP. So one of his early tasks as prime minister was to find a safe constituency in which to run.

Under the FPTP system, the highest vote-getter wins, no matter how low his or her percentage of the votes cast. A fragmented opposition benefits a dominant party like Congress, even though support for the latter may decline over time. Since part of the philosophy behind FPTP is to produce a stable governing majority (rather than to accurately represent the diversity of voter preference), it is possible for a party to win a considerably higher proportion of seats than votes. Thus, the FPTP system often inflates a party's majority, either when it has a plurality over a wide territory or when it is geographically concentrated. By way of illustration, in 1971, the year Indira Gandhi successfully appealed to voters over the heads of the senior members of the Congress Party, Congress won 68 percent of the Lok Sabha seats with less than 44 percent of the vote.[25] Even in 1991, Narasimha Rao was able to form a Congress (I) minority government when approximately 37 percent of the votes the party received translated into 44 percent of the seats.[26] Subsequently, in the 1996 elections, the BJP benefited from its tendency toward regional concentration: It received fewer votes than Congress but emerged as the largest party in the Lok Sabha, netting twenty-five seats more than its rival.

It seemed likely by the 1990s that the seat-inflating effects of FPTP would play less of a role in producing stable government majorities or even pluralities. The principal trend in the party system was toward the expanded role of regional parties. Although this trend contributed to a higher potential for government instability with coalitions, it also signaled the emergence of new political voices.

## Controversy in Japan

Japan's lower-house electoral system has long been controversial in a way not found in India. The controversy stems from two related factors: the structure of the multimember constituencies that pit members of the same party against each other in elections and the gross population inequalities in district size mentioned in Chapter 4. Both of these factors were debated for twenty years before government changes in the 1990s produced enough political will to effect reform. To understand the delay, it is necessary to understand the functioning of the system.

For the 1993 election, there were 511 seats in the House of Representatives. These seats were divided among 130 multiple-member districts, most electing three to five representatives. In each district, voters cast their ballot for only one candidate, with the top vote-getters (the number depending on the seats to be filled) to be the winners. To win a majority in the House (and thus ensure the ability to form a government), a party needed a majority of 256 representatives elected from the 130 districts. This meant, in effect, winning an average of two seats in each district, ne-

*Photo 12.1    Japanese Polling Place. Photo by author.*

cessitating competition between candidates from the same party. This intraparty competition helped perpetuate factionalism and money politics, especially in the LDP, as noted earlier.

Proposals to change this system date at least to the early 1970s, but only in the early 1990s did financial scandals force LDP leaders to address electoral reform with concrete legislative proposals that, however, never made it through the Diet. Foot-dragging by some faction leaders over reform was an important reason for the LDP's fragmentation in 1992–1993, and the desire for reform was the most important bond holding the Hosokawa coalition government together in 1993. Cabinet members and party leaders agreed that the multimember constituency system should be replaced by a combined SMC-PR system, in principle the same system earlier discussed by the LDP. Disagreement centered on how many seats would be elected under each system. Two government changes occurred before any legislation was adopted. By the time the LDP-backed Murayama government took up the issue, the seat distribution had been renegotiated to 300 SMC and 200 PR from the originally proposed 250–250, because the LDP saw proportional representation as advantaging small parties at the expense of the larger parties that could field candidates in all constituencies.[27]

As a result of the new system, which was used in the 1996 House of Representatives election, Japanese voters now cast two ballots, one for a local district candidate and the other for a party in a nationwide constituency, in elections to both the lower and the upper house. The principal differences are in election timing (in the House of Representatives, variable with a maximum of four years, and in the House of Councillors, fixed six-year terms with triennial elections) and constituency size. Photo 12.1 shows a polling place with separate ballot boxes used in a House of Councillors election.

## Local Elections in China

Chinese elections, held only at the local level so far, play a role very different from elections in India and Japan. Their purpose is to enhance the legitimacy and effectiveness of China's one-party system. (Broadly speaking, of course, elections also help legitimize governing systems in liberal democracies.) Because China does not have a true multiparty system, elections do not serve to replace one governing majority with another. Whether they serve as an indicator of the decay or the revitalization of one-party rule is a more difficult matter to judge.

The principle of competitive elections in both party and state organs was introduced as part of the reform of the late 1970s to early 1980s. Elections initially meant simply more candidates than positions, as well as (in principle) secret ballots. Even in the absence of competitive party politics, these are substantive—and substantial—reforms. Under the prereform system, candidates for the People's Congresses at different levels, for example, were nominated by CCP committees, approved by the next-higher level, then endorsed in a public vote by the congresses.[28] After promulgation of the 1979 Election Law and further reforms in the 1980s, local groups were allowed to nominate people to be placed on the ballot for election to local- and county-level congresses. Multiple candidates could contest a single position, and voting by paper ballots with varying degrees of secrecy was allowed.

In 1988, new legislation established direct elections to village committees, whose three to seven members advise township governments in their work. The goal of the system was to enhance state capacity to govern at the local level by increasing the accountability of village leaders to villages. By the early 1990s, some form of elected committees was found in most villages. Democratic competition, however, is still far from guaranteed: Party committees or township governments influence nominations, election practices are not systematized, and voting is not always secret. Nonetheless, the principle of choosing those who govern has been introduced. In the words of one observer of 1995 village elections in the northeastern province of Jilin: "Villagers were being given choices they never had before. They could vote the bad guys out of office. Their leaders were being held accountable for their behavior in office."[29] Moreover, recent grassroots surveys indicate that the electoral process is responsible for a congruence of policy views on economic issues between village leaders and village electors and also for greater responsiveness of the former to the latter.[30] In short, however limited, elections are slowly transforming grassroots politics in China.

# Summary

It would be easy to conclude that the great political dreams of a half century ago in three of the world's most important nations have failed, largely because of self-interest, corruption, and factionalism in their dominant parties. Uncertain of their authority, CCP leaders called in the army to clear Tiananmen Square of protesters in 1989; the party itself admits thousands of members have been expelled for corruption. In India, the sorrow of Mahatma Gandhi over communal and caste violence was reborn in the violence of Ayodhya; cynicism about democracy and politics permeates public debates from slum corners to middle-class living rooms, and India's best minds increasingly dismiss political parties as irrelevant. In Japan, it took party leaders more than twenty years to address the unconstitutional inequities in electoral districts, even as the momentum for political reform that seemed so promising in the early 1990s drifted away a brief six years later.

Despite these and other signs of decay accompanying the legacy of one-party and one-party-dominant rule, the political dynamics are far more complex than is suggested by the overview of parties in this chapter. Parties and elections are central to the long-term viability of liberal democracies. But they alone, even when functioning well, do not tell the full story of democratic health. Democracy is more than party competition and electoral procedures. It is reflected in other modes of political participation and citizen behavior. It is sustained (or corroded) by other institutions, notably those that maintain the coercive authority of the state: bureaucracies, police, and courts. And democracy is measured not just by procedural safeguards but also by substantive, socioeconomic progress.

But all is not bleak: Local elections in China, however limited, are a wedge that pries open the CCP's political monopoly. In India, the chaos of political parties responds in some measure to the voices of millions of new voters, most of whom were subjects of, but hardly participants in, political decisions affecting them one-half century ago. Seen this way, India's unruly political life reflects its vitality.

## Notes

1. See Chap. 10, n. 9.

2. Sheila Tefft, "Being Red No Longer Gets One Ahead in Today's China," *Christian Science Monitor*, May 25, 1995.

3. Nobuo Tomita, Akira Nakamura, and Ronald J. Hrebenar, "The Liberal Democratic Party: The Ruling Party of Japan," in Hrebenar, *The Japanese Party System: From One-Party Rule to Coalition Government* (Boulder and London: Westview Press, 1986), pp. 237–241.

4. On factions in general, see Dennis C. Beller and Frank P. Belloni, "The Study of Factions," and Raphael Zariski, "Party Factions and Comparative Politics: Some Empirical Findings," in Frank P. Belloni and Dennis C. Beller, eds., *Faction Politics: Political Parties and Factionalism in Comparative Perspective* (Santa Barbara: ABC-Clio, 1978), pp. 3–17 and 19–38, respectively.

5. Chie Nakane, *Japanese Society* (Berkeley and Los Angeles: University of California Press, 1970). See the complementary analysis by political scientist Takeshi Ishida, *Japanese Society* (New York: Random House, 1971), chap. 7, and the summary in Haruhiro Fukui, "Japan: Factionalism in a Dominant-Party System," in Belloni and Beller, *Faction Politics*, pp. 44–48.

6. Koichi Kishimoto, *Politics in Modern Japan: Development and Organization*, 3d ed. (Tokyo: Japan Echo, 1988), p. 102. For other analyses of LDP factions, see Fukui, "Japan: Factionalism," n. 11; Hrebenar, "Liberal Democratic Party"; Hans Baerwald, *Party Politics in Japan* (Boston: Allen and Unwin, 1986), pp. 16–28; and Louis D. Hayes, *Introduction to Japanese Politics* (New York: Paragon House, 1992), pp. 79–81.

7. *Japan Times Weekly International Edition* (hereafter cited as *Japan Times WIE*), September 18–24, 1995, October 2–8, 1995, and November 18–24, 1996.

8. Paul R. Brass, *The Politics of India Since Independence* (Cambridge: Cambridge University Press, 1990), p. 66.

9. Robert L. Hardgrave, Jr., and Stanley A. Kochanek, *India: Government and Politics in a Developing Nation*, 5th ed. (Fort Worth, Tex.: Harcourt Brace College Publishers, 1993), p. 199.

10. Lowell Dittmer, "Pattern of Elite Strife and Succession in Chinese Politics," *China Quarterly* 123 (September 1990), pp. 405–430.

11. See, for example, Susan L. Shirk, "The Politics of Industrial Reform," in Elizabeth J. Perry and Christine Wong, eds., *The Political Economy of Reform in Post-Mao China* (Cambridge: Council on East Asian Studies/Harvard University, 1985), pp. 216–220. Shirk linked factions to entrenched bureaucratic interests with different stakes in reform policies. See also her analysis in *The Political Logic of Economic Reform* (Berkeley and Los Angeles: University of California Press, 1993).

12. Kenneth J. Lieberthal, *Governing China: From Revolution Through Reform* (New York: W. W. Norton, 1995), pp. 183–184. Lieberthal added that the PRC appears less institutionalized as a political system than was imperial China.

13. Personal *mishu*s are overwhelmingly male, but a notable exception was Deng Rong, Deng Xiaoping's daughter. There are about 1 million *mishu*s in China. Wei Li and Lucian W. Pye, "The Ubiquitous Role of the *Mishu* in Chinese Politics," *China Quarterly* 132 (December 1992), pp. 913–914.

14. Lieberthal, *Governing China*, p. 190.

15. "How India Voted," *India Today* (May 31, 1996), p. 27.

16. For a balance sheet on the Murayama administration, see Mie Kawashima, "Murayama Solved Pending Issues; SDPJ Lost Identity as Price for Power," *Japan Times WIE*, January 15–21, 1996. In 1996, Takako Doi again assumed leadership of the party.

17. Ronald J. Hrebenar, "The Komeito: Party of 'Buddhist Democracy,'" in Hrebenar, ed., *Japanese Party System*, pp. 151–152.

18. Kishimoto, *Politics in Modern Japan*, pp. 112–113; *Japan Times WIE*, December 7–13, 1992 and August 30–September 5, 1993.

19. *Japan Times WIE*, December 11–17, 1995.

20. Bharatiya Janata Party, *Humanistic Approach to Economic Development (A Swadeshi Alternative)* (New Delhi: BJP, 1992), p. 10.

21. Thakur, *Government . . . in India*, pp. 238–239; *India Today* (May 31, 1996), p. 25.

22. Included in the eight parties is a rump-Kuomintang party (the KMT is Taiwan's long-term ruling party). For a history and description of the parties, see Chinese Academy of Social Sciences, *Information China*, comp. and trans. China Social Sciences Publishing House, ed. C. V. James, vol. 1 (Oxford, New York, and Beijing: Pergamon Press, 1989), pp. 404–409.

23. Suzanne Ogden, *China's Unresolved Issues: Politics, Development, and Culture*, 3d ed. (Englewood Cliffs, N.J.: Prentice-Hall, 1995), pp. 143–144.

24. Ibid., p. 144.

25. In the 1984 election held shortly after Mrs. Gandhi's assassination, her son Rajiv led the Congress to a victory of 48 percent of the vote—and a seat majority of over 76 percent!

26. Thakur, *Government . . . in India*, p. 259.

27. *Japan Times WIE*, September 6–12, 1993, and September 25–October 1, 1995.

28. Villagers were also allowed to vote for production team, brigade, and commune officials, but these elections were controlled by elites and were generally not effective in permitting peasants to influence policy. See John P. Burns, *Political Participation in Rural China* (Berkeley and Los Angeles: University of California, 1988), chap. 5.

29. Anne F. Thurston, "Village Elections in Lishu County," *China Focus* (Newsletter of the Princeton China Initiative) 3, no. 5 (May 1, 1995), p. 3.

30. Melanie Manion, "The Electoral Connection in the Chinese Countryside," *American Political Science Review* 90, no. 4 (December 1996), pp. 736–748.

# *thirteen*

# The Authority of the State: Civil, Security, and Judicial Bureaucracies

Indians often refer to lower-level government officials as *babu*s. Used in its most derogatory sense (as in *"babu* mentality"), the term describes petty bureaucrats filled with more self-importance than common sense, whose rigid adherence to rules and regulations is a way of asserting power. *Babu*s are found throughout the world, and public resentment toward them speaks volumes about the tension and antagonism between those who exercise the authority of the state and those who are subjected to it.

This chapter considers three important institutions that link citizens and the state: civilian administration (the civil service), security services, and the judiciary. The chapter summarizes the structure of each institution, then focuses on public policy issues of comparative significance, such as preferential hiring, bureaucratic discretion and accountability, misuse of security services, and judicial review.

# Civil Administration

The primary purpose of civilian bureaucracies is to implement, or administer, government policies. Both liberal democratic and Marxist-Leninist theories argue that policies should be made by the representatives of "the people," not by bureaucrats. These representatives may be elected legislators who pass laws and form governments, or the will of these representatives may be expressed in the vanguard role of the Communist Party. In either case, bureaucracies are presumed to operate under political priorities established elsewhere. In fact, however, even casual observation suggests a more complex picture—one in which every bureaucracy enjoys discretion in policy implementation and sometimes even in policy formulation.

## *Bureaucracies in India: Challenge of Diversity*

The Mughal and British Empires both established extensive bureaucracies to rule the Indian subcontinent, so the habits of administrative hierarchy were well established by the time of India's independence. The Indian Constitution provided for public (civil) services at both the Union and state levels. In addition, elite all-India services were created for civil administration and for the police. The all-India services are staffed by the central government, but their officials work primarily on problems specific to a state or to state-Union relations.

In addition to the all-India services, the Union-level bureaucracy includes some fifty national services responsible for executing the functions designated to the Union by the Constitution, such as the Indian Railway Service, the Postal Service, and the Foreign Service. Each of these has its own salary and promotion structures. There is also an array of government ministries and public services at the state level. In theory, political direction is provided by government ministers (both Union and state), although policy oversight encounters the problems found in other parliamentary democracies: Government ministers tend to be transitory, thus they are unable to change quickly the long-established habits and preferences of career bureaucrats.

Of all these bureaucratic establishments, the best known and most prestigious is the Indian Administrative Service (IAS). The IAS is the direct descendant of the Indian Civil Service, through which the British Raj was administered. Drawing on the British tradition, admission to the IAS is by a competitive exam that emphasizes general knowledge, reasoning and analytical skills, and written expression. Although candidates may write their exam in any major regional language, a successful IAS career also demands competency in English and Hindi. Approximately one hundred thousand candidates take the national civil service exam each year in India; about 1 percent are admitted to the various services, and of these, about 150 make it into the IAS.[1]

Like political parties and elections, the Indian bureaucracies have been transformed, for better and for worse, by democracy. State-level bureaucracies have expanded even more than the Union services, with the result that thousands of educated young Indians have public sector employment opportunities in their own language. The number of women in bureaucracies has increased (about one-fifth of IAS officers are female, for example), and the number of Scheduled Castes and Tribes has also expanded dramatically. This expansion of low-caste employment in government is the result of India's national and state "**reservations**" policies, in which a certain number of places in public institutions are reserved for applicants from designated caste groups. The percentage of reserved places varies between the union and state bureaucracies and from one state to another (each state determines its own reservation policies).

By providing opportunities for those denied any prospect of upward mobility over the centuries, reservation policies are an important strategy for fulfilling the goals of social revolution that inspired the Indian Constitution. But the policies have also become the subject of intense political controversy, for two reasons. First, low-caste groups are increasingly mobilized to use the processes made available by political democracy, including elections and public demonstrations, to press their demands for more reservations. Second, higher-caste groups ("forward castes"), seeing their traditional privileges slowly dissolve and finding themselves caught in a vicious job-squeeze, have mobilized to challenge the quotas and special advantages they see going to others at their expense. The furor over the **Mandal Commission** illustrates the dynamics of this debate.

**Mandal Commission.**   In 1980, the Backward Classes Commission, chaired by B. P. Mandal, issued its report. The commission was appointed by the Janata government in 1979, with two charges: (1) to determine the criteria for defining "socially and educationally backward classes"; and (2) to recommend steps for the advancement of the classes so identified.[2] The process of defining Other Backward Classes was politically charged because government benefits would flow to those defined as Backward Classes and there were different opinions among commission members and others consulted as to exactly which groups should be included. Should caste be the sole criterion, or should socioeconomic criteria also be used, thus opening up reservations to non-Hindus?

The question of defining OBCs encapsulated the problems posed for India's development: the pervasiveness of the Hindu caste system, widespread poverty, and minority communities, such as the Christian community, that are influenced by caste and suffer from economic deprivation.

Viewed philosophically, the Backward Classes debate resembles issues raised in any society trying to overcome historical inequities through preferential policies, and one can easily imagine substituting race or gender for caste in the debate.

The Indian Supreme Court, trying to balance preferential policies with constitutional mandates for equal treatment under the law, had stated earlier that reservations should not exceed 50 percent of the Indian population. Since the 1950s, 22.5 percent of the population in question—the Scheduled Castes and Tribes—had been entitled to preferential hiring quotas. In order to stay under the 50-percent limit imposed by the Supreme Court, the Mandal Commission recommended that no more than 27 percent of government posts be reserved for OBCs, even though by its own calculations in its 1980 report, OBCs constituted 52 percent of the Indian population. If the commission's recommendations were implemented, that would mean that 49.5 percent of the Indian population would thus qualify for preferential treatment.[3]

Both the Indira Gandhi and Rajiv Gandhi governments ignored the report, but in 1990, the National Front government headed by V. P. Singh (of the Janata Party) proposed to implement it. The decision sparked a maelstrom in Indian politics: upper-caste students set themselves on fire in protest, the Singh government was attacked for cynical vote-pandering, and many thoughtful Indians raised legitimate questions about the escalation of quotas.[4]

Although the brouhaha contributed to the fall of the Singh government in 1990, its successor, Narasimha Rao's Congress government, proposed to implement the report with the addition of a supplementary 10 percent quota for the poorest members of the forward castes. The issue was taken to the Supreme Court, which in 1992 found the Mandal Commission recommendations and Singh's implementation order constitutional but called for modification of the proposed policies. The court upheld the 50-percent cap on reservations, limited preferential treatment to hiring only (and not to promotions), and called for siphoning off the "creamy layer" of economically well-off members of the OBCs.[5] Rao's 10 percent addition was struck down, with the court simultaneously reaffirming the importance of caste and, by its reference to "creamy layers," also using economic criteria.

Ironically, the immediate, practical effect of the controversy was bound to be modest. In a country where millions are under- or unemployed, the four hundred thousand or so government jobs that were expected to become available in the 1990s would hardly transform the economic reality of India's massive poor population. Symbolically and politically, however, the Supreme Court judgment was a landmark: It pried open the issue of social justice that had been increasingly ignored and threatened the entrenched power of the upper castes throughout the Indian bureaucracy.[6]

## China's Cadre System

Those who are variously called administrators, bureaucrats, or civil servants in other countries are called **cadres** (ganbu) in China. Cadres staff both the government and party bureaucracies; not every cadre is a CCP member and not every party member is a cadre. The state Constitution is silent on the role of cadres, but the party Constitution defines them as "the backbone of the Party's cause and public servants of the people" (Article 34).

The cadre system originated in the CCP long before the party's successful capture of state power in 1949. The cadres were the party elite, whose job was to administer party directives and provide a link with the rural masses. Operating under constant military pressure and conditions of guerrilla warfare, cadres were expected to display unquestioning commitment to the revolution and to respect the top-down strictures of democratic centralism.

A government cadre system developed with the post-1949 challenges of establishing order and building a socialist society. In addition to the rapid expansion in the number of party and state cadres, new emphasis was placed on formal education and technical skills. But difficulties inevitably arose in the party-state cadre systems despite clear party directives. In the broadest sense, cadres were caught in a "red-expert" contradiction exacerbated by suspicion among top leaders about the lingering elitism associated with China's prerevolutionary Confucian bureaucracy. The emphasis on improving educational and skill levels threatened those who believed the egalitarian principles of the revolution required, above all, political correctness. The primary purpose of the rectification campaigns described in Chapter 10, for example, was to reinforce cadre ideological awareness and discipline. Another approach to combating elitism was the *xiafang*, or "downward transfer," movement developed during the 1940s. *Xiafang* required cadres to work at lower levels in rural areas. Both rectification and *xiafang* were especially widespread in the 1960s as useful ways to reeducate cadres in the "mass line." These techniques had their brutal consequences, particularly during the Cultural Revolution, but they were innovative attempts to combat a negative bureaucratic mentality by reaffirming the goals of the revolution and exposing cadres to the common people and to physical labor.[7]

The mandate to improve the cadres' expertise was reaffirmed in the 1982 CCP Constitution, which stated that cadres should "possess both political integrity and professional competence," be appointed "on their merits," and (in addition to being "revolutionary") be "younger in average age, better educated and more professionally competent" (Article 34). But as the emphasis on professionalism grew, so did the evidence that professional ethics were being rejected by cadres at every level. The CCP, both before and after 1949, had always insisted on the special responsibilities of the cadres. However, along with these responsibilities came special privileges, including household goods, cars, housing, and at the highest levels, freedom from accountability. In the early days of reform (the late 1970s), cadres were also the first to have access to the West through magazines, movies, and travel outside China. It is ironic that economic reform policies multiplied both the opportunity and the incentive for erosion of the cadres' ethical standards through favoritism, nepotism, and corruption—the bureaucratic sins that Mao Zedong had railed against during the Cultural Revolution (and that were his justification for *xiafang*).

Throughout the 1980s and 1990s, as economic modernization gathered steam, so did the attacks on cadres and "**bureaucratism**." Bureaucratism means inertia, procrastination, and arrogance.[8] As early as 1980, Zhang Jie, one of China's best-known writers, provided a vivid portrait of bureaucratism in a novel later translated with the title *Heavy Wings*. Zhang had worked as a government statistician before being sent to the countryside for "reeducation" and being given a factory job as part of the *xiafang* movement during the Cultural Revolution. Her novel focuses on the high- and midlevel cadres at the Morning Light Auto Works in Beijing, with the factory portrayed as a microcosm of the struggle between economic reformers and those resisting reform. One of the novel's chief characters is Tian Soucheng, the minister of heavy industry, who epitomizes the cautious, scheming, paper-shuffling mentality of bureaucratism. Tian "is happy to sail along with the current, signing, approving, or commenting on the documents that pass across his desk, whichever is appropriate." Throughout the novel, when it comes to important decisions, Tian hesitates, immobilized by the fear of making a wrong move. "As long as he didn't commit a major political blunder—and there was little chance of that for someone as cautious as he—the position [as minister] should be his for life." Tian epitomizes bureaucratism.[9]

## Elitism, Initiative, and Responsibility in Japan's Bureaucracy

Japan is physically smaller than India or China, has less pressure to decentralize, and of course is not a party-state system. All of these factors affect the degree of complexity in its administrative structures. Following the pattern found in other parliamentary systems, the Japanese Cabinet oversees about one dozen ministries, such as the Finance, Foreign Affairs, and Labor Ministries. Like most countries, Japan also has a variety of public agencies and commissions (for example, the Economic Planning Agency) whose heads report to the prime minister or to a Cabinet minister. With the growth of prefectural and municipal governments, administrative activities have also expanded, and more than 3 million civil service personnel are now recruited and paid by local entities.[10]

Japan is known for a tradition of bureaucratic elitism that dates to the nineteenth century, when the Meiji reformers instituted a civil service examination that gave preference to graduates of imperial universities such as Tokyo Imperial University (now the University of Tokyo). Modeling the bureaucracy after Prussia's, the Meiji oligarchs sought to protect the bureaucracy from political parties, Parliament, and local autonomy—all of which were viewed as threats to national cohesion and modernization.[11] The emphasis on elite education and insulation from party politics produced a highly capable, meritocratic civil service, but insulation from the political pressures of both the Meiji and Taisho eras "also reinforced authoritarian tendencies in Japanese government and society."[12]

This system continued until the postwar occupation, when bureaucrats were stripped of their status as officials of the emperor. The Home Ministry, held responsible for the authoritarian system of the 1930s and 1940s, was disbanded, and many of its officials purged. But most of Japan's bureaucracy remained largely intact, and it was through this bureaucracy that the occupation officials governed.

Despite the acknowledged professionalism of the Japanese bureaucracy today, its methods of administration are not without controversy. The core issue is whether the bureaucracy sustains or contradicts democratic politics, with critics citing as problem areas elitism, the bureaucracy's role in policymaking, and its (lack of) accountability.

**Elitism.**    Although elitism continues to be part of the bureaucratic ethos in both India and China, the Japanese bureaucracy is even more elitist, despite policies adopted during the occupation to "democratize" the Japanese government. As just noted, the continuity of the bureaucratic tradition facilitated implementation of occupation policies, but no effort was ever made to "democratize" the civil service or make it more representative as part of a broader mandate for political and social change.

Most civil servants are recruited by competitive exams that correspond to educational levels (high school, junior college, and university). The 10 percent or so of candidates who pass the initial tests at each level go on to take additional tests and are intensively interviewed, which further shrinks the number of successful candidates. The highest levels of the bureaucracy are dominated by graduates from the top universities: More than 50 percent of all bureaucrats hired by the ministries each year are graduates of the University of Tokyo law school alone.[13] "This narrow base of recruitment creates a tendency toward parochialism and old-boy ties among bureaucrats."[14]

The higher bureaucracy that staffs the national ministries and agencies is overwhelmingly male. Whereas 20 percent of India's prestigious IAS officials are women and between one-fourth and one-third are from the Scheduled Castes and Tribes, fewer than 5 percent of Japan's higher-level bureaucrats are female, and ethnic minorities are almost nonexistent.[15] There are more women at lower bureaucratic levels and in other public sector jobs (notably, in education and health services), but minorities are still missing. With rare exceptions, employees in public sector jobs are Japanese citizens. There is no law prohibiting foreign residents, such as Koreans, from holding civil service jobs, but the Home Affairs Ministry has taken the position that Japanese nationality is necessary for public employment.[16]

**Policymaking.**　A great deal has been written about the behind-the-scenes role of the Japanese bureaucracy in policymaking. Some have argued that bureaucrats effectively dominate the "iron triangle" of bureaucracy, politicians, and businessmen who run Japan's "developmental state." This cooperation has engendered enormous wealth for the country as a whole; but it has also eroded democracy, destroyed the environment, and encouraged corruption.[17]

One of the earliest and most influential scholars to draw attention to the bureaucracy as the "power behind the throne" was Chalmers Johnson. In his well-known study of the Ministry of International Trade and Industry (MITI), Johnson dissected the role of the state in Japan's rapid industrialization. He traced the preference for bureaucratic decisionmaking to the samurai, who were transformed from warriors into an administrative class during the Tokugawa period, then into an elite bureaucracy in the Meiji period. In linking the bureaucracy's modern power to the historic separation of power from authority (authority was lodged before 1945 in the emperor), Johnson argued that bureaucratic discretion had deep cultural roots.[18]

Bureaucratic discretion means that bureaucrats initiate and draft all important legislation, contribute to the passage of bills in the Diet, and themselves wield extralegislative ordinance powers almost on a par with statutes.[19] With MITI and the other economic ministries (such as the Finance and Construction Ministries) setting development priorities, the Diet has assumed a mediating role between the central institutions claiming to serve the "general interest" (national bureaucracy, the LDP, large business concerns) and the "particular interests" of social groups such as farmers and consumers. Johnson described the triangular relationship among the top central institutions in this way:

> The LDP's role is to legitimate the work of the bureaucracy while also making sure that the bureaucracy's policies do not stray too far from what the public will tolerate. . . . The bureaucracy . . . staffs the LDP with its own cadres to ensure that the party does what the bureaucracy thinks is good for

the country as a whole, and guides the business community toward developmental goals. The business community, in turn, supplies massive amounts of funds to keep the LDP in office."[20]

The system is reinforced by the custom known as *amakudari*, "descent from heaven." Japanese government officials retire early, usually by their mid-fifties and, having "descended," move into a second career either in business, in quasi-public corporations (created and funded by ministry officials), or as conservative (especially LDP) Diet members.[21] *Amakudari* emerged after World War II in response to a number of circumstances, but its effect has been to tighten the decisionmaking triangle described above.

**Accountability.**    Another analysis of power in Japan characterized it as a "truncated pyramid," an "elusive state," a nexus of elite organizations, and, essentially, a "system" without strong leadership, in which no one individual or institution can be held accountable for a policy. "Hence there is no place where, as Harry Truman would have said, the buck stops. In Japan, the buck keeps circulating."[22]

With the growth of citizens' movements since the 1960s (see Chapter 14) and the development of greater concern over the social and environmental costs of economic development, bureaucratic projects have been subject to greater public scrutiny. Similarly, the scandals that drew attention to the LDP and rocked the political party establishment in the early 1990s also reflected negatively on the bureaucracy. For example, in the mid-1990s, the powerful and prestigious Ministry of Finance (MOF) was criticized both inside and outside Japan for its failure to monitor several collapsed credit unions and banks. The ministry's will and competence to oversee Japan's financial institutions was widely questioned.

The escalation of public criticism is a reflection of the accumulation of disillusionment over mounting signs of the government's difficulty in handling the challenges facing the country—challenges that include economic slowdown, international strategic changes, and the problems accompanying fifty years of postwar development. Even the long-held tenet that the bureaucracy represents a higher "national interest" has been questioned, as illustrated in a 1996 political cartoon (see Figure 13.1).

The cartoon refers to three well-known failures in government oversight. "Minimata disease" was actually mercury poisoning that affected several thousand people (and from which dozens died), mostly in the 1950s. Not until 1995 did protracted court battles produce a settlement and an Environment Agency admission that the government shared responsibility for the poisoning, along with the corporation that dumped poisoned waste into Minamata Bay in Kumamoto Prefecture.

Also in 1995, the Health and Welfare Ministry acknowledged that it had failed to prevent the spread of HIV-infected blood imported from the

*Figure 13.1 "Japanese Bureaucratic Armor Through the Ages." From* Japan Times Weekly International Edition, *September 25–October 1, 1995, p. 20.*

United States, despite warnings of possible problems. Some 1,800 Japanese hemophiliacs were infected as a result of normal blood transfusions. Finally, the prototype fast-breeder nuclear reactor at Monju (Fukui Prefecture) was shut down after a leak in its cooling system was discovered. Initially, the government corporation running the reactor denied any serious accident and edited evidence of the leak from a videotape taken at the scene. When the attempted cover-up came to light, an official responsible for the investigation committed suicide. One observer concluded that these incidents were "manifestations of senility and corruption in the bureaucracy itself."[23]

## Security Forces

We turn now to a survey of institutions specializing in the use of force: the military, **paramilitary**, and police forces. Several factors account for the range and complexity of security services: the size of the country, the type of government structures, historical experience, and constitutional norms. The particular mixture of these factors has produced different security arrangements in India, China, and Japan. The primary focus of this section is on the use of coercion to reinforce state authority and its implications for the citizens of those states.

### Military

Both India and China have huge standing armies, as well as hundreds of thousands of reservists and paramilitary forces. Even Japan has close to 300,000 military personnel in the Self Defense Forces. Table 13.1 compares the estimated military, reservist, and paramilitary personnel in the three

TABLE 13.1    Military, Reserve, and Paramilitary Forces in India, China, and Japan (1994)[a]

|        | Military     | Reserve   | Paramilitary |
|--------|--------------|-----------|--------------|
| India  | 1,265,000    | 1,305,000 | 906,700      |
| China  | 2,930,000[b] | 1,200,000 | 600,000      |
| Japan  | 237,700      | 47,900    | 12,000       |

[a]Figures for different forces in India and China vary widely among sources; "police forces" are often listed as paramilitary, and governments occasionally reclassify contingents. For consistency, this table uses only International Institute for Strategic Studies totals.

[b]The PLA (People's Liberation Army, which includes army, navy, and air force) underwent continuing reductions in the 1990s.

*Source:* Adapted from International Institute for Strategic Studies, *The Military Balance 1995/96* (Oxford: Oxford University Press, 1995), p. 266. All figures are estimates.

countries in the mid-1990s. Despite the technical sophistication of the SDF and its increased importance in Japan's post–Cold War foreign policy calculations, it plays no major role in domestic politics. Therefore, the following discussion concentrates on comparing India and China.

There are several important similarities between the military establishments of India and China. First, as large, continental powers with long borders to defend, both countries have been preoccupied with threats to their national integrity, and each has been engaged in several regional conflicts over the past half century. Indian troops fought three wars against Pakistan (1947–1948, 1965, 1971) and had a major border conflict with China in 1962. In addition to the 1962 war with India, China also fought localized conflicts with the former Soviet Union (1969) and Vietnam (1979) and was heavily engaged in the Korean War (1950–1953).

A second related factor is the relatively high priority given to defense spending. The Indian government budgeted US$8.1 billion for defense in 1995, an estimated 2.8 percent of GDP. Chinese military expenditures are more difficult to determine: Official figures put defense spending at 1.4 percent of GDP in the mid-1990s, but foreign military analysts calculated the real figure to be 5.6 percent.[24]

A third similarity between India and China is the size and importance of their respective military-industrial establishments. Governments in both countries have generally given high priority to attaining self-sufficiency in military technology and arms production, although in neither case has it been realized. China, in particular, is known for the elaborate system of defense industries run by the People's Liberation Army, many of which have turned to consumer production to supplement inadequate government funding.[25]

Fourth, the armed forces in both countries are viewed as important integrating institutions for large territories and diverse populations. Historically, the army has provided opportunities for upward mobility, much as it has done in other countries. Military training in India is designed to foster national identity, and in China, it is expected to promote nationalism as well as accountability to the Chinese Communist Party. Efforts are made to assure that loyalties do not develop along regional or ethnic rather than national lines and that a cohesive, centralized command controls the armed forces. In both countries, however, a variety of problems developed in the 1980s and 1990s that hampered national cohesion and damaged military morale, including communal tensions in the Indian army, stalled professionalization of the PLA, and involvement of both armies in domestic conflicts.[26]

A fifth similarity lies in the importance attached to the maintenance of national independence in the development of nuclear forces by both countries. China is the world's fourth-largest nuclear power, whereas India is generally viewed as a threshold (or undeclared) nuclear-weapon state.[27] Given the proximity of nuclear or potential nuclear neighbors (Russia, Pakistan, and North Korea), as well as their mutual history of conflict, it is unlikely that either country will abandon its policy of nuclear independence. Japan has a large and sophisticated nuclear power industry, but the history of antipathy toward military use of nuclear technology and the reality of the American "nuclear umbrella" make Japanese policy toward nuclear weapons unique in the international system.

The most important difference between the Indian and Chinese militaries derives from historical experiences that led to different roles in politics. We have already seen that the PLA, created in the late 1920s, was central to the long Communist drive for power in China. The exploits of the Red Army during the civil war with the KMT (especially the Long March) and in the war with Japan became legendary. PLA loyalties forged during the 1930s and 1940s defined much of Chinese elite politics for half a century. Neither victory in the "liberation" struggle nor the challenges of "building socialism" can be understood without reference to the PLA, even though it does not rule directly. Put differently, the role of the military is central to Chinese political calculations, whether in time of turmoil, such as the Cultural Revolution, or in determining support during periods of political succession for preeminent leaders such as Mao Zedong or Deng Xiaoping.[28]

In contrast, the army was not central to the nationalist struggle in India, nor did it play a supporting role. After Independence, the Congress Party continued to be the most direct route to political power until the 1990s.

India adopted the British structures that concentrated political conflict in the political parties and bureaucracy and also absorbed the important principle of civilian control of the military. Most observers agree that the chances of military rule comparable to that in Pakistan or Bangladesh, for example, is unlikely. Nonetheless, despite the Indian military's apolitical tradition, the government's use of the army to handle civil conflicts in Punjab, Kashmir, and the northeastern part of the country has troubling implications.

## Paramilitary

India, China, and Japan have both reservist and paramilitary forces, as shown in Table 13.1. In India and China, the paramilitary contingents are more important for contemporary politics, whereas in Japan neither institution is directly concerned in the political process. The term paramilitary designates a wide range of armed forces working alongside of or in place of the regular military. They may have local, regional, or national responsibilities and often operate secretly. In contrast to the armed forces, which are designed to serve the external defense and foreign policy goals of a government, paramilitary services operate domestically, often against rebel groups and other (real and perceived) enemies of the state. An important exception is the coast guard, which, though armed, generally has no combat role but is assigned to defend territorial waters.

Japan's coast guard constitutes its entire recognized paramilitary force of twelve thousand personnel. China has both militia (variously categorized as reserves or paramilitary)[29] and the People's Armed Police Force (PAP). The PAP was formed in 1983, when the PLA transferred its internal security and border defense units to the Ministry of Public Security. As a national police force, the PAP was initially responsible for controlling the demonstrators in Beijing during the Tiananmen Square confrontations but was replaced by PLA units when it proved unable to handle the situation.[30]

India has almost 1 million paramilitary units, divided among a dozen different forces. The state governments separately constitute and control armed police forces (a total of about four hundred thousand) that are called in when the civil police are unable to deal with disturbances. The national contingents range from the Home Guard, men on lists with no training or resources, and India's small coast guard of five thousand to several significant, large forces with important military responsibilities. The most notable of these are the Central Reserve Police Force (120,000), the Border Security Force (185,000), and the Assam Rifles (52,000). The majority of the paramilitary forces fall under the authority of the Ministry of Home Affairs, although a few report either directly to the Cabinet Secretariat or the Ministry of Defense.[31] Several of the paramilitary contingents have become politicized through their involvement in domestic conflicts, and a few have been criticized for serious civil and human rights abuses, as explained further on.

## Police

All three of the countries discussed here have a national police force. As suggested in the discussion of China and India, a police force may properly be considered paramilitary when it has substantial responsibility to maintain domestic order or to combat insurgency. Under these conditions, it is generally left to the local police to combat individual criminal activities.

The Japanese police are highly regarded both domestically and internationally. Although recentralized after the occupation period, the police force has generally not abused its powers, nor has it been exploited for political purposes.[32] This factor alone sets it apart from the police in India and China, as well as in most Asian countries.

In contrast to Japan, where public security is the responsibility of the police, Chinese security tasks are shared by the police; cadres assigned to *danwei*, the small group that every citizen belongs to at work or at school; and neighborhood committees staffed by "granny police" (older women watching their neighborhoods). Their work is reinforced by an extensive record-keeping system that tracks the personal and work lives of citizens. Security functions are overseen by public security organizations that exist at each level of government and report to the security organ at the next-higher level. This "parasecurity network" is sufficient in most neighborhoods because its personnel know the citizens, are aware of their problems, and can therefore usually head off trouble.[33]

The police in China, as in Japan, work out of neighborhood stations and are generally stationed in large numbers only where trouble is expected. In addition to crimes such as robbery and rape, both the police and the security cadres assigned to work units identify *political* criminals, those guilty of political deviation. The tasks of both the police and security cadres are facilitated by the information kept on all Chinese citizens in the form of household registers and personnel dossiers at workplaces. Household registers, containing personal information on the residents of each household, have been used in China in one form or another (and elsewhere in East Asia) for centuries. After the PRC was founded, registers served to control rural-to-urban migration, implement family-planning policies, and administer rationing in urban areas. Work dossiers, which accompany people throughout their employment, contain detailed information on education, job performance, and noteworthy behavior patterns. Although dossier supervisors are not true "secret police," they are trusted CCP members who "function as part of the internal public security apparatus, and the dossiers that they control are shrouded in secrecy."[34]

In short, policing in China involves far more than local forces' being charged with preventing and controlling criminal activity. Local police are just one leg of a complex, national system of public security that includes CCP cadres, *danwei*, neighborhood committees, and files—all designed to maintain both social and political control. The procuracy and judiciary described later in this chapter are also part of the security apparatus.

For both historical and cultural reasons, the organization and problems of the Indian police system are different from those in either Japan or China. Structurally, multiple police forces and conflicting jurisdictions are the result of Indian federalism and the multiplication of security problems throughout the country. The central government maintains several "police forces" that serve paramilitary functions and that were included in the earlier description of paramilitary contingents in India. States also maintain armed constabularies, a reserve police force called out to deal with major disturbances to public order. The figures for these constabularies are included in the totals for paramilitary forces in Table 13.1.

The reputation of India's police forces has declined over the years as problems of corruption, politicization, and brutality have mounted. Victimization by the police has been particularly common in the case of low-caste Indians, including women, who are frequently raped while in custody. Rivals who challenge the power of local politicians on whom the local and regional police administrators depend for their careers are also frequently victimized. With the expansion of caste and communal violence, the police have been called away from normal police duties to deal with demonstrations, strikes, mob looting, murder, and other large-scale threats that they are ill equipped to handle. It has become commonplace to assume that the police are "for sale," either looking the other way when crimes are committed or even participating in them: "The police are not in fact maintaining order in either the urban or rural areas of India, but are themselves among the most dangerous and disorderly forces in the country."[35]

## Above the Law

Both China and India have been criticized with increasing frequency for abuses of civil and human rights. Information about China became more accessible in the 1980s, when freedom of movement (both domestic and international) was easier. After Tiananmen, of course, it was commonplace for the Western media and Chinese dissidents outside of China to focus on long-standing abuses (such as Chinese prison camps) as well as on widespread summary arrests or disappearances of those involved in the 1989 protests. Harry Wu, for example, became a U.S. household name in 1995 when he was arrested for illegal entry into the PRC, where he was gathering information on human rights abuses.[36]

Citizen abuse in India, although perhaps less well known than in the Chinese cases, is no less serious. It occurs in "ordinary" ways: on a daily basis against individuals, the most vulnerable of whom are low-caste individuals and *dalit*s, including women. The media widely report such incidences of police brutality, but the absence of any systematic effort to address it in structural terms (such as improving service conditions) suggests that abuse of authority by police at the local level will almost inevitably continue.

Kashmir is the most dangerous case, and the events there illustrate both abuse of force and the problems of politicization. Kashmir is the central portion of the state of Jammu and Kashmir, where the state's majority Muslim population is concentrated (Jammu is predominantly Hindu). Readers may recall from Chapter 5 that India and Pakistan disputed control over Kashmir at the time of Partition and that under pressure of invasion from Pakistan, the Hindu ruler of Jammu and Kashmir agreed to join India. India subsequently committed itself to a plebiscite to determine which country would incorporate the region permanently, but the plebiscite was never held, and India gradually came to regard Kashmir as an integral part of its own territory over Pakistan's protests.

By the late 1980s, more and more Kashmiri Muslims, "increasingly alienated by fraudulent elections, widespread corruption, and failure of the Center to develop the state economically," came to support secession from India.[37] In 1989, the center imposed President's Rule in Jammu and Kashmir in response to terrorist attacks on Hindus and the inability of the state government to control the surging violence. From the perspective of the Indian government, which fought two wars with Pakistan largely over Kashmir, civil disturbance in the state (like instability in Punjab) is viewed as an acute threat to national integrity. New Delhi is quick to point to the bombings and assassinations by terrorists, along with Pakistani support for the secessionists, as justification for its efforts to combat Muslim militants. But mounting evidence of torture, summary executions, and widespread misuse of force by Indian paramilitary and army forces had drawn international condemnation by the early 1990s.[38]

## Judicial Systems

In India, China, and Japan, the judicial systems differ from the civilian and security bureaucracies in terms of the roles they play in politics and also in their relationship to traditional social and legal values. All three countries had indigenous civil and military administrations, which were hierarchical and which predated Western influence. Western legal norms of equality were superimposed on these traditional hierarchical norms. This merging of Western and indigenous values is another reminder that history and culture, as well as government structures, help explain the different organizations and practices found in judicial systems.

This section first summarizes the organization of the judiciaries in the Indian and Japanese parliamentary systems, then compares the role of their courts in judicial review and protection of citizen rights. The section concludes with the development of the Chinese judicial system during the past two decades. The discussion here assumes that judicial systems are part of the authoritative apparatus of the state. This does not mean that the courts never dispense justice or that the law never serves the interests of average citizens, as will be seen later. On balance, however, the judiciaries in India, China, and Japan, as in many countries, play a subsidiary role in politics and often serve to reinforce state authority rather than advance citizen interests.[39]

## *Judicial Organization in Parliamentary Systems*

In a parliamentary system, popular sovereignty is expressed in an elected legislature, the legislative and executive functions are fused in a cabinet government, and there is no formal separation of powers as in the United States. Consequently, the judiciary generally plays a subsidiary role in the political system. In Britain, for example, the courts may not hold an act of Parliament unconstitutional because there is no judicial review of laws. There are parliamentary systems, however, where judicial review has been introduced, thereby altering the British pattern. India and Japan, as well as Canada, are such systems, and the reasons for and the nature of judicial review in both countries tells us much about their constitutional history and political practices.

**Japan.**   The modern Japanese legal system is patterned after that of continental Europe. The Meiji reformers Europeanized Japan's legal structures in the late nineteenth century, although the underlying values continued to be Confucian: "The new legal system was not meant to interfere with or to alter the morality of the people."[40] The dominance of codified law (in contrast to common law, found in the Anglo-American tradition) was influenced by heavy borrowing from France and Germany but was also consistent with Japanese tradition. Not until the 1947 Constitution did the principle of judicial independence become established.

As a unitary state, Japan has a single national court system, with four different kinds of courts and the Supreme Court at the apex. Local summary courts try both civil and minor criminal cases; family courts handle cases involving domestic disputes, juveniles, wills and other domestic matters, and, where possible, use conciliation; district courts have appellate jurisdiction for civil cases from the summary courts; and the eight high courts handle criminal appeals as well as appeals from the district and family courts. The fifteen-member Supreme Court exercises neither original nor advisory jurisdiction. Its job is to hear cases on appeal and to oversee the judicial system.

**India.** Although India is a federation, the country has a single, integrated judicial system in which the Union is responsible for establishing courts and determining their jurisdiction. There are no autonomous state courts in the American sense. The array of courts is complicated, with separate systems for civil and criminal cases and a different pattern of judicial administration for metropolitan and rural areas.[41] "Small cause courts" hear civil cases at the local level, and special magistrates hear criminal cases. Lower-level courts are subordinate to district courts, which in turn are subordinate to high courts. High courts are the apex of the state judiciaries, but they are controlled by the Union government in matters of appointment, transfer, and removal of judges.

The Supreme Court of India is composed of twenty-six justices (one chief justice and twenty-five associates). Like the Japanese Supreme Court, it has appellate jurisdiction, but the Indian Supreme Court also has original and advisory jurisdiction. It has original and exclusive jurisdiction in disputes between the Union government and the states and between the states themselves. Under Article 143 of the Constitution, the president of India may refer a dispute to the Supreme Court for its advisory opinion.

Both the court structure and the tradition of common law are rooted in the period of British rule. The approach taken by the Constituent Assembly was to retain the judicial infrastructure described in the 1935 Government of India Act but to enhance the power and independence of the courts. The assembly intended that the Supreme Court, in particular, would have special responsibility for defending the Constitution's fundamental rights.[42] To this end, the Constitution departed from the British precedent by conferring the power of judicial review on the court.

**Judicial Review in India and Japan.** The principle of judicial review is the same in India and Japan: Any act passed by Parliament must be in conformity with the Constitution, and the Supreme Court is the court of last resort in determining constitutionality. The implementation of this principle over the past half century has varied, however, and tells us a good deal about the way in which the two political systems have evolved.

Judicial review in India has been central to the political process and therefore controversial. The controversy results from inherent conflicts between the principles of parliamentary sovereignty and judicial review and between the fundamental rights and the goals of social revolution that are also found in the Constitution. One consequence of these conflicts has been frequent amendment of the Constitution by Parliament with the intent of circumscribing the courts' powers of judicial review.

The conflict over judicial review and, ultimately, the independence of the courts, came to a head when Indira Gandhi was prime minister. In 1970, her government's legislation to nationalize the banks was struck down by the Supreme Court. When she won a landslide victory in the 1971 elections, she pushed successfully for a constitutional amendment permitting Parliament to amend *any* part of the Constitution, including the fundamental rights section. Although the Supreme Court upheld this new amendment, it stated that any amendments that attacked the basic structure of the Constitution would be invalid. Prime Minister Gandhi's response was to intervene in the next appointment of the court's chief justice in order to elevate a candidate sympathetic to her social programs.

Finally, the period of the Emergency (1975–1977) demonstrated the vulnerability of judicial review and judicial independence in India. The 1975 high court finding that Mrs. Gandhi was guilty of corrupt electoral practices in the 1971 election catapulted the court into political controversy and precipitated the chain of events leading to the Emergency. During the Emergency, the Supreme Court, under enormous political pressure and led by a chief justice who owed his position to the prime minister, failed to defend the basic right of habeas corpus for people detained during the Emergency. This capitulation badly eroded the credibility of the court, despite subsequent decisions designed both to reinforce citizen rights and to reassert judicial authority.

In contrast to India, the Japanese Supreme Court has been largely non-controversial. Whereas Indian courts might be said to display "judicial activism," Japanese courts are conservative and, especially in the early decades, often supported the government. The Supreme Court deliberately avoids controversial issues, in part because of its understanding of the Constitution's designation of the Diet as the "highest organ of state power." In particular, the court has been reluctant to exercise judicial review of government administrative action, a pattern that privileges government bureaucrats in disputes with citizens.[43] The courts have also refused to rule on the constitutionality of the Self Defense Forces, as was explained in Chapter 8.

Despite this conservative stance, Japanese courts have exercised judicial review in a number of important instances and, in some areas, appear to play a growing role in protecting citizen rights, especially in environmental issues such as the Minimata case mentioned earlier. The Supreme Court's first case of significant judicial review occurred in 1973, when it ruled unconstitutional an article in the penal code that provided heavier penalties for the crime of patricide than for homicide, on the ground that the penal code article violated Article 14 of the Constitution, which stipulates that "all of the people are equal under the law." The treatment of patricide as a worse crime, of course, stemmed from the Confucian tradition of respect for the father as the head of the family.[44]

Given the long history of intolerance for unorthodoxy in Japan before the 1947 Constitution, freedom of expression is a good measure for judging the degree of transformation in the postwar polity. One American scholar who has made extensive study of Japanese law and citizen rights sees strong judicial support for maintenance of the broad range of constitutional freedoms.[45] Others have been more critical of specific instances in which courts support the interests of the state against individuals. In one celebrated case, for example, an Okinawan man burned the Hinomaru ("rising sun") flag at a national athletic meet in 1987 as a deliberate act of civil disobedience in protest over Japanese policy toward the prefecture. Although the Hinomaru was never designated as Japan's official flag, the Ministry of Education in 1989 made raising the flag at schools compulsory, but many Okinawans view the flag as a symbol of Japan's wartime imperialism. The flag burner claimed his act was covered by the constitutional right of freedom of expression, but in 1995 a high court rejected an appeal of his prison sentence imposed by a lower court.[46]

In addition to the different issues discussed here, Japan and India share a problem that has significant implications for citizen rights: In both countries, cases typically take years to work their way through the courts. The Japanese Minimata poisoning case and the flag-burning case, for example, took years simply to go from one court level to another. The situation is India is no better. In Japan, delays may be caused by long trials, widely spaced trial sessions, understaffed courts, and meticulous examination of evidence and issues by judges. India's problems are more frequently related to the "staggering caseload," with the result that a high court may have a backlog of fifty thousand cases.[47] Whatever the causes, "delay of justice denies justice."[48]

## The Changing Chinese Legal System

China in the 1970s and 1980s confronted a problem similar to that faced by Meiji Japan a century earlier: In order to improve its relations with other countries, it had to develop a legal system recognized and respected by foreigners. When the reform leadership under Deng Xiaoping determined to bring China into the international economy by seeking foreign investment, it quickly became obvious that China needed laws pertaining to property, joint ventures, taxes, and contracts in order to provide the level of predictability necessary for international commerce. In essence, China had no legal system as of the late 1970s. In the 1950s, the CCP had begun to develop legal codes to replace those that had existed under the Kuomintang. But the effort was halted during the political turmoil that began with the Great Leap Forward, and thereafter, the country was governed by decrees, administrative regulations, and the personal orders of various leaders. In 1978, a serious effort to create a regularized system of law and courts was undertaken.

For the past two decades, the Chinese legal and judicial system has been in a continual state of development. The 1982 state Constitution outlines a system of courts and procuratorates at each level of government and establishes their theoretical independence by stating that neither institution is "subject to interference by any administrative organ, public organization or individual" (Articles 126, 131). The system of **procuracy** is rooted both in Chinese imperial practices and in the Napoleonic civil code, which influenced the legal systems of a number of continental European states.[49] Procurators authorize the arrest of criminals, determine whether a case should be brought to trial, and if it is, they serve both as prosecuting attorney and public defender during the trial. Thus, they serve a variety of legal functions and, in principle, serve as a significant check on the arbitrary exercise of power by the police and security agencies. In fact, however, the ability of the procurators to check abuses of power is often compromised by frequent interference from government officials.[50]

Paralleling the hierarchy of procuratorates is the court system, which includes basic-level, intermediate, and higher people's courts, with the Supreme People's Court at the apex. China shares with Japan the preference for mediation rather than court trial to settle disputes;[51] once a case goes to trial, guilt rather than innocence is presumed, and defendants are under strong pressure (as in Japan) to confess and show remorse. China does not use an adversarial system in court, and lawyers are charged with determining the truth rather than with defending the accused "at all cost." "The purpose of the courts is thus not to determine guilt or innocence but to decide on punishment."[52] In contrast to India and Japan, cases are handled swiftly and seldom appealed. It is not uncommon for a case to be tried and punishment carried out within a week, even where the death sentence has been imposed and the case has been appealed to a higher level.

Despite the enormous strides made in codifying laws, training lawyers, and educating people about changes in the judicial system in China, most scholars agree that much remains to be done to protect the extensive citizen rights that are described in the Constitution. For example, there is an acute shortage of trained lawyers, defendants may not have enough time to gather witnesses, and trials (which are supposed to be held in public) often take place in secrecy. These problems are particularly serious in cases of political dissidence.

## Summary

Perhaps more than any other area discussed thus far, the topics raised in this chapter recall the importance of multiple "lenses" when trying to understand politics in other countries. India's convoluted reservations policies, the opacity of bureaucratic decisionmaking in Japan and China, the different value attached to confession and remorse in the Japanese and Chinese penal systems, and above all the controversy over human rights violations in China and India—all these issues challenge us to understand the different contexts within which politics operate. To use the single illustration of human rights in China, the debate in the United States has been dominated by two perspectives, neither of which does much to help us see the world through Chinese lenses. Some Americans argue, for example, that trade with China should be held hostage to improvements in the PRC's protection of civil rights. Others say that such a policy would likely not change Chinese behavior and certainly would damage the American economy. In contrast, the most important issues for the Chinese government and for the overwhelming majority of Chinese who share the dominant nationalist view are noninterference in the PRC's domestic affairs and the need to recognize the real progress made in the development of procedural guarantees for rights. Most Chinese would likely also think it important to acknowledge that rights must be viewed within a historical and cultural context.[53] The Western assumption that there are rights that are universal must be rethought in an Asian context, and this is a principle with strong support outside China, in both East and Southeast Asia.

## Notes

1. There are about 5,000 employees in the IAS. Ramesh Thakur, *The Government and Politics of India* (New York: St. Martin's Press, 1995), p. 166.

2. Government of India, *Report of the Backward Classes Commission*, vol. 1 (New Delhi: Government of India, 1980) (hereafter cited as the Mandal Commission Report), p. iii.

3. Mandal Commission Report, chaps. 12, 13, and pp. 63–64.

4. For an exceptionally thorough analysis of the issues surrounding the Mandal Commission Report, see Madhu Kishwar, "Beyond For or Against: Exploring the Complexity of Reservation Policy," *Manushi*, nos. 63–64 (March-June 1991), pp. 6–30.

5. *Times of India*, November 17, 1992.

6. It took the government almost another year to determine what constituted the "creamy layer" and to list some 1,300 Backward Classes eligible for reservations in government hiring. *India Today*, September 30, 1993, p. 15.

7. James C. F. Wang, *Contemporary Chinese Politics: An Introduction*, 5th ed. (Englewood Cliffs, N.J.: Prentice-Hall, 1995), p. 122, summarizes this positive assessment.

8. Ibid., pp. 124–125; Harry Harding, *Organizing China: The Problem of Bureaucracy, 1940–1976* (Stanford: Stanford University Press, 1981), discusses bureaucratism in the early years of the PRC.

9. Jie Zhang, *Heavy Wings*, trans. Howard Goldblatt (New York: Grove Weidenfield, 1989), pp. 125–126.

10. *Japan: An Illustrated Encyclopedia*, vol. 1 (Tokyo: Kodansha, 1993), p. 147 (hereafter cited as Kodansha, *Encyclopedia*).

11. Koichi Kishimoto, *Politics in Modern Japan: Development and Organization*, 3d ed. (Tokyo: Japan Echo, 1988), pp. 85–86; Kodansha, *Encyclopedia*, p. 147.

12. Kishimoto, *Politics in Modern Japan*, p. 86.

13. Ulrike Schaede, "The 'Old Boy' Network and Government-Business Relationships in Japan," *Journal of Japanese Studies* 21, no. 2 (summer 1995), pp. 297–298.

14. Louis D. Hayes, *Introduction to Japanese Politics* (New York: Paragon House, 1992), p. 61. Elite school ties, of course, are not unique to the Japanese bureaucracy. The French, for example, have their elite *"grandes écoles"* and the United Kingdom has Oxford and Cambridge (the "Oxbridge" elite). See the comments of John Creighton Campbell, "Democracy and Bureaucracy in Japan," in Takeshi Ishida and Ellis S. Krauss, eds., *Democracy in Japan* (Pittsburgh: University of Pittsburgh Press, 1989), pp. 115–116.

15. The 5 percent figure is for those admitted after passing the most prestigious A-level exam. B. C. Koh, *Japan's Administrative Elite* (Berkeley: University of California Press, 1989), p. 105. Even high-level female bureaucrats find that male superiors expect them to serve tea or clean up the office (pp. 107–108).

16. *Japan Times Weekly International Edition*, October 30–November 5, 1995, and December 18–24, 1995 (hereafter cited as *Japan Times WIE*). Both national and local government agencies have chosen to honor the Home Affairs Ministry's interpretation as policy and to restrict hiring to Japanese citizens for almost all positions.

17. See, for example, Karel van Wolferen, *The Enigma of Japanese Power: People and Politics in a Stateless Nation* (New York: Alfred A. Knopf, 1990); and Gavan McCormack, *The Emptiness of Japanese Affluence* (Armonk, N.Y.: M. E. Sharpe, 1996). The "developmental state" is discussed further in Chapter 14.

18. See especially Chalmers Johnson's *MITI and the Japanese Miracle: The Growth of Industrial Policy, 1925–1975* (Stanford: Stanford University Press, 1982), chap. 2; and his *Japan: Who Governs? The Rise of the Developmental State* (New York: W. W. Norton, 1995).

19. Ibid., pp. 123–124; T. J. Pempel and Michio Muramatsu, "The Japanese Bureaucracy and Economic Development: Structuring a Proactive Civil Service," in Hyung-ki Kim, Michio Muramatsu, T. J. Pempel, and Kozo Yamamura, eds., *The Japanese Civil Service and Economic Development: Catalysts of Change* (Oxford: Clarendon Press, 1995), pp. 213–234.

20. Johnson, *MITI*, p. 50. In a more recent study, Gary D. Allinson argued that beginning in the 1970s, the Japanese society and polity have become more fragmented, with the result that business and government relations in every arena undergo continual renegotiation; in Allinson and Yasanori Sone, eds., *Political Dynamics in Contemporary Japan* (Ithaca: Cornell University Press, 1993) pp. 17–49.

21. Johnson, *Japan: Who Governs?* pp. 133–138 and chap. 7; Schaede, "'Old Boy' Network," pp. 293–317; Takenori Inoki, "Japanese Bureaucrats at Retirement: The Mobility of Human Resources from Central Government to Public Corporations," in Kim et al., *Japanese Civil Service*, pp. 213–234.

22. Van Wolferen, *Enigma of Japanese Power*, p. 5 and chap. 2.

23. Shoichi Kobayashi, "Fooling All the People, All of the Time," *Japan Times WIE*, April 1–7, 1996.

24. The lower figure for China is quoted in Stockholm International Peace Research Institute, *SIPRI Yearbook 1995* (Oxford and New York: Oxford University Press, 1995), p. 448; the higher figure is from International Institute for Strategic Studies, *The Military Balance 1995/96* (Oxford: Oxford University Press, 1995, for IISS), p. 266. See *The Military Balance*, pp. 270–275, on the difficulties of calculating Chinese military expenditures.

25. Tai Ming Cheung, "Profits over Professionalism: The PLA's Economic Activities and the Impact on Military Unity," in Richard H. Yang, Jason C. Hu, Peter K. H. Yu, and Andrew N. O. Yang, eds., *Chinese Regionalism: the Security Dimensions* (Boulder: Westview Press, 1994), pp. 85–110.

26. Communal tensions particularly affected the Sikhs because of the army's engagement in Punjab (see Chapter 11). The Sikhs have a long tradition of prominence in the army. See Stephen P. Cohen, "The Military and Indian Democracy," in Atul Kohli, ed., *India's Democracy: An Analysis of Changing State-Society Relations* (Princeton: Princeton University Press, 1988), pp. 132–138. On China, see Jonathan D. Pollack, "Structure and Process in the Chinese Military System," in Kenneth Lieberthal and David M. Lampton, eds., *Bureaucracy, Politics, and Decision Making in Post-Mao China* (Berkeley and Los Angeles: University of California Press, 1992), pp. 151–180; and Eric Arnett, "Military Technology: The Case of China," *SIPRI Yearbook 1995*, p. 371.

27. India conducted a "peaceful" nuclear explosion in 1974; China has conducted over forty. India has opposed the Non-Proliferation Treaty (NPT), arguing that it discriminates against nonnuclear states in favor of those possessing nuclear weapons. Concerned with the principle of equal treatment, India argues that it will support nonproliferation only in the context of a clear and effective plan for nuclear disarmament by nuclear states.

28. Michael D. Swaine, "Chinese Regional Forces as Political Actors," in Yang et al., *Chinese Regionalism*, pp. 59–84.

29. In peacetime, the militia's principal tasks are economic production, periodic military training, and maintaining internal security at the local level. In time of war, the militia would supply reserves for mobilization, provide logistical support to the PLA, and conduct guerrilla operations behind enemy lines. During the 1990s, the militia underwent reorganization and downsizing. IISS, *Military Balance 1995/96*, p. 176.

30. June Teufel Dreyer, "The Military's Uncertain Politics," *Current History* 95, no. 602 (September 1996), pp. 254–255.

31. IISS, *Military Balance 1995/96*, p. 159.

32. This does not mean there is no room for criticism. One critic, for example, has described both forced and false confessions. Futaba Igarashi, "Forced to Confess," trans. with notes by Gavan McCormack, in McCormack and Yoshio Sugimoto, eds., *Democracy in Contemporary Japan* (Armonk, N.Y.: M. E. Sharpe, 1986), pp. 195–214. Both Igarashi and foreign scholars have emphasized the importance of cultural factors in confessions. See also David H. Bayley, *Forces of Order: Policing Modern Japan*, 2d ed. (Berkeley and Los Angeles: University of California Press, 1991), chap. 7; John Owen Haley, *Authority Without Power: Law and the Japanese Paradox* (New York and Oxford: Oxford University Press, 1991), pp. 129–136.

33. Suzanne Ogden, *China's Unresolved Issues: Politics, Development and Culture*, 3d ed. (Englewood Cliffs, N.J.: Prentice-Hall, 1995), pp. 174–175; Michael R. Dutton, *Policing and Punishment in China: From Patriarchy to "the People"* (Cambridge: Cambridge University Press, 1992), pp. 203–226.

34. Odgen, *China's Unresolved Issues*, p. 177.

35. Paul R. Brass, *The Politics of India Since Independence* (Cambridge: Cambridge University Press, 1990), p. 57.

36. See Harry Wu's autobiographical book, *Bitterwinds: A Memoir of My Years in China's Gulag*, with Carolyn Wakeman (New York: John Wiley and Sons, 1994); and the review essay by Jean Pasqualini, "Glimpses Inside China's Gulag," *China Quarterly*, no. 134 (June 1993), pp. 352–357. Chinese authorities suddenly released and deported Wu back to the United States in late August, on the eve of the U.N. Fourth World Conference on Women in Beijing.

37. Robert L. Hardgrave, Jr., and Stanley A. Kochanek, *India: Government and Politics in a Developing Nation*, 5th ed. (Fort Worth, Tex.: Harcourt Brace College Publishers, 1993), p. 161.

38. The Border Security Forces were one of the biggest offenders. See *Human Rights Watch 1994 Report* (New York: Human Rights Watch, 1994), pp. 162, 164; *Amnesty International Report 1995* (London: Amnesty International, 1995), pp. 157–160; and reports in *India Today*, November 15, 1993, pp. 18–29. For the official Indian position, see Subhash Kirpekar, "Hawking Half-Truths," *Sunday Times of India*, November 19, 1992.

39. I am aware of the bias I bring to this statement and recognize that in several Asian philosophies state and citizen interests are not necessarily or inevitably seen as conflictual.

40. Percy R. Luney, Jr., "The Judiciary: Its Organization and Status in the Parliamentary System," in Luney and Kazuyuki Takahashi, eds., *Japanese Constitutional Law* (Tokyo: University of Tokyo Press, 1993), p. 126.

41. See the description in Thakur, *Government and Politics of India*, pp. 51–54 including fig. 2.2.

42. Granville Austin, *The Indian Constitution: Cornerstone of a Nation* (Oxford: Clarendon Press, 1966), pp. 164–166.

43. Luney, "Judiciary," p. 139. District court judges have repeatedly held laws and government actions unconstitutional and have been subsequently overruled by a high court or the Supreme Court. See my discussion in Chapter 8. See also, in

particular, the interpretation of Frank K. Upham, *Law and Social Change in Postwar Japan* (Cambridge: Harvard University Press, 1987).

44. Hidenoru Tomatsu, "Equal Protection of the Law," in Luney and Takahashi, *Japanese Constitutional Law*, pp. 188–192.

45. Lawrence W. Beer, "Law and Liberty," in Ishida and Krauss, *Democracy in Japan*, p. 81. See also Beer's *Freedom of Expression in Japan: A Study in Comparative Law, Politics, and Society* (Tokyo: Kodansha, 1984).

46. The background and rationale of the flag burning is described sympathetically by Norma Field, *In the Realm of a Dying Emperor* (New York: Vintage, 1991), chap. 2. See also *Japan Times WIE*, November 6–12, 1995.

47. Thakur, *Government and Politics of India*, p. 66. The Supreme Court accepts some 100,000 cases a year for review, whereas the U.S. Supreme Court accepts 100–150.

48. Beer, *Freedom of Expression*, p. 139.

49. Ralph H. Folsom, John H. Minan, and Lee Ann Otto, *Law and Politics in the People's Republic of China in a Nutshell* (St. Paul: West Publishing, 1992), p. 142. The 1982 Constitution calls the procuratorates "state organs for legal supervision"; as such, they resemble the Imperial Censorate, which supervised the civil bureaucracy.

50. Ibid., pp. 143–149.

51. Ibid., pp. 203–218; Wang, *Contemporary Chinese Politics*, pp. 137–138; June Teufel Dreyer, *China's Political System: Modernization and Tradition* (New York: Paragon, 1993), pp. 221–223. Dreyer reported that about 90 percent of cases are handled through the mediation process. There were approximately 1 million mediation organizations in Chinese villages, factories, and neighborhoods in the mid-1990s. "Judiciary in Line with International Norms," *Beijing Review* 37, no. 49 (December 5–11, 1994), pp. 5–6.

52. Dreyer, *China's Political System*, p. 220.

53. See, for example, the special issue of *Beijing Review* on "Human Rights: Progress in China" (January 1996).

*fourteen*

# The Politics of Development and the Development of Politics

This chapter integrates and expands on themes introduced in earlier chapters, using comparative case studies to illustrate basic issues. The purpose of the chapter is to provoke some questions on the relationship between development and politics, and some of the points made here are deliberately controversial. The use of the "politics of development" as a theme assumes that socioeconomic development is a primary objective of Asian governments. Indian, Chinese, and Japanese politics differ in numerous respects, but all three countries have been heavily committed to modernization for at least a half century. In addition to economic development, China and India, in particular, have also pursued extensive social reforms (which in Japan occurred during the occupation). In all development policies, some people have benefited more than others, and in many cases, there have been clear winners and losers.

In order to illustrate the impact of development policies, the first section of the chapter focuses on the politics of dams. Controlling water—for irrigation, flood management, and hydroelectric power—is central to the development process. The drier the region, the larger the population, and the more ambitious the development goals, the greater the need, as those who live in regions like the American West understand.

Water resource planning is generally an elite affair, engaging mainly top-level politicians and bureaucrats, and India, China, and Japan are no exceptions. But as the following case studies show, the politicization of average citizens in recent decades has been particularly evident in environmental matters, including those involving water resources. All three countries have experienced protest movements centered on the construction of dams, and through these case studies, we will see that even the management of water resources—an area often touted as one of unquestioned national benefit—has it detractors.

Drawing on the illustrations in the case studies of dams, the second section of the chapter concentrates on the way politics has developed in response to the socioeconomic changes of recent decades. Political participation does not look the same as it did fifty years ago in Asia: Government development policies have altered economic conditions and relations, and the resulting social shifts have produced new forms of political organization and expression. These, in turn, have influenced government policy. By examining several examples of social movements and grassroots organizations, this chapter reveals an important aspect of contemporary Asian politics.

# Dam Politics

The Three Gorges project in China and the Sardar Sarovar dam in India's Narmada Valley have attracted international attention; both are controversial at home and abroad. Japanese dam projects are less well known, but they raise many of the same issues about development as do Three Gorges and Narmada.

## *Three Gorges*[1]

Thinking and planning for a dam on the upper Yangtze River dates to the Republican regime, when Sun Yat-sen and other leaders were attracted both to the potential for hydropower generation and to the possibility of controlling the river's frequent flooding. Planning in earnest began in the PRC during the mid-1950s, in part as a response to the major Yangtze floods of 1949 and 1954 (the latter claimed some thirty thousand lives). Very quickly, differences of opinion among government officials arose over the desirability and feasibility of the dam, and planning was indefinitely sidetracked.

With the Four Modernizations underway in the late 1970s, the proposed Three Gorges dam reemerged on the national agenda. Almost immediately, planning became embroiled in bureaucratic politics at the national level (between government ministries and high-ranking party

officials) and between national and provincial officials. Provincial governments supported or opposed the project according to the benefits anticipated for their regions. Hubei Province (where the dam would be located)
and Hunan Province would benefit the most from flood protection and
electricity production. But 1 million people living above the dam site, primarily in Sichuan Province, would be displaced, and Sichuan would not
benefit either from flood control (and might experience greater risks of
flooding, as noted later on) or from much of the electric power.

The decision to build the dam required a number of trade-offs, the most
important of which were crafted to win Sichuan's support. For example,
by lowering the height of the dam to approximately 600 feet and making
the reservoir smaller, the powerful Chongqing municipality would become a major trading center. Without those changes, Chongqing would
be flooded and a smaller city would emerge as an important port.
Sichuan Province also received special investment funds from the State
Planning Commission in order to offset the costs of relocating people.[2]

Despite this bureaucratic agreement and a State Council decision in the
mid-1980s to move ahead with detailed planning and construction of
Three Gorges, the project continued to generate controversy. By the late
1980s, opposition came from outside the Chinese government (from the
country's nascent environmental movement, human rights advocates,
and some Chinese scientists) and also from the international community.
The cost of the project and potential environmental damage were the two
issues generating most of the opposition. The original cost of the dam
was projected at US$12 billion, but by the mid-1990s, cost estimates grew
to US$30 billion and more, with one-third of the total cost earmarked for
resettlement compensation for those displaced by the dam and reservoir.[3]
The cost burden was a particularly serious issue because of China's difficulty in securing international financing to help with the construction.
Many international and bilateral lending agencies withheld loans because
of concern over the project's environmental impact.

Environmental issues surrounding Three Gorges were complex. Supporters of the project argued that the dam would decrease China's depen-
dency on coal for three-fourths of its electricity and thereby reduce emis-
sions of carbon dioxide and other greenhouse gases (of which China is a
major producer, second only to the United States). Critics, however,
pointed to accelerated deforestation and soil erosion, which would exacerbate landslides and flooding in the Yangtze basin. A buildup of sedi-
ment in the enormous, 370-mile-long reservoir behind the dam would
also contribute to flooding, especially upriver in Sichuan Province. Air
and water pollution would increase, both from construction and from the
factories expected to build up along the reservoir. Furthermore, given the
cost escalation, it seemed unlikely that government agencies could afford

to undertake major cleanup efforts. The reservoir would also inundate over forty thousand acres of prime farmland and destroy the natural beauty of the limestone gorges after which the project was named. When fully operational (the final phase of the project is scheduled for completion in 2009), almost 400 square miles in twenty counties and cities behind the dam will be inundated, necessitating the removal or destruction of innumerable cultural and historical sites.[4]

In early 1989, a book edited by Dai Qing (later translated into English under the title *Yangtze! Yangtze!*) was published in China. It summed up the controversy over Three Gorges, served as the rallying cry for the groups opposed to the project, and contributed to the decision later that year to postpone construction for a time. The book was banned after the democracy movement in May-June 1989 as allegedly "contributing to the political turmoil in Beijing," and some thirty thousand copies of its Chinese edition were destroyed.[5] During this same period, well-known opponents of the dam in the environmental and scientific communities were excluded from decisionmaking related to the project.

Despite this opposition, government spending on industrial plants and infrastructure, such as airports and highways, fostered new interests in support of the dam. Three Gorges thus illustrates the kinds of changes in socioeconomic classes and political power that accompany a major development project: "While project losers (farmers, small shopkeepers, local minority groups such as the Tujia) may outnumber local winners (construction workers, government bureaucrats, private entrepreneurs), the latter are concentrated in the more politically powerful towns and cities that increasingly dominate China's political landscape."[6]

At the national level, the most powerful leaders jockeying for supremacy in the wake of Deng Xiaoping, particularly premier Li Peng, hitched their political wagons to the project's successful completion. Partly because of their vision of state-centered development propelled by large infrastructure projects and partly out of concern for national cohesion in the 1990s, these leaders defended the dam as a matter of national pride and commitment. The fact that much criticism of the project's environmental costs came from outside China simply reinforced their case that completing Three Gorges was critical to the national interest.

## Narmada[7]

In 1993, *India Today* estimated that 30 million people had been made "refugees of progress" in India. Roads, industries, mines, and even wildlife sanctuaries had all displaced people from their homes and farms, but dams alone were responsible for 70 percent of the refugees.[8] When (and if) it is completed at the end of the twentieth century, the Narmada

Valley's Sardar Sarovar project (SSP), which includes an 455-foot dam, reservoir, and elaborate canal system, will have contributed another estimated three hundred thousand or more people to the total of displaced Indians.[9] As planned, the entire project to control the waters of the Narmada and its forty-odd tributaries includes thirty large (with Sardar Sarovar the biggest), 135 medium, and innumerable small dams.

The idea of damming the Narmada River system predates Independence. Planning by the Union government began in the late 1950s under Prime Minister Jawaharlal Nehru, who, like his Chinese counterparts, saw dams as an essential part of a national strategy of economic modernization. Just as the Three Gorges aggravated interprovincial competition and conflict in China, so the Narmada proposal generated conflict between Indian states. The Narmada River basin drains from three states—Gujarat, Maharashtra, and Madhya Pradesh—so one of the earliest problems to be resolved was to decide how the waters impounded by the various dams would be shared by the states. In order to resolve the interstate dispute, the Union government set up a Water Disputes Tribunal in 1969. After ten years of delays and deliberations, the tribunal made its allocations, after which the final planning phase began. As construction finally got underway in 1987, a dispute arose between Gujarat and Madhya Pradesh over resettlement of the people displaced by the project. Although the issue was nominally resolved through mediation by the central government, critics of the project argued that no systematic resettlement plan had been developed either by the states or by the central government, partly because no one knew exactly how many people would be displaced.[10]

In China, Three Gorges planning was derailed for three decades by broad political conflicts and was periodically delayed by intrabureaucratic and interregional conflicts. In India, conflicts between the states over distribution of benefits and costs were especially important in delaying both planning and construction, but disagreement occurred at the Union level also, for example, between the Ministry of Environment and Forests and the Ministry of Water Resources. The former determined that it was premature to approve the SSP and recommended the establishment of the Narmada Management Authority, giving it the authority to stop work on the project if necessary to ensure fulfillment of environmental safeguards. But the position of the Water Resources Ministry to press ahead in the absence of environmental protection measures prevailed.[11]

Narmada, like Three Gorges, generated widespread criticism of its environmental impact. Project critics pointed to the destruction of thousands of acres of valuable forests, with implications not just for commercial losses but also for soil erosion and climatic stabilization; the possibility of earthquakes; the damage to downstream ecosystems; and the likelihood that the water channels would contribute to waterborne diseases. Dams built elsewhere in India primarily for irrigation (which was the stated purpose for most of the dams in the Narmada basin) have had a poor record for increasing crop yields; at the time construction on the Sardar Sarovar was getting underway in the late 1980s, 10 percent of land irrigated from earlier projects had already been lost due to siltation and waterlogging.[12]

The issue that received the most criticism, however, was the one highlighted at the beginning of this section—the displacement of thousands of people, a large proportion of whom were members of tribal groups. A domestic protest movement, headed by an NGO called Narmada Bachao Andolan (NBA, Save the Narmada Movement), linked young and old activists, poor farmers, and tribal peoples. The anti-Narmada movement received support from other Indian NGOs, sympathetic intellectuals, and environmental and human rights NGOs outside India. The protest soon attracted international attention from bilateral and multilateral development assistance donors, including the World Bank, originally a major backer of the Sardar Sarovar dam.[13]

As a consequence of unprecedented criticism directed against the SSP, the World Bank appointed a review panel in 1991 to evaluate the status of environmental and resettlement measures before allocating the undisbursed remainder of the loan (approximately 38 percent). The Independent Review Panel issued its report in 1992, recommending that the bank "step back" from the project until concerns could be adequately addressed. But in 1993, the government of India refused the loan balance, presumably because officials knew they could not meet the bank's performance criteria.[14]

The extent of the politicization in India over the SSP distinguished this case from the Three Gorges, where domestic (but not international) criticism was curtailed after 1989. The World Bank's review noted the "strong tradition of participation of NGOs in public life" in India and observed that Gujarat, where the SSP was being constructed, was the birthplace of Mahatma Gandhi and home to strong traditions of nonviolent protest.

From the perspective of the governments committed to the Three Gorges and Narmada projects, one of the most important political defenses was the projects' significance for the process of nation building. The Chinese government, as noted earlier, used this defense against both international and domestic critics of Three Gorges. Sanjay Sangvai has argued that the Narmada project has also become embroiled in the language of nation and nationalism, to the degree that those who oppose the project are accused of being antinational. Just as economic interests are refashioned by a megaproject, so are political interests and political language. Sangvai sees a coalition of interests that includes those who will most benefit from the Sardar Sarovar dam, the agro-industrial elites of central Gujarat, state legislators from nearly every party, and all those who share the Hindutva version of Indian nationalism (represented also by the Bharatiya Janata Party)—"the upper middle class, neo-rich and aspiring class of managers, technocrats, the high caste, highly educated elites in industry, in management, in administration and education, in market."[15]

Thus, in both China and India, critics of the dams argue that the "winners" in development include those with a vested interest in state-initiated and managed development projects, including technocrat-bureaucrats, large agricultural and industrial interests, growing municipalities short of water and power, and market-driven entrepreneurs. The losers typically are small farmers, artisans, and shopkeepers displaced by water projects, landless agricultural workers, and especially indigenous peoples—in sum, all those who lack the political and economic resources to take advantages of new opportunities created by the project. At issue in both countries is the political gap between the opponents of large development projects, who seem to offer few alternatives to steady population growth, unrelenting poverty, and the galloping energy demands of industrialization, and the "developmentalists," who argue with credibility that grassroots populism, though politically satisfying, provides no viable economic solutions to the pressing problems of India and China.

## Dams in Japan's "Developmental State"

Dam construction has been central to the comprehensive national development plans that have guided Japan's economic modernization for the past century. Hydropower generation and water storage to supply urban industry and metropolitan areas were the primary goals of Japanese dam construction. Approximately one thousand dams were built between the end of World War II and the mid-1990s, and an additional four hundred were either planned or under construction. Although modern dams employ technologies deemed suitable to earthquake-prone areas, other environmental problems have appeared in the completed Japanese dams. Silting, in particular, has clogged many dams, reducing their capacity.[16]

The most controversial project was the damming of the Nagara River on Honshu Island. The river was long considered special because it hosted more known natural species than any other river. The water from the mouth of the river to approximately sixty miles upstream constituted a prize fishing area for local fishing cooperatives, and scientific and environmental groups viewed the river as important for study and conservation. Until it was dammed in the mid-1990s, it was the only free-flowing river on Honshu. Plans for dam construction dated from 1960, but local opposition from both fishing and environmental groups delayed construction for over twenty years.

The way in which the planned dam was finally approved and construction completed in the 1990s illustrates the decisionmaking bureaucracy-LDP-business triad discussed in the previous chapter. The Construction and Finance Ministries, along with LDP Deputy Prime Minister Shin Kanemaru, were the strongest supporters of the Nagara dam. Kanemaru (as a previous minister of construction) had approved the project, and contracts had been given to two large construction companies. The LDP environment minister in 1990 was opposed and was determined to suspend work on the dam, but he was opposed by his own ministry, which feared hostility from the more powerful Finance and Construction Ministries. Kanemaru also reportedly threatened the environment minister that opposition would effectively end the latter's political career. The minister of construction in the Hosokawa government, which succeeded the LDP in 1993, opposed the project, but that government fell before the new minister could overcome the opposition within his own ministry.[17] The Nagara dam was completed in 1995.

The Construction Ministry had argued that there would be no adverse effects from the dam on fishing or the environment. A year after it went into operation, however, local fisherman claimed that the number of fish caught had declined dramatically. Scientists also saw early signs of declining water quality and eutrophication. Finally, in order to curtail criticism from environmental groups, the ministry set up a panel of experts to monitor the effect of the dam on the river's ecosystem for a period of five years.[18]

## The Development of Politics

Citizens respond to government policies and, more generally, to state authority in various ways, extending from enthusiastic support through compliance, lukewarm acquiescence, resistance, and opposition. Everywhere in the world, development projects such as dams have evoked these responses at one time or another, depending on the expected impact of the project. This section of the chapter illustrates the variety of political organizations and activities that have emerged in India, China, and Japan in direct or indirect response to the development projects and in relation to overall socioeconomic changes of the past few decades.

The section on India links the proliferation of grassroots movements to socioeconomic change, the nature of Indian democracy, and the Gandhian tradition of civil disobedience. For Japan, the discussion returns to the changes in female life expectancy and work patterns explained in Chapter 4, linking these to increased grassroots political participation. The discussion on China emphasizes the role of market reform policies in making available, often unintentionally, new opportunities for grassroots political activity. In different ways, each section addresses the relationship between economic and political change.

## Social Movements and Grassroots Politics in India

"Social movements" is a generic term that includes a wide variety of groups formed for collective action purposes. Groups pool their human and material resources to influence other groups or the government, often with the intent of changing public policies. Social movements reflect the willingness and ability of people to organize for their own purposes, particularly at the local (or "grassroots") level. Their organizations may be fleeting or durable, and they use a variety of tactics and take a variety of positions with regard to collaboration with the government.

Indian political scientist Rajni Kothari has captured the significance of collective action and grassroots political participation by pointing to the contradiction between the theories of development that profess to benefit all citizens and the reality of development that advantages economic and political elites and largely ignores the poor (or leaves them worse off). Although he has written specifically about India, his argument raises questions about many political systems where development in the name of the poor proceeds largely without reference to the interests of the majority of people. Organized politics, especially political parties, are part of the problem, Kothari has argued, and their decline, along with the absence of effective government in many parts of India, has created a new political space. Grassroots movements have started to occupy this space, transforming the nature of politics.[19]

Kothari's argument is more persuasive in India, which arguably has more political action groups, nongovernmental organizations, and grassroots movements than any other country in the world.[20] India, after all, is not just a country of enormous diversity; the effects of its development policies have been felt unevenly, and its comparatively open political system offers multiple opportunities for organizing. Moreover, Mahatma Gandhi's own philosophy of collective action—satyagraha—established a tradition of legitimacy for protest movements. To protest the SSP, for example, Medha Patkar, head of the Narmada Bachao Andolan, and more than six thousand farmers and tribals undertook a 125-mile march from Madhya Pradesh to the dam site in Gujarat, a march modeled after Gandhi's famous Salt March. The leaders of the movement also fasted when denied permission to cross the Gujarat border.[21]

The rhetoric and strategies associated with both electoral politics and economic modernization have increased people's expectations. Local and

*Photo 14.1    Indian Women Demonstrating. Photo courtesy of* The Pioneer, *New Delhi.*

regional elites who have resources (such as landowning castes) are able to use informal party and government networks to achieve their goals, but those without such resources typically resort to protest methods, such as marches, sit-downs, general strikes, and sometimes violent confrontation. The middle-class women shown in Photo 14.1, for example, were protesting Hindu communalism at Ayodhya and the violence it engendered; theirs was one of dozens of such demonstrations held in North India in the wake of the Ayodhya clashes.

Social action and environmental rights groups have increased steadily in India during the past twenty-five years, most focusing on specific regional issues (such as the SSP). Many mobilize along ethnic, caste or class, or gender lines, and they are inspired by a range of philosophies, including Gandhian social transformation, Marxist-Leninist class-based resistance, and feminist consciousness-raising. Some groups have been durable, building an organizational infrastructure and a core leadership that enables them to respond to changing political contexts. Despite Kothari's optimism, noted earlier, there is little evidence yet that these social movements have significantly altered the overall development priorities of either the central or state governments. However, individually and collectively, they have had some successes and clearly represent a dynamic part of India's political processes.[22] For example, an antiliquor movement (arguing that alcohol was directly associated with domestic violence) succeeded in pressuring the state government in Andhra Pradesh to ban the production and sale of liquor, although liquor was a major source of state revenue. A Maharashtra farmers' movement, Shetkari Sanghathana (Organization of Farmers), succeeded in linking farmers from different classes, electing women to local government *panchayat*s and changing development priorities at the local level to benefit the poor.[23]

Of the thousands of movements in India, the ones with the greatest implications for the long-term transformation of Indian society are likely to be those composed of the very poor, especially the *dalits*. The economic and social conditions of most *dalits* (and backward castes more generally) are for the most part deplorable. Attacks on untouchables, including women, have continued, often as a warning against their attempts to break with traditional roles. But in the past half century, low castes and women in general have developed a political consciousness scarcely imaginable to their grandparents; they have established their own groups; and education has expanded the core of people who provide leadership and who can take advantage of opportunities provided through reservations policies. Perhaps most important, social and political action has helped the very poor shed the "deep-seated belief that oppression is part of one's *karma*."[24]

## Stratification, Citizens' Movements, and Women's Centers in Japan

Research in recent years has shown Japan to be far more socially and economically stratified than was earlier thought. This stratification helps explains both electoral politics and grassroots political participation. Using the example of changes in women's roles that was discussed in Chapter 4, for example, it becomes clearer why women were important in the citizens' movements that blossomed in the 1960s and 1970s and why they have long tended to support opposition politicians, as they did, for example, during the "madonna" revolt of 1989, when the Socialist Party surged in the House of Councillors election.

Chapter 4 noted the increased life expectancy that underlay changes in women's social and economic roles in the second half of the twentieth century. After 1970, the number of women in the workforce increased steadily, although their percentage remained at approximately 40 percent of the total labor force. In general, the gender inequalities found outside the home were reproduced in the job market, partly due to the persistence of traditional norms. Reinforcing these norms was the structure of women's employment: Women were more likely to work in smaller firms, where wages were lower, and to be disadvantaged by the seniority-based wage system prevalent in Japan. Part-time work provided the flexibility many women needed and desired, but of course it also disadvantaged them in terms of wages, benefits, and, ultimately, security. Those women employed in low-pay and low-status jobs were struggling to balance family and jobs. At the same time, approximately one-third of all adult women were full-time homemakers with upper-middle-class status residing in urban and suburban areas.

This "bifurcated pattern of life and work" divided women into two discernibly different subgroups, constituting one form of structural fragmentation in Japan.[25] This, in turn, led to different forms of gender-distinctive political participation. Many working women, especially those in low-pay, lower-status jobs in the 1970s and 1980s were attracted to centrist and progressive parties, such as Komeito and the Socialist and Communist parties, because these parties supported the public services that they needed. In times of crisis (such as the environmental crises of the 1960s and 1970s, symbolized by the Minimata case mentioned in Chapter 13), these voters were joined by women who thought of themselves as independent or had weak ties to the Liberal Democratic Party. This latter group also supported opposition parties in the late 1980s during the controversy over the LDP's introduction of a nationwide consumption tax and the party's financial and sexual scandals.

It was the second group of women, generally composed of homemakers, who were also central to the development of grassroots politics in Japan after the 1960s. During the period from 1976 to 1989, for example, the level of women's participation in local political activities, including election campaigns, doubled.[26] Those drawn into these activities were primarily the more affluent homemakers who had the time and knowledge to become involved. They also constituted the "foot soldiers" of the citizens' movements in the 1960s and 1970s.

**Citizens' Movements.** The term "citizens' movements" is associated largely with a type of social movement that arose in the 1960s primarily "to protest the rapid economic growth policies of government and their consequences at the local level, particularly pollution and the deterioration of the quality of life."[27] There were also antiwar, civil rights, and consumer rights groups, but the environmentally oriented groups have received most of the scholarly attention because they raised critical questions about the course of Japan's development and had an impact at the local level. Detailed research on the movements has suggested that they were influenced by postindustrial values and concern over the discernible effects of industrial pollution, but that as important as the intensity of the pollution problem was the preexisting network of community associations at the local level.[28] Foremost among these associations were the Federation of Neighborhood Associations and the Federation of Housewives Associations.

Women, many of whom were drawn in through contacts in the house-wives associations, played an important role in the citizens' movements. Often, they were more important as grassroots organizers than as leaders, but in some instances, they took the initiative both in researching problems and in leading the political campaigns for remedies to pollution problems. In Kitakyushu (see further on), for example, a coalition of women studied the effects of both air and water pollution, produced a film on the problems, pressured the city council, and effectively made pollution issues part of the local municipal election campaign. Representatives of the coalition subsequently served on a city council organization for the study and administration of pollution measures.[29]

Citizens' movements declined in visibility and numbers in the 1980s, leading some observers to claim that their progressive gains were not sustained and that they had been co-opted by various state agencies.[30] For elite women, in particular, however, their personal experience in these movements appears to have become part of a collective historical experience that suggests their ability to organize effectively to influence public policy.[31] The history of the citizens' movements is important also because some of the earlier activists in those movements are associated with the network of women's centers created in the 1980s.

**Women's Centers.**   Beginning in the 1970s, the Japanese government took a number of initiatives designed to improve women's legal and economic status, both in response to international pressure after the 1975 United Nations International Women's Year (IWY) and to demands from Japanese women's groups and a handful of politicians. Part of this effort was to create women's centers in prefectures and municipalities throughout Japan. The centers vary in size, staffing, and range of activities, but they share a common conceptualization and a dual purpose: to serve as an information resource and meeting place for women (and men) of all backgrounds. Inspired by the IWY, local governments, often with central government support, had constructed 170 of these centers by the late 1980s.[32] The centers were not designed specifically to develop political awareness or participation, but they typically function in an outreach capacity for women who otherwise have few contacts with public affairs or public officials. Because the centers are accessible to nongovernmental organizations and are often directed by individuals with extensive contacts in the Japanese women's movements, one may surmise that in the long term they will open up possibilities for grassroots groups to influence government policy, especially on gender issues. The Yokohama and Kitakyushu centers illustrate this potential.

The Yokohama Women's Forum, established in 1988, was one of Japan's first large centers. Administered by the Yokohama Women's Association for Communication and Networking, which is entirely funded by the City of Yokohama, the forum runs a major library and sponsors conferences and exhibitions. It serves as a policy advocate and has helped Yokohama develop a reputation for modest initiatives designed to establish gender equity.[33]

The city of Kitakyushu is located at the northern edge of Kyushu Island, where it forms an industrial zone with the western tip of Honshu Island. One of the most important centers of Meiji industrialization, the city experienced a decline in its industrial importance by the 1970s. In the late 1980s, the national government offered grants for "hometown revitalization" programs, and Kitakyushu chose a proposal for a municipal women's center. Built with both central and municipal government funds, the Kitakyushu Forum on Asian Women opened in 1990. The forum's focus on Asian women reflects the city's history as a cultural and commercial bridge between Japan and the rest of East Asia and also reflects a conscious decision by city officials to emphasize the connection with Asia in their strategy for economic modernization. Like Yokohama, the Kitakyushu forum runs research programs; it also targets environmental issues as a special area for research.[34]

Japanese women are largely absent in formal, elected positions at every level of the Japanese government. By the 1995 local elections, for example, an average of 4 percent of local assembly seats were won by women.[35] This was an increase from the previous twenty years (when most of the decisions to construct the women's centers were taken), but hardly a "feminization" of elected political posts. Moreover, women were singularly unsuccessful in winning gubernatorial and mayoral races. In the relative absence of a formal political presence, then, what accounted for the substantial commitment of energy and money to women's centers? Three factors stand out. First, all levels of government have been responsive, albeit slowly, to international influences, especially when pressured by small but able and dedicated groups of elite women. Second, the growth of citizens' movements from the 1960s and 1970s focused on local governments, and many municipalities were run by non-LDP administrations more responsive to progressive policies than national politicians and bureaucrats. In the citizens' movements, women learned how to organize at the grassroots level. Finally, linked to these factors was the growing respect of male politicians for the "women's vote." Widely heralded by the late 1980s, when women enjoyed major gains in the 1989 House of Councillors election, the women's centers symbolized a tangible commitment to women's issues.[36]

## The Developing Civil Society in China

The term "civil society" is used here to describe those areas of a society where political action occurs independently of state control. In a country such as China, where authoritarianism has been a dominant feature of the political system, the growth of independent political ideas, organizations, and activities is a sign of the profound changes occurring, partly as a by-product of the economic reforms of the last twenty years and partly as a result of the deliberate political and administrative reforms (such as decentralization and the introduction of local elections) described in earlier chapters. Although much attention outside China has been focused on dissent and events such as the democracy movement of 1989, other, more gradual, changes are likely to be more important at the beginning of the twenty-first century. Three examples of such changes follow.

**Fulian.** The All-China Women's Federation (ACWF), also known as Fulian, was one of several mass organizations established by the Chinese Communist Party after 1949 designed to mobilize people behind the goals of the party. As the only legal organization representing all the women of China, ACWF's primary purpose was to disseminate party ideology from the top down. By the early 1990s, there were over sixty-eight thousand local, county, and provincial women's federations, all under the leadership of the ACWF in Beijing.[37]

By the late 1980s, the purpose and identity of Fulian had become an issue for discussion, largely as a result of the impact of the economic reforms on women. The reforms had unintended consequences for women: The increased emphasis on productivity often worked to the disadvantage of women, who were perceived to be less productive due both to their household responsibilities and to their physical attributes; and some age-old vices, including prostitution, related to women reappeared. The question of the gender-specific implications of socioeconomic change became a legitimate topic for discussion, and many women turned to their local women's federation as the obvious organization to address their problems. Increasingly, Fulian was criticized for its willingness to sacrifice women's interests to government or party interests. Gradually, the organization began to redefine its functions and now emphasizes that serving the specific interests of women is its first priority; this shift, in turn, meant that Fulian has become more responsive to demands from the local level for legal advice, technical training, marriage and family counseling, and other services.[38]

Even while the ACWF is undergoing transformation, an independent women's movement has emerged in China. Women's studies groups, professional organizations, women's publications—all reflect a new consciousness that was given publicity and support by the thousands of nongovernmental organizations that flocked to Beijing for the NGO Forum on Women in 1995. One of the strategies used by both the independent groups and the ACWF is to encourage the development of laws and public policies that can be used to pressure the state to respond to popular criticisms and needs. This strategy is part of what one scholar has identified as "rightful resistance."

**Rightful Resistance.**   Political scientist Kevin J. O'Brien has defined rightful resistance as a form of popular action that employs laws, public policies, and even dominant values to pressure political elites to do what they are supposed to do, whether that might be implementing a policy or curbing abuses of power. The significance of this form of political action is its potential for expanding the civil society: "It is a sign of growing rights consciousness and a more contractual approach to political life. It appears as individuals with new aspirations come to appreciate common interests, develop an oppositional consciousness, and become collective actors in the course of struggle."[39]

Some examples of rightful resistance include villagers who protest procedural abuses of the election laws introduced in the late 1980s, resist unreasonable financial demands by local officials, or object to favoritism in the implementation of the birth control policy. O'Brien pointed out that resistance, particularly in the rural areas, draws on a long tradition of peasant unrest and also on Maoist exhortations to campaign against corrupt cadres at the local level. But the new strategies are different in their use of relatively new legalist means and Communist ideology to restructure villagewide governance and effect institutional change. To publicize their demands, resisters employ a variety of tactics, including making wall posters, contacting sympathetic journalists, staging sit-ins, and making appeals to higher authorities, in order to demand redress of grievances.

**Popular Culture.**   A third example of the development of Chinese civil society in the wake of socioeconomic change is the expansion of cultural opportunities and values that are not defined by and have not been created by the Communist Party and its ideological priorities. The "new" post-Communist culture may actually be a revival of traditional culture, as noted by the many observers who have reported on the revival of popular religion and the resurgence of traditional rituals, including ancestor worship. "The fastest growing sides of popular ritual . . . appear to be the most local. . . . The revival of religion not only slaps at official scientific socialism, but it highlights strictly local and family loyalties at the expense of the state."[40]

In contrast to this, a cultural pluralism is growing, particularly in the urban areas, that includes not only the proliferation of capitalist consumer lifestyles (dress, karaoke bars, and so forth) but also the development of new artistic values appearing in literature and film. Sheryl Wudunn, for example, has written a profile of satirical writer Wang Shuo, who enjoys huge popularity among young readers. Wang "writes about sex, alienation, and failure as perfectly normal things," making hoodlums larger than life and highlighting the problems of China's working-class urban society.[41]

One writer does not a revolution (or a civil society) make, but when this effort is viewed in the context of the other ongoing changes, whether rural protest, the proliferation of nongovernmental organizations, or ritual revival, it becomes clear that the political and cultural monopoly demanded—and enjoyed—by the architects of the Communist revolution for decades, is waning.

## Summary

The central question raised by this chapter is the relationship between socioeconomic change, on the one hand, and political change, on the other. Some of the changes are intentional, but many others are not, as the second half of the chapter illustrates with its focus on grassroots politics. It is impossible to predict the eventual direction of these changes as we approach the twenty-first century, but the Asian experience is an important reminder that politics cannot be understood outside of social and economic contexts.

## Notes

1. The analysis here is based on the following sources: Kenneth Lieberthal and Michel Oksenberg, *Policy Making in China: Leaders, Structures, and Processes* (Princeton: Princeton University Press, 1988), chap. 6; Lawrence R. Sullivan, "The Three Gorges Project: Dammed If They Do?" *Current History* 94, no. 593 (September 1995), pp. 266–269; Dai Qing, *Yangtze! Yangtze! Debate over the Three Gorges Project*, trans. Nancy Liu et al. (London: Earthscan Publications, 1994); Audrey R. Topping, "Damming the Yangtze," *Foreign Affairs* 74, no. 5 (September–October 1995), pp. 132–147. *Beijing Review* has followed the project from an official Chinese point of view.

2. Kenneth Lieberthal, *Governing China: From Revolution Through Reform* (New York: W. W. Norton, 1995), pp. 173–174.

3. Sullivan, "Three Gorges Project," p. 266; Sheila Tefft, "Despite Controversy, China Pushes Ahead on Colossal Dam," *Christian Science Monitor*, May 11, 1994; Topping, "Damming the Yangtze," p. 144.

4. "Three Gorges Project: Cultural Relics Protection, a Race Against Time," *Beijing Review* 39, no. 30 (July 22–28, 1996), pp. 16–18.

5. Sullivan, "Three Gorges Project," p. 267; Topping, "Damming the Yangtze," p. 143. Dai Qing was also imprisoned for ten months.

6. Sullivan, "Three Gorges Project," p. 269.

7. I am indebted to John Riley, Colorado State University, for information and references used in this section. Particularly useful sources include Claude Alvares and Ramesh Billorey, "Damming the Narmada: The Politics Behind the Destruc-

tion," *Ecologist* 17, no. 2 (1987), pp. 62–73; Rajiv Bhartari et al., "The Narmada Valley Project—Development or Destruction?" *Ecologist* 15, nos. 5/6 (1985), pp. 269–285; Thomas R. Berger, "The World Bank's Independent Review of India's Sardar Sarovar Projects," *American University Journal of International Law and Policy* 9, no. 1 (1993), pp. 33–48; Jashbhai Patel, "Is National Interest Being Served by Narmada Project?" *Economic and Political Weekly* 29 (July 23, 1994), pp. 1957–1964; and Usha Thakkar and Mangesh Kulkarni, "Environment and Development: The Case of the Sardar Sarovar Project," *South Asia Bulletin* 12, no. 2 (fall 1992), pp. 96–103.

8. Arun Katiyar, "Refugees of Progress," *India Today*, September 30, 1993, pp. 64–72. Conservative estimates claim 20 million refugees.

9. As for the Three Gorges project, estimates of numbers of people affected vary considerably, with project opponents arguing that much higher numbers of people will be adversely affected than government planners concede. The World Bank estimated that 100,000 people will be displaced from the area to be submerged by the SSP reservoir and 140,000 *families* will be displaced by the canal and irrigation system. Berger, "World Bank's Independent Review," pp. 35, 42.

10. Katiyar, "Refugees of Progress," p. 68.

11. Thakkar and Kulkarni, "Environment and Development," p. 99.

12. *India Today*, October 31, 1989, p. 84.

13. In the mid-1980s, the government of India signed an agreement with the bank for U.S.$450 million in loans to assist in construction of the dam. (China chose not to submit the Three Gorges project to the World Bank for funding consideration in view of the known opposition to the project by key member-nations of the bank. Sullivan, "Three Gorges Project," p. 268, n. 3.)

14. For a summary of the review, see Berger, "The World Bank's Independent Review." Berger was deputy chairman of the review.

15. Sangvai, "'Nation,' 'Nationalism' and Mega Projects," *Economic and Political Weekly* 29, no. 10 (March 5, 1994), p. 539.

16. Gavan McCormack, *The Emptiness of Japanese Affluence* (Armonk, N.Y.: M. E. Sharpe, 1996), p. 45. McCormack drew on Japanese sources for his discussion; I have relied heavily on his analysis for this section. See also Kodansha, *Japan: An Illustrated Encyclopedia*, vol. 1 (Tokyo: Kodansha, 1993), p. 271.

17. McCormack, *Emptiness of Affluence*, p. 47.

18. *Japan Times Weekly International Edition*, June 24–30, 1996.

19. Rajni Kothari, *State Against Democracy: In Search of Humane Governance* (Delhi: Ajanta Publications, 1988), chap. 3.

20. Estimates of the number of groups range between 50,000 and 100,000; some 15,000 are registered with the government because they receive foreign funds. Smitu Kothari, "Social Movements and the Redefinition of Democracy," in Philip Oldenburg, ed. *India Briefing 1993* (Boulder: Westview Press, 1993, with the Asia Society), pp. 134, 143.

21. Uday Mahurkar, "Battle Royal," *India Today*, January 31, 1991, pp. 66–68.

22. Jana Everett, "Incorporation Versus Conflict: Lower-Class Women, Collective Action, and the State in India," in Sue Ellen M. Charlton, Jana Everett, and Kathleen Staudt, eds., *Women, the State and Development* (Albany: State University of New York Press, 1989), pp. 152–176; Gail Omvedt, "Peasants, Dalits and

Women: Democracy and India's New Social Movements," *Journal of Contemporary Asia* 24, no. 1 (1994), 35–44; Omvedt, *Reinventing Revolution: New Social Movements and the Socialist Tradition in India* (Armonk, N.Y.: M. E. Sharpe, 1993); and Ghanshyam Shah, "Grass-Roots Mobilization in Indian Politics," in Atul Kohli, ed. *India's Democracy: An Analysis of Changing State-Society Relations* (Princeton, N.J.: Princeton University Press, 1988), pp. 262–304.

23. I am grateful to Jana Everett for her insights on these and numerous other grassroots organizations in India.

24. Kothari, "Social Movements," p. 135.

25. Gary D. Allinson, "Citizenship, Fragmentation, and the Negotiated Polity," in Gary D. Allinson and Yasunori Sone, eds., *Political Dynamics in Contemporary Japan* (Ithaca: Cornell University Press, 1993), p. 36. See also Merry White, "Home Truths: Women and Social Change in Japan," *Daedalus* 121, no. 4 (fall 1992), pp. 61–82.

26. Allinson, "Citizenship," p. 36.

27. Ellis S. Krauss and Bradford L. Simcock, "Citizens' Movements: The Growth and Impact of Environmental Protest in Japan," in Kurt Steiner, Ellis S. Krauss, and Scott C. Flanagan, eds., *Political Opposition and Local Politics in Japan* (Princeton: Princeton University Press, 1980), p. 190.

28. Krauss and Simcock, "Citizens' Movements," pp. 206–208. See also Jack G. Lewis, "Civic Protest in Mishima: Citizens' Movements and the Politics of the Environment in Contemporary Japan," in Steiner, Krauss, and Flanagan, *Political Opposition*, pp. 288–289.

29. Yoshiko Misumi, "Women of the City of Kitakyushu Environment and Anti-Pollution Movement," paper presented at the forum on Japanese and U.S. Women in the Environment, Denver, Colorado, May 4, 1996. Misumi is director of the Kitakyusu Forum on Asian Women. See also Lewis, "Civic Protest in Mishima," pp. 298–299.

30. Beverley Smith, "Democracy Derailed: Citizens' Movements in Historical Perspective," in Gavan McCormack and Yoshio Sugimoto, *Democracy in Contemporary Japan* (Armonk, N.Y.: M. E. Sharpe, 1986), pp. 157–172.

31. This is my conclusion, based on interviews with activists in the Japanese women's movement.

32. *Japanese Women* (newsletter of the Fusae Ichikawa Memorial Association, Tokyo), no. 61 (March 1, 1989).

33. Information compiled from the 1993–1996 newsletters, "Yokohama Women's Forum."

34. Interview with Yukiko Oda, senior researcher, Kitakyushu Forum on Asian Women, July 31, 1995.

35. Local assemblies include those at the prefectural, city, and town/village levels. *Japanese Women*, no. 75 (March 1, 1996).

36. Interview with Kuniko Funabashi, director, Saga Prefectural Women's and Lifelong Learning Foundation, July 27, 1995. If one views the issue from a different perspective, male politicians see women as voters and as objects of policy but not as partners in the policymaking process. Sumiko Iwao, *The Japanese Woman: Traditional Image and Changing Reality* (New York: Free Press, 1993), chap. 8.

37. Irene L. K. Tong, "Chinese Women on the Move: The Changing Face of the All-China Women's Federation," paper presented at the Association for Women in Development International Forum, Washington, D.C., October 1993.

38. Tong, "Chinese Women on the Move," p. 5; Naihua Zhang with Wu Xu, "Discovering the Positive Within the Negative: The Women's Movement in a Changing China," in Amrita Basu, ed., *The Challenge of Local Feminisms: Women's Movements in Global Perspective* (Boulder: Westview Press, 1995), pp. 34–35.

39. Kevin J. O'Brien, "Rightful Resistance," *World Politics* 49, no. 1 (October 1996), p. 34.

40. Robert P. Weller, *Resistance, Chaos, and Control in China* (Seattle: University of Washington Press, 1994), p. 217.

41. Nicholas D. Kristof and Sheryl Wudunn, *China Wakes: The Struggle for the Soul of a Rising Power* (New York: Vintage Books, 1995), pp. 283–284.

# *fifteen*

# Afterword: Asia in the Twenty-first Century

It was mentioned early in this book that by the mid-1990s, nearly 60 percent of the world's population was Asian, and by the beginning of the twenty-first century, 40 percent of all people worldwide will be Chinese or Indian. It is impossible to know what all these people think about the political changes they are caught up in, but it is clear that very few of them are left untouched by the dynamics of political life described in the preceding chapters. Perhaps the most intriguing changes are those occurring at the local level—in grassroots movements, local elections, environmental protests, women's centers, and elsewhere. The list of these locations of change is surprisingly long for countries where political activity was long viewed as largely a top-down affair. No doubt this was always an oversimplification of reality, but it is also clear that at the turn of the century we are seeing changes that are altering the fabric of political life in fundamental ways.

Viewed historically, the new political organizations, choices, and activities are the latest phase in a process of political change that dates back roughly one hundred and fifty years. The middle of the nineteenth century was replete with harbingers of the massive transformation of Asia. A nascent nationalist consciousness formed in India, as the changes introduced by the British laid the groundwork for the contradictions in Indian politics that we are seeing decades later: Western liberalism, secularism, and the English language coexisting with a Hindu renaissance, communal stirrings, and, ultimately, challenges to the dharmic order from those groups that most suffered under its strictures.

Nor have the changes in China and Japan been less momentous or less influenced by the West. Military prowess and unequal treaties were a powerful stimulus to the East Asian quest for modernization, but Western political ideas and organizations also marked the drive for national integrity. The Meiji Restoration set a new historical standard for rapid, efficient modernization, even as the declining decades of the Qing dynasty seemed to set a standard for ineptitude. One of the striking consequences of the period from the mid-nineteenth to the mid-twentieth centuries was the reversal of the long relationship between China and Japan. Whereas for centuries China set the pace for the culture, the technology, and, especially, the political norms that Japan sought to emulate, after the Meiji Restoration, Japan became the pacesetter in East Asia. But at the end of the twentieth century, we are seeing a new balance between the two countries as China flexes its economic and, increasingly, its military muscles.

The drive for socioeconomic development in Asia has extracted great costs, even as it promises improvement in the standard of living of millions of people. The industrial revolution in the West brought inhumane working conditions and environmental degradation, and these same costs are increasingly familiar to Asians. But it is crucial to remember that the world of the late twentieth century, in which the socioeconomic transformation of China and India, in particular, is occurring, is very different from the world in which countries (including Japan) modernized earlier. One of the most important differences is that the nation-state, as a form of political organization, is being undermined by global economic forces at the same time that nationalism, as a political ideology, seems to enjoy a new life.

It is perhaps a historical irony that a global economy coexists with a nation-state organization that is defined by the efforts of the state to secure territorial integrity and national identity. The tension between the policies governments follow in order to compete in and secure benefit from global economic transactions, on the one hand, and the desire to monopolize political control within the national boundaries, on the other, is amply illustrated in China. Party-state leaders introduce policies ranging from population control to decentralized economic management to local elections in order to enhance the effectiveness of socioeconomic development. But all these policies have unforeseen consequences that, in turn, threaten not just government or party control but also political stability.

As traditional values and social organizations are eroded by the pressures of social and economic change, are they transformed or replaced by new values? Japan's experience suggests an amalgam is both possible and likely. Some archaic forms of social organization, such as the samurai system, disappear, while others persist under new guises, as with the *bu-rakumin*. Loyalty and group affinity as they existed during the Tokugawa period are long gone, but related values persist in political party organizations.

The Indian experience suggests another model that may predominate in the twenty-first century. The combined effects of democracy and socioeconomic change have made it possible for formerly quiescent groups to mobilize in ways that are transforming the stakes and the meaning of Indian politics. The most obvious illustration of this is the role of caste. Arguably an archaic form of social organization, caste has acquired new life through democracy: Caste is a continuing source of identity (and in some ways, security) in an era of rapid change; it is an obvious and successful basis for election appeals and for changes in public policies, such as caste-based reservations in public institutions.

The Indian case also raises profound questions about the contradictory effects of democracy. Western democratic theory tends to anchor democracy not just in majority rule but also in the protection of individual rights. In the United States, in particular, preoccupation with individual rights has come to dominate most popular thinking and rhetoric about democracy. But the Asian polities studied in this book are grounded in cultures that emphasize the importance of community as the source of individual identity and rights. In India, this may help explain why individuals have been so quick to mobilize around traditional groups such as caste for purposes of competing in democratic politics. There are other reasons as well, including the persistence of linguistic and religious cleavages that also become fault lines for political organization.

One of the consequences of using traditional identities as a basis for political mobilization has been violence. The scale and frequency of violence appears to set India apart from both China and Japan, but it is not impossible to imagine that China, in particular, could experience increasing levels of conflict as economic and political changes spread.

India's conflicts also raise questions about national integrity and unity. Preoccupation with national unity (as well as with maintaining Congress Party control) has led to repressive, counterproductive policies in border regions such as Kashmir and Punjab in the Northwest and Assam in the Northeast. The worst scenario for India in the twenty-first century is disintegration of the country into a series of civil wars or wars of secession that, given the international relations of the subcontinent, would likely mean internationalized conflict as well. Such scenarios, however, tend to underestimate the resilience and flexibility of Indian democracy. For example, the government that took office after the 1996 Lok Sabha elections reopened the question of a new round of "states reorganization," that is, new proposals on redrawing the boundaries of the states to conform more closely to linguistic and ethnic boundaries. In the 1950s, many feared that redrawing state boundaries would lead to the breakup of the country; in the 1990s, many argued that a comparable exercise was necessary to prevent the breakup of India.

According to public opinion polls and the findings of many scholars, despite the overwhelming problems that India faces, democratic institutions enjoy widespread and growing support.[1] One of India's most thoughtful scholars has suggested that the expanse of political activity in India, coupled with the obvious problems of government institutions (including corruption), calls for a new theory of democracy, "a democratic theory that accepts the great diversity of human situations yet provides coherence to them through an active political process, opens up new and creative spaces within the framework of civil society, and at the same time restructures the State for realising these ends."[2]

Neither China nor Japan seems poised at the end of the twentieth century for a similar debate about the meaning of democracy, the role of groups versus individuals, or the need to restructure the state. Nonetheless, politics—including the potential for expanded democracy—is far from static in either country. "New and creative spaces" have been small and often hard to find, but the groups and activities described in Chapter 14 make it abundantly clear that the processes of change set in motion by the constitutional orders introduced in both countries fifty years ago, now coupled with rapid socioeconomic change, have brought new groups and new ideas into the political process. It is equally clear that the cross-fertilization that has long traveled between Japan and China, as well as among other Asian countries, will be central to the politics of the twenty-first century. The photo shown in Chapter 4, in which Korean women are protesting Japanese policies toward "comfort women" at the NGO Forum on Women in China, thus takes on new meaning as a symbol of politics in the twenty-first century.

## Notes

1. See, for example, the poll results in *India Today* (August 31, 1996), pp. 28–43.

2. Rajni Kothari, *State Against Democracy: In Search of Humane Governance* (Delhi: Ajanta Publications, 1988), p. iv.

# Glossary

**Ainu**   Indigenous people of the northern Japanese island of Hokkaido.

**Akali Dal**   Sikh political party in Punjab state.

**All-India Muslim League**   Established in 1906 to promote Muslim interests in Indian nationalist movement; later led by **Jinnah**.

*amakudari*   "Descent from heaven"; used to describe process by which Japanese government officials move into business or politics after retirement.

**Amaterasu Omikami**   Legendary sun goddess marking the origin of the Japanese imperial line.

**Ambedkar, B. R.** (1891–1956)   Indian nationalist and leader of the untouchables; critic of Hindu caste structure.

*Arthashastra*   *Treatise on Polity and Economics*; classic text on state administration from Maurya Empire, ca. fourth century B.C.E.; ascribed to **Kautilya**.

**Arya Samaj**   Indian nationalist organization founded in 1875; sought to restore ideal Hindu Aryan past.

**Ayodhya**   North Indian town; legendary birthplace of Hindu god, **Rama**; location of Muslim mosque destroyed in 1992, leading to Hindu-Muslim conflicts in India.

**Backward Classes** (BCs)   Socially and economically disadvantaged Indians; includes **Scheduled Castes and Tribes**, as well as lower strata of Shudras (see *varna*), the latter also called Other Backward Classes (OBCs).

**Bharat, Bharatiya**   Original name in Sanskrit and Hindi for India, after one of the early Aryan tribes that invaded the subcontinent around 4,000 years ago.

**Bharatiya Janata Party** (BJP)   Indian People's Party.

**Boxer Uprising** (1899–1900)   Based in Shandong Province; an attack on foreign, especially Christian, presence in China.

**Brahman**   Ultimately reality or One in philosophical Hinduism.

**Brahmin**   Member of the highest *varna* in India; traditional priestly caste (may also be spelled "Brahman").

**British East India Company**   Founded in 1600 for trade in India; gradually became the de facto ruler of India until control was officially assumed by the British Crown in 1858.

*burakumin*   Literally, "hamlet people"; traditional, pejorative name, "eta"; indigenous "subclass" of Japan.

**bureaucratism**   General term for problems of Chinese bureaucracy, such as inertia, procrastination, and arrogance.

**cadre**   Frequently used in English to describe Chinese government and party bureaucrats (*ganbu*).

**caste**   Inherited social, ritual, and class distinctions characteristic of Hindu society in India. See also *jati* and *varna*.

**Charter Oath**   Inspired by Western political ideals; issued by Meiji government in 1868.

**Chiang Kai-shek** (1887–1975)   Leader of **Kuomintang** after death of **Sun Yat-sen;** president of the Republic of China.

**collective responsibility**   Principle of parliamentary government found in India and Japan, under which government ministers share responsibility for defending government policies.

**comfort women**   Euphemism for women forced to provide sex for the Imperial Japanese Army during World War II.

**communalism**   Indian term for loyalties to and tensions between communities of faith, particularly Hindu and Muslim.

**communes**   Administrative and economic unit found in China from 1950s to 1970s; ranged in size from 5,000 to 50,000 people.

**Confucianism**   System of Chinese ethics, government, and social order derived from the teachings of Confucius (551–479 B.C.E.).

**Congress Party**   Successor to Indian nationalist movement, the **Indian National Congress**; dominant party in India from 1947 until mid-1990s.

**Constituent Assembly** (India)   Legislature responsible for writing India's Constitution, 1947–1949.

**Cultural Revolution**   Also called "Great Proletarian Cultural Revolution," peak years 1966–1969. Maoist-inspired campaigns to eliminate so-called revisionists in the party and "feudal" elements in Chinese culture. **Red Guards** mobilized for leading role.

**Dalai Lama**   Literally, "grand priest." Tibet's traditional spiritual and political leader; currently Tenzin Gyatso.

*dalit*   "Oppressed" or "downtrodden"; contemporary name for former untouchables; signifies commitment to political activism.

**declining sex ratio**   Decline in the proportion of females to males in a population.

**democratic centralism**   Leninist organizational principle for Communist Party, found in CCP; presumes consultation and exchange of views before decisions are taken, then centralized control is enforced.

**democratic parties** (China)   Small parties allowed to coexist with Communist Party as part of a "united front." No major impact on politics.

**Deng Xiaoping** (1904–1997)   Long March veteran and top Chinese leader after 1978; credited with China's policies of economic modernization.

**dharma**   Sanskrit term referring to the sacred law governing the universe as well as to codes of conduct governing relations between social groups and religions; central to the Hindu worldview.

**Diet**   Japanese national parliament.

**Directive Principles of State Policy**   Socioeconomic goals found in Part 4 of the Indian Constitution.

**Dravidian**   Language grouping and peoples based in South India; linguistic and cultural heritage distinguished from Sanskrit-based languages and culture of North India.

**dynastic cycles**   Classical Chinese theory that imperial rule moved in cyclical fashion, with socioeconomic and political well-being followed by the decline and ultimately the fall of a dynasty. See **Mandate of Heaven.**

**Edo**  Traditional name for Tokyo; on the **Edo period**, see **Tokugawa**.

**Emergency, the**  Period from 1975–1977 when the government of Prime Minister Indira Gandhi invoked a state of emergency in India, suspending constitutional civil rights protection.

**extraterritorial jurisdiction**  Characteristic provision of unequal treaties that China was forced to sign with foreign states, under which foreign residents of China were governed by the laws of their own states.

**Four Modernizations**  China's program of modernizing agriculture, industry, defense, and science and technology, begun in late 1970s, for which **Deng Xiaoping** was given credit.

**fusion of powers**  Characteristic of parliamentary systems, in which cabinet government is drawn from and reflects the majority of the legislature, hence, legislative and executive branches are "fused."

**Gandhi, Indira**  Daughter of **Nehru** and prime minister of India, 1966–1977 and 1980–1984.

**Gandhi, Mohandas K.** (1869–1948)  Indian nationalist leader known for his philosophy of nonviolence and his efforts to reform Hinduism. Called Mahatma, meaning "the Great Soul."

**Gang of Four**  Group of radical leaders, led by Mao Zedong's wife, Jiang Qing. Rose to prominence during the Cultural Revolution; were arrested and imprisoned shortly after Mao's death.

**Government of India Act** (1935)  British reform of India's political institutions; many provisions were carried over to independent India's Constitution.

**Great Leap Forward**  Maoist campaign (1958–1959) for accelerated economic production and ideological "redness"; disastrous human and economic consequences.

*guanxi*  "Personal connections"; found throughout Chinese politics.

**Gupta period**  Along with Mauyra, major ancient North Indian empire, ca. fourth to sixth century; India's "golden age."

**Han**  Ethnic majority (approximately 90 percent) of Chinese population; name derives from Han dynasty (206 B.C.E.–C.E. 222).

**harijans**  "Children of God"; Gandhi's term for untouchables.

**Hinduism**  Dominant worldview of approximately 85 percent of Indians; caste system intrinsic to Hindu social structure.

**Hindutva**  Concept of a Hindu India, supported by Bharatiya Janata Party.

**Hundred Flowers Campaign**  The 1956 invitation by CCP leaders for criticism of government and revolution; followed by purges and "reeducation" of dissenters.

**Imperial House Shinto**  Ancient Shinto rituals performed by and for the imperial family.

**Imperial Rescript on Education** (1890)  Required reading of all Japanese schoolchildren as part of their moral education; symbolized conservative, Confucian reaction of late Meiji period.

**Indian Administrative Service** (IAS)  Elite national bureaucracy in India.

**Indian National Congress**  Also called "Congress." Founded 1885; most important nationalist movement from 1880s until Independence, when it became the Congress Party.

**interlocking directorship**   Found in **party-state systems**, in which party leaders simultaneously hold government positions.

**Islam**   "Submission" to God's law or command; the Muslim religion.

**Jainism**   An Indian religion with less than 1 percent of the population as adherents; originally a movement to reform Hinduism.

*jati*   Endogamous, ritual, occupational subdivisions of *varna*; Indian castes.

**Jinnah, Muhammad Ali** (1876–1948)   Prominent Indian nationalist leader; president of Muslim League and founder of Pakistan.

*kami*   Sacred spirits found in indigenous Japanese belief system of **Shinto**.

**Kautilya**   Chief minister to Chandragupta, first Mauryan king, and reputed author of the *Arthashastra*; also called Chanakya.

*keiretsu*   Japanese company networks joined by common links to banks and trading companies.

*koenkai*   Local-level, quasi-permanent organizations that provide support for LDP politicians in Japan.

*kokutai*   National polity or essence; theory of the essence of the Japanese state developed in eighteenth and nineteenth centuries. Emphasized uniqueness of Japanese imperial tradition; foundation of twentieth-century Japanese nationalism.

**Komeito**   Clean Government Party; Japanese political party created in 1960s; merged with another party in 1990s; affiliated with **Soka Gakkai**, Buddhist lay organization.

**Kuomintang** (KMT)   Nationalist Party (successor to **Tongmeng Hui**). (In Pinyin, Guomindang [GMD].)

**Liberal Democratic Party** (LDP)   Governing, conservative party in Japan from 1955 to 1993.

**Lin Biao**   Former Chinese vice premier and defense minister; rose to top leadership during the Cultural Revolution, named "heir apparent" to Mao Zedong in 1969 CCP Constitution; allegedly died fleeing the country in 1971.

**Lok Sabha**   House of the People; lower house of Indian parliament.

**Long March**   Yearlong, six-thousand-mile march (1934–1935) of Communists from their bases in southwest China to Shaanxi Province in the North. Consolidated Communist Party leadership.

**Malthus, Thomas** (1766–1834)   Argued that Chinese population would outstrip food production in *An Essay on the Principle of Population* (1798).

**Mandal Commission**   Backward Classes Commission; issued report in 1980 recommending larger **reservations** for the **Backward Classes**; recommendations very controversial in late 1980s.

**Mandate of Heaven**   Classical Chinese imperial theory that the emperor reflected the will of heaven in his rule but through misrule could lose this mandate. See **dynastic cycles**.

**Mao Zedong** (1893–1976)   Preeminent leader of Chinese Communist movement.

**May Fourth Movement**   Name taken from Beijing demonstration against results of Versailles Conference, May 4, 1919; became major intellectual and political movement in post–World War I period.

**Meiji Constitution** (1889)   Part of conservative reaction to Meiji borrowing; established governing institutions for Japan, including the sacred role of the emperor, that remained in place until 1945.

**Meiji Restoration** (1868–1912)   Period of rapid modernization in Japan, named after the Meiji emperor (reign name: "enlightened rule") who was "restored" to the throne after the **Tokugawa shogunate.**

**Middle Kingdom**   "Central country" (Zhongguo); traditional name for China; reflection of the belief that inferior peoples and cultures surround the Chinese.

**Morley-Minto Reforms** (1909)   Important British reforms in India; created separate Muslim and Hindu electorates.

**Mughal Empire**   Muslim empire in North India (sixteenth to nineteenth centuries).

**national minorities**   Government-designated ethnic minority groups in China, many of which live in autonomous regions.

**National People's Congress**   National legislature in China.

**Nehru, Jawaharlal** (1889–1964)   Leader of Indian nationalist movement; supporter of secular constitution and strong central government; first prime minister of India; father of Indira Gandhi.

**new religions**   Japanese sects and movements derived from Buddhism and Shinto; developed in the nineteenth and twentieth centuries, attracting millions of followers. See **Soka Gakkai.**

**Operation Bluestar**   Attack by Indian army on Sikh terrorists in Golden Temple in Amritsar, Punjab (1984). Led to assassination of Prime Minister Indira Gandhi.

**Opium War**   Between China and Britain (1839–1942); British victory became a source of Chinese humiliation and motivated the Chinese nationalist movements of the nineteenth and twentieth centuries.

**Orientalism**   Western cultural and intellectual views regarding the nature of Eastern ("Oriental," or Asian) history and culture. Also title of book by Edward Said, who argued that Orientalist constructs reflect Western domination of the East.

**outcastes**   Pejorative term for Indians outside the four *varna*; see *dalit*, **untouchables, Scheduled Castes and Tribes**.

*panchayat*   Village government in India, both traditional and contemporary.

**paramilitary**   Armed forces working with or in place of regular military; usually operating domestically, often secretly.

**Parsis**   Indian Zoroastrians, found primarily in Mumbai (Bombay) region.

**Partition**   Division of the Indian subcontinent into the independent states of Pakistan and India in 1947.

**party-state system**   Form of governance characterized by penetration and control of state institutions by a single, dominant party (such as in China).

**patriarchal**   Characteristic of family and social organization in which the father or eldest male monopolizes property and legal and political authority.

**patrilineal**   Designating descent and kinship through the male, or father's, line rather than the mother's.

**President's Rule**   Indian constitutional procedure by which the central government, under presidential authorization, assumes direct control of a state government.

**private sphere**   Domestic, household, family space, to which women are often confined in traditional societies. See **public sphere**.

**procuracy**   Chinese quasi-judicial hierarchy responsible for arrest and prosecution of criminals.

**productive activities**  Production for exchange, often takes the form of paid work.

**public sphere**  Social space outside the household; viewed in many traditional societies (including China, Japan, India) as a male preserve.

**purdah**  Literally, "curtain"; seclusion or veiling, or both, of Muslim and Hindu women.

**Qing Dynasty** (1644–1912)  Last Chinese dynasty. Also known as Manchu dynasty.

**Raj**  Literally, "rule"; usually refers to the British Empire in India.

**Rajya Sabha**  Council of States; upper house of Indian parliament.

**Ram, Rama**  Indian god, hero of the classical epic, the *Ramayana*. Reputed to have been born at **Ayodhya**.

**rectification campaigns**  Chinese Communist Party method of maintaining political control and ideological discipline; typically involves self-criticism, reeducation, and purges.

**Red Guards**  Young people, primarily teenagers, called to play a leading role in the **Cultural Revolution** by attacking anything connected with prerevolutionary society and culture.

**reproductive activities**  Activities that assure the survival and well-being of the household and family, including procreation and tasks such as food procurement and preparation, child and elder care, cleaning.

**reservations**  Indian policy of establishing quotas in state or national government agencies and other public bodies (such as universities) for **Backward Classes** and **Scheduled Castes and Tribes**.

**residuary power**  The power of a national or regional government to make laws with respect to any matter not enumerated in the constitution of a federal system; this power belongs to the Union, or central government, in India.

**Ritsuryo**  System of centralized rule, derived from a Chinese model, in Japan from seventh to tenth centuries. Comprehensive legal code placed sovereign at apex of rule.

**romanization**  The respelling in the Roman alphabet of words or text from another alphabet (necessitates **transliteration** from another alphabet).

**Roy, Ram Mohan** (1772–1833)  Indian intellectual and civil servant; open to Western thought and Christianity but committed to regeneration of Hinduism; a founder of Indian national movement.

**Russo-Japanese War** (1904–1905)  Japan's defeat of Russia confirmed the former's status as a modern military power and assured Japanese interests in Korea and Manchuria.

**samurai**  Class of warrior-administrators during **Tokugawa shogunate**; also called *bushi* ("military gentry").

**Sanskrit**  Ancient Indo-European language forming the basis for contemporary spoken languages in North India.

**sati**  Self-immolation of a Hindu widow on her husband's funeral pyre.

*satyagraha*  Gandhi's concept of "soul force" and nonviolent resistance.

**Scheduled Castes and Tribes**  Castes and tribes outside four traditional Hindu *varna*. Originally listed by the British, subsequently included in the Indian Constitution. Given preferential treatment in government policies. See **reservations**.

**Self Defense Forces** (SDF)   Armed forces of Japan.

**Sepoy Mutiny** (1857–1858)   Revolt of Indian soldiers against the British.

**Shah Bano case**   Indian court case involving rights of a divorced Muslim woman; raised issues of community versus state law.

**Shinto**   Literally, "the way of the *kami*"; indigenous Japanese religion.

**Sikhs**   Followers of the Sikhism religion, founded in the sixteenth century; especially important in the northwest Indian state of Punjab.

**Sinitic**   Technically, a branch of Sino-Tibetan languages, including Chinese and its dialects. More generally, a synonym for Chinese.

**Sino-Japanese War** (1894–1895)   Conflict primarily over control of Korea. Japan demonstrated the weakness of the Qing state by inflicting decisive military defeat.

**Soka Gakkai**   Proselytizing Japanese "**new religion**," linked to Nichiren Shoshu Buddhism and to **Komeito**, the Clean Government Party.

**special administrative region**   PRC administrative subdivision designed for Hong Kong after 1997; Hong Kong SAR.

**special economic zones** (SEZs)   Chinese coastal enclaves established to attract foreign investment with preferential treatment for foreign investors.

**State Shinto**   State ideology fostered during the Meiji period; emphasized national unity focused on devotion to the emperor.

**states reorganization**   Process of redrawing the boundaries of the states in India to conform to linguistic or ethnic communities.

**Sun Yat-sen** (1866–1925)   Nationalist leader of Republican revolution in China; founder of **Tongmeng Hui**.

**Supreme Commander for the Allied Powers** (SCAP)   Occupation headquarters for Japan (1945–1952); the term referred to both General Douglas MacArthur and his headquarters.

*swadeshi*   "Self-reliance"; philosophy and strategy developed in early twentieth-century by Indian nationalist movement.

*swaraj*   "Self-rule"; central tenet of Indian nationalist movement.

**Taiping Rebellion** (1850–1864)   Massive rebellion against Qing dynasty, centered in southwestern China.

**Taisho democracy**   Japanese period (1920s) when political parties flourished; named after Taisho emperor, who reigned 1912–1925.

**Tiananmen Square**   Huge public square in central Beijing; site of student-initiated democracy movement suppressed by Chinese government in June 1989.

**Tilak, Bal Gangadhar** (1856–1920)   Leader of extremist wing of Indian nationalist movement; opposed to Western influence and British rule; proponent of traditional Hindu values.

*ti-yong* **ideology**   Characterized late nineteenth-century reform efforts in China: Adopt Chinese learning for the essence (*ti*), Western learning for practical use (*yong*).

**Tokugawa period/shogunate**   Japanese period of military rule, 1600–1867; named after Tokugawa Ieyasu, first shogun or military ruler of the period. Also called **Edo period**.

**Tongmeng Hui**   Organization that sparked revolution against Qing dynasty; known also as Alliance Society or United League.

**Tongzhi Restoration**   Effort at moral and political reform of the Qing dynasty, named after the reign title of the Emperor Tongzhi (1861–1875).

**transliteration**   The writing or spelling of words from one alphabet in another alphabet in a way that represents the same sounds.

**Treaty of Nanjing** (1842)   Marked end of **Opium War** and set pattern for unequal treaties that China was forced to sign with foreign states. Island of Hong Kong ceded to Britain.

**united front**   Collaborative Kuomintang-Communist strategy against the Japanese in late 1930s. More generally, Communist term for cooperation with non-Communist organizations.

**untouchables**   Outdated, pejorative term for *dalits*.

**Urdu**   Language used by Indian Muslims and formerly by Mughal rulers; emerged from Hindi, Persian, and Arabic but is written with Arabic characters.

**vanguard of the proletariat**   Lenin's term for the Communist Party, conceived as the leading edge of the working class.

*varna*   **Sanskrit** word meaning "color"; name for the four broad caste groupings in India (**Brahmins**, Kshatriyas, Vaishyas, Shudras).

*xiafang*   "Downward transfer"; Communist Party policy of requiring party members to work at lower levels in rural areas in order to understand the problems of the masses.

*xian*   Administrative subunit of Chinese provinces.

**Yuan Shikai**   Qing general; president and military dictator of Republican China, 1912–1916.

*zaibatsu*   Japanese industrial and financial conglomerates developed during Meiji period and broken up during U.S. occupation.

**Zhou Enlai** (1898–1976)   Early leader of May Fourth Movement and CCP; Long March veteran; after 1949, premier of PRC.

**Zoroastrianism**   Ancient Persian religion; established in India by Zoroastrians who fled Persia to escape conversion to Islam.

# About the Book and Author

*Comparing Asian Politics* presents an unusual comparative examination of politics and government in three Asian nations: India, China, and Japan. Sue Ellen Charlton artfully points out both the unique and shared features of politics in these Asian countries. The author examines the links between politics and each nation's distinctive cultural and historical contexts and, at the same time, demonstrates the intermingling and grafting of Asian traditions with the influence of Western values and institutions.

National identity, political cohesion, and socioeconomic change emerge as central to how politics have developed in each nation-state. Charlton provides insight into such topics as the significance of constitutions in the political process; the parliamentary system in Asia; the regionalization of politics and the importance of levels of government; the decay of one-party rule; state authority; and the development of grassroots politics. Selected public policy questions for each country are introduced early in the book in order to acquaint readers with political controversies that are important both domestically and internationally. Often these focus on the role of ethnic minorities, women, and regional groups in Asian political processes.

Unlike many comparative studies, this book not only illuminates the politics of India, China, and Japan in relation to one another, it also suggests to readers how their own experience of politics can be informed by understanding the politics and government of these three Asian nations.

Sue Ellen M. Charlton is professor of political science at Colorado State University.

# Index